ScottForesman Science

Discover the Wonder

Series Consulting Author

David Heil
Associate Director,
Oregon Museum of Science & Industry
Portland, Oregon

Consulting Authors

Maureen Allen
Science Resource Teacher/Specialist
Irvine Unified School District
Irvine, California

Dr. Timothy Cooney
Professor of Earth Science & Science Education
Earth Science Department
University of Northern Iowa
Cedar Falls, Iowa

Dr. Angie L. Matamoros
Science Curriculum Specialist K–12
Broward County Schools
Ft. Lauderdale, Florida

Dr. Manuel Perry
Manager, Educational Programs
Lawrence Livermore National Laboratory
Livermore, California

Dr. Irwin Slesnick
Professor of Biology
Biology Department
Western Washington University
Bellingham, Washington

 ScottForesman

A Division of HarperCollins*Publishers*

Editorial Offices: Glenview, Illinois
Regional Offices: Sunnyvale, California • Tucker, Georgia
Glenview, Illinois • Oakland, New Jersey • Dallas, Texas

Content Consultants

Dr. Linda Berne
University of North Carolina
Charlotte, North Carolina

Dr. Kurt Brorson
Laboratory of Cellular and Molecular
Immunology
National Institutes of Health
Bethesda, Maryland

Dr. Bonnie Buratti
Jet Propulsion Laboratory
California Institute of Technology
Pasadena, California

Dr. Michael Garcia
Department of Geology and Geophysics
University of Hawaii
Honolulu, Hawaii

Dr. Norman Gelfand
Fermi National Accelerator Laboratory
Accelerator Division
Batavia, Illinois

Dr. Roger Pielke
Department of Atmospheric Science
Colorado State University
Fort Collins, Colorado

Dr. Harrison H. Schmitt
*Former Astronaut (Apollo 17) and
    United States Senator*
*Geologist and Science and Technology
    Consultant*
Albuquerque, New Mexico

Dr. Richard Shippee
Department of Biology
Vincennes University
Vincennes, Indiana

Dr. David Stronck
Department of Teacher Education
California State University at Hayward
Hayward, California

Dr. Merita Thompson
Department of Health Education
Eastern Kentucky University
Richmond, Kentucky

Dr. Antonio Garcia Trejo
Arizona Department of Environmental
    Quality
Chandler, Arizona

Dr. Lisa Wagner
Department of Biology
Georgia Southern University
Statesboro, Georgia

Multicultural Consultants

Dr. Thomas Crosby
Department of Biology
Morgan State University
Baltimore, Maryland

Dr. Frank Dukepoo
Department of Biology
Northern Arizona University
Flagstaff, Arizona

Dr. Amram Gamliel (Ben-Teman)
*Educational Consultant/Professional
    Writer*
Newton Center, Massachusetts

Dr. Hilda Hernandez
Department of Education
California State University at Chico
Chico, California

Dr. Luis A. Martinez-Perez
College of Education
Florida International University
Miami, Florida

Safety Consultant

Dr. Jack A. Gerlovich
*Science Education Safety
    Consultant/Author*
Waukee, Iowa

Reading Consultant

Dr. Robert A. Pavlik
Professor of Reading/Language Arts
Reading/Language Arts Department
Cardinal Stritch College
Milwaukee, Wisconsin

Activity Consultant

Mary Jo Diem
Science/Educational Consultant
Croton-on-Hudson, New York

Math/Science Consultant

Catherine R. Ney
Teacher
Blacksburg, Virginia
1994–95 Christa McAuliffe Fellow,
State of Virginia

Acknowledgments

Photographs Unless otherwise acknowledged, all photographs are the property of ScottForesman.
Page abbreviations are as follows: (T)top, (C)center, (B)bottom, (L)left, (R)right, (INS)inset.
Cover Design Sheldon Cotler + Associates
Cover Background: Rob Badger/ROB BADGER PHOTOGRAPHY   Inset: Art Wolfe/
ALLSTOCK, INC.   Magnifying Glass: Richard Chesnut
Page iv(T) Anglo-Australian Telescope Board   **v(TR)** NASA   **v(BL)** Robert Frerck/
Odyssey Productions, Chicago   **v(BR)** Museo di Storia della Scienza, Florence
vi(B) Dominique Braud/Tom Stack & Associates   **vii(TR)** Laura Riley/Bruce Coleman, Inc.
viii(B) John Serrao/Visuals Unlimited   **ix(L)** Phil Degginger   **ix(R)** John Cancalosi/
Tom Stack & Associates   **x(T)** David Scharf/Peter Arnold, Inc.   **x(B)** Kjell Sandved/
Visuals Unlimited   **xi(B)** Allan Roberts   **xiv(T)** John D. Cunningham/Visuals Unlimited
xv(B) Tom & Pat Leeson/Photo Researchers

Illustrations Unless otherwise acknowledged, all computer graphics by Ligature, Inc.
Page vii Biomedia   **xii(T)** Jacque Auger   **xii(B)** Gary Torrisi

Acknowledgments continue on page 46.

ISBN: 0-673-40145-6
Copyright © 1996 Scott, Foresman and Company, Glenview, Illinois
All Rights Reserved. Printed in the United States of America.

910 DR 0201

About the Cover

The snowy forest with its many types of trees is
one place where you might see a gray wolf.
This gray wolf was photographed in its habitat
in Alaska. These beautiful creatures are
adapted to similar environments elsewhere,
such as the mountainous areas of Colorado
where the background photograph was taken.

Reviewers

MODULE A

Stargazing

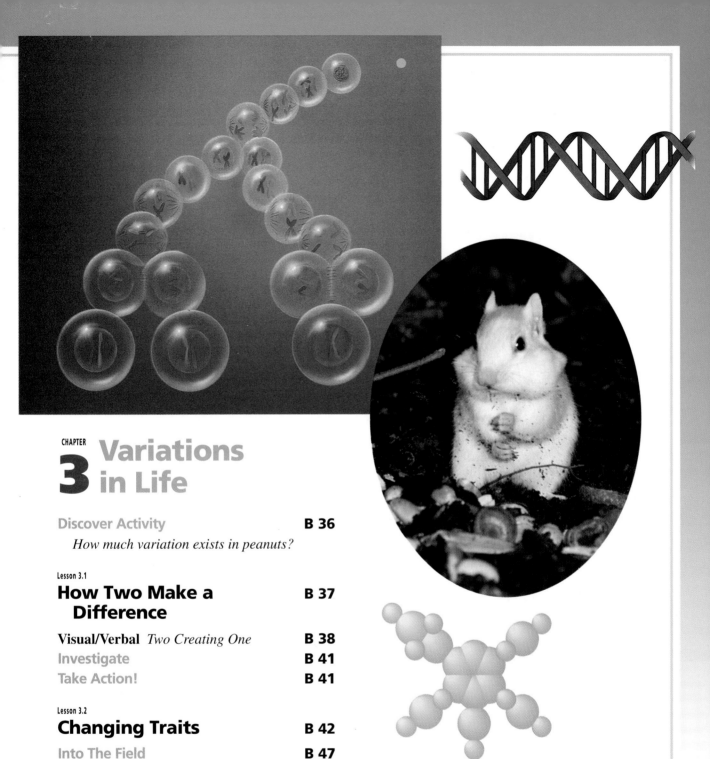

Digging for Clues

CHAPTER 1 Digging Up the Past

CHAPTER 2 Stories of Fossils

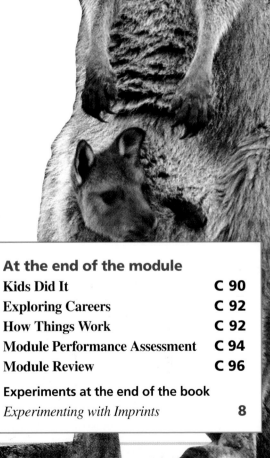

Adaptations

CHAPTER 3 Light in the Ocean

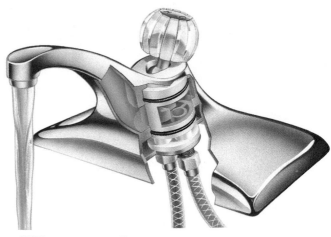

CHAPTER 3 Science and Industry

Wetlands: Making Decisions

CHAPTER
3 Applying Science

Stargazing

Stargazing

Twinkle, twinkle, little star. Astronomers wonder what you are. What are those points of light, up above the world so high? Are they really like diamonds? How do they form? Where are they located? What can they tell us about the history of the universe? You'll find the answers to these and other questions in this module.

CHAPTER 1 Stars in the Universe

Dust swirls, atoms fuse—a star is born! Stars come from dust, and to dust they return. In between, they heat up, glow brightly, and sometimes explode.

CHAPTER 2 Star Light, Star Bright

What can astronomers learn from light? Starlight gives astronomers clues about what stars are made of and how far away they are. Invisible waves from stars tell them even more.

CHAPTER
3 History of Astronomy

What do galaxies and computers have in common?
They're both objects that astronomers have used to make models of the universe. The models keep changing as people keep learning more about stars.

Stars in the Universe

It's too small. . . I can hardly see it!

Wear cover goggles for this activity.

What can you learn from stargazing?

You can be a "star" or a "stargazer." The stars should each hold a blown-up balloon and scatter themselves around the classroom. Each balloon represents a different star in the sky. The stargazers should stay in the center of the room and estimate the diameter, shape, and color of each star.

For Discussion

1. How accurate are the stargazers' estimates?
2. How can you make a map of the stars in this "sky?"

1.1 *Stardust*

▶ *Do stars have birthdays?*

Take yourself back in time to the fourth day of July in the year 1054 to the empire of China. It's nighttime, but the emperor's astronomers are hard at work, watching the night sky.

Suddenly, the astronomers notice a burst of light brighter than anything they've ever seen in the night sky. The light looks like a star, but it doesn't act like a star. The astronomers decide to call it a "guest star." The guest star is so bright that children playing can see it in broad daylight!

Telescopes haven't been invented yet, so the astronomers study this burst of light with the best tools they have—their own eyes. In a few days the guest star begins to fade. And then two years later it seems to disappear from the night sky, long before anyone can explain it.

What the astronomers witnessed was the explosive death of a star—an explosion that actually occurred 5000 years *before* they saw it! By using a telescope you can still see scattered bits of the star that died over 5900 years ago. We call those scattered pieces of star the Crab Nebula.

We know when the Crab Nebula was formed. But what about that huge star that exploded so long ago? When was it born? How did its life begin? The answers to those questions are hidden in a cloud of dust and gas.

Birth of a Star

When you look up at the clear night sky, you see twinkling stars separated by deep, dark space. That space might look empty to you, but it's not. Billions of gigantic clouds of gas and dust swirl in the gaps between the stars. The gas is mostly hydrogen atoms. The dust is made of tiny bits of matter. Scientists call this cloud of swirling dust and gases a **nebula** (neb′ yə lə), from a Latin word for mist.

▲ The Crab Nebula is an expanding mass of gas and dust.

Scientists recently observed what they believe are "newborn" stars in a nebula in the constellation Orion.

Let's pick one of these nebulas—a big one—and watch what might happen to it. Over millions of years gravity pulls the hydrogen and the dust in the nebula closer together. Slowly but surely the cloud begins to look like a giant ball. As gravity pulls the hydrogen and dust even closer together, the ball starts shrinking.

The hydrogen atoms in the center of the ball get squeezed together, causing energy conversions that make the temperature rise. First the atoms reach 100 degrees Celsius. Then they reach 1000 degrees Celsius; then 100,000 degrees; then 1,000,000 degrees.

Finally, heated to millions of degrees Celsius, the hydrogen atoms begin to join together and form new elements. The joining atoms release tremendous amounts of energy. This energy is strong enough to push the surface of the ball out as hard as gravity is pulling in. The ball stops shrinking. Some of the energy is released as light, so you now have a glowing ball in space. A star is born!

Star Power

The process by which hydrogen atoms join together to form a new shining star is called **nuclear fusion**. If you look up *fusion* in the dictionary, you'll find that it means "combining two or more things into one." That's just what's happening inside a star's glowing core. The great pressure and temperature on the inside cause atoms of less massive elements to smash against one another so hard that they fuse together, forming more massive elements. Notice in the diagram the new element produced by nuclear fusion is a more massive one.

More than one pair of hydrogen atoms fuse together in the core of a new star. Billions of hydrogen atoms fuse every second, releasing great amounts of energy.

Great pressure and much energy are needed to get nuclear fusion started. But once fusion gets going, it releases much more energy than it took to get started. The released energy spreads out from the core of the star in all directions. You see just a small part of the energy produced by the nuclear fusion within when you look at the new star. You see the visible light. The star shines through its whole life because fusion keeps producing energy, including visible light.

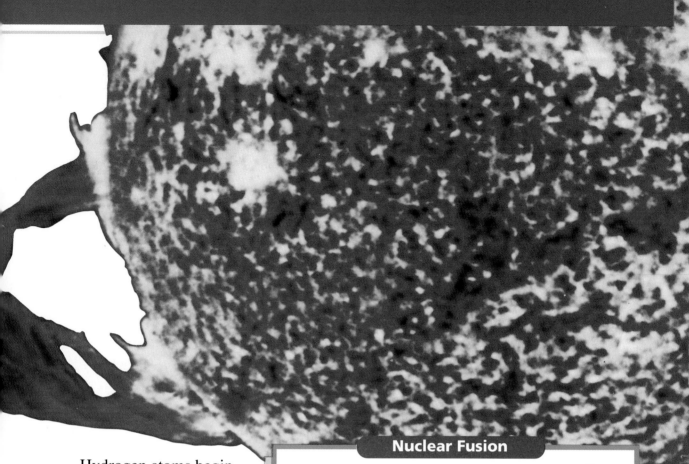

Hydrogen atoms begin the process of nuclear fusion. But they're not the only kinds of atoms that fuse together. Eventually the newly formed helium atoms fuse together from the intense pressure too. These fused helium atoms create more massive elements such as carbon and oxygen. Then those carbon and oxygen atoms fuse together, creating atoms of still more massive elements, such as silicon and iron.

Nuclear Fusion

Less massive element

Small particles

Energy

More massive element

Stars, such as our sun, get their energy from fusion.

Meanwhile in the core, the more massive elements replace the less massive elements. The core gets hotter and hotter as it fills with more massive elements. As the temperature of the star changes, so does its color and brightness. And the star expands, getting larger and larger.

Millions of years go by. With each passing year the star gets hotter and hotter, larger and larger, and brighter and brighter. Can it possibly keep expanding forever?

Star Life Cycle

The life of a star lasts for billions of years.

A star might take millions or even billions of years to form. Most stars also take millions of years to die, gradually shrinking and growing dim. So the **star life cycle**—the complete process of a particular star's life from birth to death—is impossible for humans to observe. Then how can scientists understand a star's life cycle?

When you observe different animals of the same kind in various stages of life, you can piece together the complete life cycle of that animal. Similarly, astronomers have observed millions of stars in many different stages of existence. By applying the laws of chemistry and physics, scientists have developed models of how stars live and die.

Let's look at the life cycle of just one star of medium size and medium temperature. It is about halfway through its 10-billion-year life cycle.

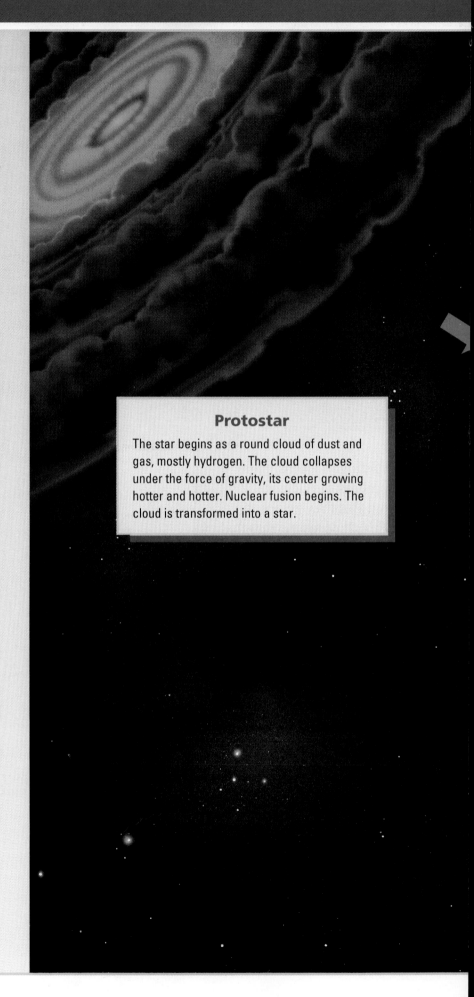

Protostar

The star begins as a round cloud of dust and gas, mostly hydrogen. The cloud collapses under the force of gravity, its center growing hotter and hotter. Nuclear fusion begins. The cloud is transformed into a star.

Mid-Life Star

Five billion years later, the star is middle-aged. It is only one of billions of medium-sized, mid-life stars. These stars are red, yellow, white, or blue, depending on their surface temperatures. Blue stars are the hottest. Red stars are the coolest. Yellow stars have medium surface temperatures. The brightness of mid-life stars depends on their mass. The largest stars, called supergiants, look brightest in the sky. Stars the size of our sun do not shine as bright.

Red Giant

Five billion years from now, the star has used up all its hydrogen. Fusion stops and the star begins to collapse toward its center. Then helium nuclei begin to fuse, producing energy that expands the surface of the star. The star becomes about one hundred times larger—a red giant.

The Death of a Star

You know the important roles gravity and pressure play in changing a cloud of gas and dust into a glowing red giant. But what happens next? The rest of a star's life story depends on its mass. First, let's look at the path above to see what happens to stars that are hotter, brighter, and more massive than the sun.

Stars more massive than the sun continue to swell even after they become red giants. Nuclear fusion continues, producing elements such as iron.

Suddenly the core can't get enough fuel and the star begins to cool down. As the core cools, the outer layers of the star are pulled in by the core's powerful gravity. Layer after layer, the star's atoms smash into the core, heating it up again. The burst of heat allows the core to create even more massive elements, such as gold and lead. Meanwhile the core grows incredibly hot, until finally an explosion occurs. Metric tons of atoms are hurled in every direction as the star becomes a **supernova.** During the supernova, the heat enables the rest of the known elements to form. The explosion spreads these elements throughout the gas and dust of the resulting nebula.

Gravity pulls outer parts of the star toward its center. Pressure and temperature increase. The outer shells of the star expand to form a cloudlike nova.

Astronomers estimate that one new pulsar is born somewhere in the galaxy about every 10 years. Pulsars live about 10 million years.

Near the middle of the newly formed nebula is a very small star. This star is both tiny—only about 20 kilometers in diameter—and dense. The star spins rapidly, giving off radio waves. At the end of its life cycle, the star has become a pulsar. Hundreds of pulsars have been observed from their radio waves.

Only massive stars turn into supernovas when they die. The pathway below shows that smaller stars have a quieter death. Read the information in the boxes and compare the death of the less massive stars to that of more massive ones.

Back in the year 1054, the Chinese astronomers saw the greatest fireworks display in the universe—an exploded supernova. That supernova became the Crab Nebula. Millions of years from now, some of the gas and stardust of the Crab Nebula may become part of a new star. The star life cycle will begin again.

Checkpoint

1. Explain how a nebula becomes a star.
2. What happens during nuclear fusion?
3. Why do stars have different temperatures and sizes at different stages of their lives?
4. How is the death of a giant star different from the death of a small star?
5. Take Action! Make a chart showing star colors and temperatures.

The center of the star continues to collapse, becoming a small, hot, and extremely dense white dwarf. As the white dwarf continues to radiate energy, its fuel is used up. Finally all that remains is a dark, dense star—a black dwarf—that no longer shines.

Looking Through a Sky Window

Counting stars seems as impossible as counting grains of sand on a beach. But you can estimate the number of stars with a sky window.

Picture A

Picture B

Picture C

Gather These Materials

metric ruler   construction paper
scissors

Follow This Procedure

Part A

1 Make a chart like the one on the next page. Record your observations in your chart.

2 To make a sky window, use the ruler to measure the length of your hand from the wrist to the end of your middle finger. (Picture A)

3 Cut a square window in the center of the construction paper. Use your hand measurement as the length of each side of the window. (Picture B)

4 Stand 2 m from the brick wall and look through the sky window. Hold the sky window at arm's length with your arm stiff. (Picture C)

5 The part of the wall you see represents a sample area. Move your sky window around the wall to estimate the number of sample areas it would take to cover the wall. Record this number in your chart.

6 Count and record the number of bricks you see in the sample area. Record this number.

7 Multiply the number of bricks by the number of sample areas. Your answer is an estimate of the number of bricks in the wall. Record this total.

Number of sample areas on wall	
Number of bricks in sample area	
Estimated number of bricks on wall	
Number of stars seen through sky window	
Estimated number of stars in sky	

Part B

1 In the same way, you can estimate the number of stars in the sky. On a clear night, go outside and view the stars through your sky window.

2 Hold the sky window at arm's length with your arm stiff. Count the number of stars you see in the sample area. Record your number.

Predict: *How many stars do you think cover the night sky in your area?*

3 To cover the sky from one horizon to the other takes 170 sample areas. Multiply the number of stars you counted in your sample area by 170. Record your answer. Your result will be an estimate of the number of stars in the sky.

State Your Conclusions

1. Count the number of bricks on the wall. How did your estimate compare to the actual number of bricks?

2. Scientists estimate that about 3000 stars are visible in the sky on a clear night. How does your estimate compare?

3. What might be a reason for the difference between your star estimate and 3000?

4. What is the advantage of using a sky window?

Let's Experiment

How do you think light from cities and towns affects the number of stars you see in the night sky? Use your sky window to find out.

1.2 *Star Clusters*

> ### *How long does it take starlight to reach you?*

That bursting supernova the Chinese astronomers saw must have been an amazing sight. The explosion was so huge you can still see bits of the star scattered throughout the night sky. And something even more fascinating about that explosion is this: When the astronomers saw the explosion, it had already taken place—around 5000 years before! Looking at starlight is looking back in time at light that left distant stars thousands of years before. And the light that is given off by most stars in the universe today won't be seen until hundreds or thousands of years from now.

Distances in space are so vast that it takes years and years for light to travel from the stars to your eyes. In fact, it's hard even to imagine how far away stars are.

▼ *Although stars in the Big Dipper appear close to each other from the earth, in space they are far apart.*

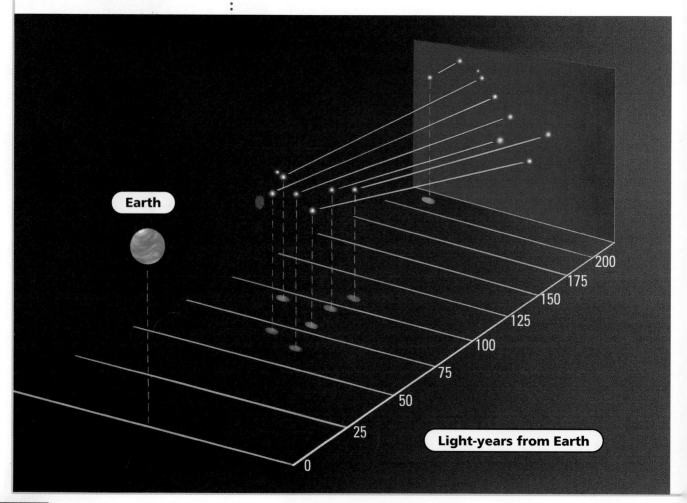

Earth

200
175
150
125
100
75
50
25
0

Light-years from Earth

Distances to the Stars

Stars are so far away that all the units used to measure distances on the earth are too small to be much help when measuring distances to the stars. If you and your classmates were to compare the distances from your desks to the classroom door, you might use meters. But would meters work as well if you were measuring even longer distances, such as from the place where you live to a city in South America? Most likely you would use a longer unit of measurement such as the kilometer.

Scientists face a similar problem when measuring the distances to stars. Using kilometers doesn't work, so astronomers created a unit especially for measuring distance in space—the **light-year**. One light-year is the distance light travels in 1 year. Light travels so fast—9 trillion 460 billion kilometers a year—that it could travel around the earth seven times in 1 second, or from the sun to the earth in about eight minutes!

The star nearest to the earth after the sun, Proxima Centauri, is more than four light-years away. Light coming from a star at that distance takes more than four years to reach the earth. Some of the stars you see are hundreds of light-years farther away than others, even though they look as if they're all about the same distance from you.

When you look up at a constellation, all the stars that make up that shape seem to be on the same plane, like a connect-the-dots drawing. But, as you can see on page 14, some stars in a constellation are light-years farther away than others.

If stars are at such different distances, why don't the stars that are farther away look smaller and those closer look bigger? After all, somebody standing a meter from you appears a lot bigger than the tiny figure of a person who is way down the road. Think back to the Discover Activity. Your observations of the size, shape, and sometimes even the color of the balloons were affected by the distance between you and the balloons. Your eyes have the same problem seeing the slightly larger appearance of closer stars. The stars are all so far away that you only see specks that look as if they are about the same size.

MATH

How Far is Long Ago?

Light moves at 300,000 kilometers per second through space. Use the following data to calculate how many kilometers light can travel in a year.

60 seconds	=	1 minute
60 minutes	=	1 hour
24 hours	=	1 day
365.25 days	=	1 year

Looking at stars that are light-years away is like looking back in time. For example, when you look at a star that is 1 light-year away, you see how the star looked 1 year ago.

The chart shows the distances to some stars.

Star	Distance in light-years
Proxima Centauri	4.3
Sirius	8.7
Megrez	63.0
Polaris	470.0
Cassiopeia A	11,000.0

What Did You Find Out?
1. *How old were you when Proxima Centauri sent the light you see now?*
2. *From which star would you notice a change in appearance that actually happened when Europeans were settling America?*

Stars in Groups

Your eyes fool you when you look into the sky and you see thousands of stars that all look equally far away. Stars aren't spread out evenly through the sky. You can't tell by looking, but stars are clustered together in groups. A group of billions of stars is called a **galaxy** (gal′ ek sē).

When you look into the sky, all the stars you see belong to our galaxy, the Milky Way Galaxy. Other galaxies appear in the sky as fuzzy blobs no brighter than a faint star.

You can see in the diagram that the Milky Way Galaxy has a center that is densely packed with stars. Curved arms seem to swirl out from the center like whirlpool waves. The earth's location within the galaxy—along with our sun and the other planets—is on one of those arms.

Gravity holds the stars and planets in a galaxy together, along with the gas and dust in the space between them. The same powerful force that plays a big role in a star's birth and death holds the star within the galaxy.

Scientists have photographed many millions of galaxies. So many galaxies exist in the universe that scientists can't even estimate how many there are! However, they have been able to classify galaxies into one of three different kinds pictured on page 17.

The Milky Way Galaxy with its sweeping arms is an example of one kind of galaxy—a spiral galaxy. Viewed from the edge, a spiral galaxy looks like a flying disc with a bulge in its center.

An elliptical galaxy is shaped like a sphere that's been stretched out at the ends. Some elliptical galaxies are flat like spiral galaxies. Others are thicker, and shaped more like an egg.

Irregular galaxies do not have the familiar shape of either elliptical or spiral galaxies. Irregular galaxies are smaller than spiral and elliptical galaxies and have more young stars than the other two kinds.

Don't let all this information about countless clusters of billions of stars make you feel small. The planet you live on fits into this enormous picture. Next, you'll see just where you live among the stars.

Milky Way Galaxy

Top View

Sun

Side View

Sun

Irregular Galaxy

Spiral Galaxy

Elliptical Galaxy

Into The Field

Where's the Milky Way in the night sky?
Observe the night sky. With the help of a field guide of the stars, locate the Milky Way. Make a sketch of what you see.

▼ You live in but one tiny part of the vast universe.

You Are Here

Now let's zoom in from deepest space to the earth and see where you live among those glittering lights in the sky. All the glowing bodies you see, as well as everything far beyond them, are part of the universe. All the matter and energy, and all the space that they fill, as well as all the empty space, make up the universe. Scientists don't know how far the universe extends. However, each year as knowledge of the universe increases, we move farther and farther into space.

The part of the universe scientists have studied is made up of gigantic clusters of galaxies separated by empty space. Find one of these clusters—the Local Group—in the diagram. It consists of 25 elliptical galaxies, four irregular galaxies, and three spiral galaxies.

The Milky Way Galaxy is one of the three spiral galaxies in the Local Group. The Milky Way Galaxy is very small compared with the whole Local Group. Yet it's 100,000 light-years in diameter. Think about what that means. Light takes 100,000 years to go from the far edge of one of the Milky Way Galaxy's star-filled spiral arms to the edge of an arm on the opposite side!

Solar System

You know one of the medium-sized stars in the Milky Way Galaxy as our sun. The distance of our sun from the center of the galaxy is about 25,000 light-years. The earth and the eight other planets in the solar system revolve around the sun. That star belongs to a spiral galaxy, that belongs to a cluster of galaxies, that belongs to a universe, that just seems to go on and on!

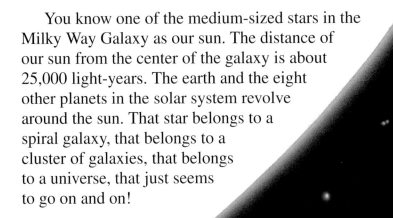

Universe

Local Group

Milky Way Galaxy

Checkpoint

1. Why do scientists use light-years to measure distances in space?
2. How are galaxies alike and different?
3. What is the earth's relationship to the Local Group?
4. **Take Action!** Scientists use astronomical units to measure distances in the solar system. Make a diagram showing distances between the planets in astronomical units.

You Can Be a Star

You read that stars that form a pattern in the sky are not all the same distance from the earth. Now try this activity and see for yourself.

Picture A

Picture B

Picture C

Gather These Materials

three identical flashlights   meter stick
masking tape

Follow This Procedure

1 Make a chart like the one on the next page. Record your observations in your chart.

2 Each of three students should hold a flashlight. They will represent stars A, B, and C.

3 Use masking tape to make a short line on the hallway floor. (Picture A) Student A should stand on this line.

4 Use the meter stick to mark off another line 60 centimeters behind Student A. (Picture B)

5 Measure 60 centimeters to the right of this new mark and make another line with tape. (Picture C) Student B should stand on this line.

6 Mark off another line 1.8 meters behind and 1.5 meters to the right of Student B. This line is for Student C.

7 The rest of your team should stand at least 6 meters away and face the students who are holding the flashlights.

8 Students A, B, and C should turn on their flashlights.

Predict: *Do you think any of the "stars" will look brighter than the others?*

Record Your Results

Observations of stars

9 Observe the three stars and record your observations in your chart. Note if any star looks brighter than the others. Can you tell if the stars are at different distances?

10 The three students are lined up in the same relation to each other as the three major stars in the handle of the Big Dipper. Ask the students to hold their flashlights at the right heights to match the shape of the Big Dipper's handle. Draw the shape you see.

11 Trade places so that everyone gets a turn at being a star and an observer.

State Your Conclusions

1. How do the three stars appear from a distance?
2. If a star that is far away appears as bright as a nearby star, how does the actual brightness of the two stars compare?
3. How has this activity shown you that looks can be deceiving when it comes to stargazing?

Let's Experiment

Now that you have learned about star distances, what are some variables that affect how bright a star looks from the earth? Use what you know about scientific methods to find out.

Chapter Review

Reviewing Words and Concepts

Write the letter of the word or phrase that best completes each sentence.

1. The changes in a star from birth to death make up a process called the _____.
2. A _____ forms when billions of stars cluster together in a group.
3. The first stage in a star's life cycle is a _____.
4. During _____, hydrogen atoms join together to form helium atoms.
5. A _____ is medium-sized and may be red, yellow, white, or blue.
6. The Crab _____ is made up of a swirling mass of dust and gases.
7. When a massive star dies, it turns into a _____.
8. The stage in the star life cycle following the mid-life phase is a very large star called a _____.
9. The distance between two stars is measured in _____.
10. The stars you see each night are part of the _____.

a. nuclear fusion
b. star life cycle
c. supernova
d. light-years
e. galaxy
f. protostar
g. mid-life star
h. red giant
i. Milky Way Galaxy
j. Nebula

Connecting Ideas

1. Copy the concept map. Use the terms at the right to complete the map about the life cycle of a massive star.

nuclear fusion   supernova
              red giant

gravity/pressure

A. nebula _____ → B. _____

↑   ↓

D. _____ ← C. _____

collapse

2. Write a sentence or two that summarizes the ideas shown in the concept map.

Interpreting What You Learned

1. What materials make up the dark space between stars?
2. What causes a nebula to release energy as light and heat?
3. Describe the star life cycle of a medium-sized star.
4. Describe the changes that take place as a red giant becomes a supernova.
5. What happens as a small star becomes a black dwarf?
6. Describe the three different kinds of galaxies.
7. How long would it take a spaceship traveling at the speed of light to reach a star eight light-years away?
8. Where in the Milky Way Galaxy is the earth located?

Performance Assessment

How can you estimate the number of stars?

Materials • sheet of paper with grid • paper circles

Collecting Data

1. Look at the sheet of paper with the grid. The grid on the paper represents part of the sky. Count the number of squares in this part of the sky and record the number.
2. The paper circles your teacher placed on the grid represent stars. Without counting, estimate how many stars are in this part of the sky. Record your estimate.
3. Count the number of stars in any two squares of the grid and record the number. Divide the number of stars you counted by two and record your answer. This calculation represents the average number of stars in one grid square.
4. Multiply the average number of stars in one grid square by the total number of squares in the grid. This calculation represents your estimate of the total number of stars on the grid paper.
5. Without moving the paper circles, count the actual number of stars and record the number. How does your estimate compare to the actual number of stars?

Analyzing Data

Explain how estimating can be more helpful than guessing or actually counting the total number of objects in a sample.

2 Star Light, Star Bright

Alright, it's a rainbow! Look at it on my hand!

Discover Activity

How can you make a rainbow?

You've probably seen a rainbow in the sky before. But did you know that you can make a rainbow with a mirror and a bowl of water? Work near a sunny window. Place the mirror in the bowl of water and move it around to catch a beam of sunlight. Look carefully at the reflected light.

For Discussion

1. *Where do you think the colors came from?*
2. *What happens when you make waves in the water?*

2.1 *Star Messages*

▶ *Just what are all those sparkles in the sky?*

Think about all that action going on in the night sky—nuclear fusion, exploding supernovas, spinning pulsars, glowing red giants! Even through the city lights you can probably see the brightest and biggest stars. Yet they look so faint, little more than tiny specks of light like this one. How did we learn so much about the universe from those tiny specks?

Believe it or not, many answers lie in the light that reaches the earth from those tiny specks in the sky. The ancient Chinese astronomers simply looked up into the night sky. But modern scientists collect and analyze starlight much like detectives analyzing secret messages. To understand how scientists decode star messages, you need to learn more about the properties of starlight.

Light Waves

The bright starlight that sparkles far off in the dark night sky may seem mysterious, but it's just like light from any lamp in your home. Light is all the same, whether it is in deepest outer space, or anywhere else. Although light seems to zoom from a lamp in a straight line, all light that you see is a form of energy that travels in waves. Whether going from a star to the earth, or from a lamp to your eye, light waves carry energy.

The rising and falling pattern of a light wave carries energy from one place to another. Imagine the waves of salt water that rise and fall in the ocean. If you've ever been knocked down by one of those waves as it broke on the shore, you know it carried lots of energy!

You can make a wave similar to a light wave by flicking one end of a rope. Attach one end of a rope to a doorknob. Then move your wrist up and down sharply. This action makes the rope move up and down in a smooth, curving pattern. Although light seems to zoom from a lamp in a straight line, every single wave travels in a curving wave pattern like that of the rope.

▲ *What can scientists learn about stars from those tiny dots of light like this one?*

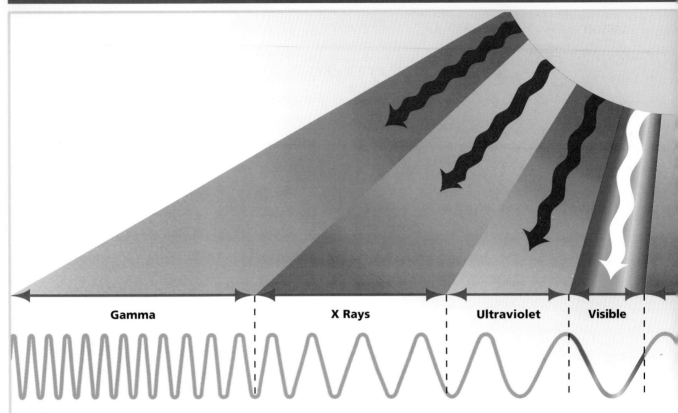

| Gamma | X Rays | Ultraviolet | Visible |

▲ *Electromagnetic waves carry energy.*

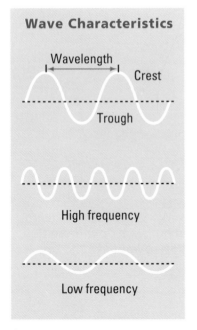

Wave Characteristics

Wavelength

Crest

Trough

High frequency

Low frequency

▲ *Properties of waves*

All waves do not travel in exactly the same curving pattern though. Study the diagram to the left. Notice in the first drawing that the wavelength is the distance from one crest to another or from one trough to another.

Wavelength is the clue to the wave's frequency, or the number of waves passing a point in a given time. A wave with a high frequency looks scrunched up like the wave in the middle. A wave with a low frequency is more spread out like the bottom one. Frequency shows how much energy each wave has. The higher a wave's frequency, the more energy it has.

The Electromagnetic Spectrum

When you gaze at the stars, the waves of starlight you see aren't the only ones reaching you. Many kinds of waves pour through space from those tiny glowing dots. The waves have a wide variety of wavelengths and frequencies, so they have different amounts of energy.

The waves stars give off don't rush through space in a neat, orderly fashion. They come to the earth from all directions in a jumbled mix. The various waves form a pattern that ranges from a very short wavelength to a very long wavelength. This pattern is called the electromagnetic spectrum. Notice the order of the waves that make up the electromagnetic spectrum shown above.

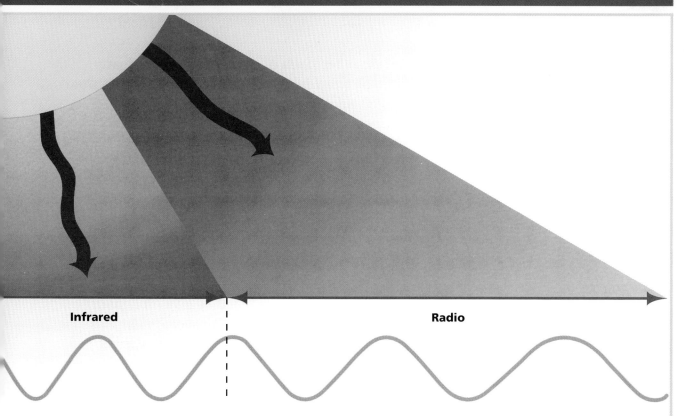

Infrared

Radio

Organizing the different kinds of waves into the electromagnetic spectrum helps scientists decode the stars' messages. By organizing the wavelengths, scientists can identify the waves, compare the amounts of energy they have, and learn some of the secrets the stars hold.

Did you find the "rainbow" in the electromagnetic spectrum? This very small part of the electromagnetic spectrum is the only part you can see, and most often you see that rainbow as white light. All of the kinds of light you found in the Discover Activity, from red light on one side to violet on the other, make up the light you see. This small range of wavelengths that humans can see is called the **visible spectrum.** What colors make up the visible spectrum?

Think about the light that's hitting the pages of this book. It's probably white, and you might think it's made up of wavelengths of white light. Yet actually white light is made of the many different wavelengths of the visible spectrum mixed together. Each color has its own range of frequencies and has a slightly different range of energies. When these colors blend together, they appear white. Notice that the visible spectrum makes up only a very small part of all of the electromagnetic waves that stars give off.

If all the other kinds of waves in the picture are reaching you from the stars, why is the visible spectrum all you see? Because your eyes' retinas perceive frequencies only within the narrow range of red to violet. Your eyes only see waves that have frequencies in the visible light range.

Analyzing Starlight

Visible light is only part of the electromagnetic waves coming from space, but it brings scientists some of the most important information they get about stars. The key to the information is this fact: When the atoms of a particular element are energized, they give off light of specific frequencies, and thus specific colors. For example, the frequencies of waves given off when hydrogen is heated are very different from the frequencies of waves given off when helium or any other element is heated.

Think of all the different colors you see when fireworks explode in the sky. These different colors burst into the sky because different elements are heated up enough to glow. The frequencies given off by the glowing elements are as unique as the fingerprints of different people. If you determine the frequencies, you can determine the element.

How can you determine the frequencies of light from stars or other objects? As the different colors come from a star, they blend together, so the starlight appears white. In order to study starlight better, scientists developed the spectrometer (spek trom′ ə tər)—an instrument that separates the different colors in a beam of light. When light given off by an element passes through a spectrometer, you can see distinct lines in the spectrum. These spectral lines tell which frequencies of light are passing through the spectrometer.

▼ *Scientists can learn about stars by studying their spectral lines.*

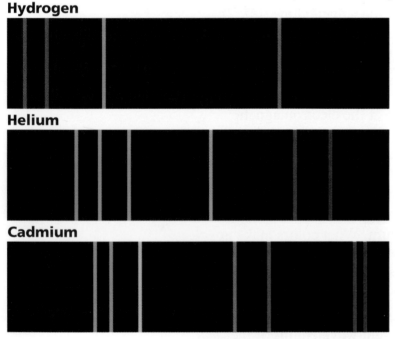

Hydrogen

Helium

Cadmium

Look on page 28 at the three sets of lines created by light from three elements that were passed through a spectrometer. Notice how different they are. The light given off by hydrogen produces sharp lines of four frequencies, three in the blue end of the spectrum and one in the red. The light given off by cadmium and helium produces spectral lines very different from hydrogen.

If every star were made up of just one element, it would be easy to look at its spectral lines and tell what the star was made of. But several elements can be found in stars. The diagram below shows the lines created when a beam of light from a particular star passes through a spectrometer. How would you go about making sense out of all those lines? No single element gives off lines in that particular pattern. It's almost as though the star were trying to tell you something about itself in a secret code. But what is it?

◄ *When light from two elements blends together, their spectral lines occur together.*

The trick to cracking the code is that when light from two elements blends together, the spectral lines of both elements appear at the same time. So compare the spectral lines of the elements on page 28 with those above. Which two of those elements are in this star? Once you've cracked the code you will have used light from a star to figure out something about the star's makeup. You will have read a message from a star!

Checkpoint

1. How is starlight like light from a lamp?
2. If you could see all the waves coming from the stars, would they look like the electromagnetic spectrum on pages 26 and 27? Explain.
3. How is starlight used to learn about stars?
4. **Take Action!** Find out how AM and FM radio waves differ. Use diagrams to explain the difference to your class.

Seeing Light's True Colors

Is the light that comes from a lamp all the same color? Find out by making your own spectroscope.

Picture A

Picture B

Picture C

Gather These Materials

cover goggles

cardboard tube from roll of
   paper towels

index card

scissors

nail

diffraction grating

masking tape

light source

Follow This Procedure

1 Make a chart like the one on the next page. Record your observations in your chart.

2 Put on your cover goggles.

3 Cut out two circles from an index card that will fit over the ends of the cardboard tube. Be careful when using the scissors.

4 Cut one of the circles in half. Tape the two halves over one end of the tube but separate them slightly so they form a slit. (Picture A)

5 Use tape to seal the spaces between the tube and the circle. Do not cover the slit. (Picture B)

6 Punch a small hole in the middle of the other circle using a nail.

7 Cover the hole with the diffraction grating. A diffraction grating separates light. Tape the circle and grating over the other end of the cardboard tube. (Picture C)

8 Use tape to seal the tube so that no light can enter except through the hole and slit.

Predict: *What will you see when you look at a light source through the diffraction grating?*

9 Aim the tube with the slit end toward a light source. Look through the other end and record what you see. *CAUTION: Do not look directly at the sun with your spectroscope.*

State Your Conclusions

1. What kinds of patterns or colors appear through the grating? Make a drawing of what you see.
2. What part of the electromagnetic spectrum can you see through the diffraction grating?
3. What does your spectroscope do to the light that comes from the lamp?

Let's Experiment

Do all indoor light sources give off the same light spectrum? Use what you know about scientific methods to find out.

LESSON 2.2 *Collecting Light*

How can you gather lots of starlight?

You couldn't have pulled off that discovery about the elements in a star just by staring up at the starlight. You needed the spectrometer. You might have used another instrument scientists use to collect and study starlight: a telescope. With even the simplest telescope, you can look up at the stars and get a lot more clues about the stars than you can by just staring with your eyes. How do telescopes gather starlight? Let's find out.

The Bending of Light

One of two ways a telescope can gather light is by bending it. Light bends as it changes speed while passing from one material to another. Scientists call this bending of light **refraction.** You see refraction when you stick a straw into a glass of water. The straw looks like it's bending, but it isn't. Actually the light from the straw bends as it passes from water into the air.

Look at the lenses in the pictures below. What do you notice about the shape of the lenses? How do they differ? The lens with the middle thinner than the edges is a concave lens. The other lens whose middle part is thicker than its edges is a convex lens. Now take a look at the waves of light being refracted as they pass from the air into the glass lenses. The light bends in this way because light travels more slowly through glass than it does through air.

▼ The shape of a lens determines how light passing through it will bend.

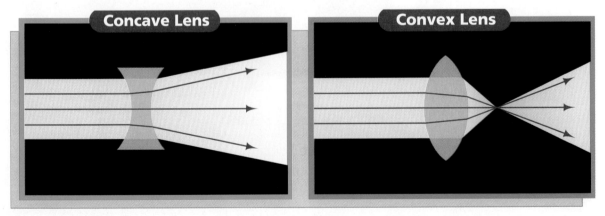

A 32

To understand how a lens bends light, look at the arrows that go through the convex lens. With its smoothly curved shape, a convex lens bends the light waves as they pass through it in such a way that the light comes together in a single point—the focal point.

A concave lens also uses refraction to direct the light's path. But notice how the light doesn't come together in a focal point. In a concave lens the light spreads apart as it passes through the lens.

The first telescopes gathered light from the stars by using lenses. Today many telescopes use the same method to gather starlight. A telescope captures lots of light coming from an object and focuses it for your eye by putting lenses together in different combinations.

The picture shows one way lenses can be organized in a telescope. A simple refracting telescope uses a pair of convex lenses. A large lens in front collects light and bends it to form an image. A smaller convex lens works with the larger one. This combination gives you a much clearer picture of those faraway points of light than you could ever get using just your eyes.

The Italian scientist Galileo (gal′ ə lē′ ō) was the first person ever to use a telescope to gather starlight. In 1609, Galileo ground two small pieces of glass into lenses. Then he put them at opposite ends of a tube and peered into the heavens. Galileo was able to make some thrilling discoveries. He could see ten times as many stars as anyone had ever seen before!

▼ *A refracting telescope collects starlight by using lenses.*

Convex lens

Convex lens

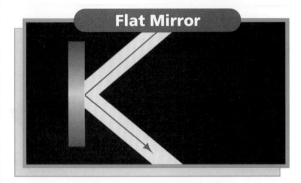

Flat Mirror

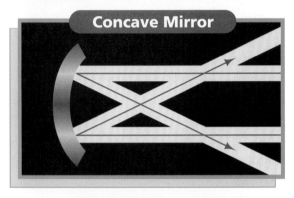

Concave Mirror

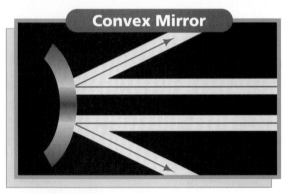

Convex Mirror

Curved mirrors change the direction of light.

The Bouncing of Light

For almost 400 years scientists have been following in Galileo's footsteps, using telescopes to collect light from the stars. But not all scientists have chosen to go about their collecting in the same way as Galileo.

Along the way some scientists thought there must be a better way than using lenses to gather starlight. After all, bending isn't the only way light can form an image. At least once each day you probably see an image of yourself that was created not by bending light through lenses, but with reflecting light from mirrors!

A second method scientists use to gather light is based on what happens when you look in a mirror. You know how light bends when it passes through a glass lens that is transparent. But light also bounces off the surfaces of many objects, especially those that are shiny. This bouncing of light off a surface is called **reflection** (ri flek′ shən).

Study the three pictures to the left. They show light reflecting off differently shaped mirrors. As you can see, light is almost completely reflected when it hits a polished surface like a mirror. Each of the three mirrors is very good at bouncing back light, but the shapes of the mirrors cause the light to bounce in different directions.

When a beam of light strikes the flat mirror, the light bounces back at the same angle that it hit the mirror's surface. Light always reflects off a smooth surface at the same angle that the light strikes it.

Now see what happens when the mirror is curved. Curved mirrors change the direction of light because of their shapes. Light that strikes a concave mirror bounces toward the center to a focal point. When light strikes a convex mirror, it bounces outwards and spreads farther apart. Note that the light does not come together in a focal point.

The second type of telescope—called a reflecting telescope—takes advantage of the way concave mirrors bounce light. Study the picture to see how a reflecting telescope uses mirrors instead of lenses. Mirrors in this kind of telescope bounce starlight together to form a clear, magnified image, and focus it to your eye.

Can you imagine two ways to collect light that are more different than refracting telescopes and reflecting telescopes? One kind of telescope bends light through a convex piece of clear material and the other bounces it off a concave piece of material that's not clear at all. Reflection and refraction are two properties of light that help scientists decode those star messages.

Comparing Telescopes

Although both types of telescopes are used by scientists, each has advantages and disadvantages. A reflecting telescope is usually cheaper than a refracting telescope because mirrors are easier to make than lenses. If you own a pair of glasses or contact lenses, chances are you're careful not to lose or break them. You know those carefully crafted lenses can cost a lot.

On the other hand, a problem with reflecting telescopes is that the mirrors need to be cleaned and recoated from time to time. But telescopes that use mirrors have an advantage that makes them much more useful to scientists for viewing faint, faraway objects. Mirrors can be made much larger than lenses.

Why should the size of a lens or mirror matter so much? Because as lenses and mirrors get bigger, their light-gathering power increases dramatically. For example, when the diameter of a lens or mirror is doubled, its light-gathering power is 4 times greater. If the diameter is made 4 times larger, the light-gathering power is 16 times greater!

Into The Field

What do you see on each side of a spoon? Observe your reflection on each side of a shiny metal spoon. Record your observations. How does each side look like a concave or a convex mirror?

▼ *A reflecting telescope uses mirrors to collect starlight.*

Flat mirror

Concave mirror

Recall that the nearest star beyond the sun is over four light years away. With those great distances, no wonder scientists need to gather as much light as possible when it comes to studying the stars. New problems arose as engineers constructed bigger and bigger mirrors for reflective telescopes. For one thing, the huge mirrors were so heavy that they sagged under their own weight and warped. So scientists built telescopes like the Keck, which are made up of many small mirrors arranged in such a way that they act like one large mirror.

Have you ever seen a mirror that's been cracked into pieces? If the pieces are still right in place in the frame, you can see an accurate reflection of yourself. But bits of your face appear distorted if some of the pieces are twisted in the frame. That's why all the small pieces that make up the mirror in a large telescope must be placed in just the right spot, and carefully kept there.

▲ Thirty-six individual mirrors work together in the Keck telescope to form a single image.

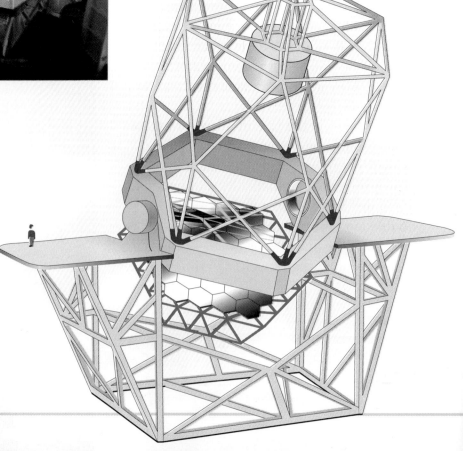

▲ *The Keck telescope sits over 4 km above sea level.*

The Keck telescope sits on top of Mauna Kea, a large volcanic mountain in Hawaii. The Keck is 10 meters in diameter, making it the world's largest light collector. The mirror with which the Keck collects light is really 36 hexagonal mirrors, each about 2 meters wide. Notice in the picture on page 36 that the mirrors fit together like tiles on a floor. Each individual mirror rests on a movable support. A computer adjusts every support twice each second. This adjustment assures that the Keck's 36 hexagons always work together as one single, gigantic concave mirror.

Look how far scientists have come in collecting waves of light. They've gone from Galileo's two tiny lenses that could see craters on the moon to the Keck's 36 mirrors that can see beyond billions of stars!

Just remember, stars give off lots of other kinds of waves than the light that you see. Lenses and mirrors can make small things look bigger, but they can't help you see things that are invisible. Next, you'll find out how scientists are collecting those invisible waves from outer space.

Checkpoint

1. How can refraction be used to gather light?
2. How does the shape of a mirror affect the way light is reflected?
3. Why are scientists interested in developing telescopes with larger lenses or mirrors?
4. **Take Action!** A periscope uses mirrors in a similar way as a telescope. Use a cardboard tube and mirrors to construct a periscope.

It's All Relative!

Isaac Newton invented one of the first reflecting telescopes. Compare the relative Light Gathering Power (LGP) of Newton's mirror to the LGP of his unaided eye at night.

$$LGP = \left(\frac{\text{diameter of mirror}}{\text{diameter of pupil}}\right)^2$$

$$LGP = \left(\frac{0.210 \text{ m}}{0.007 \text{ m}}\right)^2 = (30)^2$$

Then square that number. $(30)^2 = 900$

So Newton could gather about 900 times more light with his telescope than with the unaided eye.

The graph shows the diameters of some large telescopes.

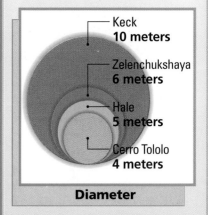

- Keck **10 meters**
- Zelenchukshaya **6 meters**
- Hale **5 meters**
- Cerro Tololo **4 meters**

Diameter

What Did You Find Out?
1. *How many times more powerful is the Cerro Tololo than your unaided eye?*
2. *Compare the LGP of the largest and smallest telescopes in the chart.*

Make a Light Trap

Light travels in straight lines. But if you trap light and cause it to reflect many times, it will look like it's bending. Try this activity to see how this happens.

Picture A

Picture B

Picture C

Gather These Materials

cover goggles

clear plastic 1-liter bottle
  with label removed

bottle cap for plastic
  bottle

water

funnel

black construction paper

tape

pan or pail

pushpin

flashlight

Follow This Procedure

1 Make a chart like the one on the next page. Record your observations in your chart.

2 Put on your cover goggles.

3 Use the funnel to fill the plastic 1-liter bottle with water. (Picture A) Replace the bottle cap.

4 Cover the bottle with black construction paper leaving an opening of about 3 centimeters. Secure the paper with tape.

5 Place the bottle over a pan or pail.

6 Use the pushpin to carefully make a hole somewhere on the lower part of the bottle directly across from the opening in the paper. (Picture B) Twist the pushpin to enlarge the hole slightly. Take the pushpin out.

Predict: *What would happen to the water if you twisted off the cap?*

7 Dim the lights in the room. Shine a flashlight through the opening in the paper and twist off the cap. (Picture C)

8 What do you see in the water streaming from the bottle? Record your observations.

9 Trace the path of the light from the flashlight to the water. Put your finger in the beam of light.

Observations of light

State Your Conclusions

1. If light travels in a straight line, how did the stream of water light up?

2. How can this property of light be useful to people?

Let's Experiment

Will the number of holes in the bottle make a difference in how the light acts? Use what you know about scientific methods to find out.

2.3 *Invisible Waves*

▶ *How can you learn from waves you can't even see?*

You learned how powerful telescopes gather visible starlight. But what about all those invisible waves stars give off? Scientists are just as anxious to gather as many of the invisible waves as they can. Invisible waves help unlock the secrets of the stars.

Waves Beyond the Violet

Scientists have developed specialized detectors that reveal the invisible radiation stars give off. In this way scientists get much more information about what's going on in space than they could from studying only visible starlight. Since the earth's atmosphere blocks out most waves with frequencies higher than visible light, few of these high-frequency waves reach the earth. So scientists send detectors above the atmosphere to collect these waves. Scientists have been collecting high-frequency waves above the atmosphere for only about 20 years. But they've already learned some incredible things from the invisible waves they've studied. Let's look at some of them and how they affect your life.

▼ *Gamma rays are used to preserve foods.*

Gamma | X Ray | UV

Did you know that one kind of high-frequency wave, gamma rays, is used in food-processing plants, hospitals, and factories? Food-processing plants send those high-energy waves through foods, such as those in the picture, to kill bacteria. Doctors send them through people's bodies to destroy tumors. Factories send them through metals to see how strong the metals are. Gamma rays are very useful here on the earth.

Scientists also use gamma rays to learn about space. At first, gamma ray detectors were sent up into the atmosphere on balloons. Now the detectors are launched into space on space shuttles.

When gamma rays enter the special chambers of a gamma ray telescope, they give images of distant stars, some of which can't even be seen by visible light telescopes. Gamma ray images give clues about what these stars are made of and how old they are.

▼ X rays and UV waves can be both beneficial and harmful.

Just as doctors use X rays to figure out what's going on inside your body, scientists use X rays to get clues about what's happening in distant stars. X-ray detectors pick up X rays coming from parts of the universe where the temperature is over one million degrees Celsius! Scientists have been watching clusters of mysterious, extremely bright stars billions of light years from the earth. These clusters, called quasars, give off large amounts of energy in the form of X rays. Scientists are getting new clues about how the universe was formed by studying the X rays coming from quasars. Many known quasars also give off radio waves and infrared radiation.

The child in the picture is using sunscreen to help prevent the harmful effects of ultraviolet radiation. But that same ultraviolet radiation gives scientists clues about certain stars that can barely be seen by telescopes that collect X rays or visible light.

Gamma **X Ray** **UV**

In 1991, the space shuttle *Columbia* brought back photographs made by ultraviolet radiation from huge groups of stars. Since ultraviolet photographs give sharper images for hotter stars than cooler ones, those pictures told not only about the positions of the stars but about their temperatures, too. Those ultraviolet photographs are yet another example of how invisible high-frequency waves can help you discover the makeup of the stars.

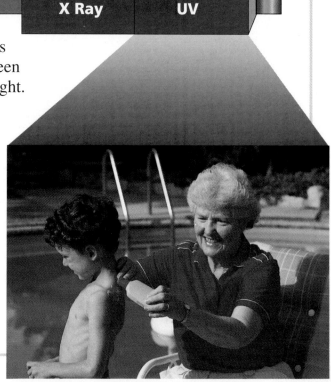

Galaxy Images

How does faint radiation give information about the stars and space?

Optical telescopes, radio observatories, infrared satellites, and gamma-ray telescopes all capture wave patterns from different parts of the electromagnetic spectrum. How do astronomers interpret these rays to get the "big picture" of outer space?

Computer systems change electromagnetic waves into electrical impulses that can be used by computers to form images. Scientists interpret the images using their increasing knowledge of astronomy.

Compare these images of the Milky Way Galaxy from four telescopes. Visible-light images become more detailed. Invisible radiation is converted into a visible image. Colors show the intensity of radiation.

Astronomers can focus on one type of radiation or combine information from all parts of the spectrum. The result? A bigger big picture!

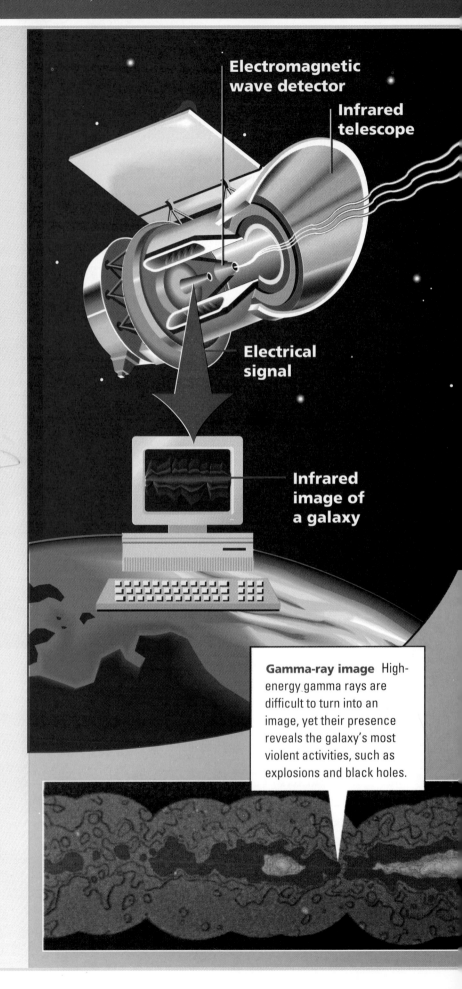

Electromagnetic wave detector

Infrared telescope

Electrical signal

Infrared image of a galaxy

Gamma-ray image High-energy gamma rays are difficult to turn into an image, yet their presence reveals the galaxy's most violent activities, such as explosions and black holes.

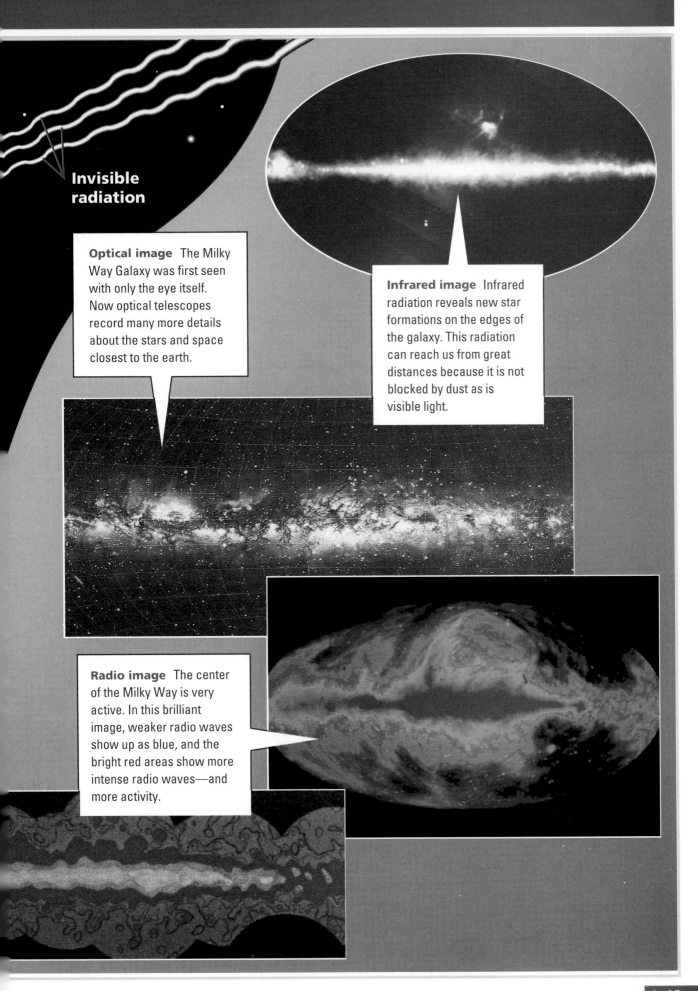

Invisible radiation

Optical image The Milky Way Galaxy was first seen with only the eye itself. Now optical telescopes record many more details about the stars and space closest to the earth.

Infrared image Infrared radiation reveals new star formations on the edges of the galaxy. This radiation can reach us from great distances because it is not blocked by dust as is visible light.

Radio image The center of the Milky Way is very active. In this brilliant image, weaker radio waves show up as blue, and the bright red areas show more intense radio waves—and more activity.

Waves Beyond the Red

Though electromagnetic waves with lower frequencies than those of visible light have less energy, they're of no less use in learning about the stars. In fact, since many of these waves are not blocked out by the earth's atmosphere, scientists didn't have to wait for the invention of the satellite to start collecting these waves. For almost a hundred years now, scientists have been able to learn about outer space by collecting low-frequency waves.

The camera that took the infrared photograph of the human body on this page used infrared radiation coming from the body, instead of reflecting visible light off it. Because the amount of infrared waves an object gives off is based on how hot or cold the object is, the photograph shows patterns of heat.

Scientists also use infrared waves to learn about objects that don't give off much light. Some of the cooler objects in the universe, such as large planets, don't give off light of their own and reflect very little light from nearby bodies. But the infrared waves that these dark objects give off help scientists find them.

Infrared waves are also helpful in studying stars just forming. Young stars may be hidden among seas of brighter, older stars. The light coming from the newborn stars can be almost impossible to see. But since the new stars are much cooler than their full-grown neighbors, infrared telescopes can pick them out of the crowd.

Chances are you benefit from radio waves several times a day. Every time you turn on a radio or TV you're inviting radio waves to provide instant communication over incredible distances.

▼ How do infrared and radio waves help scientists learn about stars?

Infrared **Radio**

Today's telescopes, such as the Very Large Array at the left, have changed much from the first telescopes.

Galileo's first telescope

Radio waves from outer space provide information to scientists too. An advantage of radio waves' low frequency is that it allows the waves to travel through vast distances, making them useful for studying faraway stars. Radio waves were emitted by stars long ago, so radio waves that reach astronomers are like fossils found by geologists. They tell astronomers about stars that exploded long ago, and pick up radiation that may have been created when the universe began.

The Very Large Array telescope pictured here collects invisible signals from deepest space and feeds them through computers. How different from Galileo's first little refracting telescopes! But the goal is the same—to gather as many waves coming from space as possible so people can interpret those sparkling dots.

Checkpoint

1. Where are detectors best located for receiving high-frequency waves? Why?
2. Why are scientists interested in "seeing" invisible waves?
3. What kind of information can scientists get from low-frequency waves that they cannot get from high-frequency waves?
4. **Take Action!** Make a list of objects around your home that use electromagnetic waves.

2.4 Bang!

How did it all begin?

Detectives might dust for fingerprints, test the ink samples, or photograph the paper to look for hidden clues that might tell them the origin of a secret document. Astronomers also search for clues to answer their questions. They take "fingerprints" of elements with spectrometers and photograph the electromagnetic waves from all over the universe. They too, are searching for origins—how all the galaxies, stars, and planets that make up the universe got to the positions where they are now.

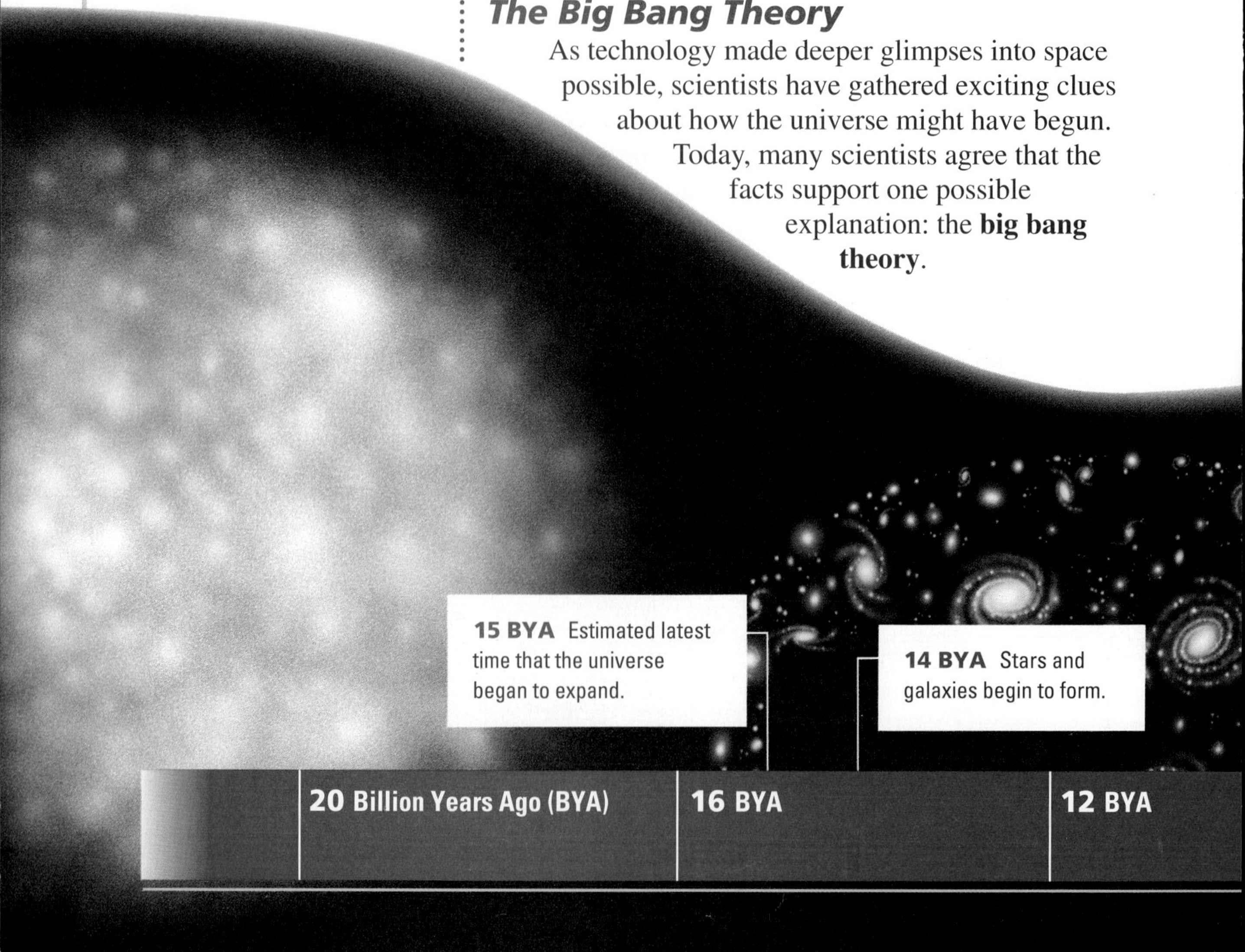

▼ Some scientists think the universe began its expansion suddenly with a big bang.

The Big Bang Theory

As technology made deeper glimpses into space possible, scientists have gathered exciting clues about how the universe might have begun. Today, many scientists agree that the facts support one possible explanation: the **big bang theory**.

15 BYA Estimated latest time that the universe began to expand.

14 BYA Stars and galaxies begin to form.

| 20 Billion Years Ago (BYA) | 16 BYA | 12 BYA |

According to the big bang theory, the entire universe started out as a clump of dense, hot matter. About 15 billion years ago, this clump shattered in a huge explosion that sent pieces of matter zooming in all directions. As these pieces flew apart, they formed the clusters of galaxies that make up the universe.

When did the galaxies stop flying apart and settle into place? They haven't! According to the big bang theory, the universe has been expanding since the moment it began.

In the Milky Way Galaxy, a supernova explosion left behind a cloud of gas and dust enriched with all the known elements. About 4.6 billion years ago, gravity caused that cloud to collapse into a ball at the center that became the sun. Chunks of the remaining materials in the cloud began to rotate and collide, forming larger bodies that finally became planets. Astronomers think many other stars have orbiting planets that were formed in the same way.

The big bang theory is an exciting idea. But how could anyone ever find evidence to support a theory that explains how galaxies far beyond the Milky Way Galaxy are drifting apart because of an event that happened 15 billion years ago?

4.6 BYA Gravity pulls matter together to form the solar system.

8 BYA

4 BYA

Today

Cosmic Tail Lights

What clues tipped scientists off that the universe might have begun with a big bang? Again, light helped. Recall that the spectral lines for any element appear at a very specific place on the spectrum. The location of each line is determined by its wavelength. For example, the top diagram shows the spectral lines for helium coming from a source here on the earth. Now compare those spectral lines with the lines in the bottom diagram. How do they differ?

Scientists have found that light given off by distant stars produces spectral lines that have shifted toward the red end of the spectrum. The spacing of the lines is exactly the same. But the lines are in a different location on the spectrum.

Helium

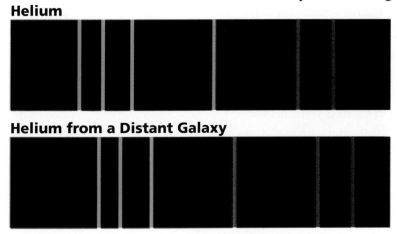

Helium from a Distant Galaxy

Scientists hypothesize that the universe is expanding by observing red shift in starlight. Red shift is caused when light waves spread out as stars move apart in space. Spectral lines from stars farthest away from Earth show the greatest shift. That is because the farthest stars are moving away fastest and their waves are spread out more.

Scientists studying spectral lines of many stars conclude that all galaxies in the universe are moving away from one another. They can estimate how quickly galaxies are moving apart—some at speeds as fast as 20,000 kilometers per second. This information leads scientists to think the big bang occurred, and the spreading began, about 15 billion years ago.

Predicting the Future

While the big bang theory explains the history of the universe, it also raises a big question: Will the universe expand forever? The answer might lie in the relationship between the universe's mass and gravity.

One idea is that galaxies would keep drifting apart. Space would get emptier and emptier. Galaxies would grow dim. Our universe that began with a *bang* would die with a *sigh*.

◄ *Dr. Stephen Hawking thinks that scientific research over the next 20 years will uncover many secrets of the universe.*

On the other hand, if the universe has enough mass, its gravity might be strong enough to stop all the galaxies from drifting apart and start pulling them in. If this happens the universe could crash in on itself until all the galaxies are squashed back into the same original clump. That would be the end of the universe. Then, perhaps another big bang would occur!

The brilliant British scientist Stephen Hawking, shown here, is one of many searching for a link between the force of gravity and forces that hold the parts of atoms together. He thinks this link will be the key to understanding how the universe began, and thus how it will end. For now, Hawking has yet another idea about the universe—that it had no beginning and will have no end. So don't worry that the universe will begin dying out or come crashing back in on itself tomorrow! No doubt scientists will debate this question for many years.

Checkpoint

1. According to the big bang theory, how did the universe get started?
2. What evidence supports the big bang theory?
3. What could affect the future of the universe?
4. **Take Action!** Find out some new theories that explain the formation of the universe. Present these to the class as a TV news show.

Chapter Review

Reviewing Words and Concepts

Write the letter of the word or phrase that best completes each sentence.

1. A reflecting telescope uses mirrors with a _____ shape.
2. The bending of light is called _____.
3. Most scientists use the _____ to explain how the universe began.
4. The bouncing of light off a surface is called _____.
5. The range of light you can see is the _____.
6. The frequency of a wave increases as its _____ decreases.
7. A lens that is thicker in the middle than at its edges is _____.
8. A _____ is used to study the light given off by elements.
9. Light is a form of energy that travels in _____.
10. Quasars give off large amounts of energy in the form of _____.

a. waves
b. wavelength
c. spectrometer
d. convex
e. concave
f. refraction
g. reflection
h. big bang theory
i. visible spectrum
j. X rays

Connecting Ideas

1. Copy the concept map. Use the terms at the right to complete the map about the electromagnetic spectrum.

infrared waves   colored light
electromagnetic spectrum
gamma rays   radio waves
ultraviolet radiation   X rays

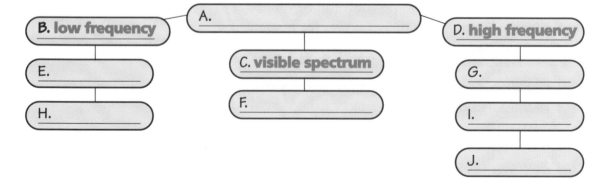

2. Write a sentence or two that summarizes the ideas shown in the concept map.

Interpreting What You Learned

1. Which colors in the visible spectrum have the least energy? the most energy?
2. Describe how the spectral lines created from the visible light of a star are as unique as a fingerprint.
3. Explain how the reflection of a beam of light changes when the angle changes.
4. How is refraction used in telescopes?
5. Why are concave mirrors rather than convex mirrors used in reflecting telescopes?
6. How has technology enabled scientists to make larger reflecting telescopes?
7. What information do scientists obtain by studying gamma rays, radio waves, and infrared waves?
8. What parts of the electromagnetic spectrum do scientists use to study quasars?
9. In which direction does the big bang theory suggest galaxies are moving?
10. What do scientists think causes the red shift in starlight?

Performance Assessment

How does changing energy affect a wave?

Materials • piece of string (about 3 meters long)

Collecting Data

1. Tie one end of a piece of string to a stationary object such as a doorknob or the back of a chair.
2. Holding the free end of the string in your hand, move away from the stationary object. Leave a small amount of slack in the string.
3. Flick your wrist in a rapid up-and-down movement. Observe the wavelength and frequency of the wave formed by the string. Draw a diagram that represents the wave's wavelength and frequency.
4. Create another wave along your string using a slower, gentler, up-and-down movement of your entire arm. Observe the wavelength and frequency created by this movement. Draw a diagram that represents the wave's wavelength and frequency.

Analyzing Data

Compare the two diagrams you made. Explain the effect that the changing energy of your arm had on the frequency and wavelength of the waves.

How's it know the difference between a nickel and a penny?

Discover Activity

What Goes on in This Machine?

It seems simple enough. You put in a coin, turn a crank, and out drops a handful of nuts. But is it really that simple? Think about all the things that must take place inside this machine for the nuts to come out. Draw a diagram of what you think takes place. Explain your diagram to your classmates.

For Discussion

1. How does the machine know which coin you put in?

2. Explain why your diagram is a good model.

3.1 *Guiding Stars*

▶ *How did people learn from stars long ago?*

In the last two chapters you learned how scientists found out so much about stars. But did you know that much of the equipment researchers use to study the stars is less than 75 years old? So how did people who lived long before that equipment was invented learn about the stars? They used their eyes!

For example, the star map to the right was made in the 900s by Chinese astronomers. Other cultures throughout history used similar star maps. Why did they create such maps?

Myth Makers

One way ancient cultures made sense out of the night sky was by creating myths—stories about how things came to be the way they are. Myths helped people organize what they knew in a way that was easy to remember.

For example, ancient Greeks noticed a group of stars clustered together in a shape they thought looked like a big bear. You might recognize the Big Bear constellation, shown on page 54 because of the Big Dipper—a group of stars that is part of the constellation.

Ancient Greeks created a myth to explain the birth of the Big Bear constellation: Once there was a young woman named Callisto (Kə lis′tō) who was so beautiful that Zeus (Züs), the Greek king of the gods, fell in love with her. Zeus turned Callisto into a bear to hide her for himself. But a hunter almost killed the bear with his spear! So Zeus lifted Callisto up into the sky where she would be safe from hunters. She remains there today!

Maybe ancient people thought stories such as these really happened. But whether they believed every word or not, myths were important. They satisfied the curiosity people had when gazing at those mysterious dots in the sky, and helped them in their everyday lives.

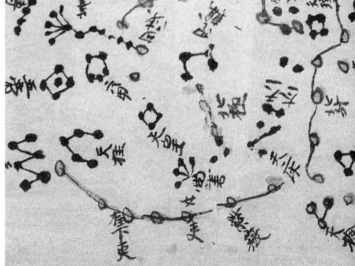

▼ *This Chinese star map shows many constellations we recognize today.*

North Star

▲ *Ancient travelers used the Big Dipper to determine directions.*

➤ *The Bighorn Medicine Wheel (right) and Stonehenge (below) were constructed to track the movements of the sun and stars.*

Compasses, Calendars, and Clocks

You might wonder how a myth could be useful in everyday life. If you connected myths with stars, and stars with sailing, you're moving in the right direction.

The diagram shows how sailors used the myth of Callisto: The North Star is a guiding star that, because of its position relative to the earth, doesn't seem to change position in the sky. You can figure out where you are and the direction in which you're headed if you know how to find the North Star. Sailors and travelers can always find the North Star by remembering to look for the Big Bear in the sky. Two of the stars in the Big Bear constellation always point to the North Star.

Ancient cultures also could read the stars like a calendar. Myths about certain constellations reminded them that particular stars shifted when the seasons changed. Clues about the change of seasons were very valuable since many ancient people were hunter-gatherers or farmers. Even today Hopi Indians in Arizona use this system.

Stone structures still stand that ancient cultures made to tell the time of year by measuring the position of stars and planets. You can see three of those stone calendars on these pages. Stonehenge was built by Bronze Age people in England. The Bighorn Medicine wheel dates from about 1400 and was made by the Native Americans of present-day Wyoming. Both structures were used to determine the beginning of important times of the year, such as summer or winter. These important times were determined by aligning stones with the directions of the sun at its rising and setting. The third stone calendar was made by the Aztecs, an ancient civilization who were the ancestors of some of today's Mexicans. This calendar, too, was based on the orbit of the earth around the sun.

In a way, each of the ancient constructions is like a clock. The rocks are like the circle of numbers that go around the clock. But the hands of these ancient timepieces are waves of light from the sky. The earth in its orbit around the sun is the machinery that moves the hands!

▲ *This Aztec calendar was based on the earth's orbit around the sun.*

Checkpoint

1. Why did ancient people construct myths?
2. How did the ancient cultures make practical use of the stars?
3. **Take Action!** Design a simple water clock that has ten drops per minute. Hint: An empty milk carton and pin holes might work.

Activity

Tell Time With a Star Watch

How can you tell the time if you are not wearing a watch? On a starry night you can tell time by the stars. Find out how with this activity.

Picture A

Picture B

Picture C

Gather These Materials

cover goggles
copy of star watch
   patterns A and B
scissors
glue

thin cardboard
brass paper fastener
large rubber band
directional compass
flashlight

Follow This Procedure

1 Put on your cover goggles.

2 Your teacher will give you a copy of two circular star watch patterns like the ones on the next page. Circle A shows some stars and Circle B shows the names of the months. Cut out the circles. (Picture A)

3 Glue each circle onto thin cardboard.

4 When the glue is dry, trim each circle neatly and carefully cut out the window in Circle A.

5 Use a brass paper fastener to carefully poke a hole in the center of each circle. Then place Circle A on top of Circle B and line up the holes.

6 Fasten the circles with the brass paper fastener. (Picture B)

7 Twist a large rubber band around the fastener a couple of times. (Picture C) Then put the rubber band loosely on your wrist. You are now wearing your own star watch.

8 Take your star watch outside on a starry night. Use your directional compass to find north.

A 56

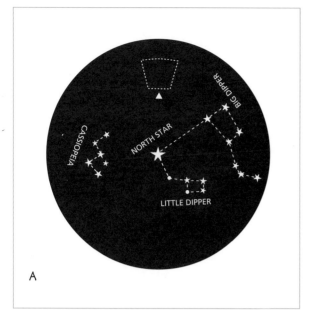

A

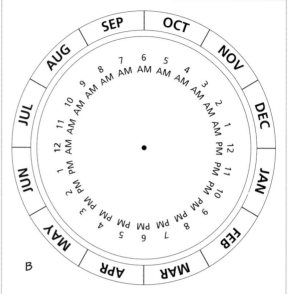

B

9 Face north and hold your star watch so that the current month is at the top. Leave the month dial in that position.

10 Look up at the stars and find the Big Dipper.

Predict: *How should you position your star dial as you look up at the stars?*

11 Turn the star dial until it matches the position of the stars as you see them in the sky. Look through the window on the dial to tell the time. You might need your flashlight to read it.

State Your Conclusions

1. What time did your star watch show? Is it accurate?
2. Why does your star watch work? Why does the position of the stars change each month?
3. What are the advantages and disadvantages of telling time by the stars?

Let's Experiment

Use your star watch at two different times during the evening. How accurate are the readings? Compare them to the actual times.

3.2 *The Big Picture*

▶ **What did ancient cultures think about the universe?**

Today, scientists travel widely to study the ancient stone calendars. They hope to get clues about what the ancient cultures thought about their world.

Getting clues to how people think about the earth today is a lot simpler—just look at a globe! The globe helps us understand how the earth is like a ball covered with huge bodies of water separated by irregularly shaped pieces of land. However, our picture of the earth and how it fits into the universe has come a long way since ancient times.

Ptolemy's Picture

One ancient picture of the universe was developed by the Greek scientist Ptolemy (tol′ə mē) who lived in the second century. Forming a picture of how the universe fits together was a lot easier in Ptolemy's time than it is today. People thought the solar system and only about a thousand stars made up the universe. Ptolemy didn't have to deal with the many billions of stars we now know are out there. The picture shows Ptolemy's idea of the universe. Notice the earth was at the center of everything. The sun, planets, and all the stars revolved around the earth.

➤ *In Ptolemy's universe the earth was at the center.*

In Ptolemy's picture, the deepest parts of space weren't very far away. They were even closer in other ancient pictures. The ancient Egyptians believed that the sky hung just above the earth like a canopy. Four mountains at the corners of the world acted like bedposts holding up this canopy of sky. To get closer to the canopy, Egyptian astronomers climbed mountains to study the stars.

The Aztec and Mayan civilizations thought the universe was made of a series of layers. Every layer contained a different kind of object. A layer above the earth held the moon, the next layer held the clouds, and then layers above those held the stars, the sun, Venus, the comets, and on and on. Besides the 13 layers that were stacked above the earth, these people thought 9 more layers went deep beneath the ground.

Ptolemy was wrong, but his idea that the earth was the center of the universe made sense to him and many other people. In fact, all across Europe most people thought Ptolemy's idea was correct for about 1500 years. Then in the early 1500s, Nicholas Copernicus, (kə pėr′ne kes) a Polish astronomer, studied the existing theories of the universe and developed his own ideas. How did Copernicus's universe, shown below, differ from that of Ptolemy?

Ptolemy, the Aztecs, the Maya, and Copernicus all lived on the same planet and saw the same bright lights in the sky. Why did they all come up with quite different ideas of how the parts fit together?

Into The Field

Why did Ptolemy think the earth was the center of the solar system?
Observe the sky. Figure out what Ptolemy saw that made him draw his conclusion. Record your observations.

◄ *In Copernicus's universe, the planets revolved around the sun.*

Models

Today, it's easy to point out Ptolemy's mistakes. But he did give people an idea of how the parts of the universe they knew fit together. Because Ptolemy was able to bring together the available information about the universe into a single picture, you can say he created a **model**—a representation of how something looks or works. You made a model of the nut machine in the Discover Activity. Every culture throughout history has had some sort of model of the universe.

When you start a jigsaw puzzle, the finished picture is unclear. But with each new piece, the picture becomes clearer. Similarly, when putting together a model of the universe, you have to learn how all the pieces—the bodies in the sky—make one big picture.

You might not think of the ancient models of the universe as very scientific. The Egyptian picture of the sky draped over the earth may seem more like fantasy than science. But people only had their eyes and some primitive measuring tools to study the stars. Stare into the sky and imagine the stars draped over you, just a kilometer or two away. It's not so hard!

➤ *Astronomers in the late 1600s used tools such as these to study stars.*

Technology helps people make models. In the past, people have developed models using simple tools, such as those shown on these pages. You have learned about some of the improved tools, machines, and devices that enable scientists to gather more information. The more information scientists collect, the more complete their models can be and the more complete a model is, the more useful it is for explaining the universe.

A model is limited by the way people think. For example, some Europeans thought the universe was perfect. If anyone noticed spots on the sun, they assumed something must be blocking their view—since the sun had to be a perfect ball. But the ancient Chinese didn't hold this view of perfection. That's why they discovered sunspots long before the Europeans did.

The way people think can change. Technology can change even faster. Models of the universe are bound to change too. Sometimes a model is adjusted slightly. Other times the whole model is discarded, making way for a new one.

▲ This astronomical quadrant was used to determine the location of stars.

The Model of Today

In the centuries since Ptolemy's day, breakthroughs in technology have transformed our model of the universe many times. In some ways, today's model is completely different from Ptolemy's. For example, the earth doesn't play nearly as big a role in our universe as it did in Ptolemy's. The earth has gone from being the main attraction, at the center of everything, to being a tiny, dark speck orbiting a rather small star in a remote part of a rather ordinary galaxy!

Another striking difference between today's model of the universe and the ancient models is size. In most ancient models, the night sky extends just a little beyond the earth. In today's model, the universe might be endless. Astronomers have seen stars about 14 billion light years away—and they don't think the universe stops there.

Although scientists can't estimate how big the universe is, they can estimate how old the part we see is. You know they think this part of the universe was born at least 15 billion years ago during the big bang.

Today's model of the universe presents more kinds of bodies than the ancient models did. Among the unusual bodies scientists have found are mysterious black holes, shown below, that might be the remains of huge stars. The force of gravity coming from these black holes is so powerful that it pulls in everything that comes near them. That's why black holes are invisible—they even pull in light shining past them.

Astronomers cannot see a black hole directly because no light escapes from it. The black hole seems visible because it pulls gases from a nearby star into it.

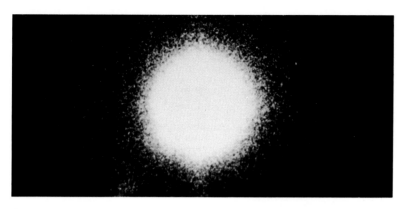

▲ *Astronomers think quasars are the farthest objects from us in the universe.*

The picture shows another kind of stellar body that belongs in our model of the universe. These incredibly bright objects—called quasars—have the largest red shifts known. Therefore, astronomers think quasars are the farthest objects from us. The fact that quasars are so far away and we can still see them tells scientists that they give off amazing amounts of light. Quasars are so far away and so bright that scientists wonder whether they could have possibly come from the same clump as everything else. As new space telescopes provide scientists a closer look at quasars, scientists may find information that proves the big bang theory—the basis of today's model—is wrong!

Therefore, even though today's model of the universe is based on thousands of years of knowledge, there's no guarantee that it's right. Just as the ancient pictures of the universe might seem silly to you, a thousand years from now, someone may look at your picture of the universe as silly. Models are always changing as new information is gathered.

Checkpoint

1. What was Ptolemy's idea of the universe?
2. Why does a model change?
3. How is our present model of the universe different from the ancient ones?
4. **Take Action!** Research some ancient models of the universe. Then construct a bulletin board comparing some of those models.

What's in the Box?

How can you design a model of something you cannot see? Let's investigate.

What To Do
A. Ask a classmate to put an object in a shoe box.
B. With the lid on, pick up the box and tilt it from side to side.
C. Draw a model of what you think is inside the box.
D. Without looking in the box, run the end of a pencil over the object.
E. Change your model of what you think is in the box, if you want to.

Record Your Data

First Model

Second Model

What Did You Find Out?
1. *Were your two model drawings based on a guess or evidence? Explain.*
2. *How can scientists make a model of something they cannot see?*

Activity

The Expanding Rubber Band Universe

Use a rubber band to make a model showing how galaxies travel away from the earth at different speeds in our expanding universe.

Picture A

Picture B

Picture C

Gather These Materials

cover goggles
pen

rubber band
metric ruler

Follow This Procedure

1 Make a chart like the one on the next page. Record your observations on your chart.

2 Put on your cover goggles.

3 Use your pen to make two marks at the opposite ends of a rubber band. (Picture A) These marks will represent Galaxies A and B.

4 Place the metric ruler on your desk. Lay the rubber band against the ruler so that one end is on the 0 centimeter line. (Picture B) The earth in this model is at the 0 centimeter mark.

5 Measure the length of the rubber band to the nearest 0.5 centimeter. Record your measurement in the chart.

6 Record the positions of Galaxies A and B to the nearest 0.5 centimeter.

Predict: *Will Galaxies A and B move the same distance as you stretch the rubber band?*

7 Hold the rubber band at the 0 centimeter end with your left hand and pull the rubber band to the right. Stretch it to about three times its length. (Picture C) Record its length. This stretching represents the expansion of the universe.

Record Your Results

	Length of rubber band	Position of Galaxy A	Position of Galaxy B
Unstretched			
Stretched			
Total Change			

8 Record the new positions of Galaxies A and B. The marks will stretch out, so use the middle of the mark to measure its new position.

9 Record the differences between the old and new positions for Galaxies A and B.

State Your Conclusions

1. How far apart were the two galaxies when you started? How far apart were they after the "universe" expanded?

2. Suppose you were at the 0 centimeter mark on the ruler observing the galaxies move. How far away did Galaxy A move from you? How far away did Galaxy B move from you?

3. How does this activity fit in with the current model of the universe?

Let's Experiment

How might the rubber band thickness change your results? Use what you know about scientific methods to find out.

3.3 *Deeper Space*

How did today's model get made?

The model of the universe has come a long way since Ptolemy's day. But this change didn't happen overnight. It happened bit by bit over the years. As people gazed deeper into space, a new model of the universe came together piece by piece.

Decades of Discovery in Space

During this century, change has hit the model of the universe like an avalanche. New technology has led to new discoveries and more technology. Nowadays, every decade brings more change than entire centuries did in ancient times. Look below at some of those advances.

One scientist who helped start this century's avalanche of discovery was Edwin Hubble. When Hubble began his work in the 1920s, scientists thought the Milky Way Galaxy was the only galaxy. But Hubble noticed fuzzy patches of light coming from beyond the Milky Way Galaxy! Soon the model of the universe changed to feature many galaxies. When scientists studied different galaxies, they found that the galaxies were moving apart. The Big Bang theory was born.

1923 Edwin Hubble discovers light from beyond the Milky Way Galaxy.

1937 Grote Reber builds the first radio telescope used for astronomical observation.

1920

1940

In 1937, about 13 years after Hubble's discovery, an American radio engineer named Grote Reber made history by collecting another kind of wave—radio waves. Reber's first radio telescope—made in his own backyard in Illinois—proved that scientists could study the universe by collecting electromagnetic waves other than visible light.

Although scientists couldn't wait to start collecting other waves coming from space, they faced a big obstacle: the earth's atmosphere. Remember, most electromagnetic waves are blocked out by the atmosphere. Scientists knew that if they could position their telescopes above the atmosphere, they could collect all kinds of waves from space. But how…?

In 1957, the Russian Sputnik—the first artificial satellite—orbited the earth above the atmosphere. Soon bigger and better satellites were being built as quickly as possible, carrying technology above the atmosphere to pick up waves from distant objects in the universe.

In the 1970s, scientists developed a new detector chip called the charged couple device, or CCD. The CCD has millions of tiny electronic parts that work together to make incredibly clear images of distant objects.

Since Hubble discovered other galaxies, the model of the universe has grown so fast it's hard to keep up with it. But remember, it's still just a model. No one has ever visited any of those distant galaxies!

1957 The Russian Sputnik orbits the earth above the atmosphere.

1970's Scientists develop the charged couple device, which makes clearer images.

1960

1980

Eyes on the Universe

Technology helps us expand our knowledge of the universe.

If you've ever looked through a telescope at the nighttime sky, you know how surprising the view can be. Suddenly stars appear where you see only darkness with your naked eye.

The telescope is a tool of discovery. The instruments shown on these pages are among the most advanced tools of discovery in the world. With them, astronomers can learn more about objects and events in the deepest reaches of space.

What advances in technology led to the development of these instruments? One advance in the 1970s and 1980s was the development of electronic devices that allowed spacecraft to be remotely controlled from the earth. Other advances involved improvements in computer systems and solar energy.

Think about how the "eyes in space" shown here will add data to the model of the universe.

Hubble Telescope
Launched by the space shuttle *Atlantis* in 1990, the Hubble is being used to search for planets orbiting nearby stars and to see into the centers of nearby galaxies.

Gamma Ray Observatory
Launched by *Atlantis* in 1991, this telescope performed the first all-sky survey of gamma rays over a two-year period. It has detected gamma-ray bursts across the universe.

Advanced X-Ray Astrophysics Facility
This instrument will be launched around 1998. Its mission will be to gather radiation that reveals new information about the age of the universe.

The Space Infrared Telescope Facility is scheduled to be launched around the year 2000.

► In the near future scientists may have instruments on permanent space stations.

The Stargazing of Tomorrow

The avalanche of discovery in space isn't over. In fact, it's probably just starting. In the decades ahead, scientists think they'll get much closer to answering the big questions about the universe. How big is it? What are its parts? How did it begin? What is its future?

Soon some scientists may be trying to answer those questions from work stations out in space! Imagine yourself on a permanent space station, like the one in the picture below, where scientists will do daily research beyond the earth's atmosphere. These stations will also be a place to launch or repair artificial satellites.

Most scientists will still be studying the universe from the earth. But they'll see farther than ever before because of new technology such as the Space Infrared Telescope Facility, pictured to the left. The SIRTF is a space telescope that will be able to collect infrared rays from galaxies billions of light-years away. After its launch, this super-powerful telescope will take clear pictures of distant, dim objects in space.

Remember, light that reaches you from a billion light-years away was given off a billion years ago. By collecting infrared rays from a billion light-years away, the SIRTF will be able to give pictures of objects that are farther away—and therefore older—than any other objects seen by telescopes before.

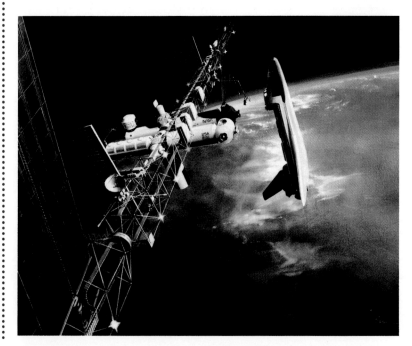

Believe it or not, discoveries about events that took place long ago and far away could have a big effect on you, right here on the earth. By learning about the lives of stars, scientists will better understand how the sun— which you depend on for your survival—will change over time. By discovering planets that orbit other stars, scientists may learn much about the history of life and the future of the earth. By studying the weather on other planets, such as in the atmosphere of Venus, scientists will learn more about weather on our planet.

By collecting rocks from other planets and moons, such as this one from the earth's moon, scientists may find out more about energy and other resources on the earth and about the origins of life. And if scientists discover intelligent beings in a distant corner of the universe, just think how much those beings could tell us! They might be able to tell us what they've learned from their stargazing. Maybe they've even learned a thing or two from "earth-gazing"!

Scientists are bound to make shocking and unexpected discoveries. Do you think Hubble was planning to find a new galaxy on that historic night? His discovery took him completely by surprise. The telescopes of the future could uncover a new kind of object or material in space that's even more plentiful than stars. Think what a tremendous change that would bring to our ever-changing model of the universe!

Checkpoint

1. How has information discovered in this century changed the model of the universe?
2. What is the advantage of having telescopes in Earth's orbit instead of on the ground?
3. How might future discoveries in space help people living on the earth?
4. **Take Action!** Research future projects planned to study the universe. Design an information pamphlet to inform the public.

▲ *Moon rocks like this one give scientists clues about the origin of our planet.*

Chapter Review

Reviewing Words and Concepts

Write the letter of the word or phrase that best completes each sentence.

1. The scientist who suggested that the sun was at the center of the solar system was _____.

2. The first satellite launched into space was _____.

3. The model of the universe developed by _____ placed the earth at the center.

4. The Aztecs created a _____ based on the earth's orbit around the sun.

5. Early sailors used the _____ to guide their travels.

6. Scientists are able to obtain information about the origin of the earth by studying the makeup of _____.

7. Scientists often use a _____ to show how something works or looks.

8. A _____ is a computer chip that helps provide scientists with very clear images of distant objects.

9. Quasars have the largest _____ known.

10. Strong gravitational forces in space create unusual bodies called _____.

a. North Star
b. calendar
c. Ptolemy
d. black holes
e. model
f. Sputnik
g. red shifts
h. moon rocks
i. CCD
j. Copernicus

Connecting Ideas

1. Copy the concept map. Use the terms at the right to complete the map about universe models.

expanding galaxies   ancient

earth-centered system   modern

A. models of the universe

B. _____

C. _____

D. _____

E. _____

2. Write a sentence or two that summarizes the ideas shown in the concept map.

Interpreting What You Learned

1. What evidence shows that ancient cultures used objects in the sky for practical purposes?
2. Explain how the Aztec and Mayan models of the universe differed from the model developed by Copernicus.
3. List some advances in technology that have led to the newest telescopes in the earth's orbit.
4. How have artificial satellites expanded our view of the universe?

Performance Assessment

How can the universe be modeled?

Materials • cover goggles • 2 pieces of cardboard • 3 pushpins • string (about 30 cm long) • metric ruler • pencil • paper

Collecting Data

1. Put on your cover goggles. Place one piece of cardboard on top of the other. Fold the paper in half by width and then by length. Unfold the paper and place it on top of the cardboard.
2. Push a pushpin through the center of the paper into the cardboard. Push a second pushpin into one of the fold lines 2 centimeters away from the center. Push the third pushpin into the same fold line, 2 centimeters away from the center in the opposite direction, to make a line of pushpins.
3. Tie the ends of the string together to make a loop. Place the loop around the pushpins.
4. Place the tip of your pencil inside the loop. Pull the loop tight so the pencil is at one end of the loop. Draw a curved line on the paper by moving the pencil within the loop all the way around the pushpins. Pull the loop tight as you move the pencil around the pushpins.

5. Move the pushpins so they are on the same fold line 3 centimeters from the center. Repeat step 4.
6. Move the pushpins so they are on the same fold line 5 centimeters from the center. Repeat step 4.
7. Remove the pushpins and draw a small circle at the center of your diagram. Label the circle either *Sun* or *Earth*. Based on the label you added to the circle, title your diagram *Copernicus' Model of the Universe* or *Ptolemy's Model of the Universe*.

Analyzing Data

How is Copernicus' model of the universe different from the model developed by Ptolemy? How are the two models similar?

Where No One Has Gone Before

Space exploration has been an exciting and rewarding field for thirty years. We have gained information that helps us in many ways, including nautical charts, global communications, surveying, weather prediction, and understanding more about the origins of the universe. However, project failures and rising costs have caused a re-evaluation of the space program. Many people wonder whether we should continue to explore space. There are also questions as to whether space exploration should go forward with spacecraft that carry people or with less expensive space probes. A probe is a remote-controlled spacecraft that can gather information but does not carry people.

Project failures and rising costs have caused a re-evaluation of the space program.

Needs and Goals

To consider what might be a good course for the space program, here are some questions to think about:

- What projects are planned for the future?
- What options are there for completing those projects?
- What are the problems and risks?
- What are the expected costs?
- What do we hope to learn?
  - How valuable is the information that we hope to discover?

Gathering Information

Make a table like the one shown on the next page. In this table, list the projects being considered for the space program. Then find out what you can about each.

Possible Alternatives

- NASA (National Aeronautics and Space Administration) has proposed building a space station that would orbit the earth. It would cost $30 billion. Many long-term experiments that provide information about the environment could be conducted more easily from a space station than from the shuttle spacecraft, where they are presently done. However, those experiments can now be done for much less money.

- The probe *Viking* explored Mars in 1976 and provided a wealth of information about the surface of the planet. A mission to Mars that would carry people would permit more extensive exploration of the planet. NASA has not estimated the cost of such a mission.
- An exploration of Mars with probes would be less expensive than a mission with astronauts but might result in less conclusive information. Several missions to Mars without crews have been successful.

Crew or No Crew?

Mission	Problem/risks	Cost	Knowledge potential
Space station (with crew)			
Flight to Mars (without crew)			
Flight to Mars (with crew)			

Evaluating Alternatives
Fill in the table with your ideas about the costs, problems, and knowledge potential of each mission.

Making the Best Choice
Now decide which of the possible missions makes the most sense to you.

Now You Do It

1. Which of the missions seems to be the most valuable one for the cost? Explain.
2. Which missions seem to be the least valuable? Explain.
3. *On Your Own* See what you can find out about other missions that are ongoing or under consideration, including orbiting power stations, the Hubble Telescope, and the Earth Observing System.
4. *Critical Thinking* Many people disagree over whether or not the money that is spent on space exploration should be spent on other problems, such as medical research. What do you think?

Studying the Stars

Dr. Ron Taam

Occupation: Astrophysicist
Current Project: Studying white dwarves and black holes
Job Bonus: Getting to know scientists throughout the world

Ron Taam thought he'd be a pilot when he grew up. So he used binoculars to identify planes flying overhead. And when there were no planes, he would look at other things in the night sky. He was surprised to see that the twinkling white stars now appeared red or blue or yellow. Why? He wanted to learn more about the stars and planets. Today Dr. Ronald Taam still wants to learn more about stars—he is an astrophysicist.

How do you study the stars now?
"Instead of using optical telescopes, my research uses computers to study the data we get from X-ray telescopes."

What can you learn from X rays?
"One type of object that gives off X rays is a black hole. A black hole is very dense so all its mass is compressed into a very small space. Because it's so dense it has an extremely strong gravitational pull. This pull is so strong that nothing, not even light, can escape. Instead of seeing a speck of light in the sky, we see only blackness."

But how do you see a black hole against a black sky?
"You can't. Scientists identify a black hole by the way it affects other stars around it. For example, sometimes a star seems to be orbiting around an invisible object. This object could be a black hole." If certain patterns of X rays are found in this area, Dr. Taam concludes that he has found a black hole.

Why study the universe?
"We can learn from what is happening in the cosmic laboratory of space. The pressures and temperatures within stars are so great that events that do not occur on the earth take place constantly in space." From these events, scientists can learn basic physics—about the tiny particles that make up atoms. What is learned from this research can be used in many types of new technology.

What do you like best about your job?
"Teaching. Students ask good questions. Sometimes I have answers, sometimes I don't. There's much more to learn."

Spectrometer: Breaking Up Light

Each substance has its own spectrum, or rainbow of light, that is as unique as fingerprints. By interpreting the pattern of color in a spectrum, scientists can recognize what a substance, such as a star, is made of. A spectrometer is used to make this pattern.

4 A lens at the end of the tube is an eyepiece that focuses the spectrum for the viewer to see.

3 The series of prisms breaks the white light into the colors of the spectrum.

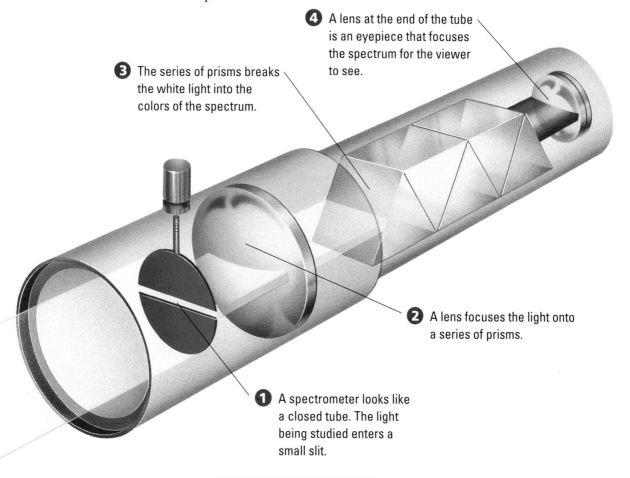

2 A lens focuses the light onto a series of prisms.

1 A spectrometer looks like a closed tube. The light being studied enters a small slit.

Find Out On Your Own

Use a prism to break up light into a band of colors.
Paint and label the colors in the visible spectrum.

Module Performance Assessment

The Planetarium

Using what you learned in this module, help prepare exhibitions and presentations that could be used at a local planetarium. Complete one or more of the following activities. You may work by yourself or with others in a group.

Art

Make a drawing to show your ideas about the universe. Label galaxies, galaxy clusters, the Local Group, and the Milky Way Galaxy. Add a dot to show our solar system.

Social Studies

People of several early cultures used sundials to keep track of time. Construct a simple sundial to show time during daylight hours. Ask permission to place your sundial somewhere on school grounds. Mark the position of the shadow on the sundial several times during the day.

Math

Focal length is the distance between a lens and the focused image that passes through the lens. You can measure focal length using a sheet of white paper, a tape measure, and a hand lens. Hold a piece of paper near a window. Hold a lens between the window and the paper so light is refracted onto the paper. Move the lens to focus the image. Then measure the distance between the lens and the paper. Draw a diagram that shows the window, lens, paper, and focal length.

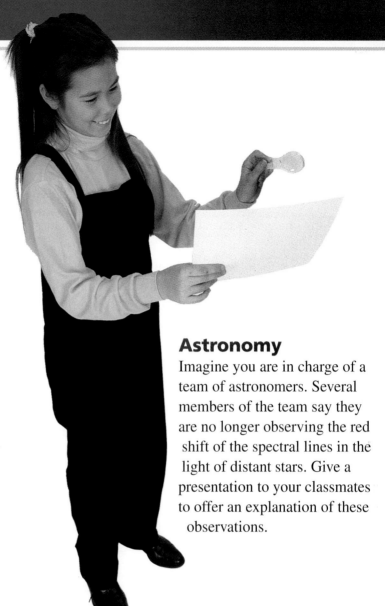

Astronomy

Imagine you are in charge of a team of astronomers. Several members of the team say they are no longer observing the red shift of the spectral lines in the light of distant stars. Give a presentation to your classmates to offer an explanation of these observations.

Technology

Determine what effect the amount of artificial lighting in an area has on your ability to observe stars in the night sky. Observe the light from a flashlight in your classroom with the lights on. Then observe the light from a flashlight with the classroom lights turned off. Finally, place the flashlight in a shoe box with the lid on. Cut a hole in the side to view the flashlight. Write about how bright the light appears to be in different conditions.

Module Review

Reviewing Words and Concepts

Write the letter of the word or phrase that best completes each sentence.

1. All the changes a star undergoes from its formation until its death are part of the _____.
2. A _____ is made up of dust and gas.
3. The _____ explains how the universe formed.
4. Proxima Centauri is about four _____ from the sun.
5. Copernicus' _____ of the universe places the sun at the center.
6. Light bouncing off the surface of a mirror is illustrating _____.
7. During _____, hydrogen atoms join together to form helium atoms.
8. The apparent bending of a straw placed in a glass of water results from _____.
9. A large group of stars makes up a _____.
10. White light makes up the _____.

a. model
b. visible spectrum
c. big bang theory
d. reflection
e. refraction
f. nebula
g. galaxy
h. light-years
i. nuclear fusion
j. star life cycle

Interpreting What You Learned

1. What causes a star to give off light?
2. What process forms more massive elements within a star?
3. How does starlight provide evidence that the universe is changing?
4. Name and describe the current theory about the origin of the universe.
5. Explain how models help people organize their observations.
6. List several factors that led to the many changes in the model of the universe.
7. If one object is emitting gamma rays and another is emitting infrared rays, which object is hotter?

Applying What You Learned

1. Observe one of the constellations in the night sky. Write a myth about the constellation that people of an ancient culture may have told.
2. What do the mirrors and lenses used in telescopes have in common?
3. Which have a shorter wavelength, X rays or radio waves?
4. What elements might astronomers find when using a spectrometer to analyze a supernova?
5. Explain why spectral lines shift toward the red end of the spectrum.
6. What characteristics of the Milky Way led scientists to call it a spiral galaxy?
7. Why are radio wave receivers curved?

The Living Planet

The Living Planet

Imagine a planet without life—a planet without trees, birds, insects, or people. All the planets we know of are just like that. All except one. Thanks to its place in the solar system, the planet Earth is bursting with life. In this module, you'll survey the amazing variety of life on Earth and learn about the remarkable code that allows living things to reproduce.

CHAPTER

2 Code of Life

It's as easy as ACGT! Long, thin DNA molecules carry the complex code of life. Yet these molecules contain just four types of bases: A, C, G, and T.

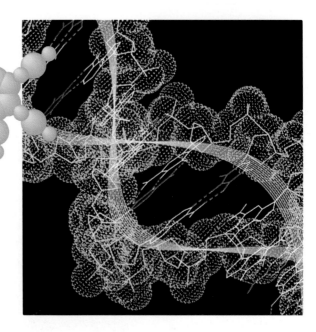

CHAPTER

1 Life on Earth

What's so special about species? Our planet is home to millions of different species of living things. Each one is unique—including your own.

CHAPTER

3 Variations in Life

Do you have an identical twin? If not, that makes you one of a kind because you have a set of traits unlike anyone else.

Life On Earth

How about freckles, do they count?

What are the effects of sunlight?

Sunlight can melt ice, make flowers bloom, and fade house paint. Think about something that changes because of the sun. Then demonstrate and explain this change to your classmates.

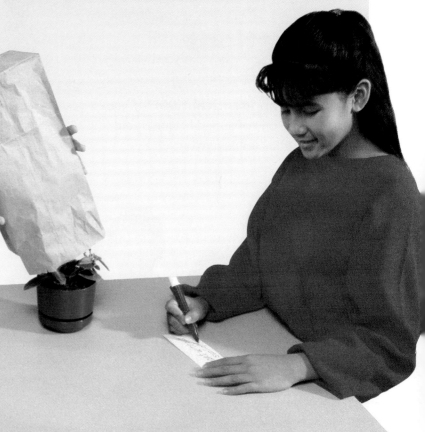

Plant with sunlight

For Discussion

1. Classify the changes you demonstrated as helpful/harmful, permanent/temporary, and so on.

2. How might life be different without these changes?

LESSON

1.1 Diversity of Life

▶ *How is Earth special?*

Earth is just one of nine planets in the solar system. It is neither the largest planet nor the smallest. It is not the fastest nor the slowest; not the hottest nor the coldest. Yet Earth has one quality that sets the planet apart from all the others. Earth seems to be the only planet in the solar system where life exists.

Third Planet From the Sun

What is it about Earth that makes life possible? For one thing, Earth's position in the solar system is ideal. As you might have learned in the Discover Activity, sunlight heats Earth. If Earth were closer to the hot sun, as Mercury is, living things would burn up. If Earth were farther away, like Pluto, living things would freeze. Even near the South Pole where Earth is coldest, the temperature doesn't fall lower than about –90°C. Compare that to Pluto's temperature of about –233°C!

Most organisms on Earth rely on sunlight for the energy they need to perform life functions. Plants and other producers capture the sun's energy, using it to make sugars through photosynthesis. Producers use some of the sugars for living and growing. Animals that eat producers also use the energy stored in the sugars.

Gases in Earth's atmosphere play a role in this transfer of the sun's energy through living things. For example, producers use carbon dioxide to carry out photosynthesis. And most living things use oxygen to release the chemical energy in sugars.

So oxygen and carbon dioxide in Earth's atmosphere are very important! Although other planets in the solar system have these gases in their atmospheres, only Earth's atmosphere has the right amount of oxygen and carbon dioxide to support the many kinds of living things on the planet.

▲ *Why do you think Earth is called both the living planet and the water planet?*

B 5

→ Beetle in the Namibian desert

⋏ Mushrooms growing on a dead tree in a forest

▽ Musk oxen in an Arctic region

Yet even with all the sunlight, carbon dioxide, and oxygen, life could not exist on Earth without one more substance—water. Although you might find it hard to believe, you and all other organisms are made mostly of water. This important substance helps living things carry out photosynthesis and other life functions. Three-fourths of Earth's surface is covered with water, making the planet an ideal home for organisms that need this vital liquid.

An Amazing Array of Life

Although organisms have similar needs for water, a quick look around will tell you that not all organisms are the same. Earth supports many different kinds of living things. In other words, Earth supports a great diversity of life.

Each different kind of life is called a **species** (spē′shēz). Only members of the same species can mate and produce offspring, which can also produce offspring. About 30 million species share the "living planet." New species are constantly being discovered!

▲ *Lichens growing on rock*

More amazing than the number of species on Earth is their endless diversity. They range in size from microscopic to mammoth, and come in every imaginable color and shape, as well as some you'd never imagine.

The species on these pages have characteristics and structures that enable them to live in places where few other species could survive. For example, the Namibian beetle lives in the desert where water is scarce. By sucking in morning dew left in the sand, the beetle meets its water needs in an extremely dry environment.

The colorful mushrooms grow from the dead trunk of a tree. The mushrooms get food by breaking down the dead material of the tree.

Notice the orange and green mat on the surface of the boulder above. The "mat" is a living thing—a lichen. Actually, lichens are two kinds of organisms— an alga and a fungus—living together. The fungus gets nutrients from the alga, which produces these nutrients during photosynthesis.

Except in flowing lava, hardly a spot exists on Earth where some form of life can't be found. So no matter where you go—whether it is hot, cold, dark, light, wet, or dry—some kind of life probably exists there!

Checkpoint

1. What features of Earth make life possible?
2. How do species differ?
3. **Take Action!** Make a mobile that shows the tremendous array of life on Earth.

INVESTIGATE

Comparing Species

How might one fly species differ from another? Let's investigate.

What To Do
A. Study the characteristics of the fly in the diagram. Its characteristics make this fly a particular species.

B. Make two tracings of the fly diagram.
C. Change some of the traits in each tracing to make two new, different species.
D. Give each new species a name that fits its new characteristics.

What Did You Find Out?
1. *What characteristics do you think identify the original fly as a species?*
2. *Describe how your two new species differ from the original one.*
3. *How could the changes you made affect the way the new species live?*

Activity

Teeming with Life

What about all the life you can't see? A drop of water might seem lifeless, but an invisible zoo is waiting for exploration.

Picture A

Picture B

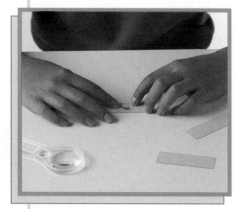
Picture C

Gather These Materials

pond water   hand lens
dropper   coverslip
microscope slide   microscope

Follow This Procedure

1. Make a chart like the one on the next page. Record your observations in your chart.

2. Move the container of pond water gently so you do not disturb the mud that has settled to the bottom. Obtain a water sample from just above the mud. Place a drop of water in the center of a clean microscope slide. *CAUTION: Handle the glass slide carefully.* (Picture A)

3. Observe the drop of water with the hand lens. (Picture B) Record your observations.

4. Place the coverslip onto the slide. (Picture C) Put one edge of the coverslip flat along the side of the water drop. Then slowly lower the coverslip over the drop. *CAUTION: Handle the glass coverslip carefully.*

5. Carefully put the slide on the stage of the microscope. Focus the light through the slide. Then, observe the water drop.

6. Look at the zoo! Use the picture on the next page to identify some of the living things in your water drop. The organisms in your drop will not match exactly the ones in the picture. You might see the same organisms or different ones. Record what you see in the drop.

State Your Conclusions

1. Compare the observations you made with the hand lens with those you made with the microscope.
2. How many different species do you think you observed in that tiny drop of water?
3. How do your observations compare to those of your classmates?
4. What factors do you think might affect the number and kinds of organisms you observed in your drop of pond water?

Let's Experiment

If living things exist in a drop of pond water, would they also exist in a temporary body of water such as a mud puddle? Use what you know about scientific methods to find out.

Record Your Results

	Description of organism (color, shape, size, movement, etc.)
Organism 1	
Organism 2	
Organism 3	
Organism 4	

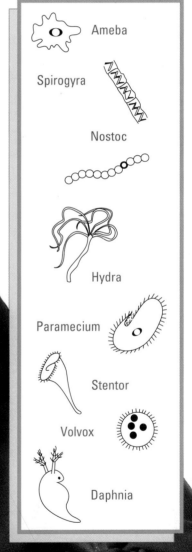

Ameba

Spirogyra

Nostoc

Hydra

Paramecium

Stentor

Volvox

Daphnia

1.2 *Materials of Life*

> ### How do organisms differ from one another?

You know that Earth was formed from the enriched "stardust" of a supernova. So you might be thinking that organisms are made up of those same elements, which is true. But look around at the many species of living things. Some appear to have nothing in common. For example, where one organism has feathers another has fur or leaves; where one has legs, another has tentacles or roots. Could different species be made up of different combinations of elements? Let's find the answers.

Chemicals of Life

Notice the two species on this page. One has a large head, arms, and legs that help it walk or run. The other has a tiny head, antennae, and wings that enable it to fly. The human and the butterfly appear very different. However, what does the pie chart tell you about their chemical makeups? Yes, both species contain the same percentages of carbon, nitrogen, oxygen, hydrogen, phosphorus, and sulfur. When it comes to *chemical* makeup, you're not so different from a butterfly after all!

The six elements that are most plentiful in the human and the butterfly are plentiful in most other kinds of organisms as well. Those six elements are found in nonliving things too, but usually in smaller percentages.

To see what nonliving matter such as rock is made of, study the pie chart on the next page that tells you about the makeup of Earth's crust. As you can see, the surface of Earth is made mostly of oxygen, silicon, aluminum, magnesium, iron, calcium, potassium, and sodium.

▼ *Six elements—carbon, hydrogen, oxygen, nitrogen, phosphorus, and sulfur— make up 99% of all living things.*

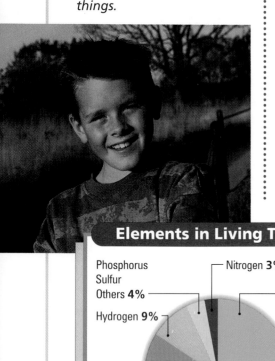

Elements in Living Things

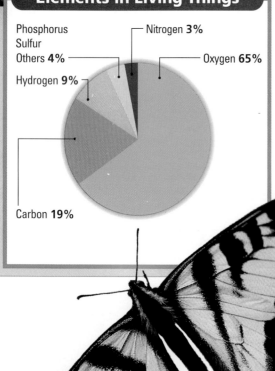

Phosphorus
Sulfur
Others **4%**

Hydrogen **9%**

Nitrogen **3%**

Oxygen **65%**

Carbon **19%**

◁ Of all the elements in nonliving things, which element is found in the greatest amount?

Elements in Earth's Crust

Potassium **3%**

Calcium **4%**

Iron **5%**

Aluminum **8%**

Sodium **2%**

Magnesium **2%**

Oxygen **47%**

Silicon **29%**

Compare the elements commonly found in the earth's crust with those found in living things. Only one element—oxygen—is common in both. The other elements that make up the earth's crust are found only in very small percentages in organisms. Those percentages are too small to show in the pie chart with the boy and the butterfly.

You might have been surprised earlier to learn that living things are made mostly of water. Besides covering most of the earth's surface, water accounts for between 50 to 95 percent of the weight of any organism. So why doesn't water appear on the pie charts? You might remember that water is not an element, but rather a compound made up of oxygen and hydrogen. Both of these elements appear on the charts. In organisms, elements are almost always combined with one another to form compounds.

But wait a minute! Many nonliving things have a lot of water too. All those elements that make up organisms are found in nonliving things, even if only in small percentages. So how do organisms differ from nonliving things? The answer lies in certain characteristics that all living things share.

It's Alive!

All living things carry out processes that nonliving things don't.

In the middle of this patch of gravel, a grasshopper rests, camouflaged by its color and pattern. If you didn't look closely, you might not have seen it at all. But the grasshopper is very different from the gravel that surrounds it.

You know the basic unit of all living things is a **cell**, similar to the one in the diagram below. These cells maintain life by carrying out six basic life processes.

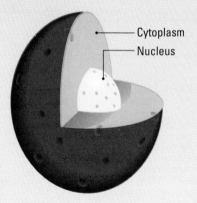

— Cytoplasm
— Nucleus

Pebbles and sand might move and change because of the forces of wind and moving water. But only living things like this grasshopper are made of cells and can carry on all of these life processes.

Getting Energy and Nutrients

Living things must get energy. Plants trap energy from sunlight to make sugars. Animals eat plants or other animals to get the energy and nutrients they need.

Responding to Change

Living things respond to change in their environments. For instance, some animals eat extra food in late summer. They store the chemical energy from the food in layers of fat. They then slowly release this stored energy while they sleep through the long winter months.

Using Energy

Through the process of respiration, plants and animals use oxygen to release the chemical energy stored in sugars. This "burning" process enables them to use the nutrients they take in.

Releasing Wastes

As cells carry out life processes, wastes are produced. These waste products can be poisonous, so they must be released from the cells or the organism will die.

Reproduction

Only living things can reproduce others of the same kind. While not every individual of the species reproduces, some must or the species will die out and become extinct.

Growing

Trees get taller and thicker. You get larger and stronger. Growth is the process of making more living material by taking in energy and nutrients.

Into The Field

Is it alive?

Make a chart to list the characteristics of living things. Go outdoors and observe 10 objects. Use your chart to determine if each object is living or nonliving.

Molecules of Life

The pictures show some basic parts that go into building a car. Each part serves the car in a different way. A living thing is built out of basic parts that serve different purposes too. But an organism's parts aren't big slabs of metal—they're building-block molecules.

When you first studied atoms, you learned how they join together. Atoms combine in different ways to form molecules that make up all the structures in a living cell. Remember the six most common elements found in living things? The building-block molecules of all cells are made mostly of atoms of those six elements. Those molecules can be very large—sometimes with thousands of atoms! Organisms are made of billions of these building-block molecules.

Of the building-block molecules three types are especially common, and important—proteins, carbohydrates, and nucleic (nü klē′ik) acids. Although your body assembles these molecules, you might recognize two of them as nutrients in food you eat.

DNA molecule

➤ *Just as parts of a car have certain functions, building-block molecules have certain functions in an organism.*

Carbohydrate molecule

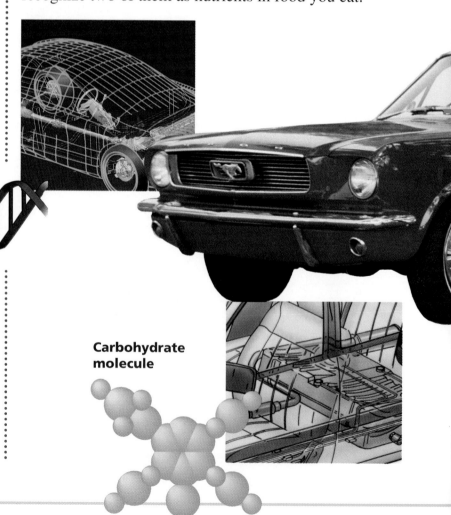

Each kind of building-block molecule has a specific function. Proteins are one kind of building-block molecule in living things. Proteins form the basic structure of an organism, just as the chassis (chas′ē) makes up the basic framework of a car.

Carbohydrates are a second kind of building-block molecule. Carbohydrates serve an organism in the same way fuel serves a car. A car gets energy from its fuel, just as most living things release energy from carbohydrates. The carbohydrates you eat provide your body with the energy it needs.

Nucleic acids are the third kind of building-block molecule. Nucleic acids control the activities of a cell. A special kind of nucleic acid is called deoxyribonucleic (dē ok′sə ri′bō nü klē′ik) acid or **DNA.** This building-block molecule contains the instructions that control how an organism takes shape and grows. The molecule carries information about how the parts of an organism are put together, just as a blueprint shows how the parts of a car are put together.

Protein molecule

Checkpoint

1. How is the chemical makeup of a tree different from that of a mountain?
2. List the six basic life processes.
3. What basic building-block molecules make up an African elephant?
4. Take Action! Find out about viruses. Make a chart that explains how viruses are different from living things.

Activity

Carbohydrates: Fuel of Life

Carbohydrates such as starch and glucose, one kind of sugar, provide fuel for living things. Try this activity to identify some foods that contain these building-block molecules.

Picture A

Picture B

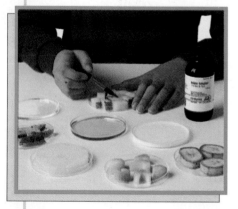

Picture C

Gather These Materials

cover goggles
food samples: apple juice,
   onion, water, banana,
   potato, milk, celery, bread

8 small dishes
glucose test paper
dropper
weak iodine solution

Follow This Procedure

1 Make a chart like the one on the next page. Record your observations in your chart.

2 Put on your cover goggles.

3 Place the food samples in separate dishes. *CAUTION: Do not taste any of the samples.* Add a small amount of water to the bread sample and mash up the bread. All the samples should be moist. (Picture A)

> **Predict: Which foods contain glucose? contain starch? contain both? contain neither?**

4 To test for glucose touch a glucose test paper to each of the food samples. Use a separate piece of test paper for each food.

5 The test paper will change color if glucose is present in the food. Record if a color change occurred. (Picture B)

6 Test the food samples for starch by adding 2–3 drops of the weak iodine solution to each sample. *CAUTION: Do not get any iodine solution on your skin or clothing.* (Picture C)

Record Your Results

Food	Test paper change in color?	Glucose present?	Iodine change in color?	Starch present?

7 The iodine solution will change color from red-brown to blue-black if starch is present. Record if a color change occurred.

State Your Conclusions

1. Which foods contain glucose? How do you know?
2. Which foods contain starch? How do you know?

Let's Experiment

People eat many seeds, such as beans, nuts, and grains. Do seeds contain carbohydrates? Use what you know about scientific methods to find out.

Chapter Review

Reviewing Words and Concepts

Write the letter of the word or phrase that best completes each sentence.

1. Earth supports a great _____ of life.
2. Plants use the sun's energy to make sugars during _____.
3. Most living things use molecules of _____ to release the energy in sugars.
4. DNA is an example of a _____.
5. Molecules called _____ form the basic structures of organisms.
6. Organisms release the energy stored in sugars in the process of _____.
7. The instructions that control how an organism takes shape and grows are contained in molecules of _____.
8. Each different kind of life is a _____.
9. The basic unit of all living things is the _____.
10. The types of molecules living things use as fuel are _____.

a. DNA
b. oxygen
c. respiration
d. photosynthesis
e. species
f. cell
g. nucleic acid
h. proteins
i. carbohydrates
j. diversity

Connecting Ideas

1. Copy the concept map. Use the terms at the right to complete the map about living things.

elements   carbohydrates
living species   DNA
proteins

A. _____
B. building blocks
F. _____
C. _____
D. _____
E. _____

2. Write a sentence or two to explain similarities among species' chemical makeup shown in the concept map.

Interpreting What You Learned

1. Explain how Earth would be different if it were located where Mercury is located.
2. Explain why no life exists on Mars even though its atmosphere contains carbon dioxide, oxygen, and water.
3. What is the role of DNA in organisms?
4. Which basic building-block molecule provides energy for an organism?
5. List the six elements that are most plentiful in living things. Place a check beside each element that is also present in the earth's crust.
6. What life processes are shared by a house plant and a canary?
7. Using water as an example, explain the relationship between atoms and molecules.

Performance Assessment

How do members of the same species differ?

Materials   • 2 ears of corn   • metric ruler   • piece of string   • marker

Collecting Data

1. Examine one ear of corn. Count the number of kernels in one row on the ear of corn. Then count the number of kernels in another row. Record the numbers.
2. Examine another ear of corn. Count the number of kernels in two different rows on the ear of corn. Record the numbers and compare them to the first ear of corn.
3. Measure the length of both ears of corn to the nearest millimeter. Record the measurements.
4. Place one end of the string on the widest point of an ear of corn. Wrap the string around the corn. Make a mark on the string where the part you wrapped around touches the end of the string.
5. Unwrap the string and measure the distance from the mark to the end. Record the measurement.
6. Repeat steps 4 and 5 for the other ear of corn. Record the measurement and compare it to the first ear of corn.
7. Count the number of rows of kernels around the circumference of an ear of corn. Count the rows of kernels around the other ear of corn. Record the numbers and compare them.

Analyzing Data

How are the two ears of corn you examined similar? How are they different?

Code of Life

Babies all look alike.
No they don't!

What characteristics make people alike and different?

Collect magazine pictures of people from various countries. Study these pictures carefully. List as many characteristics as possible that show how people are alike and different.

For Discussion

1. *Which of the characteristics on your list do you think were inherited, or came from the parents?*
2. *List the range you observed in one characteristic.*

2.1 *Chemicals that Copy*

▶ How much information does a DNA molecule carry?

If you think that bigger is better, then the DNA molecule will astonish you. This tiny molecule carries a tremendous amount of information. In fact, human DNA from one cell carries more information than all of these encyclopedias put together! Yet a DNA molecule is about one million times thinner than a human hair.

Information Molecules

DNA carries information about all your traits, or characteristics. It controls what makes you *you*. It has information about how tall you are, what color eyes you have, what your voice sounds like, and even whether you are right- or left-handed. When you did the Discover Activity, you investigated some of the traits of people. Information about their traits is carried by DNA.

The same is true for every other living thing. DNA carries information about the color of a tulip's petals, the length of a tiger's fangs, when a robin will build a nest, and the number of seeds in a squash. The information in DNA is like a set of instructions that controls how traits develop in an organism.

▼ *To print all the information in human DNA would take 13 sets of encyclopedias.*

Your Unique DNA

Almost every cell in your body carries a chemical pattern that makes you unique.

Every DNA molecule in your body is just like the others. Take a closer look to see where DNA is and how it's structured.

1. Let's start by magnifying a single cell from the tip of your finger. Inside the cell you'll find the nucleus, or control center of the cell.

2. Inside the nucleus, you'll see **chromosomes**, structures made mostly of DNA molecules.

3. These long DNA molecules look like spiralling ladders.

4. The ladders have millions of rungs. These "rungs" are smaller molecules, arranged in specific patterns.

5. The twisting DNA ladders are divided into sections a few hundred to a few thousand rungs long. Each section of DNA is called a **gene**.

Each gene controls one or more traits. How? Read on to find out how two scientists "cracked the code."

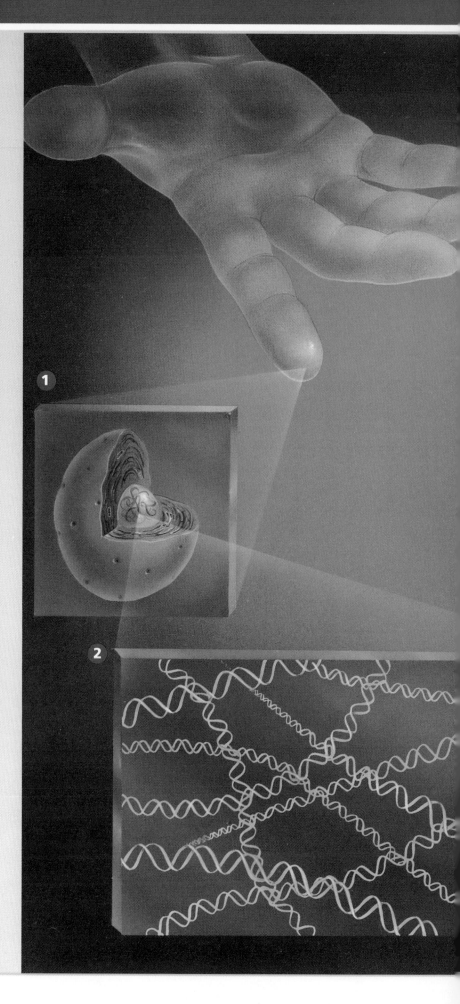

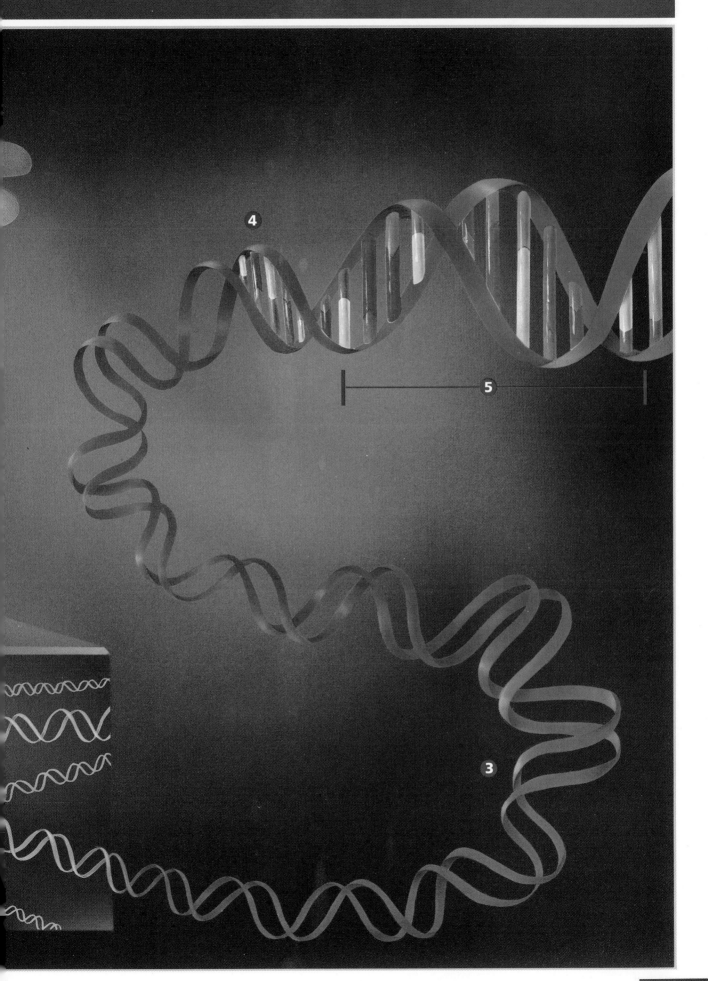

A T C G

▲ *Use the key to see how the bases pair up when DNA makes a copy of itself.*

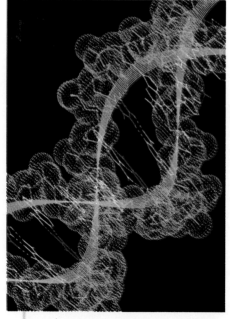

▲ *A computer designed this model of the DNA molecule.*

Making DNA Copies

In 1953, biologists James Watson and Francis Crick discovered the structure of the DNA molecule and how it works. Their discovery was sensational news. Why was their discovery so important? Because Watson and Crick showed how the structure of DNA allows the molecule to make copies of itself. In this way, the information about traits can be passed from parent to offspring. Watson and Crick also discovered that the information in DNA is "spelled out" in a language represented by just four letters—A, T, C, and G.

If you look at the computerized model of DNA to the left, you may wonder how anyone could have figured out its complicated structure. But as you read and study the diagram above, you will discover that DNA has an orderly and simple arrangement of parts.

Notice that the DNA molecule is made up of two long strands held together in the form of a spiral ladder. The steps of the ladder are made of pairs of smaller molecules called bases. The letters *A, T, C,* and *G* stand for these bases.

Like puzzle pieces, the bases have shapes that allow them to fit together in only certain combinations. A fits only with T, and C fits only with G. The bases must pair up in these combinations to form the steps of the ladder.

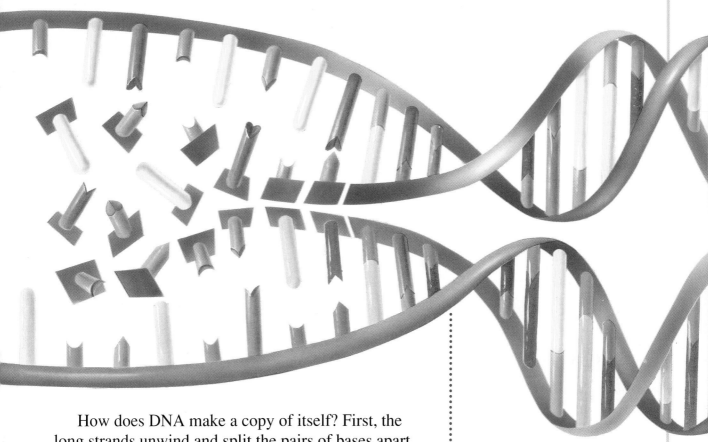

How does DNA make a copy of itself? First, the long strands unwind and split the pairs of bases apart. Then, the unpaired bases on each strand join with bases present in the cell. As the bases snap into place like puzzle pieces, two new DNA molecules form. Each of the two new DNA molecules is an exact copy of the original DNA molecule. And because they are exact copies, the new DNA molecules contain exactly the same information as the original DNA molecule.

The bases in the DNA molecule form a code that the cell "reads." Every set of three bases tells the cell to make a part of a protein, or to start or stop the protein-building process. You know that proteins are your structural bulding blocks. That's why DNA is called the "code of life."

Checkpoint

1. How does DNA control an organism's traits?
2. Compare chromosomes and genes.
3. How does DNA make a copy of itself?
4. **Take Action!** Find a picture of a human karyotype. How many chromosomes do humans have?

Into The Field

How is a zipper a model of DNA replication?

Observe a zipper as you unzip and zip it. Record how it is like a DNA molecule copying itself. Describe how it is different.

Activity

Making Copies: DNA Model

You know that a DNA molecule is shaped somewhat like a twisted ladder and that it can make an exact copy of itself. Make a model to show how this process works.

Picture A

Picture B

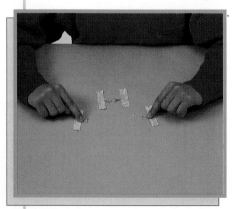

Picture C

Gather These Materials

colored pencils: red, blue,
    purple, green, orange
DNA pattern pieces

scissors
white paper

Follow This Procedure

1 Make a chart like the one on the next page. Record your observations in your chart.

2 Color each DNA pattern piece in the same colors shown in the pattern pieces on the next page. Label each piece. You should have 2 blue A shapes, 2 green C shapes, 2 purple T shapes, 2 red G shapes, and 8 orange ladder side pieces. Notice that the ladder side pieces are the same shape, but flipped with the open side notch facing inward. You will need 4 ladder sides with the side-notch opening facing right and 4 ladder sides with the opening facing left.

3 Cut out your colored pattern pieces. (Picture A)

4 Assemble a short model of a DNA molecule using 4 of the ladder sides and one each of the base molecules A, T, G, and C. Notice that each of the base molecules will combine with only one other base molecule. These paired combinations of base molecules will make 2 rungs of your ladderlike model. (Picture B)

Predict: *How can you create an exact copy of your DNA molecule?*

Record Your Results

Observations

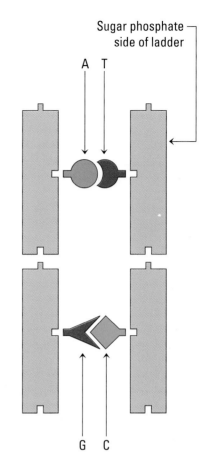

Sugar phosphate side of ladder

A T

G C

5 To make a copy of your model, split your molecule apart by opening the model down the middle vertically, right between the 2 base molecules that make up the rungs.

6 Pull the two halves of your ladder model completely apart. (Picture C)

7 Using the extra puzzle pieces you have, fit them to each side of your split-apart ladder model to create 2 DNA molecules that are exactly the same.

State Your Conclusions

1. How does your DNA model resemble a ladder? How does it resemble a puzzle?

2. Are the 2 final DNA molecule models exact copies of each other?

3. Using what you have learned, what can you conclude about how DNA's structure allows it to make copies of itself?

Let's Experiment

You have made a colored-paper model of a DNA molecule. The real DNA molecule is twisted like a spiral staircase. What could you use to make a model DNA molecule that could show how DNA is twisted?

2.2 *It Takes One to Make One*

How is DNA passed to new cells?

Right this very minute the cells in your body are making new cells. Without these new cells, you wouldn't be growing "like a weed." Imagine that one of these new cells did not receive the information in DNA. Without any instructions, how could that new cell do what it is supposed to do?

Producing New Cells

Many cells in an organism are frequently making new cells. The new cells can replace worn-out cells and allow a young organism to grow in size. In most cases, a cell reproduces by forming two new offspring cells.

Before a cell forms two new cells, each DNA molecule makes an exact copy of itself. After all the DNA molecules have been copied, each chromosome consists of two identical parts attached together.

After the DNA and chromosomes are copied, the cell goes through mitosis (mī tō′ sis). **Mitosis** is a process by which a cell's nucleus divides to form two identical nuclei. As you read, follow the steps of mitosis on these two pages.

▼ *Mitosis is a continuous process. If you could look through a microscope and observe a living cell go through mitosis, it would be like watching a movie.*

1. **Parent cell**

2. **Twin chromosomes become visible**

3. **Twin chromosomes line up**

4. **Twin chromosomes split apart and move**

Notice that at the beginning of mitosis the chromosomes are attached to their copies as twin chromosomes. They look like Xs. Twin chromosomes contain the same DNA. As mitosis continues, the twin chromosomes separate and move to opposite ends of the cell. Toward the end of mitosis the cell has two nuclei. That's right—one cell with two nuclei! And each nucleus has a complete set of single chromosomes. This one cell is now ready to become two cells.

When mitosis is complete, the cell goes through cell division. **Cell division** is a process by which a cell divides into two nearly equal-sized cells. As you can see, the cell pinches apart until it divides in two. Notice that each of the two offspring cells receives one of the nuclei formed during mitosis.

Now think about the chromosomes in the offspring after cell division. Each of the two new cells has a complete set of chromosomes. The chromosomes in each offspring are exactly the same. The DNA in a parent cell makes an exact copy of itself before mitosis. So the entire set of DNA molecules in each offspring cell is identical.

Almost all the cells in your body are formed by mitosis and cell division. Each body cell has 46 chromosomes. So, how many chromosomes does a body cell have after DNA copies itself? How many chromosomes would each cell have after cell division?

5. Cell divides in two

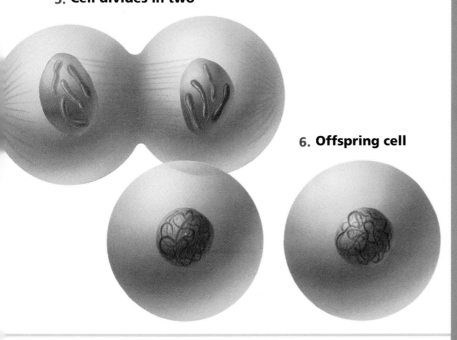

6. Offspring cell

Population Explosion

Bacteria are one-celled organisms. They are among the smallest living things and they exist almost everywhere.

When bacteria reproduce, one bacterium splits into two. Then two split to become four, and so on.

The majority of bacteria reproduce quickly. For instance, the species *E. coli* reproduces about every 15 minutes. So these bacteria double their number in that period of time.

The chart shows how quickly a population of *E. coli* could grow, if it were growing in the best conditions possible.

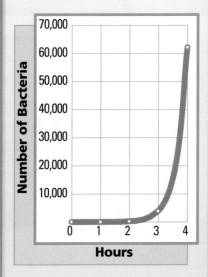

What Did You Find Out?
1. *About how many* E. coli *exist in 3 hours? 4 hours?*
2. *Calculate how many would exist after 5 hours.*
3. *What do you think might cause a population of* E. coli *to grow more slowly?*

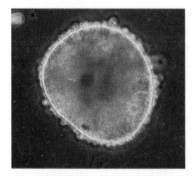
Reproduction By One Parent

Like you, the ameba in the picture is an organism. But you're an organism made up of many cells. The tiny ameba is an organism made up of a single cell. When an ameba reproduces, it does so in much the same way as the cells of your body do. It divides in half, forming two offspring cells. In other words, one parent produces two offspring. At the end of this process, the parent cell no longer exists. Reproduction by one parent is called **asexual** (ā sek′shü əl) **reproduction**.

Look carefully at the two single-celled offspring of the ameba. What differences do you see between them? Be sure to check out everything—their shape, color, size, and body parts. Notice that the cells look almost exactly the same. Now compare the offspring cells to their parent. Not only do the two offspring look alike, they also closely resemble their parent! It may seem strange to find parents and their offspring looking almost exactly alike. But if you think about how these offspring form, it makes sense that they look just like their parent.

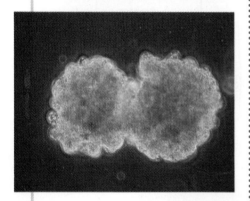

Before the parent cell begins to reproduce, it makes two identical copies of its DNA. Then the parent cell goes through mitosis and cell division. During cell division each new offspring cell receives one of these identical sets of DNA. Remember, the order of bases along the DNA molecule is a set of instructions that determines traits. Because each cell has identical instructions, the cells share the same traits.

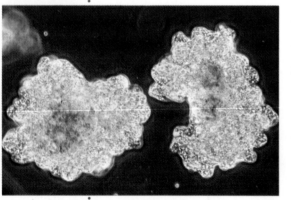

Is it a little confusing to read about identical DNA, identical chromosomes, identical offspring, and an identical parent? What does *identical* mean, really? The picture shows what your class could look like if people were all formed from identical DNA. Your friends would be hard to tell apart! Everyone would have the same kind of hair, the same eye color, the same smile. Everyone would have the same traits.

Remember this idea too: if your classmates formed by asexual reproduction, they would also look exactly like their one parent. In asexual reproduction, the parent and offspring have identical DNA, unless, for some reason, the DNA is changed. In the next chapter, you'll learn how that might happen.

▼ *The children are wearing masks to show the results of having identical DNA.*

Checkpoint

1. How does a cell pass DNA to new cells?
2. In what way are organisms formed by asexual reproduction exactly the same?
3. **Take Action!** Make several drawings of the steps in mitosis on separate sheets of paper. Put them together to make a flip book of mitosis.

Activity

Splitting Cells

You have learned what happens to chromosomes when cells make copies of themselves during mitosis. Make this model to help you understand this important process.

Picture A

Picture B

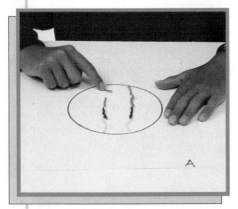
Picture C

Gather These Materials

small lid about 10 cm in
diameter
paper

one 3-cm strand each of
red, green, yellow, and
blue yarn

Follow This Procedure

1 Make a chart like the one on the next page. Record your observations in your chart.

2 Use the lid to trace the circular shapes shown below on separate sheets of paper. They will represent cells in different stages of mitosis. Label the drawings A, B, C, and D.

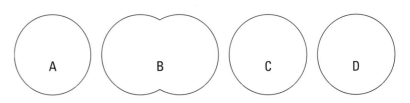
A   B   C   D

3 Place the 4 strands of yarn in the middle of cell A. The strands represent chromosomes.

4 Before a cell divides, its chromosomes make exact copies of themselves. Model this process by unraveling each strand of yarn so that you have 2 thinner strands for each color, but leave the thin strands connected at the middle. (Picture A)

5 Place the yarn strands back in the middle of cell A. What happens to the membrane of the nucleus in real cells during this stage of mitosis?

Record Your Results

	Number of cells	Number of chromosomes
Beginning of activity		
End of activity		

6 Line up the strands of yarn in the cell. (Picture B)

> **Predict: *What should you do with the strands next as you continue your model of mitosis?***

7 Completely unravel the strands and move each thin strand to opposite sides of the cell. (Picture C)

8 Drawing B represents a cell dividing in two. Move each group of strands to the middle of each part of this dividing cell. Record your observations about the model.

9 Drawings C and D represent 2 new cells after division takes place. Move each group of strands to the middle of each new cell. Record your observations about the model.

State Your Conclusions

1. In this model, how many chromosomes did the cell contain before mitosis began?
2. How many chromosomes did each of the 2 new cells contain after mitosis?
3. A human cell has 46 chromosomes. How many chromosomes are in a human cell after it undergoes mitosis and cell division?

Let's Experiment

You have made a model of mitosis using 4 chromosomes. Now show this process starting with 8 chromosomes.

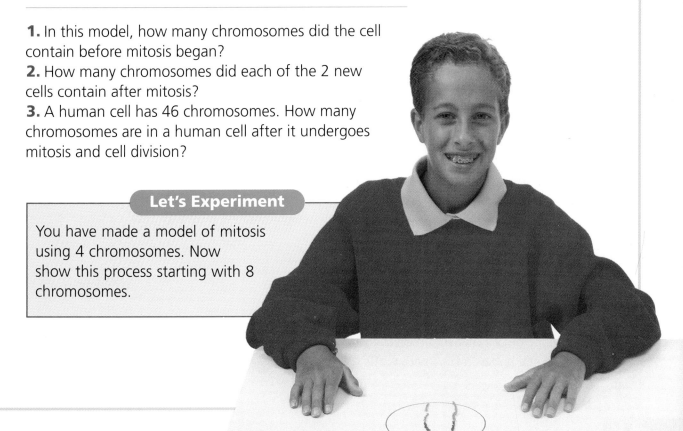

Chapter Review

Reviewing Words and Concepts

Write the letter of the word or phrase that best completes each sentence.

_____ 1. Information about the traits of organisms is carried by chromosomes of _DNA_.

_____ 2. The structures within a cell that are made mostly of DNA molecules are called Chromosomes

_____ 3. The steps of the DNA ladder are made up of pairs of molecules called _____.

_____ 4. In your body, a cell's nucleus divides to form two identical nuclei during _____.

_____ 5. When one parent cell reproduces, the process is called _____.

_____ 6. When mitosis begins, the chromosomes of a cell exist as _____.

_____ 7. The cells produced through asexual reproduction are _____.

_____ 8. A _gene_ is a small section of DNA that controls one or more traits.

_____ 9. The process in which a cell divides into two nearly equal-sized cells is _____.

_____ 10. DNA molecules have the shape of _____.

a. chromosomes
b. spiralling ladders
c. gene
d. identical
e. mitosis
f. twin chromosomes
g. cell division
h. bases
i. asexual reproduction
j. DNA

Connecting Ideas

1. Copy the concept map. Use the terms at the right to complete the map about reproduction.

mitosis   DNA copies itself
          cell division

A. parent cell

B. _____

C. _____

D. _____

E. new cell

F. new cell

2. Using the concept map above, write a sentence or two that summarizes the way a cell passes traits to new cells.

Interpreting What You Learned

1. Describe the relationship among genes, chromosomes, DNA, and traits.
2. Imagine you had one side of the DNA ladder with the following unpaired bases: AACTG. Describe what the opposite side of this section of the DNA ladder would look like.
3. How is a newly formed cell in your body able to carry out its correct functions?
4. If an organism's body cell contains ten chromosomes, how many chromosomes will be present in each offspring following cell division? Explain your answer.
5. How is the asexual reproduction of an ameba similar to mitosis and cell division in a human body cell?
6. List ten traits for which a DNA molecule carries information.

Performance Assessment

How do cells multiply during cell division?

Materials • 2 sheets of paper

Collecting Data

1. Use one sheet of paper to make a data table with two columns and seven rows. Write the following headings at the top of the columns: *Generation Number* and *Number of Cells*. Fill in the rows of the column labeled *Generation Number* as follows: *1st, 2nd, 3rd, 4th, 5th, 6th,* and *7th.*
2. The sheet of paper represents a cell. The entire sheet will be the parent cell. Fill in *1* in the first row of the column labeled *Number of Cells.*
3. Fold the sheet of paper in half. Unfold the paper and count the sections to see how many cells result from the second generation of cell division. Record the number in your data table.
4. Refold the paper. Fold the folded sheet of paper in half again. Unfold the paper to see how many cells result from the third generation of cell division. Record the number in your data table.
5. Repeat step 4 four more times, adding one more fold to the paper each time. Determine how many cells result from the fourth, fifth, sixth, and seventh generations of cell division.

Analyzing Data

Use your data to predict how many cells would result from the eighth, ninth, and tenth generations of cell division.

Variations in Life

Hey, this one's got three!

How much variation exists in peanuts?

Just like the students in your class, peanuts come in all shapes and sizes. To find out how much peanuts can vary, examine a handful of unshelled peanuts. Measure and compare the lengths of the peanuts.

For Discussion

1. Summarize the results using a graph.
2. List other variations you found among your peanuts.

3.1 *How Two Make a Difference*

▶ *What difference do two parents make?*

You know how an ameba can produce a large group of amebas. Thanks to asexual reproduction, it can form offspring all by itself. But sometimes an ameba reproduces in another way—with a partner. This process can make quite a difference in the offspring!

Reproduction by Two Parents

Just by glancing at this family of cats, you can pick out the two parents and their offspring. Now take a closer look. Notice that the kittens are not identical to either of their parents. Although the offspring resemble their parents, not one of the kittens is an exact copy of either parent.

Why are the kittens different from their parents and from each other? They were produced by **sexual reproduction**—or reproduction by two parents.

Offspring produced by sexual reproduction are not exactly like either parent. Sometimes the differences between offspring and parents are easy to see—like differences in fur color between these kittens and their parents. But often, the differences are inside an organism where they can't be seen! You'll find out more about these hidden differences later.

▼ *Notice how these kittens have traits of both parents.*

Two Creating One

Parents produce sex cells by a process called meiosis.

Many organisms produce offspring by sexual reproduction. Such organisms reproduce through sex cells. Male sex cells are called sperm. Female sex cells are called eggs. When a sperm joins with an egg, a new organism forms.

Both female and male sex cells are produced by **meiosis** (mī o′sis). During meiosis, the nucleus of the beginning cell divides twice. Because the nucleus divides two times, the final sex cell contains only half the amount of DNA as was in the beginning cell. So, a sex cell contains one-half of one parent's genetic code.

You know that chromosomes contain DNA. When two sex cells combine, the chromosomes from one parent pair with the chromosomes of the other parent. Then the offspring has a complete set of DNA, and traits from both parents!

Egg Formation A cell that forms eggs divides twice to form four cells. Each egg cell has half the number of chromosomes, and thus half the DNA, of the original cell.

Sperm Formation A cell that forms sperm divides twice to form four cells. Each sperm cell has half the number of chromosomes, and thus half the DNA, of the original cell.

Fertilization A sperm cell enters the egg cell. The chromosomes from both cells pair up. This first cell of the new offspring now has a complete set of DNA.

Variations

Look at the children in the picture. Do you recognize them? You've seen them before. On page 31 they were hidden behind identical masks to show the results of asexual reproduction. With the masks put aside you can see that their real faces are anything but identical!

Notice that the children differ in many other ways, too. They have different heights, weights, skin colors, and foot sizes. They're different in more ways than you can count! The children in the picture look different from one another for one main reason—they were formed by two parents instead of one.

▼ *Just like the variations in these children, you can look around at your classmates and see the variations caused by sexual reproduction.*

Having a second parent sure makes a big difference. With one parent the offspring are identical. With two parents the offspring are different in countless ways. Why should the number of parents matter so much? The answer to this question is DNA. When two parents reproduce, DNA is passed to offspring in a very different way than it is when one parent reproduces.

Remember, in asexual reproduction an offspring gets all its DNA from its one parent. That's why each offspring looks like its parent. But when an organism forms from two parents, half of its DNA comes from the male parent and the other half comes from the female parent. Do you remember how an offspring gets this combination of DNA? If not, take another look at pages 38 and 39. In plants and animals, DNA in the egg and DNA in the sperm combine during fertilization.

The kitten on those same pages looks like each of its parents in certain ways. That's because the kitten inherits half its DNA from its mother and half from its father. Look closely at the kitten. Find a trait the kitten inherits from its mother and a trait the kitten inherits from its father. You have just observed the results of DNA the kitten got from each of its two parents!

Sexual reproduction accounts for most of the differences between a kitten and its parents. It also accounts for differences among the peanuts you measured in the Discover Activity. It accounts for most of the differences among humans. Many kinds of organisms on the earth produce offspring by sexual reproduction. That's why so many variations, or differences, exist among members of a species.

Checkpoint

1. How is sexual reproduction different from asexual reproduction?
2. What kinds of cells are formed by meiosis?
3. Why does a kitten have some traits that are like traits of each of its parents?
4. **Take Action!** Make a chart that compares mitosis and meiosis. Use pictures or words in your chart.

Variations on a Bean

What variations can you find in pinto beans? Let's investigate.

What To Do
A. Arrange 20 pinto bean seeds in order of length. Record the length of the shortest and longest seed in millimeters.
B. Sort the seeds by color. Record how many are light or dark.
C. Sort the seeds by number of spots present. Record the number that have many spots and the number that have few spots.

Record Your Results

Length	Short =
	Long =
Color	Light =
	Dark =
Spots	Many =
	Few =

What Did You Find Out?
1. *How did the pinto beans you observed vary?*
2. *List other variations that you did not measure or count. Add them to your chart.*
3. *How do you think each variation might affect the germination and survival of the bean?*

LESSON

3.2 *Changing Traits*

> *How can humans change other species?*

Since ancient times, farmers have been providing people with tasty, nutritious foods. One important way to improve foods was discovered during the early days of agriculture. Back then, farmers noticed many variations among the plants and animals they raised. This should not surprise you. Remember, plants and animals are formed by sexual reproduction.

Ancient Choosing and Changing

Ancient farmers noticed that certain plants had desirable traits, such as better taste or larger size. Certain animals also had desirable traits, such as better health or thicker hair. By choosing those animals or those plants with the desired traits as parents, farmers produced offspring with those traits. The practice of mating plants or animals with certain traits to produce offspring with those traits is **artificial selection**.

By choosing parents for many generations, farmers could produce offspring quite different from the original plants or animals. So, as you'd expect, over time, artificial selection can bring about a big change in a species of plant or animal.

One example of a species changed by artificial selection is the corn plant. The first corn that people ate did not look anything like the corn you eat today. Look to the left at the life-size drawing of an early corn plant. Indians of Central and South America were among the first to grow this corn.

Scientists have found five thousand-year-old corncob fossils of this early corn. These ancient cobs were only two and one-half centimeters long—about one-tenth the size of a modern corncob! An ancient cob had about fifty kernels, compared with hundreds on a modern corncob.

▼ *The ancient Incas were one culture using artificial selection to change traits in corn.*

➤ *An early corn plant*

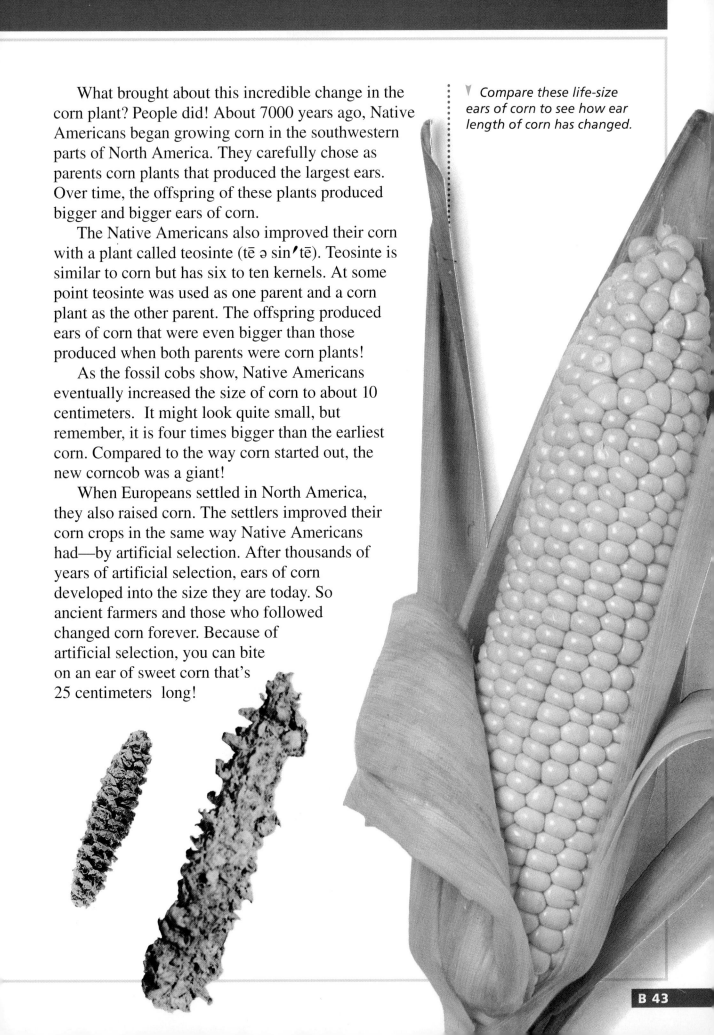

What brought about this incredible change in the corn plant? People did! About 7000 years ago, Native Americans began growing corn in the southwestern parts of North America. They carefully chose as parents corn plants that produced the largest ears. Over time, the offspring of these plants produced bigger and bigger ears of corn.

The Native Americans also improved their corn with a plant called teosinte (tē ə sin'tē). Teosinte is similar to corn but has six to ten kernels. At some point teosinte was used as one parent and a corn plant as the other parent. The offspring produced ears of corn that were even bigger than those produced when both parents were corn plants!

As the fossil cobs show, Native Americans eventually increased the size of corn to about 10 centimeters. It might look quite small, but remember, it is four times bigger than the earliest corn. Compared to the way corn started out, the new corncob was a giant!

When Europeans settled in North America, they also raised corn. The settlers improved their corn crops in the same way Native Americans had—by artificial selection. After thousands of years of artificial selection, ears of corn developed into the size they are today. So ancient farmers and those who followed changed corn forever. Because of artificial selection, you can bite on an ear of sweet corn that's 25 centimeters long!

Compare these life-size ears of corn to see how ear length of corn has changed.

Artificial Selection Today

Today, artificial selection is a science that is practiced quite differently than it was in ancient times. For example, livestock breeders are now using new methods to produce new varieties of animals.

Suppose you're a livestock breeder who has a superior male animal with many desirable traits. You might want to increase the number of offspring that this animal could father. About 50 years ago, breeders discovered a method to do just that. They collected semen—liquid containing sperm—from a selected male and placed it inside many female animals. In this way, breeders increased the number of offspring that the selected male can produce.

But suppose your superior animal is a female. In the 1970s breeders found a way to increase the number of offspring that a female animal might produce. A breeder removes eggs from a prize female and fertilizes them in a glass dish. Then the breeder places the eggs inside other females. While the eggs grow inside the other females, the superior female is able to produce more eggs that can be fertilized. In this way a prize female can have several offspring every year.

▲ *The baby Bengal tiger above was actually mothered by a Siberian tiger like this one!*

An endangered species is a species that might die out because so few are left on the earth. Scientists who work in zoos are trying to save endangered species by borrowing methods livestock breeders use. For example, researchers at the Henry Doorly Zoo in Omaha, Nebraska, are helping to save Bengal tigers. This species is decreasing because their habitats are disappearing. Study the graph. Fewer than 4000 Bengal tigers are left in the entire world!

At the Doorly Zoo, scientists are trying to increase the numbers of Bengal tigers using the breeding methods you learned about. In one procedure, scientists collected semen from a male Bengal tiger. They used this semen to fertilize the eggs of two

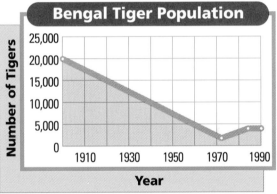

female Bengal tigers. Next, the scientists placed each of the fertilized eggs inside a female Siberian tiger. Siberian tigers are a related species of tiger. The Bengal tiger eggs developed inside the Siberian tiger mother. Eventually, the Siberian tiger gave birth to two Bengal tiger cubs.

The breeding program at the Doorly Zoo allows female Bengal tigers to produce additional eggs that can be fertilized. So a female Bengal tiger might produce several offspring in a single year. It won't be easy to save the species. But artificial selection made a big difference in the size of corn. Perhaps it can make a big difference in the numbers of Bengal tigers!

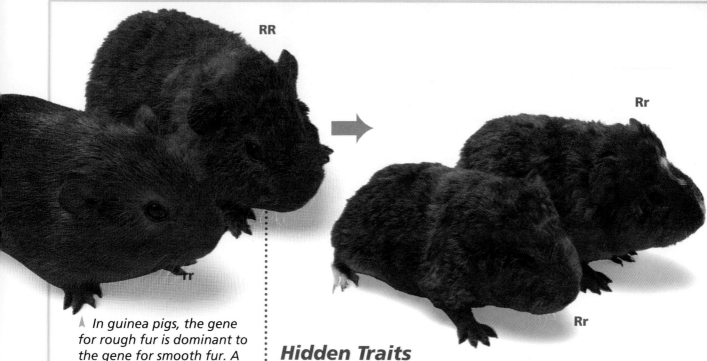

RR

Rr

Rr

▲ *In guinea pigs, the gene for rough fur is dominant to the gene for smooth fur. A dominant gene is represented by an upper case letter. A recessive gene is represented by a lower case letter.*

Hidden Traits

Sometimes an offspring's traits surprise breeders. Think how surprised a breeder would be to discover that two big corn plants produce a small offspring. How can an offspring have a trait that is unlike the traits of both parents? To answer this question, you need to know more about genes.

Remember, the DNA in genes controls the traits of organisms. In plants and animals, an offspring inherits at least two genes for every trait. One gene is inherited from the male parent; the other gene is inherited from the female parent. The genes are passed to the offspring when the egg and sperm cells join during sexual reproduction.

But how do genes control traits? Genes from both parents work together to determine the offspring's traits. Sometimes a gene completely hides the effect of another gene. A gene that hides another gene's effect is a **dominant** (dom′ə nənt) **gene.** A gene whose effect is hidden by a dominant gene is a **recessive** (ri ses′iv) **gene**. A dominant gene controls a trait whenever a dominant gene and a recessive gene pair together.

To see how dominant and recessive genes work, take a look at these guinea pigs. Notice the texture of their fur. The mother has two genes for rough fur *(RR)* and the father has two genes for smooth fur *(rr).* No matter how many offspring these parents produce, all of the young will have rough fur; not one will have smooth.

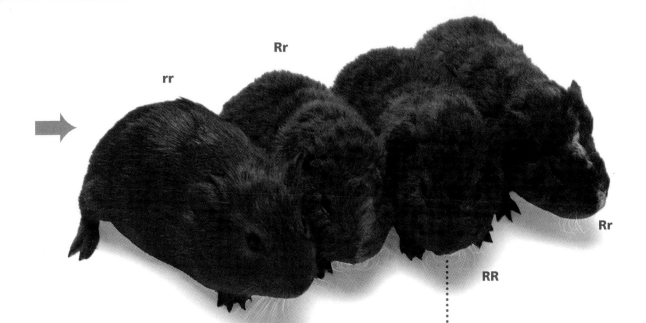

rr

Rr

Rr

RR

So why do all the offspring have rough fur? To solve this mystery you need to consider the parents' genes. Remember, the female guinea pig has two genes for rough fur. She is said to be purebred. The male guinea pig has two genes for smooth fur, and is a purebred too. Each of the offspring inherits one gene for rough fur and one gene for smooth fur. Which gene must be dominant? Which gene is hidden? These offspring with one dominant gene and one recessive gene are hybrids.

Suppose the hybrid offspring reproduce with other hybrids. What kind of fur would *their* offspring have? An offspring might have rough fur if it inherits one gene for rough fur from each parent. In what other way could it inherit rough fur? Notice that an offspring can also have smooth fur. This offspring inherits one gene for smooth fur from each parent. So it wouldn't look like either parent. It would look like one of its grandparents!

Checkpoint

1. Why is corn bigger now than it used to be?
2. How could a breeder increase the number of offspring produced by a prize bull?
3. Compare dominant and recessive genes.
4. **Take Action!** Make a timeline that shows how people have developed different breeds of dogs through artificial selection.

Into The Field

How does the eye color of the parents affect the color of their offspring's eyes?
Survey ten people about their eye color and their parents' eye colors. Record the results.

Dominant and Recessive Genes

You can demonstrate how dominant and recessive genes interact to determine flower color. Try this activity to find out how.

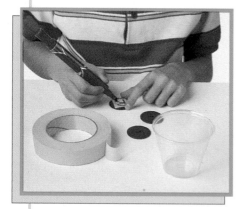

Picture A

Picture B

Picture C

Gather These Materials

masking tape   marker
3 large, flat buttons   cup

Follow This Procedure

1 Make a chart like the one shown on the next page. Record your observations in your chart.

2 Place a small piece of masking tape on each side of each of the 3 buttons.

3 On both sides of one button, print a capital letter *R* with the marker. This button represents a parent pea plant that is purebred for flower color. A purebred plant has 2 genes of the same kind. This button represents a plant that has 2 genes, or is purebred, for red flowers. (Picture A)

4 On one side of the other 2 buttons, print a capital letter *R*. On the other side of each button, print a lowercase letter *r*. These buttons represent parent pea plants that have 2 different genes, or are hybrid for flower color. These plants have one gene for red flowers and one gene for white flowers. These plants have red flowers because in pea plants, red flower color is dominant and white flower color is recessive.

5 Place the purebred (*RR*) parent and one of the hybrid (*Rr*) parents in the cup. Cover the cup with your hand, and shake it a few times. When you spill out the buttons on the desk, the letters that are face-up will represent the genes of one offspring of the 2 parents.

Predict: *What flower color will the offspring have?*

6 Spill the buttons out. Note which letters are face-up. Use a check to record which genes the offspring has.

7 Do steps 5 and 6 a total of 40 times. (Picture B)

8 Add the number of checks in each box. Record your total for each box.

9 Try the activity again, but this time use the 2 hybrid (*Rr*) buttons. Record your data. (Picture C)

Record Your Results

Parents	Offspring		
	RR	Rr	rr
RR x Rr			
Total			
Rr x Rr			
Total			

State Your Conclusions

1. How many red-flowered offspring and how many white-flowered offspring were produced when you crossed the purebred and hybrid parents? when you crossed 2 hybrid parents?

2. How many purebred and how many hybrid plants were produced when you crossed the purebred and hybrid parents? when you crossed 2 hybrid parents?

Let's Experiment

Now that you have tried one kind of cross, try a cross in which the gene for dark hair is dominant. Represent this gene with an *H*. Light hair is recessive. Represent this gene with an *h*. What would the results be if you crossed an *HH* male with an *Hh* female?

3.3 *Unexpected Traits*

▶ *How can new traits come from nowhere?*

What do you think about when you hear the word *mutation?* Do you remember a freaky-looking monster that you saw in a horror movie? Well, life isn't like the movies! Mutations happen in the real world, not just in science fiction. And mutations aren't freaky either— they happen all the time.

DNA Change

A recessive gene can cause an offspring to have traits that neither parent has. Sometimes a new trait pops up! The new trait sometimes results from a **mutation** (myü tā′shən) or change in the DNA.

Mutations happen by chance when DNA makes a copy of itself. The change can be a rearrangement of a whole section of the DNA strand. More often the change is as small as a single T, A, C, or G molecule that's out of place. Because of this change, a different DNA message is passed along to the offspring. Some changes in DNA might not change its message very much. The change might not even be noticed in the offspring. But other changes might result in a trait that has never been seen before.

▼ *This peacock's white coloring isn't bright enough to attract a mate.*

This Northern Pine snake is normally colored green and brown.

Imagine how much better this chipmunk would blend in with its surroundings if it were its normal brown, striped color.

An example of a mutation is albinism (al'bə niz'əm). Organisms that have this mutation are called albinos. They cannot make a chemical called melanin. Because melanin gives color to skin, hair, feathers, and eyes, an albino organism is usually colorless, or without color.

Albino animals, like the ones shown here, usually do not survive as well as other members of their species. Because albinos are easy to see, hiding from an enemy might be a problem for this albino chipmunk. A hawk might easily spot a white chipmunk on the dark forest floor. The albino snake has another problem. Without melanin, the snake doesn't absorb heat from the sun. So the snake may not be able to stay warm enough to survive in cool weather. The snow-white peacock is unlucky in still another way. It has no bright purple, blue, and green feathers that would help it attract a mate.

Mutations and Variations

Hiding from an enemy isn't easy for an albino chipmunk living in a green forest. But what would happen if the chipmunk's surroundings changed? During the Ice Ages thousands of years ago, parts of the earth were covered with ice and snow. In this environment, albinism might be a useful trait.

Mutations can be harmful or helpful to an individual; most often, a mutation has no effect. But no matter what the effect on an individual organism, mutations are important to the survival of the whole species. By adding new traits to a species, mutations help the species survive changes in its surroundings.

Over time, a trait that began as a mutation might cause a great change in a species. If the individual with the mutation survives long enough to reproduce, the mutant gene will be passed to its offspring. If the offspring survive and reproduce, the mutant gene can be passed along again. In time, many individuals of the species will inherit the mutant gene.

Sickle-cell is a trait caused by a mutant gene that has spread through a human population. This gene affects the shape of red blood cells, which can affect the person's health. Study the chart below to learn about the effects of having one or two sickle-cell genes.

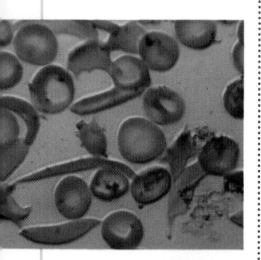

▲ *This blood was taken from a person with sickle-cell trait. Notice the two different shapes of the red blood cells.*

Sickle-cell Mutation

Genes	Red Blood Cells		Effects on Body
Normal gene Normal gene		Cells are round. They carry oxygen to body tissues.	No blood disease
Normal gene Mutant gene		Some cells are round. Some cells are curved and twisted – or sickle-shaped. Sickle-cells do not carry oxygen well.	No blood disease Resistance to tropical disease malaria
Mutant gene Mutant gene		All blood cells are sickle-shaped. Sickle-cells do not carry enough oxygen to body tissues.	Sickle-cell anemia. People feel weak. Not treated, causes death at a young age.

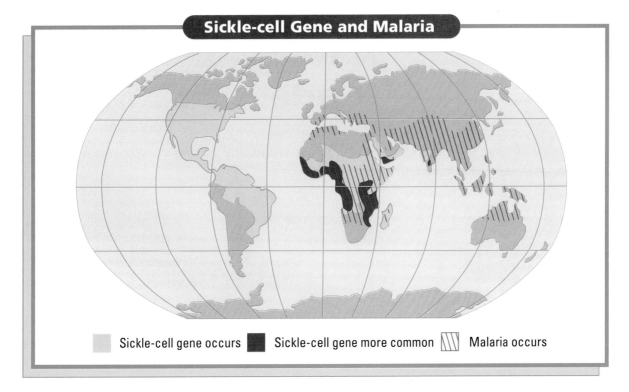

Sickle-cell Gene and Malaria

☐ Sickle-cell gene occurs   ■ Sickle-cell gene more common   ⫽⫽⫽ Malaria occurs

If you consider the effects of the sickle-cell genes on the red blood cells, do you think having one mutant gene is helpful, harmful, or has no effect? The answer to this question depends on where a person lives.

Having one mutant gene has little effect on a person who lives in the United States. But the gene can be helpful if a person lives in tropical regions of Africa and Asia. There, people who have the gene can be resistant to malaria, a deadly tropical disease. Mosquitoes carry the disease, passing it from person to person.

The map shows the parts of the world where malaria is found. It also shows areas where people carry the sickle-cell gene. Notice that in areas where malaria is found, more people have the mutant gene. Why do you think the gene has spread through the population in these regions?

Checkpoint

1. What produces an albino squirrel?
2. How can the mutant gene for sickle-cell be both harmful and helpful?
3. **Take Action!** Using a map, list countries where people have the sickle-cell gene.

Activity

A New Code

How does a change in the DNA code produce a mutation? In this activity you'll model a similar process by making letter changes in words.

Picture A

Picture B

Picture C

Gather These Materials

paper
pencil

10 index cards
scissors

Follow This Procedure

Part A

1 Make a chart like the one on the next page. In the "Original words" column of the chart, write five words that include the letter *a*.

2 When you complete your list, substitute the letter *e* for each *a* in the list of words. Write the new words with the substituted *e* in the "New words" column of the chart. (Picture A)

3 Read aloud each original word and each new word from the chart. How do the meanings of the words change as you substitute letters?

Part B

1 Print the word *rat* in large letters on each of two index cards. Cut apart the letters on one card. (Picture B)

2 Rearrange the cut-apart letters to make a new word. You must use all the letters. (Picture C)

3 Place the card with the original word beside the new word. Write the word *rat* in the "Original words" column of your chart. Then copy the new word in the "New words" column. Compare the meaning of the original and new word.

Record Your Results

Original words	New words

4 Repeat Steps 1-3 with the words *eat, rate, own,* and *gear.*

State Your Conclusions

1. How does changing or rearranging a letter in a word affect that word's meaning?

2. How is what you did in this activity similar to what happens to DNA when a mutation occurs?

Let's Experiment

How else might you model how mutations occur? Design a procedure and present it to the class.

Chapter Review

Reviewing Words and Concepts

Write the letter of the word or phrase that best completes each sentence.

___ **1.** Male sex cells called _____ are formed during meiosis.

___ **2.** The process of _____ involves two parents.

___ **3.** Organisms of the same species produced through sexual reproduction often have _____.

___ **4.** In _____, plants with certain traits may be mated to produce offspring with the same traits.

___ **5.** The female sex cells produced through meiosis are called _____.

___ **6.** A _____ hides the effect of a recessive gene.

___ **7.** A change in an organism's DNA may result in a _____.

___ **8.** Most often, a mutation does not _____ an individual.

___ **9.** When a dominant gene and a _____ pair together, the dominant gene controls the trait.

___ **10.** During _____, the nucleus of the beginning cell divides twice.

a. sexual reproduction
b. dominant gene
c. affect
d. artificial selection
e. sperm
f. mutation
g. eggs
h. recessive gene
i. variations
j. meiosis

Connecting Ideas

1. Copy the concept map. Use the terms at the right to complete the map about variations.

sexual reproduction
mutation   **artificial selection**
variety in species

A. _____ + B. _____ + C. _____ = D. _____

2. Using the concept map above, write a sentence or two that summarizes the reasons for the great variety of living things on Earth.

Interpreting What You Learned

1. If a cell with 46 chromosomes undergoes meiosis, how many chromosomes will there be in the egg or sperm cells that result? Why?
2. Explain why offspring produced by sexual reproduction are not exactly like either parent.
3. If a brown rabbit and a white rabbit produce offspring that are all brown, is the gene for brown fur dominant or recessive?
4. How would the world be different if most plant and animal species reproduced through asexual reproduction instead of sexual reproduction?
5. How is the way artificial selection is used today different from the way it was used in ancient times?
6. When might a mutation be helpful to an organism?

Performance Assessment

How do traits pass through generations?

Materials • masking tape • 2 large, flat buttons • marker • plastic cup

Collecting Data

1. Place a piece of tape on each side of the two buttons.
2. Print a capital letter *R* on one side of each button. The *R* represents rough fur, a dominant gene in guinea pigs. On the other side of each button, print a lowercase *r*. This *r* represents smooth fur, a recessive trait in guinea pigs.
3. Place both buttons in a cup. Shake the cup, then spill the buttons. The letters on the buttons represent the genes of one parent. Record the letters.
4. Repeat step 3 to find the genes for a second parent guinea pig. Record the letters next to the first pair you wrote. Draw a line connecting the pairs of letters you recorded. This is the beginning of a family tree.
5. Replace the tape on the buttons. On one button, write the letters of the genes from one parent (one letter on each side). Write the letters for the other parent on the other button.
6. Spill the buttons four times to find the traits for four offspring of these parents. Draw four lines down from the line connecting the parents' genes on your family tree. Write each offspring's genes at the end of a line.
7. Look at the genes of the parents and offspring. Write *rough* or *smooth* next to the genes you recorded.

Analyzing Data

Examine the offspring on your chart. Write whether each of the offspring could possibly have offspring of their own with smooth fur or with rough fur. Explain your answer.

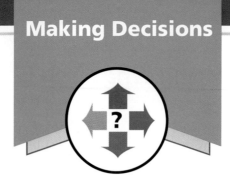

Breeding a Companion

The first dogs looked like wolves. Early variations in size or color were caused by mutations. Later, people used artificial selection to cause these changes and created breeds.

Needs and Goals

Suppose you have a purebred golden retriever, and you want puppies. What kind of dog will you choose as the other parent? Several possibilities exist:

- Another purebred golden retriever.
- A different purebred.
- A mixed-breed, or mixture of two known breeds.
- A mutt, or mixture of so many breeds that you can't identify them.

Consider the traits you would prefer the puppies to have. Then pick the kind of dog most likely to assure these traits in the greatest number of puppies.

Pick the kind of dog most likely to assure desired traits in the greatest number of puppies.

Gathering Information

Consider the traits commonly found in golden retrievers. They are large but not huge, about 55–61 cm at the shoulders. They have a mass of about 27–32 kg. They have long golden fur and floppy ears. They are intelligent, active, and good natured.

- If you want these traits in the puppies, choose another purebred golden retriever.
- If you want puppies with a variety of traits, but don't require certain ones, choose a mixed-breed dog or a mutt.
- Suppose you want puppies with traits different from those of the golden retriever. Then choose another purebred. Examples of purebreds follow.

Newfoundlands are huge—65–70 cm, 54–68 kg —with long black fur and floppy ears. They are intelligent, sweet, patient, and brave.

Dalmatians are medium size—50–60 cm, 25 kg — with black spots on short white fur and floppy ears. They are alert and playful.

German shepherds are large—55–60 cm, 35–40 kg. They have long hair with black, tan, and grayish markings. They have upright, pointed ears. They are intelligent, bold, protective of their master, but distrustful of strangers.

Standard poodles are medium size—38 cm or more, 22 kg. They can be a variety of solid colors from black to white. Their fur is long and curly, but they don't shed. Their ears flop. They are cheerful and very intelligent and trainable. They must be bathed.

Possible Alternatives

Think about your needs. Would a large dog be too big for your home? Is long fur a problem? Do you have a baby brother or sister who might upset an excitable dog?

Evaluating Alternatives

Copy and complete the table. Choose any two pure breeds, or a mixed breed. You can write down the specific characteristics you want, such as "floppy" for the ears, or you can write your opinion or rating of each characteristic. It's your choice.

Making the Best Choice

Use the table to help you make a final choice.

Breeding Dogs

	Breed 1	Breed 2	Mixed Breed
Ear type			
Personality			
Intelligence			
Fur length			
Size			
Markings			
Color			

Now You Do It

1. Which type of dog did you choose? Why?

2. Which traits of each parent would you most want your puppies to have?

3. *On Your Own* In an encyclopedia or dog book, look up some other dog breeds. If you could choose any purebred, which would you most like as a pet? Why?

4. *Critical Thinking* Most types of dogs were bred for a purpose, such as herding, water rescue, pulling sleds, or guarding property. What traits might be most useful for each of these four jobs?

The Frozen Zoo

Dr. Betsy Dresser

Occupation: Animal Breeder
Best part of her job: "The privilege to work with and learn from animals."
Pets: Horses, cats and birds

When Betsy Dresser was little, she visited zoos to learn about animals. Today, Dr. Dresser's trips take her to Africa or China to study endangered species. She is the Director of Research at the Center for Reproduction of Endangered Wildlife at the Cincinnati Zoo.

How do you help endangered animals to reproduce?

"One way is by giving animals special drugs called hormones. The Puerto Rican crested toad had not bred in North America for 25 years. Using hormones, we got 500 tadpoles from a single female—double the total number of toads in this endangered species."

Toads sound easy. Can you help larger animals?

"One way we can help endangered larger animals is with our 'frozen zoo.' The frozen zoo is a collection of embryos from many different species. These embryos can be frozen until they are needed. Then an embryo can be placed in a female of a related species and [after birth] grow up another member of the endangered species."

That sounds like science fiction. Does it work?

"Yes, it does work. When freezing an embryo, you're dealing with just a few cells. As you probably know, cells are made up of about 90% water. If the water freezes, it forms sharp crystals that tear the cells. So we take the water out of the cells and replace it with something like an antifreeze. It makes a kind of slush inside the cells. So far embryos have been frozen for about 15 years, but there's no reason to think that they can't be frozen for hundreds or even thousands of years."

How would we use embryos that were frozen for a long time?

"As long as we have frozen embryos, we should be able to keep a species alive and off the endangered list. It would be a real help to have frozen embryos from each endangered species—a real frozen zoo. Just think, if we had their embryos, we could bring back the dinosaurs!"

DNA Fingerprinting: Solving Crimes

Did you know that DNA can be used to identify a criminal? When radioactive DNA probes are combined with a person's DNA, DNA fingerprinting results.

1 Human DNA contains areas, or "genetic fingerprints" that are unique for every person. Scientists developed a set of probes that attach to these unique areas.

2 Samples are subjected to an electric current in the gel slab, causing the molecules to separate.

3 When DNA probes are combined with the DNA in a sample of blood, it will bind only to matching DNA.

4 DNA from the victim and from the suspects is each combined separately with the DNA probes and tested on a gel slab. Compare the samples.

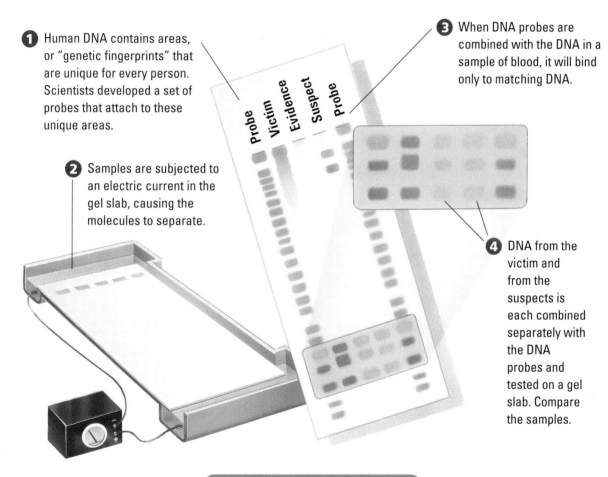

Find Out On Your Own

Draw a model of a DNA fingerprint collected as evidence in a crime. Then draw models of DNA fingerprints from the people involved. Write a detective's report.

Module Performance Assessment

Science Fair

Using what you learned in this module, help prepare exhibitions to be used at a science fair. Complete one or more of the following activities. You may work by yourself or with others in a group.

Environment

Find out whether an endangered species lives in your state or local area. Try to find out reasons why the species is endangered and make a poster to alert your community about the problems the species faces. Include a suggestion for how the species might be saved from extinction.

Biology

Use four strands of yellow yarn, four strands of blue yarn, scissors, and paper to demonstrate that when a cell undergoes meiosis, the four new cells produced have half the number of chromosomes as the original parent cell.

Art
Create a concept map that shows the reasons mentioned in this module for the great variety of living things on Earth. Add drawings to your concept map to illustrate each idea.

Language Arts
Make a bulletin-board display of newspaper clippings about scientific or medical research or applications that are possible due to the current understanding of chromosomes, genes, and DNA. Underline the parts of each article that refer to chromosomes, genes, or DNA.

Drama
In 1962, James Watson, Maurice Wilkins, and Francis Crick shared the Nobel prize for physiology and medicine for their work explaining the structure of the DNA molecule. Plan a skit of the presentation ceremony. Have a presenter from the Nobel committee speak first, and then have Watson, Wilkins, and Crick give their acceptance speeches.

Module Review

Reviewing Words and Concepts

Write the letter of the word or phrase that best completes each sentence.

1. A trait carried by a _____ may be hidden by a dominant gene.
2. An organism that has two parents was produced through _____.
3. The parts of the nucleus made up mostly of DNA are the _____.
4. When mitosis is complete, a cell goes through _____.
5. The traits an organism has are determined by _____.
6. Reproduction by one parent is _____.
7. Sperm and eggs are formed through the process of _____.
8. Organisms with specific traits are produced using _____.
9. A new trait in an organism sometimes results from a _____.
10. All living things are made up of one or more _____.

a. artificial selection
b. meiosis
c. cell division
d. sexual reproduction
e. asexual reproduction
f. cells
g. recessive gene
h. mutation
i. chromosomes
j. DNA

Interpreting What You Learned

1. What characteristics do you share with a blade of grass?
2. How is the DNA in your cells related to your appearance?
3. Why might one say that no "typical" life form exists?
4. List factors that contribute to the diversity of life forms on Earth.
5. Why can you predict the traits of cells formed through asexual reproduction?
6. How might chance play a role in the development of traits that can help an organism survive in its environment?
7. On what basis do scientists place organisms in the same species?

Applying What You Learned

1. How are proteins like the wood and glass used to build a house?
2. Explain the relationship between an organism's resemblance to its parent and method of reproduction.
3. From smallest to largest, state the correct order of the following: organism, gene, nucleus, chromosome, cell.
4. Write a paragraph to explain the importance of the discovery of DNA.
5. If the offspring of a purebred short plant and a purebred tall plant are all tall, which gene is dominant?
6. Why might many people think mutations are always harmful?

Digging for Clues

Digging for Clues

Can you crack the Case of the Ancient Eggs? In this module, you'll follow the adventures of a detective who's hot on the heels of one of the most baffling mysteries of modern science. Can he solve the riddle of the missing babies? Can he put together the puzzle of the fossils? Read on and find out!

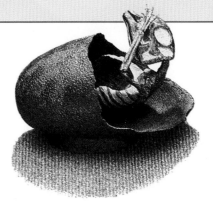

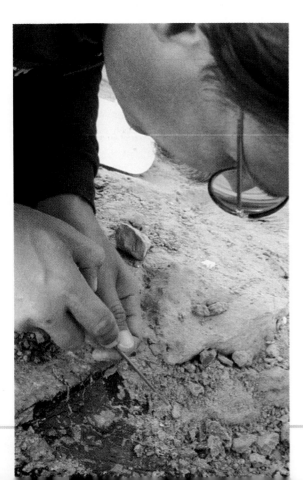

CHAPTER
3 Building on the Past

Guess what, you're on the move! The earth's constantly moving plates change life as well as land.

Digging Up the Past

What can you learn from bones?

Obtain some bones from your teacher. What do the bones tell you about the animal they came from? Use what you already know about animals and their bones to make a list of information you can infer from your bones.

For Discussion

1. What kinds of information did you infer from your bones? What clues did you use?
2. How does your information compare to that of the rest of the class?

1.1 *Looking for Answers*

Where can you find baby dinosaur bones?

Jack Horner—the man in the picture—is famous. You can see him on television and read about him in newspapers and magazines. Dozens of people work for him, and he's even written a book about his life.

How did Jack get to be so famous? By asking a question and finding the answer. Back in 1978, he began wondering why scientists had dug up so few baby dinosaur bones. Adult dinosaur bones were easy to come by, but baby bones were very rare. Given this fact, Jack asked himself a simple question: Where could he find the bones of baby dinosaurs?

Jack knew that around 1900 someone had dug up the bones of young duckbill dinosaurs near Billings, Montana. That seemed like a good place to begin, so he went to Montana in July, 1978. While trying to figure out where to start digging, he took an unplanned detour to a small town called Bynum. It was a pretty quiet town, but it did have a store that sold rocks and fossils.

That simple, little store shown below changed Jack Horner's life. When he walked in, he was still asking his simple question. When he walked out, he had found the beginning of an answer.

▼ *Jack Horner didn't know when he visited this rock shop in Bynum, Montana, that it would be the start of an exciting adventure.*

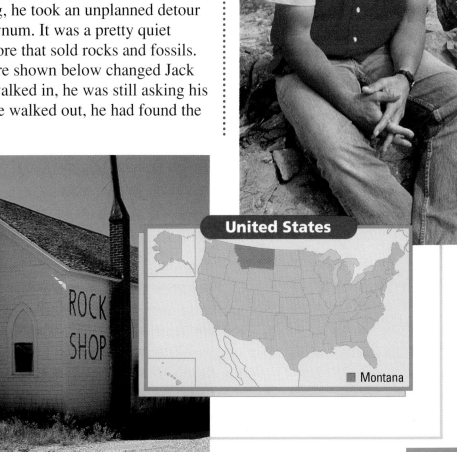

United States

■ Montana

> The Mantells were among the first people to study dinosaur fossils.

> These fossilized teeth were the first fossils the Mantells found.

Learning the Ropes

Dinosaurs died out about 65 million years ago, but their fossils—remains such as bones, teeth, eggs, and footprints—are still buried in the earth. Jack Horner and other scientists who study these fossils are called paleontologists (pā′lē on tol′ə jists). Not all paleontologists study dinosaurs, however. Some study the fossils of plants, algae, or other animals that were very different from dinosaurs.

Modern paleontology began in 1796, when the French scientist Georges Cuvier realized that fossils resulted from plants and animals that are now extinct. Thanks to Cuvier's discovery, people of all ages began digging into the ground, looking for the fossils of extinct animals. Two of those people were an English doctor named Gideon Mantell and his wife Mary Ann.

Gideon and Mary Ann dug up many fossils in the South Downs area of England, including the large fossilized teeth you see on this page. Gideon realized these teeth came from some unknown plant-eating animal. But what that animal might have looked like was a mystery. So Gideon included sketches of the fossilized teeth drawn by Mary Ann in his book, *The Fossils of the South Downs*, published in 1822.

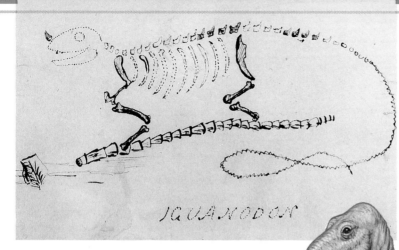

◀ *Compare the Mantells'
sketch of Iguanodon to
today's model, below.*

Gideon and Mary Ann soon found more unusual fossils. Gideon was particularly interested in one set of very large fossils, which he described as "the teeth, vertebrae, bones, and other remains of an animal of the lizard tribe." He didn't know it at the time, but Gideon had just become the first person to write about the fossils of a dinosaur!

Gideon sent the unusual teeth and bones to Cuvier and other experts. One declared they came from a rhinoceros; another from a fish. Unhappy with these answers, Gideon took the teeth to a natural history museum, where he compared them to all the teeth in the museum's collection. At last he found what he was looking for.

The teeth resembled those of a reptile called an iguana lizard, but they were much larger. Gideon decided that the teeth must have come from an extinct reptile that he named *Iguanodon*. *Odon* means "tooth" in Greek, so an Iguanodon is an "iguana-tooth."

Gideon or Mary Ann drew the above sketch of an iguanodon based on the fossils they had found. The dotted lines show missing bones. Since that time, paleontologists have learned that the sketch contains several mistakes. Iguanodons didn't have horns, for example, and they didn't walk on four legs.

The picture to the right shows a more modern version of Iguanodon, but we still don't know exactly what Iguanodon and other dinosaurs looked like. Like the Mantells, today's paleontologists can only guess at the dinosaurs' appearance. As they uncover more fossils, their view of dinosaurs keeps changing.

➤ *Until the 1970s, models and illustrations of dinosaurs often showed them as slow and clumsy.*

Doubting the Experts

Jack Horner learned about dinosaurs as he was growing up in Montana in the 1940s and 1950s. He read about dinosaurs in his school textbooks and looked for dinosaur fossils in his spare time. He also might have visited museums to see dinosaur fossils, just as the boys in the picture from that time are doing. And he most likely studied illustrations of dinosaurs such as the one in the 1950s textbook above.

The dinosaurs in the illustration look slow and clumsy. Their colors are bland, and their tails drag on the ground; they also seem to live by themselves. The artist who drew the illustration probably got these ideas about dinosaurs from the paleontologists of the time.

The more Jack learned about dinosaurs, the more he came to doubt illustrations such as the one above. He knew that the ideas of paleontologists and other scientists are mostly hypotheses—explanations based on evidence. He also knew that hypotheses are only as good as the evidence that supports them. If not enough evidence can be found, a new hypothesis must be made or the old one changed. In the 1940s and 1950s, paleontologists hypothesized that dinosaurs were just like the lizards, turtles, and other reptiles of today. In fact, the very word *dinosaur* means "terrible lizard" in Greek.

On the left is a flying reptile. On the right are some of the first birds.

HISTORY OF LIVING THINGS 275

Missing Any Pages?

Can you figure out a story's main idea if given only a few pages of the book? Let's investigate.

What To Do

A. Obtain part of a page from a short story.

B. Read your part of the page. What can you tell about the story from your part?

C. Work in a group to arrange the group's story pieces in their proper order.

D. Name the story's main characters.

E. Decide on the main idea of the story.

Record Your Data

Main Characters	Main Idea of Story

What Did You Find Out?

1. *Could you have figured out the main idea with only one story piece? How?*

2. *How did each additional piece help?*

3. *What else might have helped you answer the above questions?*

4. *How is answering questions like the ones in this activity similar to working like a paleontologist?*

Since reptiles are generally slow and clumsy and drag their tails, paleontologists of the 1940s and 1950s hypothesized that dinosaurs had similar characteristics. They also thought that all dinosaurs were cold-blooded loners who did not take care of their babies.

As Jack grew up and went on to college, some paleontologists began to challenge these ideas. They pointed out that dinosaurs could stand upright, like birds, while the legs of reptiles, such as lizards, usually sprawl out to the sides. Paleontologists also showed that certain dinosaur bones were more like bird bones than reptile bones. And some even found fossilized feathers.

For these and other reasons, paleontologists began to agree that some dinosaurs were more like birds than reptiles. But they still disagreed about whether dinosaurs were cold- or warm-blooded, whether they took care of their babies, and whether they lived alone. To solve these disagreements, paleontologists needed more evidence, particularly about baby dinosaurs. That's exactly the kind of evidence Jack Horner was looking for when he walked into the rock shop in Bynum, Montana.

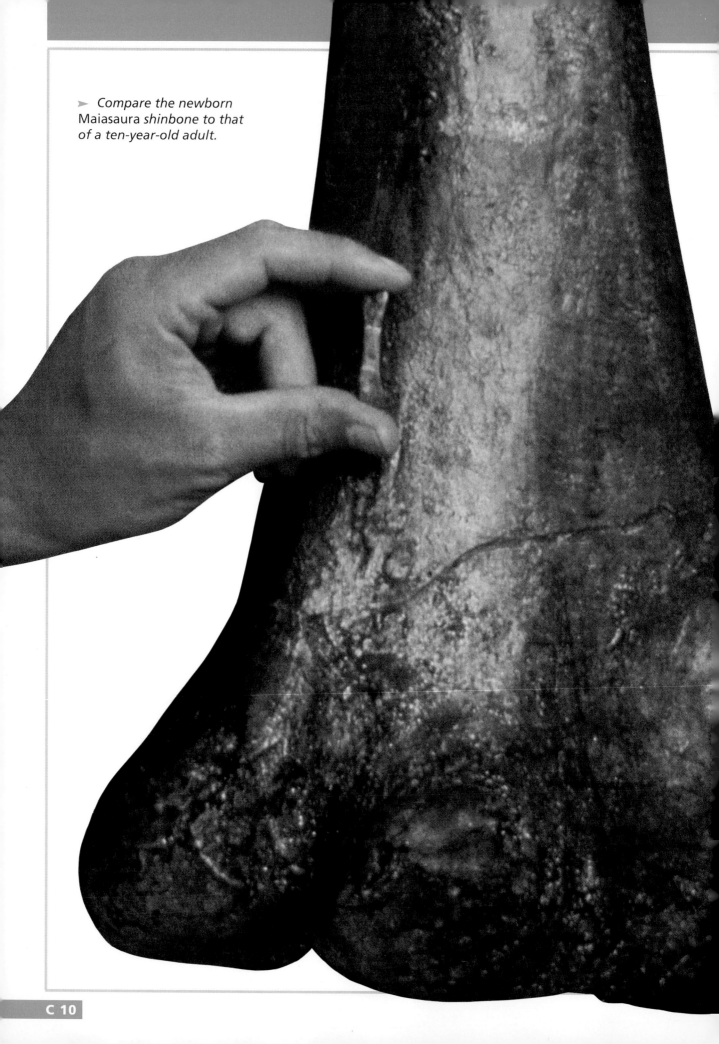

➤ *Compare the newborn Maiasaura shinbone to that of a ten-year-old adult.*

Finding a Clue

Like all paleontologists, Jack Horner is skilled in many areas of science. He knows a lot about rocks and about living things. He knows how the lands and the climate have changed over millions of years. He knows where to look for fossils and how to identify them.

When Jack looked at the fossils in the rock shop, he could tell that many came from duckbill dinosaurs. The owners asked him to identify two small gray bones they had dug up. As Jack examined the first bone, he realized that it looked just like the femur, or thigh bone, of a duckbill dinosaur, but with one important difference. If the femur had come from an adult dinosaur, it would have been about 120 centimeters long. This femur, however, was less than 3 centimeters long.

Why was the femur so small? To Jack, the answer was obvious: It was the femur of a baby duckbill dinosaur. The picture shows the size difference between baby and adult dinosaur bones. Jack had found a baby dinosaur bone right here in the rock shop. He asked the owners if they had any more small bones. They did! The owners gave Jack a whole coffee can full of bones. As Jack separated the pieces, he found bones from at least four baby duckbill dinosaurs.

Jack had found part of the answer to his simple question about baby dinosaur bones, but now he needed the rest. He turned to the shop owners and asked them where they had dug up the tiny bones.

Checkpoint

1. Why did Gideon Mantell use the name *Iguanodon* to describe the animal whose fossils he and his wife had found?
2. How have ideas about dinosaurs changed since the Mantells wrote about them?
3. Why does a paleontologist like Jack Horner need to understand many areas of science?
4. **Take Action!** Find pictures of dinosaurs prior to the mid-1970s. Construct a bulletin board display to show how ideas about those dinosaurs have changed.

1m = 39 inches
3ft + 3inches

How Much Time Is That?

Scientists think the earth is about 4.6 billion years old. How can you get a better picture of this long time span? In this activity, you'll make a proportional time line to show the relative lengths of time between major events in the earth's history.

Picture A

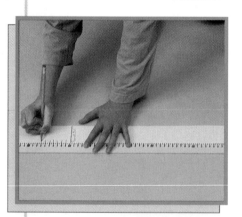

Picture B

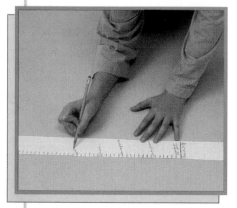

Picture C

Gather These Materials

adding-machine paper   meter stick
2 pieces masking tape   pencil

Follow This Procedure

1 Make a chart like the one on the next page. Record your observations in your chart.

2 Using the scale 1cm = 10,000,000 years, cut a piece of adding-machine paper 5 m long.

3 Tape the ends of the paper to the floor with masking tape.

4 Draw a vertical line at the left end of the paper and label it *4.6 billion years ago.* Measure 4.6 m to the right of the line and draw another verticle line. Label this line *Present day.* (Picture A) The space between the 2 lines represents the time period of the earth's history.

5 Make lines 1 cm apart in the space between the 2 end lines. Each 1 cm distance between 2 lines equals 10,000,000 years. (Picture B)

6 Using the same scale, determine the distance that each event in the chart should be located from the "Present day" line on your adding-machine paper. Record each distance in your chart.

7 Use the information from your chart to mark the appropriate place on the time line where each event occurred. Label the events. (Picture C)

Record Your Results

Event	Approximate number of years ago	Distance on time line from present day
First plants	3, 200, 000, 000	320 cm
First animals	1, 200, 000, 000	120 cm
First land plants	440, 000, 000	44 cm
First dinosaurs	250, 000, 000	25 cm
First mammals	250, 000, 000	25 cm
First birds	195, 000, 000	19.5 cm
First flowering plants	140, 000, 000	14 cm
Extinction of dinosaurs	65, 000, 000	6.5 cm
Earliest human-like species	10, 000, 000	1 cm

SCALE: 1 cm = 10,000,000 years

State Your Conclusions

1. For what percent of geologic time has each of the following existed on the earth: life in any form, human-like species, dinosaurs?

2. Based on what you learned in this activity, what would you say about the dinosaurs' success as a group of organisms?

Let's Experiment

How might you show geologic time on a 24-hour clock? Design an activity that would show the same events and times in the chart on a 24-hour clock.

1.2 *Evolving Life*

> ### How has life on the earth changed?

Just where do Jack Horner's duckbills fit into the "parade" of life on the earth? Let's track the changes in species over time to see.

From Water to Land

Scientists use fossil evidence to divide the earth's history into units of time called the **geologic time scale**. It shows the process of **evolution**, or the change in species over time. Follow this geologic time scale over the next six pages.

Notice on the time line that the longest period of time is called Precambrian (prē′kam′brē ən) time. What time period did it span? Life evolved in the ocean during Precambrian time. For hundreds of millions of years, bacteria dominated. Over time, ancestor bacteria evolved into small floating and weak-swimming, simple ocean organisms, such as algae and jellyfish.

Geologic Time Scale

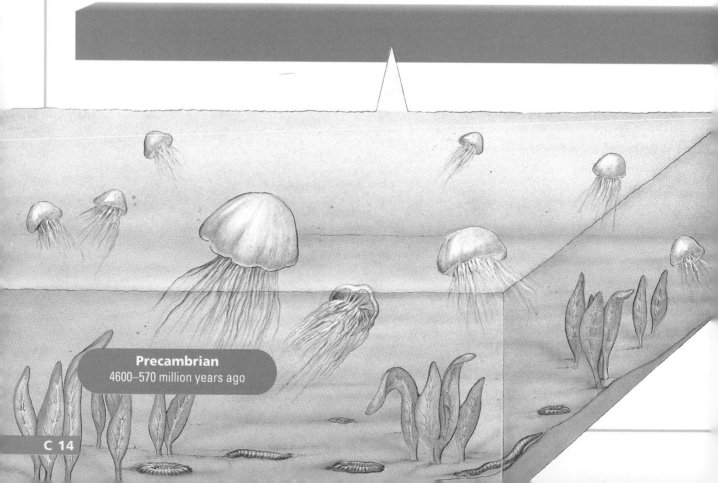

Precambrian
4600–570 million years ago

The Paleozoic (pā′lē ə zō′ik) Era began when the first complex animals appeared about 570 million years ago. The oldest animal fossils come from the beginning of this era, when all living things still lived in the ocean. These fossils include the remains of sea stars, mollusks, and trilobites. These animals were invertebrates—they lacked a backbone. Instead, they were protected by hard outer shells. These shells formed impressions in many materials.

Fish were the first vertebrates—animals with backbones—to evolve. Because their internal backbones provided better attachments for muscles, they could move faster and grow larger. By the middle of the Paleozoic Era, fish replaced trilobites as the dominant consumers in the ocean.

While fish were conquering the ocean, plants and insects were appearing on the land. Lobe-finned fish may have left the water and crawled on the land for short distances. But amphibians were the first vertebrates to actually live on the land. Ancestors of frogs, toads, and salamanders hatched in the water and grew up on the land. By the end of the era, they had been joined by land-dwelling reptiles and dinosaurs.

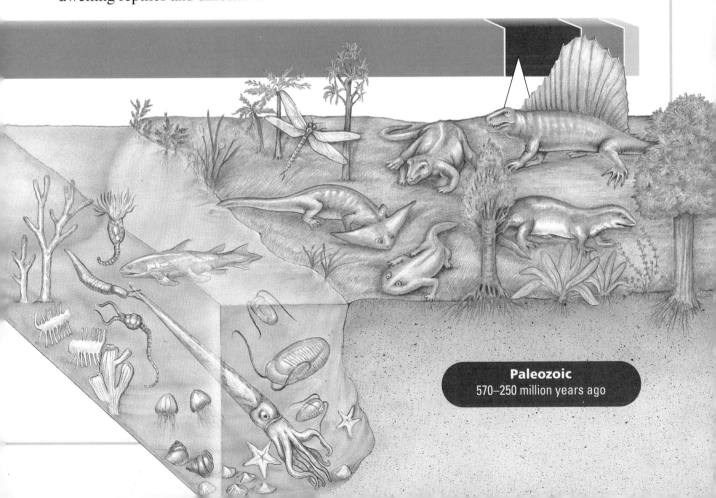

Paleozoic
570–250 million years ago

Drawing On Fossil Evidence

Life in the Mesozoic Era was diverse.

At the end of the Paleozoic Era, glaciers covered much of the land. Many kinds of organisms became extinct. But during the Mesozoic Era, the earth warmed. Many insects evolved, and reptiles became the major kind of land animal. The first mammals and birds also evolved at that time.

Plant life changed too. Cone-bearing trees evolved. Later in the Mesozoic, flowering plants appeared.

This era is often called the Age of Reptiles because reptiles were so large and numerous. And among reptiles, dinosaurs ruled. In fact dinosaurs were the dominant life form on the earth for about 150 million years!

The picture shows what life during the Mesozoic might have looked like. But no human has ever seen a living dinosaur. So how did the illustrator know what to draw?

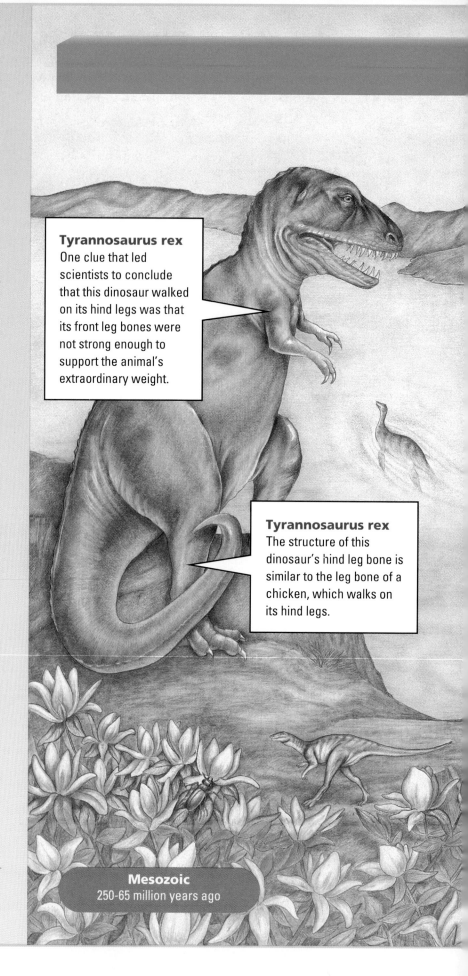

Tyrannosaurus rex
One clue that led scientists to conclude that this dinosaur walked on its hind legs was that its front leg bones were not strong enough to support the animal's extraordinary weight.

Tyrannosaurus rex
The structure of this dinosaur's hind leg bone is similar to the leg bone of a chicken, which walks on its hind legs.

Mesozoic
250-65 million years ago

Pteranodon The bone structure of the front forelimbs of this flying reptile provides scientists with evidence that pteranodons could fly.

Triceratops The position in which scientists found fossil bones led them to think these huge beasts traveled in herds. Also bone scars show evidence of frequent fights. Such injuries are common in modern herding animals.

Staying Warm

Most dinosaurs and other large reptiles became extinct at the end of the Mesozoic Era. Only a few small reptiles, such as lizards, snakes, turtles, and alligators, survived the dramatic changes in land and climate that began the next era, the Cenozoic Era.

But two other types of vertebrates that evolved during the Mesozoic Era—birds and mammals—survived. The earliest bird fossils suggest that they evolved from small, meat-eating dinosaurs. Like reptiles and dinosaurs, birds and some primitive mammals lay eggs. But as the mammals continued to evolve, almost all began giving birth to live babies.

You're still living in the Cenozoic Era, which is often called the Age of Mammals. At the beginning of the era, the earth turned cool and dry. Fur and feathers protected the warm-blooded mammals and birds of that time from cold winters.

Unlike the huge organisms of the Mesozoic Era, early mammals were small. For example, the first horses were about the size of today's foxes, and the first elephants were only about the size of pigs today. Find other early mammals in the timeline. How are they similar to the animals of today?

By the middle of the Cenozoic Era, temperatures warmed. The first tigers and apes appeared, along with rodents. Near the end of the era humans evolved.

About 1.5 million years ago, ice covered large areas of the earth. Humans survived but many other mammals became extinct. In fact, of all the different species that have lived on the earth, most are now extinct. The species that survive continue to evolve. Millions of years in the future the species around you now probably will look much different than they do today.

Checkpoint

1. What advantages did vertebrate fish have over invertebrates?
2. What evidence enables scientists to recreate conditions during the Mesozoic Era?
3. What features of mammals helped them survive during the early Cenozoic Era?
4. **Take Action!** Gather information about the organisms of part of one era. Make a poster, and then combine it with other posters to form an illustrated geologic time scale.

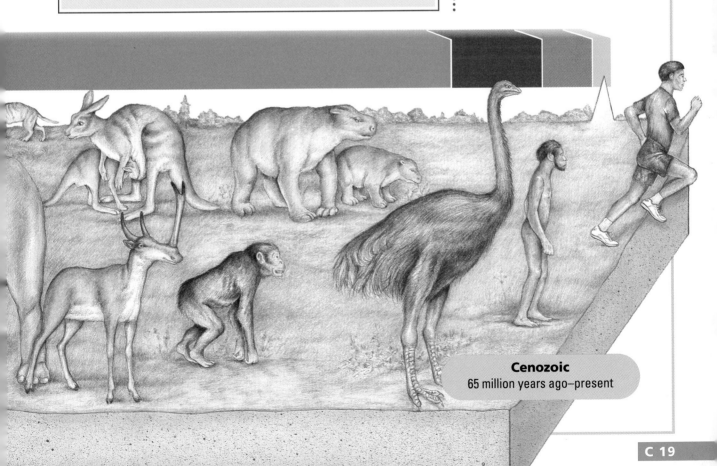

Cenozoic
65 million years ago–present

1.3 *Mysteries of Life*

▶ *Does research always begin with a question?*

Throughout history, scientists have used questions about the world as a starting point for their research. Jack Horner, for example, started his work by asking where he could find the bones of baby dinosaurs. Then he went to Montana to search for evidence.

However, for an English naturalist named Charles Darwin, the evidence came long before the questions. When Darwin sailed away on the *Beagle* in 1831, he had no idea that the voyage would coax him into asking some of the most dazzling questions in science history.

Darwin had not done well in medical school or law school, but he had excelled in observing the organisms of England's countryside. So he was very excited to be asked aboard the *Beagle* as the ship's naturalist. In exchange for his cabin and his food, Darwin wrote journals describing the different species the ship encountered on its journey, shown on the map below.

Darwin's Route

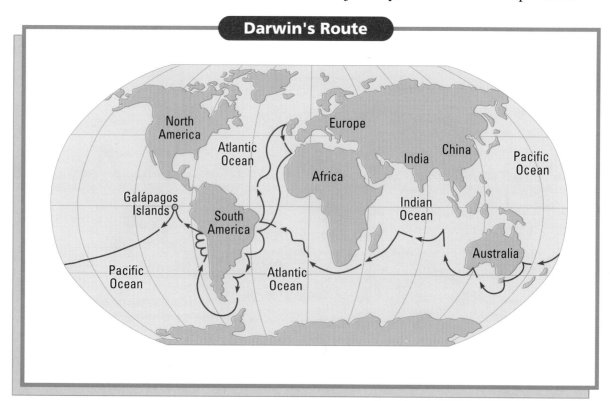

As the *Beagle's* voyage stretched from months into years, Darwin's journals—one of which is shown above—continued to grow. The journals contained detailed descriptions of hundreds of different species of plants and animals. And as the journals grew, they began to provide Darwin with the evidence that would eventually enable him to ask the questions about why species differed.

The Land of the Tortoises

Of all the places Darwin visited, none prompted more questions than the Galápagos, a group of islands about 1000 kilometers off the west coast of South America. Darwin spent only about five weeks visiting the different islands, but observations he made on the islands later changed his view of the entire world.

Darwin was amazed by the islands' unusual animals. He soon realized that many were unique species found nowhere else in the world. Although the animals resembled other species that Darwin had seen and described, they had their own unique qualities that set them apart.

The tortoises that gave the islands their name— *galápagos* means "tortoise" in Spanish—were much larger than any other species of tortoise. As you might guess from the picture, their shells were more than a meter long, and they tipped the scales at 250 kilograms. Even more astonishing was the fact that each island had its own particular kind of tortoise. Some had round shells; others had shells that looked like saddles. Some were dark; others were light.

The tortoises were not the only animals that differed from island to island. At least 13 different species of finches flew about the Galápagos Islands. But on each island, the species present had different types of beaks, which they used in different ways. One species cracked nuts with its short, wide beak. Another caught insects in its long, narrow beak. "One might really fancy," wrote Darwin, "that one species had been . . . modified for different ends."

Darwin didn't yet know how the different species evolved, but he sensed that he was close to an answer. "We seem," he wrote, "to be brought somewhat near to that great fact—that mystery of mysteries—the first appearance of new beings on this earth."

The Survival of the Fittest

It was 1835 when Darwin wrote that he was "somewhat near" to solving the mystery of mysteries; but it was not until 1859 that he finally explained his answer in a book titled *On The Origin of Species.* In the 24 years between his visit to the Galápagos Islands and the publication of this book, Darwin studied his specimens, conducted experiments, analyzed his observations, and wrote his slowly developing ideas.

During that time, Darwin became particularly interested in how farmers used artificial selection to change their livestock. Recall that dairy farmers, for example, can choose to mate their best milking cows with their strongest bulls. The offspring of those cows and bulls often give more milk and are stronger than offspring from other livestock. Darwin wondered if nature was like those dairy farmers. He thought that perhaps some kind of artificial selection process was going on in nature—one where *nature* selects the traits.

The speed of this leopard enables it to catch the slower-moving bush pig.

Through his careful study and analysis, Darwin made two main observations about the natural world. The first observation is that offspring inherit many individual traits from their parents. Recall that, because of sexual reproduction, offspring are never exactly like their parents. Nor is a given offspring like any other offspring of the same two parents. Each one inherits its own unique combination of traits.

The second observation is that living things produce more offspring than can survive. A mallard duck, for example, may lay and hatch dozens of eggs during her lifetime. Most of those offspring, however, will die long before they become adults. If all the offspring survived and reproduced, the world would soon be covered with nothing but mallard ducks.

From these two observations, Darwin drew two main conclusions. First of all, he concluded that life was a constant battle for survival. "As more individuals are produced than can possibly survive," he wrote, "there must in every case be a struggle for existence." And who survives that struggle?

The answer to that question led Darwin to his second conclusion. Based on all his evidence, he concluded that the individuals with the best combination of inherited traits were the most likely to survive and reproduce. Another scientist summarized this conclusion as a simple phrase: Survival of the Fittest.

Taken together, Darwin's observations and conclusions show how a new species develops over time. The pictures show a leopard chasing a bush pig. The pig's parents gave birth to many offspring. Each one was slightly different. Some offspring had stronger leg muscles, and some had weaker ones. This offspring with the weaker leg muscles couldn't outrun the leopard. So, this pig lost its struggle for existence.

However, the pigs with the stronger leg muscles did survive. They were the fittest. Over time, they too might give birth to offspring and their offspring would be more likely to have strong leg muscles. As this pattern repeats, the offspring become more and more likely to have strong leg muscles. Over thousands of years, the bush pigs might slowly change from slow runners into fast ones. These "new" bush pigs might be so different from the old ones that they would become a new species and no longer be able to reproduce with the original ones. Meanwhile, the last of the slow-running bush pigs might die out and become extinct.

Few extinctions are as simple as that, however. Not even Darwin could explain all the extinctions he discovered while sailing on the *Beagle*. "No fact in the long history of the world," he wrote, "is so startling as the wide and repeated exterminations of its inhabitants." And of those "exterminations"—or extinctions—none is so interesting as that of the dinosaurs.

The Last of the Dinosaurs

In many places, you can see some of the layers of rock that make up the earth's crust. In areas where the layers are undisturbed, the farther down you dig, the older the layers become. By knowing which layer a fossil comes from, you can figure out about how old it is.

Luis Alvarez worked with his son Walter to hypothesize why the dinosaurs became extinct.

How do scientists know that most of the dinosaurs became extinct by the end of the Mesozoic Era, 65 million years ago? They know because they have found few dinosaur fossils in the layers of rock above the Mesozoic layers. These higher layers—which were laid down in the Cenozoic Era—contain many mammal bones but few dinosaur bones. Look at the diagram that highlights different layers. Notice that shells, bones, and other fossils are trapped inside the various layers.

Back in 1977, the geologist Walter Alvarez discovered a thin layer of reddish-gray clay between the Mesozoic and Cenozoic layers. This layer is shown on the diagram as a black band. Walter and his father Luis, a physicist, began to study it. They soon discovered that the clay contained a high level of iridium, a rare element on the earth, but one that is common in meteorites.

Could the iridium explain why the dinosaurs became extinct? The Alvarezes thought so. They hypothesized that a giant meteorite collided with the earth 65 million years ago, sending up a cloud of dust that blotted out the sun. According to the Alvarezes' idea, the months of darkness that followed resulted in the death of much plant life. As a result, the dinosaurs died off since plants were the source of food for many dinosaurs.

The impact of a meteorite was a startling hypothesis, and scientists around the world tried to investigate it by examining the rock layers. They too found iridium between the Mesozoic and Cenozoic layers at the sites shown in the map at the top of the next page.

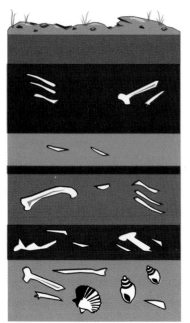

Layers of rock laid down after the iridium layer, shown in black, do not contain dinosaur fossils.

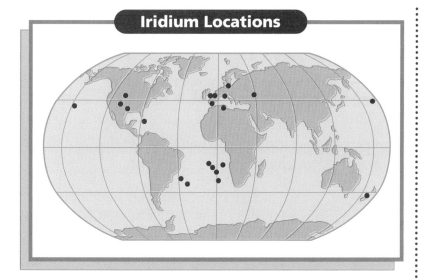
Iridium Locations

Other scientists were not convinced. They pointed out that the Alvarezes had not found any craters formed by the meteorite. And even if a meteorite had hit the earth, how had the mammals and other species survived the months of darkness? If it were that dark, they argued, every species would have become extinct.

That argument continues to this day. Some scientists think the meteorite killed off the dinosaurs. And they think they have found remnants of the impact in craters in Mexico and Iowa. Others suggest the dinosaurs became extinct because they couldn't adjust to other changes in the environment. Scientists have noted that mass extinctions seem to occur every 26 million years or so. More evidence may someday resolve the argument. Until then one fact remains beyond dispute: The dinosaurs died out over a very short period of time.

Checkpoint

1. How did the beaks of the Galápagos finches relate to their eating habits?
2. Use Darwin's observations and conclusions to explain how a new species develops.
3. What are some arguments against the Alvarezes' hypothesis?
4. **Take Action!** Find pictures of the finches Darwin found on the Galápagos Islands. Draw each species and the food they eat.

Activity

Developing a Classification System

Organisms are classified by characteristics that show how closely related they are. In this activity you will use similarities in characteristics to classify cards.

Picture A

Picture B

Picture C

Gather These Materials

poster board   string
3 identical sets of cards   glue

Follow This Procedure

1 Make a chart like the one on the next page. Record your observations on your chart.

2 Place a sheet of poster board on your desk.

3 Lay one set of cards together across the top of the poster board. Examine each of the cards carefully. This is your unsolved reference set. (Picture A)

4 Record the characteristics of the cards, such as color, size, or shape.

5 Use a second set of cards. Divide the cards into two groups based on a characteristic such as shape. (Picture B) Identify the characteristics you used to divide the cards into two groups.

6 Repeat Step 5 using a third set of cards so that each of these two groups is divided into two more groups. Once again use a characteristic that separates each group from every other. Identify the characteristics that divided each group into two. (Picture C)

7 Use the string to connect the groups.

Predict: *How many more times do you think you can divide each of the smaller groups?*

Record Your Results

Characteristics of objects	
Characteristics used for first classification	
Characteristics used for second classification	

8 Divide your groups into smaller and smaller groups. Each time identify the characteristic that separates the groups.

9 Glue the string and cards to your poster board.

State Your Conclusions

1. What characteristics did you use to divide the cards?

2. How many ways could the cards be divided according to characteristics you can see?

Let's Experiment

Could trees be grouped according to the characteristics of their leaves? Use leaves or pictures of leaves to design a system to classify trees.

1.4 *Filling in the Blanks*

▶ **Why are dinosaurs saurs?**

As Jack Horner learned about dinosaurs, he read the Greek word *saur* over and over again. Why? Because when the scientist Richard Owen named the newly discovered animals back in 1841, he thought they looked like monster lizards. Owen therefore combined the Greek word *dino,* meaning "terrible," with the Greek word *saur,* meaning "lizard." The result was *dinosaur,* the "terrible lizard."

Dinosauria is the name given to a group of extinct animals, and the different types of dinosaurs are all members of this group. Many of their names combine *saur* with another Greek word. *Tyrannos,* for example, is a Greek word meaning "cruel." A tyrannosaur, therefore, is a "cruel lizard."

Scientists around the world continue to call dinosaurs by these Greek and Latin names so that everyone will know exactly which organism is being talked about. These Greek and Latin names represent a system that all scientists understand. And you can understand it too. For example, scientists sometimes call a housecat a cat; but when they want to be exact, they use the Latin name *Felis domesticus.* That way they know someone will not mistake the housecat for a bigger cat such as a lion. The name *Felis domesticus* not only describes a certain species but gives other information as well. This naming system is an important part of taxonomy—the science of classifying organisms.

From Kingdom to Species

The chart shows how scientists use evolutionary relationships to group organisms. The five major groups are called kingdoms. In addition to plants and animals, the kingdoms include monerans (bacteria and blue-green bacteria), protists and other kinds of algae, and fungi (molds, mushrooms, and yeast).

➤ **Five-kingdom classification**

Ⓐ Christmas fern fiddleheads
Ⓑ Scarlet cup fungi
Ⓒ Spotted lady beetle
Ⓓ Showy lady's slippers
Ⓔ Bread mold fungus
Ⓕ Grevy's zebra
Ⓖ *Volvox, Spirogyra*
Ⓗ *Ameba*
Ⓘ *Borrelia*
Ⓙ *Micrococcus*

Plant

A

D

Many-celled, undergo photosynthesis, reproduce by seeds, cones, or spores

Fungus

B

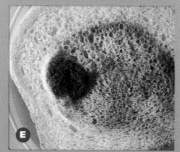
E

Many-celled, absorb food from dead or living organisms, reproduce by spores

Animal

C

F

Many-celled, get energy by consuming other organisms, have specialized sex cells

Protist

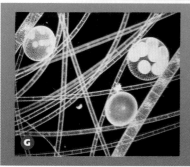
G

Most one-celled, get food by eating other organisms; some many-celled, undergo photosynthesis

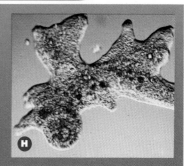
H

Moneran

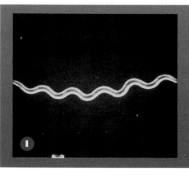
I

One-celled, no distinct nuclei, some undergo photosynthesis, some get energy from other organisms

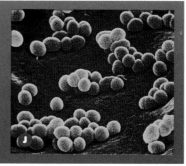
J

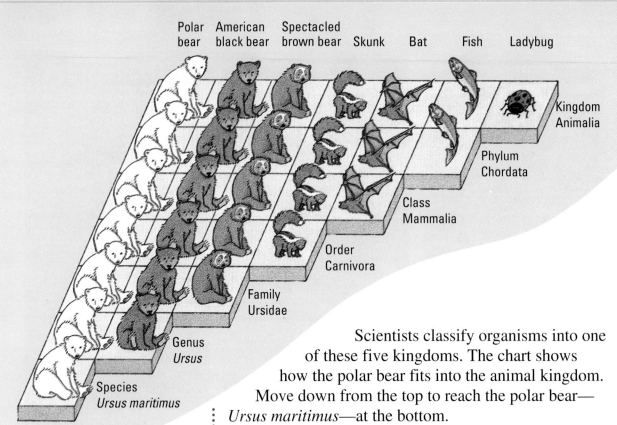

Polar bear | American black bear | Spectacled brown bear | Skunk | Bat | Fish | Ladybug

Kingdom Animalia

Phylum Chordata

Class Mammalia

Order Carnivora

Family Ursidae

Genus *Ursus*

Species *Ursus maritimus*

▲ *Classification of a polar bear*

Scientists classify organisms into one of these five kingdoms. The chart shows how the polar bear fits into the animal kingdom. Move down from the top to reach the polar bear—*Ursus maritimus*—at the bottom.

Scientists subdivide each of the five kingdoms into smaller groups called phyla (fī′lə). Scientists have named more than 30 animal phyla, each with its own unique characteristics. The polar bear belongs to the phylum of chordates. Most chordates have vertebrae, or backbones. You also are a member of the chordate group because you have a backbone.

The next smaller group is the class. The seven classes of vertebrates are mammals, birds, reptiles, amphibians, and three classes of fish. Polar bears belong to the mammal class. Just like all other members of the mammal class, polar bears are warm-blooded, have fur or hair, and feed milk to their young. To which class do humans belong?

Scientists divide living mammals into 18 smaller groups called orders. These orders include primates (apes and monkeys), marsupials (kangaroos and koalas), and rodents (rats and mice). Polar bears belong to the order of carnivores.

The carnivores are made up of several families, including the bear family, Ursidae. The members of the bear family—black bears, grizzly bears, and polar bears—look fairly similar, but they differ greatly in size, color, and habits.

Within the bear family only polar bears and brown bears have a certain jaw structure that is different from that of other bears. So they're put together in the next smaller group: the genus *Ursus*. Members of a genus are very much alike but can't breed with each other.

The smallest group is the species, and each species has its own unique name that combines the genus name and another descriptive name. The polar bear's name is *Ursus maritimus,* which means "ocean-going bear" in the Latin language. Like all other species, polar bears are unique in at least one way.

A Species of Debate

Polar bears became a species through evolution. Their ancestors lived in temperate regions, but over millions of years, as the bears moved toward the arctic, they developed certain traits and polar bears evolved. When polar bears were no longer able to breed with other bears, they became a separate species.

Scientists often disagree about how certain species evolved. Some scientists, for example, hypothesize that both brown bats and flying foxes are closely related to flying lemurs. Others hypothesize that they had different ancestors. As with many science debates, no one is yet absolutely sure of the answer.

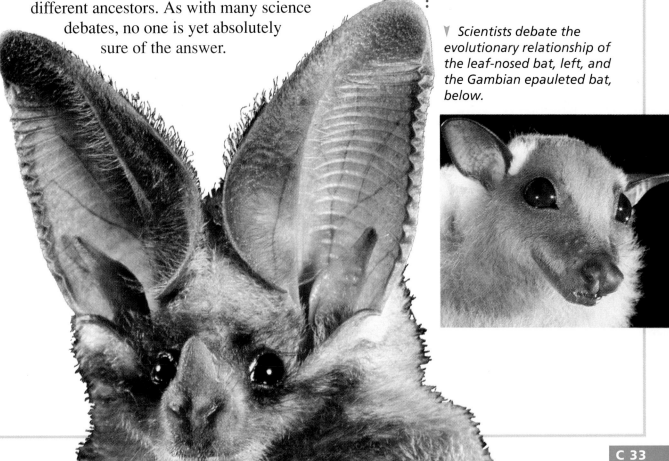

▼ Scientists debate the evolutionary relationship of the leaf-nosed bat, left, and the Gambian epauleted bat, below.

▼ *Felis domesticus*

Debates over taxonomy are nothing new. When people first classified organisms thousands of years ago, they used only two categories: useful and harmful. The ancient Greek philosopher Aristotle replaced those categories by dividing organisms into plants and animals. He further divided animals into those with red blood and those without red blood. As to plants, he identified three kinds: herbs, shrubs, and trees.

Aristotle's classification system lasted for more than 2000 years. But in the 1700s, the Swedish scientist Carolus Linnaeus developed the system that scientists use today. Linnaeus devised the seven-level method— kingdom, phylum, class, order, family, genus, species. He gave each species a unique Greek or Latin name. Thanks to Linnaeus, this pet cat is a *Felis domesticus*.

Naming the Living World

What are the differences among a puma, a cougar, a panther, and a mountain lion? That's a tricky question, because they're all the same animal. People in different parts of North America use those names to describe the animal shown below. By using the animal's scientific name—*Felis concolor*—scientists avoid confusion. Since no two species have the same scientific name, there can be no doubt about which animal *Felis concolor* refers to.

▼ *Felis concolor*

Every species' name has two parts, just like your own name. *Felis concolor* and *Felis domesticus* are two species that evolved from a common ancestor. So they're grouped in the same genus: *Felis*. Their names use Latin words to describe their characteristics. *Felis concolor* means "one-color cat"; *Felis domesticus* means "household cat."

Sometimes species get part of their names from the people who discovered the species. For example, one species of duckbill dinosaur—*Hadrosaurus foulkii*—is named for William Foulke, who discovered it in 1858.

The name of a species can change if scientists learn more about how that species evolved. Lions, for instance, used to be called *Felis leo,* which means "lion cat." Then scientists decided that, because of ancestral differences, roaring cats such as lions belong to a different genus than cats that meow. So lions became *Panthera leo,* which means "lion roaring cat," and were grouped with the tigers, *Panthera tigris.*

One interesting name change involved the person who devised the system of species names. His real name was Carl von Linne. But von Linne became so famous for the books he wrote in Latin that he "Latinized" his name, changing it to Carolus Linnaeus. His brilliance helped explain the name of the species to which he belonged—*Homo sapiens*, or "wise human being."

Into The Field

If you discovered a new organism, what would you name it?
Imagine that you discovered a new organism. Draw it. Describe it. Tell what you would name it.

▼ *Panthera tigris*

How can this girl identify the skull she has dug up?

A classification guide aids in identifying organisms.

Winning the Race

It's possible that anyone might dig up the remains of a living thing. All you need is a plot of ground, a shovel, some muscle power, and a little luck. If you pick the right spot, you might even find a skull. That's what Sandra found when she went digging with her grandfather in their back yard. The photograph shows what the skull looked like when they dug it up.

Then came the hard part. They wanted to identify what species the skull belonged to. Grandfather wrote a seven-level list, beginning with *kingdom* and ending with *species*. If they could fill in all seven levels, they'd know what species the skull represented.

The first two levels were easy. Sandra and Grandfather knew the skull came from the animal kingdom, because only animals have bones. And they knew the skull came from a vertebrate, because only vertebrates have skulls. But what class of vertebrate was it? To answer that question, they used a reference book that showed the different classes of skulls. After much debate, they decided their skull belonged to a reptile, because it had the characteristics of a reptile skull.

By using the reference book, Sandra and Grandfather figured out that the skull was too small to be a crocodile's and too large to be a local lizard's or a snake's. And the skull had no teeth—a characteristic of turtles. Therefore, it had to belong to the fourth order of reptiles: turtles. But then Sandra read that 13 families and more than 200 different species of turtles have been classified. How could they ever identify the species of their skull?

Sandra and Grandfather looked at the skull again and noticed the powerful jaws. At that moment, both of them realized that the skull must have come from the family of snapping turtles, which is famous for its powerful jaws. Now the detectives were hot on the trail, because only two species of snapping turtles exist: common and alligator. Each species is the only member of its genus.

The alligator snapping turtle is the largest freshwater turtle in the world. Its skull is angular and wedge shaped. But the skull that Sandra and Grandfather had dug up was fairly small and more rounded. At last they agreed that it belonged to a common snapping turtle. They had found the remains of a *Chelydra serpentina*—the "snake-like turtle."

Turtles are one of the oldest living groups of reptiles. They trudged over the land and swam in the ocean millions of years ago when dinosaurs ruled the earth. The snapping turtle of today is far different from those ancient turtles, but it still provides a kind of living link with the earth's astonishing past. The huge dinosaurs may have died out, but the turtles just keep trudging along.

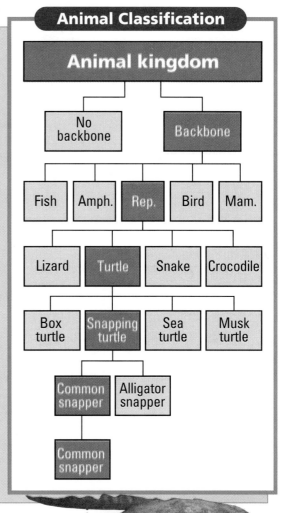

Animal Classification

Animal kingdom

No backbone | Backbone

Fish | Amph. | Rep. | Bird | Mam.

Lizard | Turtle | Snake | Crocodile

Box turtle | Snapping turtle | Sea turtle | Musk turtle

Common snapper | Alligator snapper

Common snapper

Checkpoint

1. Why are polar bears classified as a species?
2. What disagreement do scientists have about brown bats and flying foxes?
3. Why did the name of the lion species change?
4. What piece of evidence convinced Sandra and Grandfather that their turtle skull came from a snapping turtle?
5. **Take Action!** Choose an organism and make a mobile showing its classification. Include information about its habitat and characteristics.

▲ *Common snapping turtle*

Chapter Review

Reviewing Words and Concepts

Write the letter of the word or phrase that best completes each sentence.

1. A scientist who studies fossils is called a _h_.

2. During the _a_, dinosaurs existed in great numbers.

3. Most species that have ever lived on the earth are now _f_.

4. The first animals with backbones to evolve were _g_.

5. The process in which species change over time is called _e_.

6. Scientists know dinosaurs became extinct about 65 million years ago because of the lack of _h_ in rock layers younger than 65 million years.

7. The _c_ divides the earth's history into units of time.

8. The earliest and longest period of time on the geologic time scale is called _d_ time.

9. All of the earth's organisms are classified into five large groups called _c_.

10. The smallest classification group is the _b_ group.

a. Mesozoic Era
b. species
c. geologic time scale
d. Precambrian
e. evolution
f. extinct
g. fish
h. paleontologist
i. dinosaur fossils
j. kingdoms

Connecting Ideas

1. Copy the concept map. Use the terms at the right to complete the map about the geologic time scale.

Paleozoic Era   trilobites
simple ocean life   Mesozoic Era
Cenozoic Era   humans

A. Precambrian — C. _____ — E. _____ — G. _____

B. _____   D. _____   F. dinosaurs   H. _____

2. Write a sentence or two that summarizes the ideas shown in the concept map.

Interpreting What You Learned

1. How did the Mantells determine that the teeth and bones they found came from an extinct reptile?
2. What evidence caused scientists to change their views about dinosaur traits?
3. Describe the climatic changes that took place during the Cenozoic Era.
4. Why did Darwin find the species on the Galápagos Islands so interesting?
5. What were the two main observations Darwin made about the natural world?
6. Describe how scientists name organisms.
7. What are some hypotheses about the cause of the extinction of dinosaurs?

Performance Assessment

How are the five kingdoms similar and different?

Materials
- markers
- 2 pieces of string (each about 1 meter long)
- 9 index cards

Collecting Data

1. Use five of the index cards to make the following labels: *Plant, Animal, Fungus, Protist,* and *Moneran.*
2. Use the remaining index cards to make four other labels: *many-celled, one-celled, undergo photosynthesis,* and *eat other organisms.*
3. Make two overlapping circles using the pieces of string.
4. Place the label *many-celled* in one circle and *one-celled* in the other circle.
5. Place each of the five cards with labels of the kingdoms in one of the circles. If any kingdom contains both *many-celled* and *one-celled* organisms, place that card in the overlapping space between the circles.
6. Draw a picture that shows the arrangement of the cards.
7. Remove all the cards from the yarn circles. Place the label *undergo photosynthesis* in one circle and *eat other organisms* in the other circle.
8. Place each of the five cards with labels of the kingdoms in one of the circles. If any kingdom contains organisms that both *undergo photosynthesis* and *eat other organisms,* place that card in the overlapping space between the circles.
9. Draw another picture showing your arrangement of the cards.

Analyzing Data

Choose two or more kingdoms and write a short description telling how they are alike or different.

2

Stories of Fossils

I give. What is it?

What can you learn from clay impressions of an object?

Work where others can't see what you're doing. Remove a mystery object from the bag. Press one side of it into a lump of clay. Show the impression to the group. Have them guess what the object might be. Repeat with each side of the object until someone guesses what it is.

For Discussion

1. *How many guesses were needed to identify your objects?*
2. *What types of objects are most difficult to identify?*

2.1 Bones, Eggs, and Nests

Where did baby dinosaurs live?

Jack Horner's startling discoveries about baby duckbill dinosaurs began in the Brandvolds' rock shop in Bynum, Montana. The discoveries continued a few days later, when Jack, his friend Bob Makela, and the Brandvolds all drove out to the cattle ranch where Marion Brandvold had first dug up the baby dinosaur bones Jack had seen in the rock shop.

Like much of central Montana, the ranch—owned by the Peebles family—consisted of windswept grasslands with low rolling hills and small mounds made of mudstone. Marion pointed to a mound about one meter high and three meters across. On the surface of the mound, Jack and Bob found limestone pebbles, pieces of mudstone, bits of rock—and the fossils of baby duckbill dinosaurs, like those to the right.

Soon afterwards, Jack and Bob returned to the ranch with bags and shovels. They dug down into the green mudstone at the top of the mound and turned up more and more fossils of baby duckbills. And then they noticed something unusual. About one meter down, the green mudstone turned red and the fossils disappeared. The red mudstone contained no fossils.

Jack and Bob dug all the green mudstone out of the mound. When they finished, they had uncovered a big bowl about two meters wide and one meter deep, as shown in the picture. They asked themselves a question: Why were all the fossils inside the bowl? The answer seemed obvious: Because the bowl was a nest.

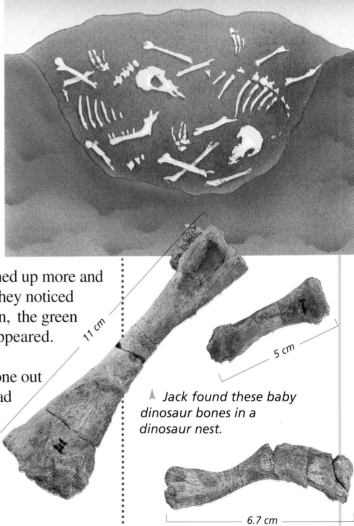

11 cm

5 cm

6.7 cm

Jack found these baby dinosaur bones in a dinosaur nest.

At The Dig

***Life at a fossil dig can be
simple, hard, tedious—
and exciting!***

Imagine the thrill of
finding fossils! But life at
a fossil dig is not always
exciting. Life can be
hard, and the job tedious.

At first Horner's crew
was small—about 13
people. The crew worked
six days a week. On the
seventh day they went to
town for supplies, a hot
shower, and telephone
calls. The camp consisted
of teepees, small tents,
trailers, and a collection
of cars and trucks.

In later years as more
money became available,
the size of the crew
increased and the camp
improved. A permanent
tent served as a kitchen
and a device made from a
truck inner tube served as
a hot shower.

An observer of the
camp would have seen
scattered tools—maps,
hammers, picks, dental
tools, and brushes. As
one observer noted, "It
looked like a group of
scientific hoboes had
found a place to hide
until the police came to
roust them out."

Housing at a dig can range
from cabins to these simple, but
comfortable, teepees. Many crew
members used teepees because the
teepees are airy and very sturdy. In fact, they
can withstand the 128-kilometer-per-hour winds
that move in from the nearby Rocky Mountains.

Finding and removing fossils from
rock is a slow, tedious job. Often
crew members crawled around
for two or three days and still
found nothing important. Even
after finding a fossil, removing it
from the rock can take months.

The most common way to look for fossils is to walk along and look at the ground. But Jack's crew members spent most of the time on their knees, their noses seldom more than 46 centimeters from the ground. Even when wearing knee pads, rocks dug into their knees.

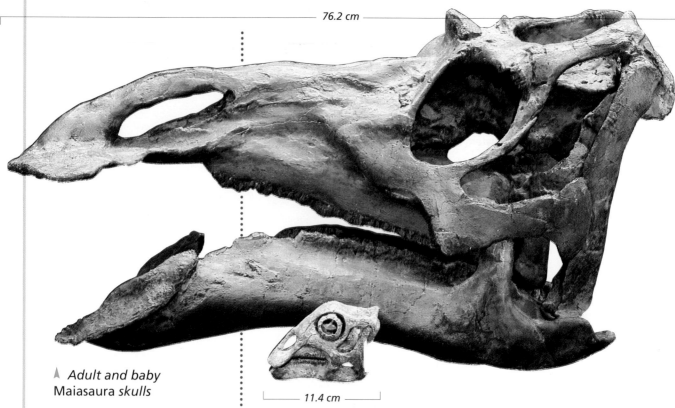

76.2 cm

11.4 cm

▲ *Adult and baby*
Maiasaura *skulls*

The Good Mother

While Jack and Bob dug up the nest of baby duckbills, the Brandvolds shoveled into another patch of ground. They too found a fossil, but it was much larger than the baby bones. It was the skull of an adult duckbill dinosaur, like the one above.

"If I had only one part of an animal," Jack said later, "I'd rather have a skull than anything else." Like other duckbill skulls, this one had a wide, duck-like bill in the front and rows of teeth along the upper and lower jaws. But the nose was longer than other duckbill noses, and the nose holes were smaller.

After studying the skull at length, Jack and Bob realized that the Brandvolds had found a *Maiasaura* fossil; but, it was one of a new species of duckbill dinosaur. It was the same species as the babies in the nest. They decided to call the species *Maiasaura peeblesorum,* meaning "the good mother lizard from the Peebles ranch."

What kind of animal was *Maiasaura peeblesorum?* By studying the skull and other bones, Jack was able to figure out what *Maiasaura* probably looked like. The picture below shows the complete skeleton of an adult maiasaur.

Maiasaurs were about seven meters long and had a mass of about two metric tons. They walked on their long back legs. They may have used their front legs to support their weight when resting or bending down. Unfortunately, *Maiasaura* skeletons don't give any clues about their color.

The maiasaurs used their long rows of teeth to grind and chew plants. They probably made bleating or honking noises by blowing air through their large upper jaw bones.

The skeleton, however, doesn't show the most unusual feature of *Maiasaura*. Because the skull and the nest were so close, Jack concluded that the maiasaurs may have been taking care of the babies in the nest when all were killed. Dinosaurs weren't supposed to do that. According to the experts, most dinosaurs just laid their eggs and left. But it seemed to Jack that the maiasaurs acted differently. If only he could get more evidence, he might be able to prove his point.

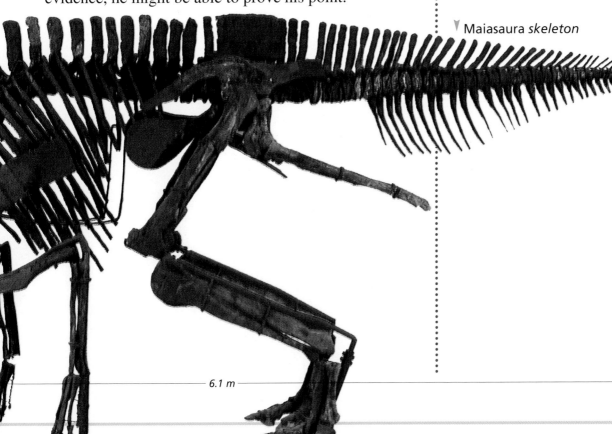

▼ Maiasaura *skeleton*

6.1 m

Hatching Tough Questions

The discoveries at the Peebles Ranch in 1978 might have satisfied some paleontologists. But for Jack Horner the discoveries were just the beginning. He went back to Montana the next summer and the next and the next. At last he moved his whole family to Montana in order to be closer to the *Maiasaura* fossils.

Recall that during those first summers, Jack and his helpers lived in tents and teepees on or near the Peebles Ranch. Every day they crawled around the rocky, windswept land on their hands and knees, looking for dinosaur fossils. The photograph below shows the kind of ground they worked on.

By 1983, Jack's crew had found 14 nests and the bones and teeth of 31 baby maiasaurs. They had also uncovered 42 *Maiasaura* eggs, along with many bits of eggshell. In two of the nests, they found eggs arranged in neat circles and stacked on top of each other. The eggs were oval, rough to the touch, and about 20 centimeters long. Millions of years ago, those eggs held *Maiasaura* embryos—unhatched babies. But time had turned most of the embryos to dust. The picture on the next page shows what a *Maiasaura* embryo might have looked like while still inside the egg.

▼ *Jack Horner and his crew worked on this barren land of Montana called the "Badlands."*

◄ Maiasaura *embryo and egg*

Through their careful digging, Jack and his crew had found an impressive number of fossils. And, in turn, those fossils prompted an impressive number of questions. For example, why were the baby maiasaurs in some nests so much larger than the embryos? Why were the teeth of those babies worn down? Why were the bottoms of the nests covered with broken eggshell?

The nests themselves were even more puzzling. As the crew dug up more and more nests, it became clear that many of the nests were evenly spaced. Each of these nests was about seven meters away from its neighbor. Not only that, but evidence from the surrounding rocks showed that many of the nests may have been built in the same year. What did it all mean? Why were the nests evenly spaced? Those were tough questions, and they needed answers.

Checkpoint

1. How is working at a dinosaur dig different from working in a typical science lab?
2. What evidence led Jack Horner to think that maiasaurs took care of their babies?
3. What evidence about *Maiasaura* was Jack Horner able to collect at the Peebles Ranch?
4. **Take Action!** Write a newspaper advertisement seeking people to work at a fossil dig.

Activity

Scaling Things Down

Whenever Jack Horner and his crew found fossils, they made detailed drawings and notes about their discoveries. In this activity you'll work with a team to make a scale drawing of a bed of "dinosaur footprints."

Picture A

Picture B

Picture C

Gather These Materials

graph paper   meter stick
pencil   metric ruler

Follow This Procedure

1 Make a chart like the one on the next page. Record your observations in your chart.

2 Use a meter stick to measure the length and width of your classroom. (Picture A) Record the measurements in the "Actual distance" column of your chart.

3 Make a scale drawing of the room floor plan on a sheet of graph paper. Decide on the scale of your drawing. For example, 1 cm on your graph paper might represent 1 m of room length. Use a scale that will allow you to draw the whole room on your graph paper. Write your scale in your chart.

4 Locate Footprint 1 on the floor of your classroom. Measure the distance from the closest side wall to the footprint. Record your measurement in your chart. Now measure the distance from the front wall in the classroom to the footprint and record your data in the chart. (Picture B)

5 Repeat Step 4 for all the footprints in the room.

6 Fill in the "Scale distance" column of the chart to show how long each measurement should be in your scale.

Record Your Results

Scale:	Actual distance (in classroom)	Scale distance (on graph paper)
Room length		
Room width		
Footprint 1 • Distance from closest side wall • Distance from front wall		
Footprint 2 • Distance from closest side wall • Distance from front wall		

7 Using your scaled-down measurements, draw the footprints in the proper location on your graph paper. (Picture C)

State Your Conclusions

1. How did your scale drawing help you study the footprints?
2. How would a scale drawing be helpful to a paleontologist?

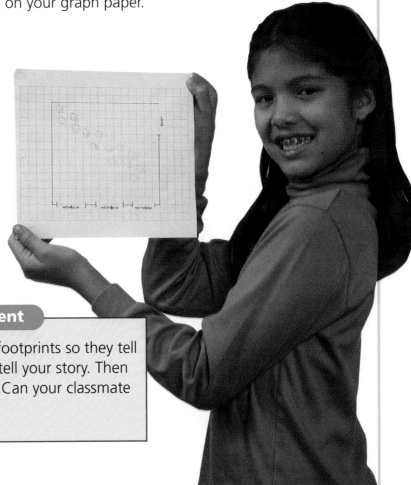

Let's Experiment

How could you arrange dinosaur footprints so they tell a story? Make a scale drawing to tell your story. Then give your drawing to a classmate. Can your classmate figure out the story?

2.2 *Impressions in the Earth*

▶ ***When is a rock not a rock?***

Jack Horner can't answer every question about *Maiasaura*. But he does know how the baby maiasaurs became fossils.

Leaving a Mark

The process of fossilization began when the *Maiasaura* babies died. After the babies died, their flesh began to rot and fall away, leaving only their skeletons. Then the ligaments that held the bones together also rotted away, and the skeletons fell apart. The disconnected bones lay in a heap at the bottom of the nest, as shown in the first picture to the left.

The bones themselves could have rotted away next, but then something happened. As shown in the second picture, mud and water from a spring flood swept into the nest and covered the bones. Now the bones were buried under the mud, which slowly hardened into rock, as shown in the third picture. Over millions of years, water and silica minerals from the rock seeped into pores in the bones, as shown in the last picture. Through a chemical process, the silica minerals gradually replaced the materials that the bones were made of. Eventually, the bones turned into objects made of silica minerals. These objects looked just like the original bones, down to the tiniest detail. They weren't rocks, but they weren't bones either. They were fossils.

▼ *How some fossils form*

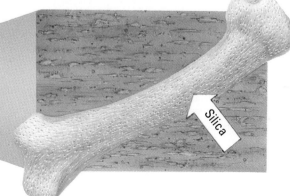

Silica

Even as the baby maiasaurs were dying in their nests, billions of other living things were dying all over the earth. But very few of those living things have been preserved as fossils. Why? Because most living things die without leaving a trace. Their flesh rots and their bones erode or dissolve. Soon nothing is left—no flesh, no bones, no fossils. All parts are recycled in nature.

Then how did the baby maiasaur bones become preserved? They were buried by mud. Fossils form by different processes, but all those processes begin when a dead organism comes into contact with mud, sand, or some other mineral substance. Often only the hardest parts of the plant or animal—stems, bones, teeth—turn into fossils. However, sometimes traces such as footprints or burrows, or even the entire organism become fossils.

Compare the living dragonfly in the picture below to the fossilized dragonfly on the side. You can see that the fossil preserves the outlines of the dragonfly's body, down to the finest detail. Missing are the blood and organs that bring the dragonfly to life.

The dragonfly fossil began to form after the dragonfly came into contact with mud or some other type of sediment. The dragonfly soon decayed, but it left behind the impression, or outline, of its body in the mud. As the mud hardened into rock, so did the impression. In some ways, this type of fossil is like the handprints that children make in wet cement. Both leave behind an impression that hardens into rock.

Into The Field

Can you find imprints outside?

Look for things imprinted in mud, concrete, or snow. Draw what you observe. Infer what made each impression.

▼ Compare the dragonfly fossil to the living dragonfly.

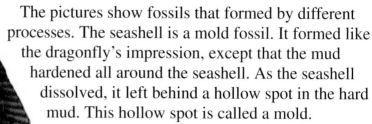

The pictures show fossils that formed by different processes. The seashell is a mold fossil. It formed like the dragonfly's impression, except that the mud hardened all around the seashell. As the seashell dissolved, it left behind a hollow spot in the hard mud. This hollow spot is called a mold.

People have understood the principle of molding for many years. They make their own molds in order to manufacture a wide range of products, including plastic dinosaurs. Workers at toy factories begin making plastic dinosaurs by forming a mold in the shape of a dinosaur. Then they fill the mold with liquid plastic. When the plastic hardens, the workers open the mold and out pops a "cast" of a dinosaur.

The trilobite fossil is a cast fossil, formed in a way similar to that plastic dinosaur. Like the seashell, the trilobite left behind a hollow mold in the rock. But then water containing minerals filled up the mold. Over time, the minerals formed into the shape of a trilobite, just as the plastic hardened into the shape of a dinosaur.

Water and minerals also played a role in forming the petrified tree. First the tree was buried in mud, volcanic ash, or sand. Then water with dissolved minerals seeped into the tree replacing the tissues of the tree. As the minerals hardened, the entire tree turned into stone.

A mold of an ammonite

A cast of a trilobite

➤ *Petrified wood*

Mud isn't the only material that can cover dead organisms. The insect at the right got stuck in the sap of a tree. The sap hardened around the insect. The hardened sap is called fossilized amber.

People have found remains of animals that were stuck in tar pits or frozen in blocks of ice. The tar and the extreme cold can preserve not only the animals' bones, but also their skin and even their hair. Usually these remains are not nearly as old as the fossils you see on this page. In 1991, German mountain climbers found the well-preserved body of a man who lived 5300 years ago. He was preserved in a glacier in the Alps.

Stacking Up

The trilobite fossil probably began to form after a layer of mud buried the animal at the bottom of the ocean. As that layer of mud hardened into rock, more mud settled out of the water and buried other animals. This process repeated over and over, and the layers of rock slowly built up. The diagram shows how each layer contained its own set of fossils.

As long as nothing disturbs the rock layers, the fossils in the bottom layers are much, much older than the fossils in the top layers. By looking at certain fossils in a particular layer of rock, scientists can get an idea of when that layer formed. These fossils are called **index fossils.** Trilobites, for example, are organisms that lived only during the Paleozoic Era. When scientists dig up a rock layer that contains trilobite fossils, they conclude that the rock layer formed during the Paleozoic Era. Therefore, any other fossils in that layer must also be from the Paleozoic Era.

Fossils in undisturbed rock layers show the order of events in the past. Index fossils give scientists clues about the relative age of fossils. But exactly how old are the fossils themselves? In order to answer that question, scientists have to use other clues.

▲ *A termite preserved in amber*

▼ *Certain fossils only appear in certain rock layers.*

> Radioactive dating equipment

▼ Radioactive potassium atoms change to argon atoms, shown in black, over time.

The Shifting Sands

Not so long ago, people used hourglasses such as the one below to measure time. An hourglass consists of two bulbs of glass with a small opening in between. One of the bulbs is filled with an exact amount of fine, dry sand. When that bulb is placed on top, the sand begins to pour into the empty bulb below. In an hourglass, it takes exactly one hour for all the sand to pour from the top bulb into the bottom bulb.

Certain elements in the earth work a little bit like hourglasses. These elements are radioactive, which means that the nuclei of their atoms naturally break apart, changing them into atoms of different elements. Radioactive uranium, for example, slowly changes into lead. Radioactive potassium changes into argon.

The diagram compares the changes in radioactive potassium to the action of the hourglass. When this type of potassium first forms, it is made of only one kind of atom—radioactive potassium atoms. Over time, however, these potassium atoms change one by one into argon atoms, just like the grains of sand pouring one by one into the lower bulb of the hourglass. At the end of a certain period of time, a certain number of the radioactive potassium atoms have changed into more stable argon atoms.

Scientists know exactly how long it takes for a certain amount of potassium to change into a certain amount of argon. By measuring the amount of potassium and argon in a piece of rock, scientists can figure out how old the rock is. This technique is called **radioactive dating.**

Radioactive dating can be used to measure the age of rocks, fossils, and even the earth itself. Because of radioactive dating, scientists have determined that the earth is about 4.6 billion years old. Written out, that number comes to 4,600,000,000 years.

The picture above shows a scientist using radioactive dating to determine the age of a fossil. Instead of measuring the fossil itself, the scientist measures the amount of radioactive potassium and argon in the rock around the fossil. Since the rock and the fossil formed at about the same time, these measurements tell the scientist how old the fossil is.

Potassium-argon dating is used for fossils that are more than 50,000 years old. Another method, called radiocarbon dating, can show the age of newer fossils and other objects. By using index fossils, radioactive dating, and other clues, scientists can begin to piece together the 4.6 billion year story of the earth.

Checkpoint

1. What is the difference between a mold fossil and a cast fossil?
2. How can undisturbed layers of rock give clues about the ages of fossils?
3. Explain how a radioactive element is used to date a fossil.
4. **Take Action!** Use clay and common objects to construct a model of fossils in rock layers.

Decay Dating

How can you use a model to show radioactive decay? Let's investigate.

What To Do?
A. Shake 25 pennies in your hands. Drop them on your desk. Remove all coins that show tails. Record your number of heads as *Flip 1*.
B. Shake the remaining heads coins. Remove all tails. Record the number of heads as *Flip 2*.
C. Continue counting flips and removing tails until you have no heads left.

Record Your Data

Flip	Number of Heads
1	
2	
3	
7	
8	

What Did You Find Out?
1. *If the heads represent potassium atoms and the tails represent argon atoms, how many flips were needed to get rid of all potassium atoms?*
2. *Assume that each flip equals 8000 years. How long did it take to change all potassium atoms to argon atoms?*

Activity

What's That Footprint Say?

Scientists learn about dinosaurs by studying their footprints. In this activity you will work with a group of students to make and interpret footprints in trackways.

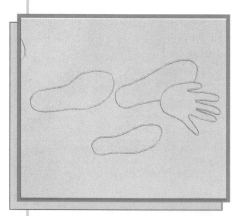

Picture A

Picture B

Picture C

Gather These Materials

large sheet of paper
masking tape

pencil
colored markers or pencils

Follow This Procedure

1 Make a chart like the one on the next page. Record your observations in your chart.

2 Use masking tape to tape a large sheet of paper to the floor. Your group will make student trackways on the paper.

3 Begin by having one student remove his or her shoes and move slowly across the sheet of paper in some manner. For example, the student might walk, jump, crawl, or hop. As the student moves across the paper, he or she should stop each time his or her body touches the paper. Other members of the group should use pencils to trace the outline of any part of the body that contacts the paper. (Picture A)

4 Repeat Step 3 as each member of the group makes his or her own trackway. Your sheet of paper should have a trackway for each group member. (Picture B)

5 Exchange trackways with another group. Your group's job is to interpret the other group's trackways. Begin by identifying a single trackway made by one person. Use a colored marker to color each track in the trackway.

Record Your Results

Trackway	My interpretations
1	
2	
3	
4	

6 Continue identifying and coloring all the trackways on the paper. Each trackway should be colored with a different colored marker or pencil. (Picture C)

7 When all the trackways have been colored, interpret each trackway. Record what you infer about how the trackmaker moved across the paper. Then identify which student made each trackway.

8 Compare your group's interpretations with the group that made the trackways to see how accurate your interpretations are.

State Your Conclusions

1. What additional information might have made interpreting the trackways easier?
2. How might this activity be similar to the process scientists use to interpret dinosaur tracks?
3. What kinds of information might scientists get from dinosaur trackways?

Let's Experiment

How might you use trackways to determine how fast an animal was moving? Use what you know about scientific methods to find out.

2.3 *Building a Better Dinosaur*

▶ *How do you move a dinosaur nest?*

When Jack Horner found 18 eggs inside a *Maiasaura* nest in 1983, he knew just what to do. Slowly and carefully—very carefully—he and his crew dug a trench around the nest. They had to be slow and careful because they kept finding more and more fossils. Each time they found a fossil they stopped digging the trench and started digging up the fossil.

With all the delays, they needed two years to dig the trench. Then they soaked burlap strips in wet plaster of Paris and laid the strips over the nest. The strips hardened and formed a protective plaster cast around the nest. The covering looked a little bit like the plaster casts that doctors wrap around broken arms and legs.

After the plaster hardened, Jack and his crew began chipping away at the rock underneath the nest. They soon formed a kind of stem that supported the nest. When they were finished, the plastered nest and stem looked like a giant mushroom.

The nest was heavy; in fact, it had a mass of about two metric tons. So Jack had a new problem to solve. How do you lift a two-metric ton mushroom off the ground? You call in a helicopter! While waiting for the helicopter, Jack and the crew broke the nest off its stem and rolled the nest into a strong net. The helicopter then tried to lift the net and the nest. After much effort, the nest rose into the air and began its long journey. Like the other *Maiasaura* fossils, it was headed for the laboratory.

▼ *Crew members apply a plaster cast to a fossil.*

The Library of Bones

Paleontology laboratories are found in museums, universities, and other research centers. They're usually big rooms with lots of sinks, tables, tubs, and trays. The fancier labs may also have microscopes.

People called preparators work in these labs, cleaning the fossils and preparing them for study. Some of the tools the preparator uses are shown at the top of this page. Some are the same tools that dentists use to scrape teeth.

Preparators work on many different kinds of fossils, including dinosaur bones. When they get a bone, the first thing they do is to remove the plaster cast from around the bone. Then the preparators begin to chip away the rock that is sticking to the bone. Because of the way dinosaur fossils form, they are often covered with a layer of rock.

Sometimes the rock can't be removed by chipping. When that happens, the preparators soak the rocky bone in a bath of weak acid, such as vinegar or lemon juice. The acid dissolves the rock but not the bone.

Once the bone is clean, the preparators repair any cracks or breaks and then coat the bone with varnish. The varnish preserves and protects the bone. Finally the preparators identify the bone and put it into storage.

When paleontologists decide to study a particular fossil, they go to a laboratory, take the fossil out of storage, read all the information, and begin their work. A good fossil collection is like a library, except that most of the "books" are millions of years old.

▲ Cleaning and preparing fossils at the paleontology laboratory

14 cm

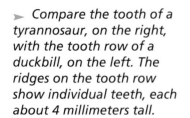
➤ *Compare the tooth of a tyrannosaur, on the right, with the tooth row of a duckbill, on the left. The ridges on the tooth row show individual teeth, each about 4 millimeters tall.*

14 cm

Clues from Every Corner

Fossil collections are great places for research. Just as you were able to guess many things about the object that made the impression in the Discover Activity, scientists learn many things about organisms and their environment from the fossils they collect. For example, the teeth in the pictures tell a story. They show two basic types of dinosaur teeth: those of an herbivore, or plant-eater, and that of a carnivore, or meat-eater. Can you figure out which is which? Here's a hint: Some herbivores chew their food by sliding their teeth back and forth, like when you chew vegetables. Use this hint to examine the teeth.

As you look down on the top of the tooth row to the left, you can see it is nearly flat. Two of them could slide back and forth over each other. The tooth row belonged to a plant-eating dinosaur. The pictures show some of the plants that the dinosaur might have eaten.

But what about the tooth to the right? This side view shows it's sharp and curved, like a knife. Those teeth couldn't slide back and forth. Instead, it's designed to cut and tear flesh. It's the tooth of a meat-eater.

Not all fossils can be moved to fossil collections. The footprints of dinosaurs are sometimes impossible to move. To study them, paleontologists often travel to where the footprints are.

▼ *Dinosaurs probably ate plants similar to these.*

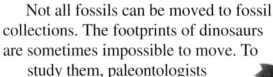

Footprints also can tell quite a story. The ones to the right show that certain dinosaurs held their tails up in the air while walking. If the dinosaurs had dragged their tails behind them, the tails would probably have left tracks. But no tail tracks can be found next to these footprints. And since no tail tracks exist, the tail was probably up in the air.

Paleontologists can only guess what dinosaur flesh looked like, because flesh rots away quickly. But on rare occasions they get a chance to see dinosaur skin. One of those occasions happened back in 1908, as George Sternberg and his two brothers dug up the skeleton of a duckbill dinosaur in southern Wyoming.

"When I removed a rather large piece of sandstone from over the breast," wrote George, "I found, much to my surprise, a perfect cast of the skin impression beautifully preserved. Imagine the feeling that crept over me when I realized that here for the first time a skeleton of a dinosaur had been discovered wrapped in its skin. That was a sleepless night for me."

Under the skin, however, it's a different story. Here paleontologists must use evidence from the bones to figure out how the skeleton fit together, how the muscles tied in, where the organs were located, and how the whole contraption moved around. Every little mark on a dinosaur bone may have some meaning. The insides of some bones, for example, have a series of rings, just like the rings on a tree stump. By counting the rings, paleontologists get some idea of how old the bone's owner was when it died.

▲ Footprints and fossilized skin give scientists clues to what dinosaurs looked like.

Putting the Pieces Together

Complete dinosaur skeletons are hard to come by, because not every bone turns into a fossil. Instead, paleontologists often uncover a jumble of bones with many missing parts. In order to reconstruct those bones—put them together again—the paleontologists must sort them out and fit them together like the pieces of a three-dimensional puzzle. The missing parts make the puzzle all the harder to solve.

Paleontologists can either reconstruct the entire dinosaur skeleton or use the skeleton as a basis for restoring the complete original dinosaur: skin, bones, and all. Skeletal reconstructions are called free mounts; restorations are called models. You can see how the model builds on the free mount in the picture.

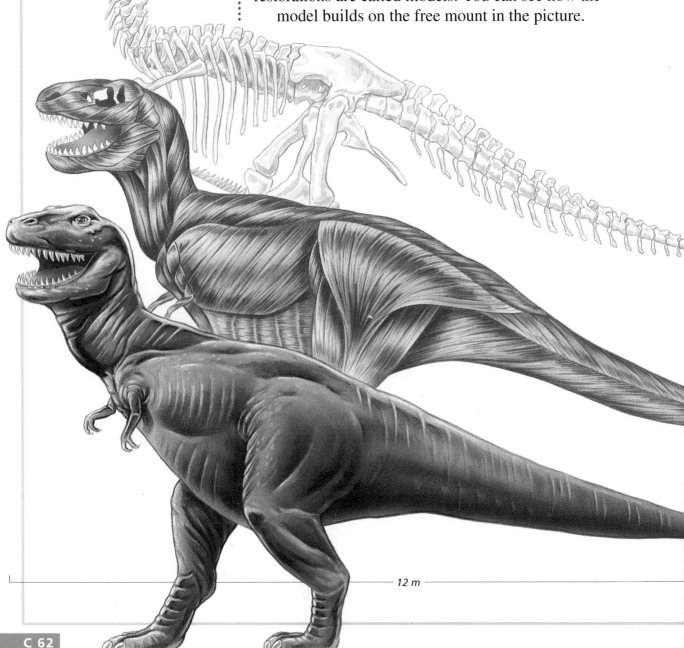

▼ *Paleontologists make models of dinosaurs using the completed skeleton as a base.*

12 m

In order to build a free mount—just the skeleton—workers first make a strong frame out of steel or plastic. Then they attach as many original bones as possible to the frame. If bones are missing, they make replacements out of fiberglass, plaster, or plastic. Sometimes an entire free mount will be made out of these replacements, because they are lighter and less easily damaged than the original bones.

When the free mount is completed, the entire skeleton can be displayed for study. The top picture on the previous page shows a free mount of a *Tyrannosaurus rex.*

Models begin where free mounts leave off. Since the bones will be covered by other materials, workers simply build a metal frame that resembles the original skeleton. Paleontologists then use evidence from the bones to figure out how the muscles and other body parts attached to the bones. In order to do so, they may compare the skeleton to those of similar species. Since modern birds, for instance, evolved from certain types of dinosaurs, those birds may provide clues to the dinosaurs' muscles and organs.

The middle picture shows *Tyrannosaurus rex's* muscles. Workers add the shape of these muscles to the metal frame by using wire and screen. Then they're ready for the last step: covering the model with skin-like material and painting it. The last picture shows the completed model, sharp teeth and all. One can only wonder what the original *Tyrannosaurus rex* would do to its copy.

Checkpoint

1. How is a fossil collection like a library?
2. How do the shapes of dinosaur teeth give clues to what they ate?
3. Why do paleontologists compare the skeletons of certain dinosaurs to the skeletons of modern birds?
4. **Take Action!** Find pictures of animals that show the shapes of their teeth. Classify them as herbivores or carnivores.

Chapter Review

Reviewing Words and Concepts

Write the letter of the word or phrase that best completes each sentence.

1. Fossilized teeth with flat surfaces suggest that an animal was a _____.
2. Sharp, pointed teeth suggest that an animal was a _____.
3. A fossil called a _____ forms when materials fill in a mold and harden.
4. Scientists use _____ to measure the ages of rocks, fossils, and the earth itself.
5. Petrified wood forms as _____ replace the living tissue of a tree.
6. The assembled skeleton of an animal is called a _____.
7. A _____ is one example of an index fossil.
8. Fossils sometimes form in hardened tree sap called _____.
9. As an organism buried in rock dissolves, it may leave a hollow area called a _____.
10. Fossils that can be used to decide when a layer of rock formed are _____.

a. cast
b. trilobite
c. radioactive dating
d. mold
e. free mount
f. index fossils
g. carnivore
h. minerals
i. herbivore
j. amber

Connecting Ideas

1. Copy the concept map. Use the terms at the right to complete the map about how dinosaur fossils form.

silicates replace bone
dinosaur dies
mud covers bones
fossil

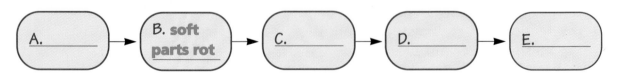

A. _____ → B. soft parts rot → C. _____ → D. _____ → E. _____

2. Write a sentence or two that summarizes the ideas shown in the concept map.

Interpreting What You Learned

1. How are the tools used at a dinosaur dig different from other scientific tools?
2. What evidence led Jack Horner and Bob Makela to think they had found a new species of duckbill dinosaur?
3. Explain what information an index fossil can tell scientists about other fossils in the same rock layer.
4. Why do very few examples of skin from ancient organisms exist?
5. How are free mounts used to construct models of dinosaurs?

Performance Assessment

What clues can fossils provide about organisms?

Materials   • 2 cutout fossil teeth   • 2 cutout fossil footprints   • cutout fossil shell
• metric ruler

Collecting Data

1. Look at the two cutouts that represent fossil teeth. Using a metric ruler, determine the actual size of each tooth. Record your measurements.
2. Carefully observe the shape of each tooth. Based on shape, identify each tooth as the tooth of a plant-eating dinosaur or a meat-eating dinosaur. Record your observations.
3. Study the two cutouts that represent fossil footprints. Using a metric ruler, determine the actual length and width of each footprint. Record your measurements.

4. The footprints were discovered in the same place. One footprint made an impression 8 centimeters deep in the mud. The other footprint made an impression 12 centimeters deep. Choose which footprint you think made each of the impressions. Record your response.
5. Look at the cutout that represents a fossil shell. Using a metric ruler, determine the length and width of the shell. Record your measurement.
6. The fossil shell was found in a layer beneath the fossil footprints and the fossil teeth. What does this tell you about the age of the shell? Record your answer.

Analyzing Data

What are some different kinds of information that fossils can provide about the past?

3

Building on the Past

Hey! We're making history!

What can you learn from a time capsule?

A time capsule is a container that holds materials to tell about a particular time. Make a time capsule that tells about you at this time. Think of ways to describe yourself. Next, think about things you like to eat and do. Collect objects that represent these things and put them into a covered can.

For Discussion

1. *How does this capsule compare to one you might have made a year ago?*
2. *How do your classmates' time capsules differ?*

3.1 *Putting It All Together*

▶ **Who spread the news about Maiasaura?**

Soon after Jack Horner and Bob Makela dug up the first *Maiasaura* nest on the Peebles ranch in 1978, the story leaked out to television, radio, and newspaper reporters. They quickly spread the news about the amazing discovery. All of a sudden, Jack was famous.

Jack didn't mind his sudden fame, but he was more interested in sharing his discoveries with his fellow scientists. Therefore, in 1979, after a review by other paleontologists, Jack published an article about the *Maiasaura* nest in a highly respected science magazine.

Because he kept making new discoveries, Jack wrote more and more articles for scientific journals. Finally in 1988 a professional writer helped Jack write and publish a book. Notes, such as those below, that Jack and his crew made while looking for fossils were a valuable tool in writing the book. The book presents Jack's conclusions about how maiasaurs lived and grew up. To find out what those conclusions were, read on.

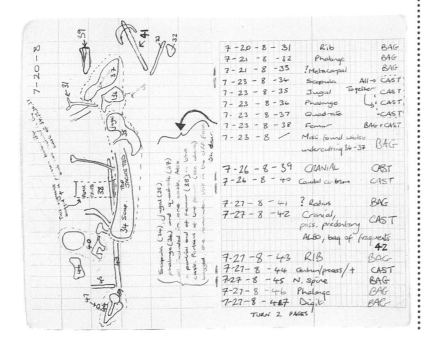

◀ *An important part of a paleontologist's job is keeping detailed notes. These notes were made by one of Jack Horner's crew members.*

What's It Mean?

Scientists draw conclusions from information they gather.

Small bones, crushed egg shells, worn teeth—what does it all mean? That's the problem Jack Horner was faced with when he began to put together the information he gathered. Like all scientists, Jack came to his conclusions by carefully observing characteristics of an object or event and then relating the observations to other scientific information.

Often this process involves information from many areas of science. For example, to make conclusions about dinosaur bones, Jack needs to know about animal structure, the history of the earth, and chemical processes that take place in the earth.

Study the pictures to review Jack's evidence. Then, on the next page, read what he already knew and about his conclusions. Match each of Jack's conclusions to his evidence.

Bones The bones had the features of duckbill femur bones. But they were much smaller than the duckbill bones Jack had seen before. The bones at the base of the spine weren't fused together.

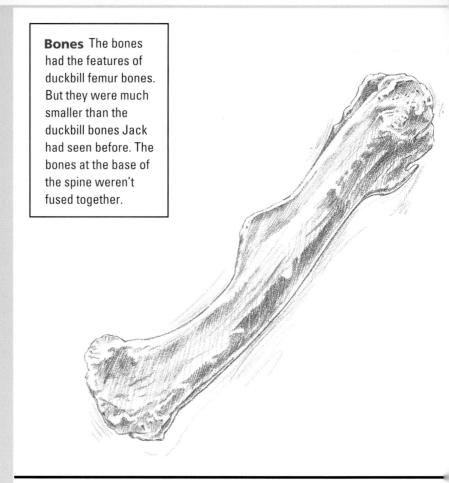

Hollows The bones were in green mudstone hollows of similar shapes. Each hollow contained eggshells or bones of the same size.

Teeth The teeth were worn. In some cases, three-fourths of the tooth was worn away.

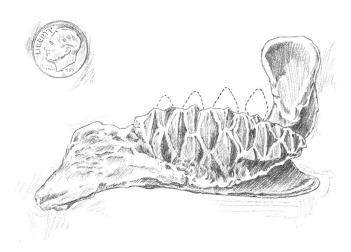

A. Prior knowledge: The only place mudstone was found was in the hollows. **Conclusion:** The baby dinosaurs were in nests.

B. Prior knowledge: Dinosaurs wore out their teeth as they ate. New teeth replaced worn ones throughout their lives. **Conclusion:** The baby dinosaurs had been eating for some time and, therefore, had not just hatched from the eggs.

C. Prior knowledge: Birds nesting in colonies separate nests by the length of an adult's outstretched wings. Seven meters is the average length of the adult female duckbill. **Conclusion:** The nests were made and the babies all hatched within one nesting season.

D. Prior knowledge: In adult dinosaurs the vertebrae at the bottom of the spine join together. **Conclusion:** The bones were those of baby duckbill dinosaurs.

Now that you've been a dinosaur detective and drawn conclusions, it's time to put all the pieces together. Read on!

Spacing The nests did not overlap. They were equally spaced about 7 meters apart.

Evidence indicates that Maiasaura *built nests in large nesting grounds.*

Into The Field

How do careful observations lead to inferences?

Go outside and make four observations. Write an inference for each observation that you make.

Maiasaur Toddlers

In the Discover Activity your time capsule gave clues about you at a particular time. The evidence Jack Horner collected was like a time capsule telling about dinosaurs. This evidence suggests that baby maiasaurs were born and grew up in nests. The evidence also indicates that the maiasaurs nested in groups, with equal spacing between the nests. The shape of the nests suggests that the maiasaurs first used their powerful hind legs to sweep dirt into mounds. Then they may have used their front legs to form the mounds of dirt into large bowl-shaped nests.

Maiasaura mothers laid their eggs in neat circles. Unlike lightweight birds, the heavy maiasaurs would have crushed the eggs if they had tried to sit on them. Instead, they may have kept the eggs warm by covering them with grass and leaves, as shown in the picture. Once the babies hatched, *Maiasaura* parents probably fed them berries and other plant food. All day long, the babies toddled around the nest, crushing the eggshells—which explains why the bottoms of the nests were covered with broken eggshells.

The baby maiasaurs almost tripled in length—from 35 to 100 centimeters —before leaving the nests. But how long did that take? In order to answer that question, Jack compared *Maiasaura* to modern reptiles and birds.

Baby reptiles grow slowly because they are cold-blooded. They don't grow up in nests, and they need at least a year to double in size. But because baby birds are warm-blooded, they double in size in just a couple of months, while staying in their nests.

It seems highly unlikely that the baby maiasaurs could have stayed in their nests for more than a year. No animal that scientists know of stays in a nest for that long. Therefore, it appears that the baby maiasaurs grew quickly, like birds. And that means that *Maiasaura* may have been warm-blooded.

So far, so good, except for one small problem: Scientists always believed that dinosaurs were cold-blooded reptiles. To change other scientists' minds, Jack knew that he had to find more evidence. And in his search, he stumbled across evidence that led him to an even more startling conclusion.

The Thundering Herd

Maiasaura nests weren't the only fossils that Jack Horner and his crew dug up. Not far from the nests, but in a different layer of rock, they found 4 different piles of adult *Maiasaura* bones. One pile contained about 200 bones; another had more than 4000. The sheer numbers were startling. But the many similarities among the bones were even more amazing: They were all black, they were all broken, and they were all facing the same way. Not only that, but it seemed as if they all came from maiasaurs who had died at the same time.

By using a special measuring stick, Jack figured out that all 4 piles of bones were part of a much larger pile that stretched over more than a square kilometer. He calculated that the large pile contained more than 30 million bones—enough for about 10,000 maiasaurs!

The figures were astonishing. No one had ever found so many dinosaurs gathered so closely together. What were they doing there? And what powerful force could possibly have killed them all? The answer to the first question seems to be that *Maiasaura* lived in herds, much like the herds of bison that roamed the Great Plains millions of years later.

▼ *Jack's find of the large number of fossil bones in one area suggested that* Maiasaura *travelled in herds.*

Like the bison, *Maiasaura* may have migrated from north to south, eating the ripening berries and grasslike sedges. Eighty million years ago, what is now Montana was part of the home where herds of *Maiasaura* roamed.

But what killed this particular herd of *Maiasaura*? The answer might lie about 45 centimeters above the bones, in a layer of volcanic ash. The ash was everywhere, and it could only have come from one source: a gigantic volcano. The volcano might have erupted and killed the maiasaurs with a deadly mixture of gas, smoke, and ash. The constantly changing Earth unleashed its awesome power. Like so many animals before and since, the maiasaurs could do nothing to stop it. And like so many other times, forces within the earth have influenced the history of life on the earth.

Checkpoint

1. How did Jack use the information he gathered at the dig?
2. Why were the *Maiasaura* nests filled with broken eggshells?
3. How were *Maiasaura* like bison?
4. **Take Action!** Be a television reporter. Have another student be Jack Horner. Interview Jack about his conclusions.

Puzzling It Out

How can you simulate a paleontologist piecing together bits of fossil evidence? Try this activity to find out.

Picture A

Picture B

Picture C

Gather These Materials

cover goggles
2 large sheets of white construction paper

crayons, markers, or colored pencils
scissors

Follow This Procedure

1 Make a chart like the one on the next page. Record your observations on your chart.

2 Put on your cover goggles.

3 On the construction paper, draw a picture of a real or imaginary animal of your choice. Make the picture large to fill the paper.

4 Color your animal. (Picture A)

5 Draw lines on your picture to represent puzzle pieces. Make at least 25 pieces, all different sizes and shapes, just like a jigsaw puzzle. Write in the number of pieces at the top of the chart.

6 Use the scissors to carefully cut out all the pieces of your animal puzzle. (Picture B)

Predict: *Will a "paleontologist" be able to draw your animal if some pieces are missing?*

7 Mix up the pieces of your puzzle. Choose 15 pieces at random. Write the number of pieces on the chart.

Record Your Results

Total number of pieces_____

Partners	Number of pieces shown	Correct guesses	Incorrect guesses
1	15	15	0
2	10	7	0
3	5	2	3

8 Give the 15 pieces to a partner. Ask him or her to try to put the puzzle together on top of a clean sheet of construction paper. (Picture C)

9 Instruct your partner to guess what the picture is if he or she can.

10 Try steps 7–10 twice more, with different partners. Describe the results in your chart.

State Your Conclusions

1. Were your partners able to draw in the missing pieces? What clues did your partners use?
2. How were your partners able to "supply" the missing pieces?
3. How are your partners like paleontologists?

Let's Experiment

What would happen if you mixed the pieces from two puzzles? Use what you know about scientific methods to find out.

3.2 *Creeping Crust*

▶ *How is Africa like South America?*

The salty Atlantic Ocean—6,679 kilometers wide—separates Africa and South America. These two continents are far apart and vastly different, except for a few striking similarities. For one thing, the Atlantic coasts of Africa and South America seem to match like the pieces of a jigsaw puzzle. For another, fossil hunters have found the remains of *Mesosaura,* shown to the left. The fossils of this genus of ancient freshwater reptiles was found in both continents, and nowhere else in the world.

Could the *Mesosaura* fossils—and also the fossils of *Glossopteris,* an ancient plant found on both continents—help to explain the matching coasts? Scientists began asking that question back in the nineteenth century. The answer was a long time in coming, but when it arrived, it changed our view of the earth.

▼ Glossopteris *fossil*

—— 7.6 cm ——

▼ Mesosaurus *fossil*

—— 5 m ——

➤ *Pangaea*

🌿 Mesosaurus fossils

🌱 Glossopteris fossils

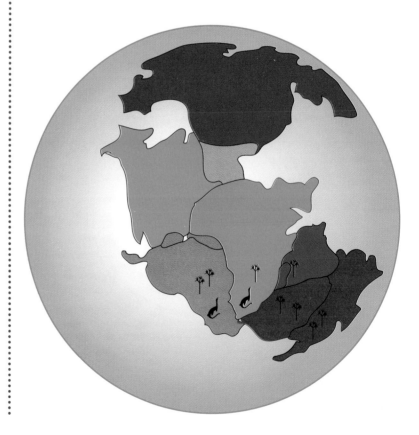

Drifting Apart

In 1924, the German meteorologist Alfred Wegener (vā′ gə nər) published the third edition of a book titled *The Origin of Continents and Oceans.* Within the book's few pages, he explained his hypothesis that all the earth's continents had been part of a single super-continent 300 million years ago. He called this super-continent Pangaea (pan jē′ ə), meaning "all lands."

According to Wegener, Pangaea began to break up about 200 million years ago, and the continents slowly drifted to their present locations. The map on the previous page shows Pangaea; the map below shows the drifting continents about 80 million years ago, during the time of *Maiasaura*.

To support his theory, Wegener pointed to the matching coastlines and fossils of Africa and South America. The freshwater mesosaurs, for example, could not have swum across the salty Atlantic. They must have lived and died on a single land mass, which then split apart. So too with *Glossopteris* and with other bits of evidence linking Africa and South America. As Wegener wrote, "It is just as if we were to refit the torn pieces of a newspaper by matching their edges."

Key	
■	Africa
■	Antarctica
■	Asia
■	Australia
■	Europe
■	India
■	North America
■	South America

Indicates Present-day Land Masses

◄ *Earth about 80 million years ago*

➤ *Use this key to identify the tectonic plates. The arrows indicate the direction of movement of each plate.*

Ⓐ North American Plate
Ⓑ Eurasian Plate
Ⓒ African Plate
Ⓓ Indian-Australian Plate
Ⓔ Antarctic Plate
Ⓕ South American Plate
Ⓖ Nazca Plate
Ⓗ Pacific Plate
Ⓘ Philippine Plate

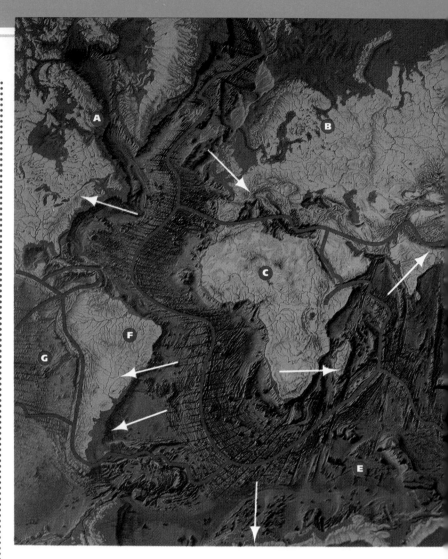

Wegener's evidence was powerful, but how could continents possibly move? He was still puzzling over that question when he died in a blizzard in Greenland in 1930. Almost 40 years passed before scientists discovered the answer.

Mapping the Boundaries

During the late 1950s the map maker Marie Tharp used information gathered from research ships to draw the first detailed relief map of the Atlantic Ocean floor. Before that time scientists could only guess what kinds of landforms lay beneath the ocean's dark waters.

Tharp's maps startled scientists around the world. For the first time, they saw that a long chain of mountains ran right down the middle of the Atlantic Ocean. The east slopes and the west slopes of the mountains were remarkably similar, as can be seen in the map above. Scientists called the mountains the Mid-Atlantic Ridge.

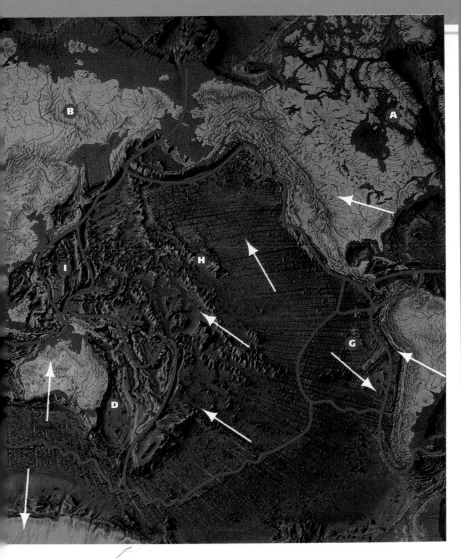

To map the ocean floor, oceanographers send sound waves down into ocean waters using a process called SONAR. As these sound waves hit the ocean floor, their echoes reflect back. Scientists use information about how long it takes the echoes to return to the surface to measure land formations on the ocean floor.

The chart shows the depth of some of the world's oceans.

Body of Water	Maximum Depth (meters)
Pacific Ocean	11,034
Indian Ocean	7725
Atlantic Ocean	8648
Arctic Ocean	5450

What Did You Find Out?
1. *Sound in ocean water travels about 1531 meters per second. At the Indian Ocean's deepest point, how soon would sound waves return to the surface?*
2. *The height of Mt. Rainier is about the same distance as the depth of the Gulf of Mexico. SONAR would take about 5.62 seconds to reach the ocean floor and return to the surface at the Gulf of Mexico's maximum depth. How high is Mt. Rainier?*

The explanation for the Mid-Atlantic Ridge arrived in the late 1960s, when a trio of American geologists proposed the theory of plate tectonics. According to the **theory of plate tectonics**, the earth's rocky outer skin—called the lithosphere—is made up of at least a dozen gigantic moving plates. These plates are between 70 and 150 kilometers thick.

The plates, which float on a partly molten layer of the mantle, travel a few centimeters every year. Each one moves differently. Study the map to see how in some places, the plates are pulling apart. In others, they are sliding under or crashing into one another.

The theory of plate tectonics finally answered Wegener's question about how continents could move. For example, Africa and South America are riding on two separate plates that are slowly pulling away from each other. And as those plates pull apart, molten rock erupts along the fracture between them, forming the Mid-Atlantic Ridge.

Great earthquake activity indicates that the Himalayas are still forming, as the plate carrying India collides with the Eurasian plate.

The photographs on these pages show where crust is deleted from and added to the earth's surface. This action occurs at **plate boundaries**—the places where plates meet. The landform above is a part of the Himalayan Mountains, which rose up when one plate collided with another, slowly crumpling the continental crust into soaring mountains. The photograph on the next page depicts the Great Rift Valley of east Africa, where two plates are pulling apart, adding new crust to the earth. Far in the future, ocean water will flow between the valley walls, just as the Atlantic Ocean now flows between the continents of Africa and South America.

The photographs demonstrate that evidence of plate movement is all around us. But they don't explain exactly how the plates move. For that matter, neither does the theory of plate tectonics. The causes of plate movement are still not fully understood. Many scientists, however, conclude that slow convection currents in the earth's mantle provide the answer.

Going With the Flow

Convection currents are circulation patterns that occur when air or liquid heats, rises, cools, and falls back down. Some electric room heaters, for example, heat the surrounding air. The heated air rises to the ceiling where it spreads out and cools off. Then the cold air falls back down to the floor, where it is heated once again by the electric heater. This pattern of heating and cooling forms a convection current within the air of the room.

A similar process may be occurring inside the earth's mantle. A current of hot, soft rock flows up to the gaps between plates at the top of the mantle. Some of the hot molten material may flow through the gaps, forming mountains such as the Mid-Atlantic Ridge. But most of the molten rock spreads out under the plates. As the magma currents spread out, they carry the plates along— like a conveyor belt. Eventually, the molten rock cools and sinks back down in the mantle. There some is melted again only to reheat and rise again millions of years later.

The main problem with this explanation is that scientists have never seen the mantle. And without that kind of solid evidence, convection currents remain an unproven hypothesis. Thus scientists continue to search for ways of peering beneath the earth's plates, hoping for an answer to the riddle of their movement.

⋏ *The Great Rift Valley is one place where boundaries are spreading and new crust is being added to the earth's surface.*

Checkpoint

1. According to Alfred Wegener, how were Africa and South America like the torn pieces of a newspaper?
2. How does the theory of plate tectonics explain the Mid-Atlantic Ridge?
3. What is the pattern of movement inside a convection current?
4. **Take Action!** Besides spreading and colliding, plates also slide past each other. Use clay to demonstrate these movements.

3.3 *Mothering Mammals*

▶ *Can babies grow in pouches?*

Humans are placental mammals, which enables them to give birth to well-developed babies. A human baby spends nine months in its mother's uterus nourished by a placenta before it emerges into the world.

On the other hand, kangaroos, and the animals on this page, are marsupial mammals, and they give birth to incompletely developed babies. A baby kangaroo grows inside its mother's body for just one month. When it emerges, it is blind and only a few centimeters long. For the first three minutes of its life, the baby kangaroo must crawl along its mother's body groping for the safety of her pouch. There it spends the next eight months feeding on its mother's milk, finally growing large enough to live on its own.

Placental babies, such as the baby gorilla, are far more likely to survive than marsupial ones. In the continuing struggle for existence, placental mammals have usually defeated the marsupials. Yet in Australia, where the kangaroos live, nearly all native mammals are marsupial. Why have the marsupials fared so well in Australia? The answer to that question comes not from the animals themselves but rather from the continent on which they live.

▲ *The little pygmy possum, above, and the long-nosed potoroo to the right are marsupial animals.*

Going It Alone

About 275 million years ago, Australia formed part of the super-continent Pangaea. At that time, tiny, egg-laying mammals already scurried across Pangaea's vast

surface, lurking in the shadows of the dinosaurs. When Pangaea split into smaller continents a few million years later, the mammals were cut off from each other.

◄ This three month old baby lowland gorilla will stay with its mother for about three and a half years.

◄ The kangaroo is the largest member of the marsupial group.

Because the lands and climates of the new continents differed, the mammals on those continents evolved in different ways. The mammals in the northern continents generally evolved into placentals. But the mammals in Australia evolved into marsupials. When the dinosaurs died out across the world about 65 million years ago, the marsupials quickly took their places in the ecosystems of Australia. Kangaroos, wallabies, wombats, bandicoots, koalas, and opossums ruled the land. They had no contact with the placental mammals on the other continents.

But modern times have brought human settlers from other continents into Australia; and with them have come sheep, foxes, rabbits, dogs, and other large placental mammals. What will happen to the marsupials? We may already know the answer to that question, because marsupials and placentals have met before—in the continents of the Americas.

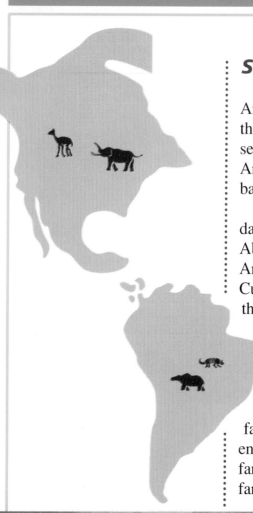

Struggling to Survive

When the dinosaurs died out, North and South America were still separate continents. As in Australia, the mammals on each continent began evolving in separate ways. Placental mammals ruled North America, but in South America they struck an uneasy balance with the marsupials.

That balance might have continued to the present day, were it not for the earth's constantly moving plates. About three million years ago, North and South America joined together at the Isthmus of Panama. Curious mammals from both sides began investigating their new neighbors and invading their territory.

As the years passed, the northern placentals—bears, llamas, deer, weasels—won more and more of these battles with the native marsupials and the total number of mammal species began to decline. Before the continents joined, North America had 29 families of mammals and South America had 27 entirely different ones. After the joining, only 22 families survived on both continents. And of those families, the southern marsupials fared the worst.

The marsupials may have lost out because growing up inside a pouch, as a marsupial does, is riskier than growing up inside a placental uterus. Of all the families of marsupials in South America, only one survived the joining of the continents. But that family—the opossums—did very well indeed. As time passed, opossums spread throughout both North and South America. With its bald, thick tail and its long, pointed snout, the common opossum of North America looks like a cat-sized rat. But the opossum is far different from cats and rats. It carries its young in a pouch and it uses its tail to hang from trees. It hunts for food at night, eating almost anything that crosses its path, including frogs, insects, worms, and fruit.

Opossums are a hardy breed. In the constant struggle for existence atop a constantly moving earth, they are one of evolution's winners. They are famous for knowing how to play dead, but in the end they may outlast even people. Only time will tell.

Checkpoint

1. Before the modern age, why didn't Australian marsupials come into contact with large placentals?
2. What advantages did North American placentals have over the South American marsupials?
3. **Take Action!** Make a map of the world. Draw pictures of marsupials on the map to show where they live around the world.

Activity

Predicting the Shape of a Supercontinent

Scientists use evidence to conclude that the continents were once joined to make a supercontinent. You can model the process by creating your own supercontinent.

Picture A

Picture B

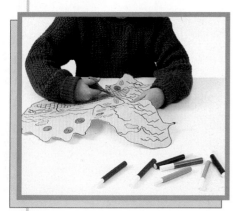

Picture C

Gather These Materials

large sheet of
  construction paper
scissors

large sheet of white paper
pencil or pen

Follow This Procedure

1 Make a chart like the one on the next page. Record your observations on your chart.

2 Draw the outline of a make-believe supercontinent on the construction paper.

3 Outline 5 continents within your supercontinent. (Picture A)

4 Add land features, such as mountains, and fossil deposits to your supercontinent. Be sure that your land features cross your continent borders. (Picture B)

5 Use the scissors to cut out the supercontinent.

6 Trace your supercontinent and its outlines of the smaller continents onto a large sheet of white paper. Keep this record for later use.

7 Cut apart the continents of the construction paper supercontinent. (Picture C)

8 Trade supercontinent puzzles with a teammate.

Predict: *What clues will a teammate use to combine your continents into a supercontinent?*

Record Your Results

Your teammate's supercontinent

9 Arrange your teammate's continents to form a supercontinent. Try to fit the continents together until they form one you think matches your teammate's original supercontinent. Draw your teammate's supercontinent on the chart.

10 Compare your results with your teammate's original drawing of a supercontinent.

State Your Conclusions

1. How many ways did your teammate's continents fit together?
2. What clues did you use to fit your teammate's continents into the correct supercontinent?

Let's Experiment

Could the continents of the earth join together in other ways besides the form of Pangaea? Design different supercontinents from different arrangements of earth's continents.

Chapter Review

Reviewing Words and Concepts

Write the letter of the word or phrase that best completes each sentence.

1. A _____ occurs at the place where two plates meet.
2. Humans and gorillas are examples of _____.
3. When air or a liquid heats, rises, cools, and falls back down, _____ occur.
4. The idea that the earth's continents have moved from their original locations was first suggested by _____.
5. Kangaroos and opossums are modern-day examples of _____.
6. New _____ forms at the earth's surface where two plates are pulling apart.
7. The first detailed relief map of the Atlantic Ocean floor was made by _____.
8. Animals roamed from continent to continent when the earth's land masses were joined in one supercontinent called _____.
9. A mountain range called the _____ is located in the Atlantic Ocean.
10. According to the _____, the earth's outer skin is made up of huge moving plates.

a. Pangaea
b. crust
c. Mid-Atlantic Ridge
d. plate boundary
e. placental mammals
f. convection currents
g. Marie Tharp
h. marsupials
i. theory of plate tectonics
j. Alfred Wegener

Connecting Ideas

1. Copy the concept map. Use the terms at the right to complete the map about how evidence is used to form conclusions.

   plate tectonics   30 million bones
   supercontinent   ridge maps
   herds of maiasaurs

   Evidence —————— *Explanation*

   A. coastlines fit like a puzzle — B. _____

   C. _____ — D. _____

2. Write a sentence or two about the ideas shown in the concept map.

   E. _____ — F. _____

Interpreting What You Learned

1. How did Jack Horner's prior knowledge help him interpret his evidence and draw conclusions about the maiasaurs?
2. Why did Jack Horner think *Maiasaura* may have been a warm-blooded animal?
3. How does the theory of plate tectonics differ from Wegener's theory?
4. Give an example of a structure that is found at a plate boundary and explain how it formed.
5. What structures would scientists need to observe to have solid evidence of convection currents inside the earth?

Performance Assessment

How can plate movement be modeled?

Materials • cover goggles • piece of cardboard • scissors • metric ruler • 2 sheets of white paper • colored construction paper • tape • sharpened pencil • 6 thick books

Collecting Data

1. Put on your cover goggles. Using a sharpened pencil, poke a hole in the center of a piece of cardboard. Then use scissors to cut a slit about 20 centimeters long in the middle of the piece of cardboard.
2. Measure and cut out two strips of white paper about 15 centimeters wide and 20 centimeters long.
3. Using construction paper, make cutouts of Africa and South America. Tape the cutout of Africa to the right end of one strip of paper. Tape the cutout of South America to the left end of the other strip.
4. Make two stacks of books the same height. Move the stacks 20 centimeters apart. Put the cardboard on top of the books so it connects the stacks.
5. Hold the strip of paper with the Africa cutout in your right hand. Hold the strip with the South America cutout in your left hand. Push the ends of the strips without cutouts through the slit in the cardboard until the two cutout continents are next to each other. Separate the pieces of paper so you can see the continents.
6. Under the cardboard, hold the strips of paper together. Push the strips up through the slit. Observe how the continents move as you push up on the paper. Record your observations.

Analyzing Data

Over time, what might happen to an animal or plant species that lived on Africa and South America when they were connected?

Fossil Finds

Our knowledge of dinosaurs comes mainly from their fossilized remains—their bones, their petrified eggs, their footprints. Therefore, finding dinosaur fossils of any kind is a very exciting event. Sometimes scientists find fossils because they go out looking in likely places. Other times, they are lucky enough to find fossils by accident. But fossils don't always have to be found by scientists. Some of the most interesting fossils have been found by kids.

Adam Kahle, a ten-year-old Texan, and his father go on hunts to find fossils of an ancient reptile, the phytosaur. This animal looked like a crocodile. Most phytosaur fossils they find are in tiny pieces, including bits of bone and teeth. Adam knows that the pieces they find in one place probably belonged to the same animal, so he keeps them together in a bag. At home, the fun begins. Once the fossils are clean, Adam tries to fit them together into skeletons. "I feel like I'm working a jigsaw puzzle," he says. "It's a thrill to see a phytosaur take shape."

Like dinosaurs themselves, dinosaur tracks come in all different sizes.

Other fossil-finders were not out deliberately looking when they made their finds. Wesley Williams, 16, and Sean Ramp, 15, of Maryland, made an important discovery by accident. They found the ancient remains of a sperm whale on the beach. As Sean says, "I sat down on something, and it stuck me." Scientists from the Smithsonian Institution in Washington, D.C., later visited the spot. They unearthed a two-meter-long jaw, some teeth, vertebrae, and ribs. The fossils had probably been buried for about 16 million years. They will now be used to figure out where different kinds of whales once lived.

Kids who are lucky enough to find fossils often feel that they have discovered a fascinating window through time. Charity Ann Gardner and her father explored dozens of dinosaur tracks while they were on a summer vacation in Arizona.

Like dinosaurs themselves, dinosaur tracks come in all different sizes. "Some . . . were so small that I could cover them with one hand," Charity says. "A couple . . . were big enough to sit in!" By tracing tracks onto clear plastic that she puts over them, Charity now has "dinosaurs at home—walking all across the walls of my room," she says, laughing.

Scientists can tell a lot from these fossils. The length of a dinosaur track, for example, can tell a scientist how big that animal was. A fossilized tooth can give an idea of what that dinosaur ate. Sometimes, scientists are lucky enough to get hold of an entire set of dinosaur bones that can be put together. Then we are all able to see how huge, majestic, and frightening some of these animals were.

On Your Own

To learn where you can see fossils near your home, talk to your state's geological survey office or the geology department at a local college. Or take your family on a trip to see the fossils at one of the spots famous for them, such as Dinosaur National Monument in Utah.

A Scientific Detective

Occupation: Paleoecologist
Words to Remember: "You have to try things, make that first step, and maybe make that step a lot of times."

Dr. Julio Betancourt

Julio Betancourt came to the United States when he was ten years old. Fleeing Cuba, his family had to leave everything they knew and owned. His family was seeking a better life in a new country. What Julio found was a rough welcome. Kids teased him about his accent and for being different. Julio's solution was to learn to speak perfect English.

Julio now sees many advantages in speaking two languages. His interest in English made him think more about words, and led to his first work as a writer. In college, Julio's interest in the differences among people led him to study anthropology—the science of human history and cultures. Julio's interests further evolved from the Social Sciences to biology and geology and to his present career.

What do you do now?
"A lot of different things. If you need a label, you could call me a paleoecologist—a historian of the environment. And to find out what the environment was like in the past, you have to be a little bit of a detective. You find many bits and pieces and then put them all together. For example, you can find out about past weather by looking at ice that formed many years ago."

Does that work in warm areas?
"Yes, all you need is a high elevation. In the mountains of New Mexico you can find very old ice in lava tubes—deep holes in the ground where lava once flowed. With only a few hand tools you can get ice that formed 3000 years ago."

What can you learn from that?
"Some people look at bubbles in the ice to see what the air was like. I look at the oxygen that makes up the water molecules. From that oxygen I can figure out the temperature of an area thousands of years in the past."

What's the best part of your job?
"The best part is the freedom to be creative. Being a scientist means daring to ask questions. First you form a question, then you find answers."

Radiocarbon Dating

A technique called radiocarbon dating helps scientists determine the age of living things when they died.

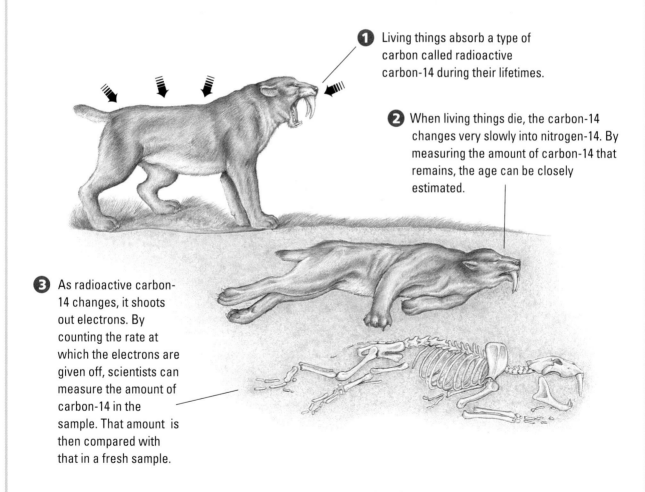

1 Living things absorb a type of carbon called radioactive carbon-14 during their lifetimes.

2 When living things die, the carbon-14 changes very slowly into nitrogen-14. By measuring the amount of carbon-14 that remains, the age can be closely estimated.

3 As radioactive carbon-14 changes, it shoots out electrons. By counting the rate at which the electrons are given off, scientists can measure the amount of carbon-14 in the sample. That amount is then compared with that in a fresh sample.

Find Out On Your Own

How does radiocarbon dating differ from potassium-argon dating? When is each type used?

Module Performance Assessment

The Museum

Using what you learned in this module, help prepare exhibitions to be used at a local museum. Complete one or more of the following activities. You may work by yourself or with others in a group.

Drama

Survey adults and other students to construct a profile of what most people think is a "typical" scientist. Write a skit or create a presentation to compare that scientist with a real scientist such as Jack Horner.

Biology

Use 20 pea pods, a metric ruler, and your ability to group and count to make a display demonstrating Darwin's idea that in each species there is great variation among organisms.

Geology

Look at a map that shows the areas of volcano and earthquake activity in the Western Hemisphere. Find out what preparations must be made in homes and schools that are located in these areas. Make a poster that identifies precautions that should be taken by people who live in these areas.

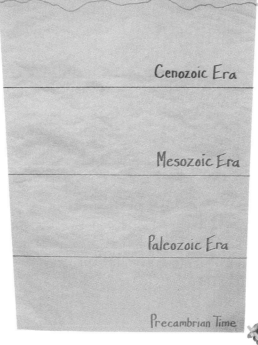

Cenozoic Era

Mesozoic Era

Paleozoic Era

Precambrian Time

Art

Imagine walking downward through layers of rock that contain older and older fossils. On a long, vertical sheet of paper, draw and label the geologic time periods and some of the fossils you would find in each.

Environment

Imagine that a construction company excavating to build a new supermarket in your town finds fossil bones in the soil. Should the company ignore the find and proceed with the excavation? What would you want the company to do? Write a set of rules to be followed in these types of situations.

Rules for Fossil Finds

1. Notify people of fossils.

2.

3.

4.

5.

Module Review

Reviewing Words and Concepts

Write the letter of the word or phrase that best completes each sentence.

1. The _____ shows the earth's history divided into units of time.
2. Scientists use _____ to determine the ages of rocks and fossils.
3. Babies of placental mammals are more likely to survive than babies of _____.
4. The movement of the earth's rocky plates may be caused by _____ below the plates.
5. Trilobites are _____ that can be used to determine the age of a rock layer.
6. Moneran, protist, fungus, plant, and animal are the names of the five _____.
7. The _____ states that the earth's outer "skin" is made up of gigantic moving plates.
8. Organisms change over time through _____.
9. The place where two plates meet is called a _____.
10. The smallest group used by scientists to classify organisms is the _____ group.

a. theory of plate tectonics
b. convection currents
c. plate boundary
d. index fossils
e. radioactive dating
f. geologic time scale
g. evolution
h. kingdoms
i. marsupials
j. species

Interpreting What You Learned

1. What is the relationship between classification and evolution?
2. Describe how life on the earth changed during the Paleozoic Era.
3. How has plate tectonics affected evolution?
4. Species produce more offspring than can survive. Explain why some offspring are more likely to survive than others.
5. What information do paleontologists use to construct models of dinosaurs?
6. Give an example that supports the theory of plate tectonics.

Applying What You Learned

1. By radioactive dating, a scientist places the age of a rock at about 95,000 years. How old is a fossil found in the rock?
2. Draw a chart to show the correct order of the following taxonomic groups from largest to smallest: species, order, family, genus, kingdom, class, phylum.
3. Draw a diagram showing a convection current in a liquid that is being heated. Use arrows to show direction.
4. Name two characteristics you would use to classify an animal as a mammal.

Adaptations

Adaptations

Could you live at the top of the world or the bottom of the ocean? Only with great difficulty. Yet thousands of species have adaptations that help them survive these hostile environments. In this module, you will discover how light and color played roles in the evolution of the endless diversity of species on the earth.

CHAPTER 1
Seeing and Being Seen

Can bees see what we see? Human eyes and bees' eyes differ in many ways. Each is adapted to a particular use.

CHAPTER 2
Rainforest to Arctic

Come out, come out, wherever you are! From the lush green rainforest to the snowy white Arctic, species of all kinds use color to compete and to hide.

CHAPTER
3 Light in the Ocean

Is there life without sunlight?
In the blackest depths of the
ocean, life lights its own way.

1

Seeing and Being Seen

Oh neat . . . spin the wheel and then blink your eyes really fast!

Wear cover goggles for this activity.

What can color wheels teach you about colored light?

Cut a circle with a diameter of 10 centimeters out of white cardboard. Divide the circle into two or three equal sections. Color each section a different color. Poke a sharp short pencil through the center. Be sure to wear your cover goggles. Tape the cardboard to the pencil. Spin the color wheel. What happens?

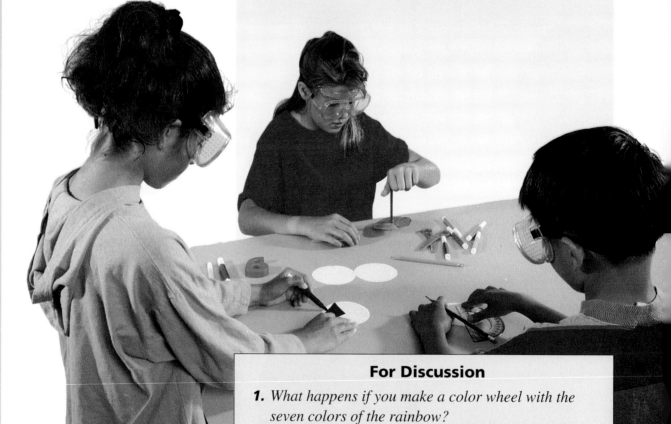

For Discussion

1. *What happens if you make a color wheel with the seven colors of the rainbow?*
2. *Do paint colors mix the same way as colored light?*

1.1 Color Choosers

▶ *Why does the bee visit certain flowers?*

Have you ever watched a bee going from flower to flower? It might go from one flower to the next. Then it might skip six flowers and go to the seventh. Why does the bee visit some flowers, but not others?

The bee sees something you can't see. The picture to the right shows black-eyed Susans as a human with normal vision would see them. Compare it to the picture below that shows the same flowers as a bee would see them. Notice the difference in the center of the flower. The design in the center of the flower—called a nectar guide—seems to guide the bee to the area of the flower where it can find nectar. Many other flowers also have nectar guides that the bee can see but humans can't.

▼ *Black-eyed Susans as seen by the human eye*

Color and Light

What humans see and the way they see it are adaptations that the human species has made to its environment. An **adaptation** is an inherited trait that enables a species to survive in its environment. For example, bees' eyes are adapted to see the nectar guides. The adaptation helps the bee find the food it needs. Species have adapted over millions of years to the many different habitats on the earth.

▼ *Black-eyed Susans as a bee might see them*

Adaptations help organisms survive in many ways. Some adaptations protect organisms from hazardous conditions in the environment or from enemies. Other adaptations help organisms find mates or raise their young. And many adaptations help organisms find food.

Absorption-Reflection

▲ *The girl sees light that is reflected from the flower.*

For example, as the food for bee ancestors became more specific to nectar, bees' eyes were changing or evolving. Some began to see nectar guides, so they found more food—and lived to reproduce. Eventually most bees could see nectar guides.

To understand why you don't see the same thing the bee sees, let's look at how color, light, and sight work together. Most people say an apple is red. But is the red color *part* of the apple? People over 3000 years ago thought so. Since then, scientists have learned that color is *not* a part of an object. Color comes from light—no light, no color. But a light like the sun looks white. So how can colors come from light?

You know that visible light is made up of a combination of colors. But in visible light you don't see the colors because they're mixed together to give white light. The combined colors make light appear white. If that seems strange to you, think about the Discover Activity. When you mixed colored light, the result was white light.

You know white light is made of all the wavelengths of light. When light strikes some objects, the objects absorb some of the wavelengths. But the objects reflect others. Your eye sees the reflected wavelengths.

Light made up of all wavelengths strikes this flower. The yellow parts of the flower absorb all the light striking them *except* the yellow wavelengths. The yellow parts reflect those yellow wavelengths, and the reflected light travels to your eye. As a result, your eye sees the parts as yellow. Use the diagram to tell why you see the leaf as green.

But what about the center of the flower? You see it as black. You know that black light can't be reflected from an object because black isn't one of the colors that makes up visible light. So why does an object appear black? Objects appear black because *no* light is being reflected from them. The black center of the flower absorbs all the light that hits it. As a result, no light from the black center is reflected to your eye. What do you think happens to light when it reaches an object that appears white?

All the color you see in the world comes from light, whether you're looking at grass, a tiger-striped cat, or the black-eyed Susan to the left. But what makes some objects absorb certain wavelengths and reflect others? What makes one flower absorb red wavelengths while another one absorbs yellow or purple? In living things the answer is in the cells.

Pigments

Within some cells of living organisms are special chemical molecules called **pigments**. Pigments absorb light energy. Cell structures containing pigments are easy to see under the microscope because they appear colored. Most plant and animal cells have pigment molecules. In fact, almost everything has pigment molecules.

Pigments appear colored because they absorb some wavelengths of light and reflect others. Remember the black-eyed Susan? The pigments in the cells of the yellow parts give those parts their yellow color. The pigments absorb all the wavelengths of light except yellow. The center of the flower has black pigments that absorb all wavelengths of light.

Pigments do more than give color to organisms. As you know, light waves carry energy. Shorter wavelengths carry more energy than longer wavelengths. When a pigment absorbs light, it is also absorbing the energy light carries. An organism uses this energy in different ways. Let's look at some of those ways.

One important kind of pigment—chlorophyll—is found in plants. Plant structures containing chlorophyll appear green. As you can see below, chlorophyll is found in structures called chloroplasts. Chloroplasts use the light energy absorbed by chlorophyll to produce molecules of glucose in the process of photosynthesis.

▼ *Chlorophyll captures light energy to produce glucose molecules.*

Glucose molecule

Chloroplast

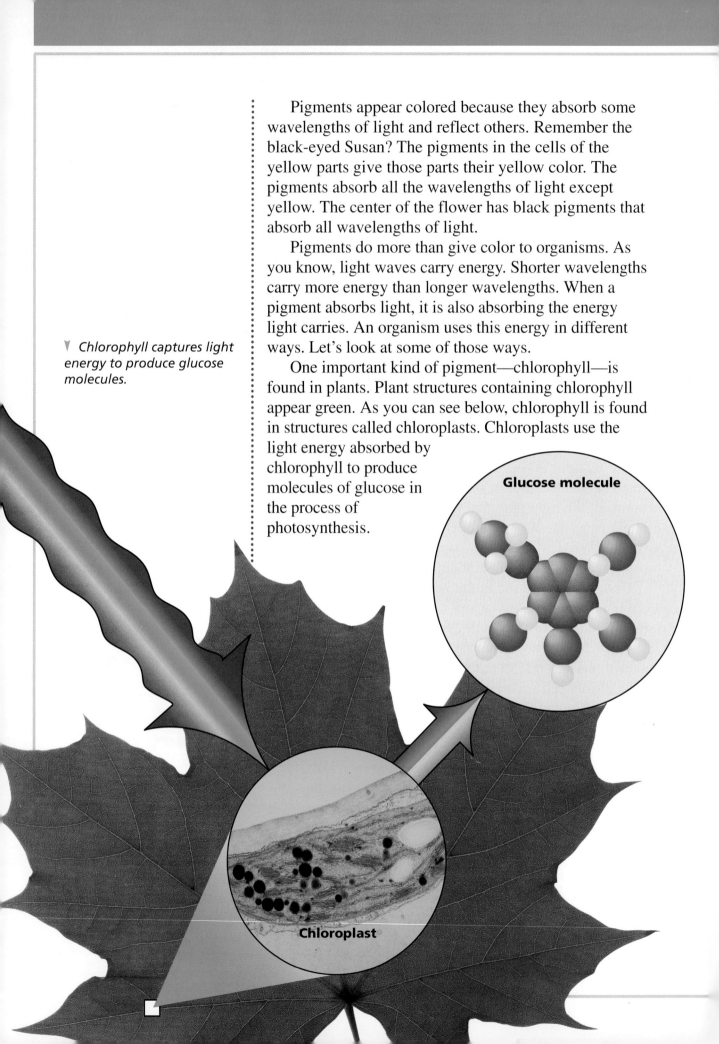

Carotene (kar′ə tēn′) is a yellow-orange pigment found in many plants. You see it in carrots. But it's also hidden in the green leaves of trees. Because carotene absorbs different wavelengths of light than chlorophyll, it enables plants to absorb greater amounts of light energy.

▲ *The skin colors of these children vary because their skin cells have different amounts of melanin.*

Another important group of pigments—phycobilins (fī′kō bi′linz)—is found in the red algae and blue-green bacteria that live below the ocean's surface. Not all wavelengths of light penetrate into the same ocean depths. Phycobilins absorb those wavelengths of light that penetrate into deeper water. As a result, the red algae and blue-green bacteria have a source of energy for photosynthesis.

Plants contain many other pigments as shown by the variety of colors found in the plant kingdom. But what about animals? What kind of pigments do they have?

Animal cells have a variety of pigments. Among them is melanin (mel′ə nən)—a brown pigment that helps determine the colors of many animals, including the skin colors of the children in the picture. If large amounts of melanin are produced, the skin will be dark. If small amounts are produced, the skin will be light. Melanin absorbs harmful ultraviolet light from the sun. Exposure to the sun causes skin cells to produce more melanin. So if you stay out in the sun long enough your skin will become darker.

Checkpoint

1. How are color and light related?
2. Explain two ways that pigments benefit organisms.
3. **Take Action!** Mixing colors of paint is different than mixing colors of light. Use paints to illustrate this idea to your class.

Into The Field

Is the top or underside of a leaf darker?
Look at many different kinds of green leaves to discover which side of a leaf is darker. Make a chart to record the data you collect.

Activity

Find the Hidden Colors

What color is a leaf? In this activity, you will separate the pigments in leaves so you can see the hidden colors.

Picture A

Picture B

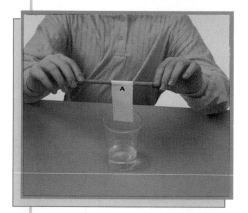

Picture C

Gather These Materials

cover goggles
Leaf Extract A
2 toothpicks
2 filter paper strips
2 pencils

Leaf Extract B
2 clear plastic cups
alcohol
paper towel
masking tape

Follow This Procedure

1 Make a chart like the one on the next page. Record your observations in your chart.

2 Put on your cover goggles.

3 Use a toothpick to place a small drop of Leaf Extract A near the bottom of a filter paper strip. (Picture A)

4 When the drop is dry, place a second drop of the same extract on top of the first. Do the same for two more drops. Label this strip *A*.

5 Repeat Steps 3 and 4 with Leaf Extract B. Label the strip *B*.

6 Fill each of 2 clear plastic cups with about 1 cm of alcohol. Cap the alcohol promptly. *CAUTION: Alcohol is very flammable. Never use it near a flame.*

7 Tape each strip to a pencil, as shown in Picture B.

8 Use the pencils to hold the paper strips in the jars so that the bottom of each paper is just touching the alcohol. The drops of pigment should not be touching the alcohol. (Picture C)

Predict: What will happen to the drops of leaf extract on the filter paper?

Record Your Results

Paper strip	Colors and distance each traveled
A	
B	

9 The paper will soak up the alcohol. Allow the alcohol to rise up the paper about 7 cm from the bottom.

10 Remove each strip, and lay it out to dry on a paper towel. You may notice lines of color at different distances along the filter paper strip. Each line is a different pigment. Your teacher can help you identify them. Make a drawing of what each strip looks like.

11 Measure the distance each color has traveled. Record your measurements in your chart.

State Your Conclusions

1. Leaf Extract A was from green leaves. What colors did you see on the paper strip with this extract?

2. What colors did you see on the paper strip with Leaf Extract B? From what color leaf do you think this extract was made?

3. Why do you think you don't see all the colors that are present in a leaf?

4. What factors might cause the color change in some leaves in autumn?

Let's Experiment

Now that you have seen what colors are found in leaves, what colors do you think might be present in the petals of flowers? Get an extract of flower petals from your teacher. Then use what you know about scientific methods to find out.

1.2 Perceivers of Light

▶ *Why don't you see the same thing as the bee?*

The same reflected wavelengths reach the bee's eyes as your eyes. So why do you see things differently? The eye structure of a species varies according to the lifestyle of the species. The bee uses its eyes mostly for finding nectar. Humans use their eyes for many purposes, such as finding food, reading, and recognizing others. As a result human eyes have evolved different structures than bee eyes.

▼ Rods, shown in orange, enable you to see in black and white. Cones, shown in yellow, detect color.

Eyes are Different

How is one species' eye structure different from another? How an organism sees an image depends on two parts in its eye structure: the kinds of **receptors**—or cells that receive light in the eye—and the kind of lens it has. The human eye has two kinds of receptors. These receptors are called rods and cones because of their shapes, as shown below.

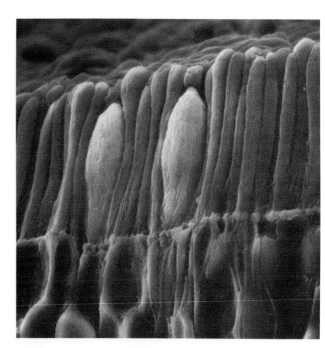

Rods are receptors that enable you to see black and white images. If you had only rods, your vision would be like black and white television. Cones detect the color your eyes see. Your eyes have three types of cones. Each kind of cone has a particular kind of pigment—called a visual pigment—that is sensitive to either red, blue, or green light. All other colors we see are a combination of these three colors of light.

The process of vision works much the same for bees, even though the bee's eye has a different structure than yours. But the bee's receptors are sensitive to a different range of wavelengths in the electromagnetic spectrum. Bees can see ultraviolet light, which you can't. But they can't see wavelengths in the red range. Therefore, the bee sees color differently than you do.

The human eye, as well as the eyes of many other animals, has a single lens. The lens changes shape and brings images into sharp focus. As a result, you see clear single images.

Bees, like most insects, crabs, and lobsters, have compound eyes. You can see in the picture below that the compound eye has many lenses. Each lens sees only a part of an object. The bee's eye can detect motion better than a single-lens eye can. Detecting motion quickly probably helps the bee escape predators.

▼ *The compound eye of the bee might have thousands of separate lenses.*

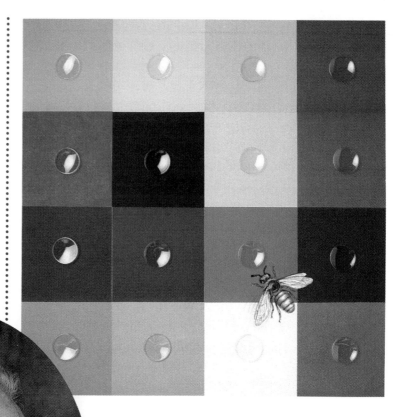

➤ *Karl von Frisch used a series of cardboard squares to find out what colors bees see.*

▼ *Karl von Frisch*

Colors Animals See

In the early 1900s, many biologists thought that the evolution of brightly colored flowers was most important in attracting insects for pollination. But not all biologists agreed. Some thought bees were color-blind, that they found a flower by its scent.

In 1910 Karl von Frisch, the scientist in the picture, began a series of experiments with bees to see if they could see color. Data from those experiments led scientists to think that bees can recognize colors.

Dr. von Frisch began his tests by putting out red and blue cardboard squares. On the blue square, he put a few drops of honey. He wanted to train the bees to eat from the blue square. When the bees repeatedly flew straight to the blue square to get food, von Frisch changed the squares around. He put the blue square in a different place. This time, he did not put honey on either square, but the bees continued to return to the blue square. He wondered: Did that mean bees could tell which square was blue?

"Maybe the blue square smells differently," somebody suggested. So von Frisch put the squares under glass so the bee wouldn't be able to smell any odor. Still, the bees flew directly to the blue square.

Did the bees really see blue, von Frisch wondered. Or did they see only different shades of gray? To find out, the scientist put a blue square in the midst of gray cards as shown to the left. The cards were many shades of gray, from almost white to almost black. On each square he placed a small glass dish. Each dish was empty except the one on the blue square. In that dish, von Frisch put a few drops of odorless sugar water rather than honey. He wanted to make sure odor didn't influence the bees' choice.

Once the bees again were trained to find food on the blue card, they returned directly to the blue square every time. Whenever the bees left, von Frisch changed the location of the blue square. Still the bees flew to it. So von Frisch concluded that the bees could see blue as a color and that it was different from any shade of gray.

With similar experiments, von Frisch went on to use other colors. The results showed that bees are blind to crimson shades of red. When food was put on a red square, the bees flew to various squares of black and gray before they finally located the red square with the food. When a bluish red color was tested, bees had no trouble finding the square. Experiments indicated, too, that bees see yellow clearly. However, the bees had trouble distinguishing orange or yellow-green from yellow. But the bees had no problem distinguishing a blue-green square from a blue one.

Next von Frisch investigated why bees went to white flowers but had trouble finding a hive that was painted white. He learned that white flowers reflect ultraviolet light, which the bee's eye appears to see as a shade of blue-green. When a hive was covered with a paint that reflected ultraviolet light, the bees had no trouble finding the hive. Bees seem to see ultraviolet as a separate color that they can distinguish from other colors. Because bees see ultraviolet wavelengths as a separate color, they can see the nectar guides on the black-eyed Susan.

What Do Animals See?

Different animals see things in different ways.

It's nighttime and you're alone in the forest. You're hungry. But you haven't brought any food with you. The only way you can get something to eat is to hunt for it. How successful do you think you would be? If you are like most people, you might be hungry for a while—at least until morning brings light.

Food is hard to find when you can't see it. So how do animals that are nocturnal—active at night—find it? Many nocturnal animals have vision that is adapted to see in the dark. Some have enlarged eyes or more light receptors. Both enable them to collect more light.

Not all visual adaptations help animals see at night. Some animal species have evolved structures that help them see better in light. Let's look at some adaptations and at how they make animals better suited to their environments.

Pit vipers have normal day vision, as well as infrared sensing organs. Those organs allow the snake to form images from heat given off by other organisms, even in complete darkness.

Raccoons, like many other nocturnal animals, can see only in shades of gray and white. To your eye yellow is the brightest color. To the raccoon green is the color that appears the brightest.

Prairie dogs can see best in shades of blue and yellow. Such vision requires brighter light than regular color vision. Prairie dogs can see in light that is so bright it would hurt your eyes.

What Animals See

What Humans See

Placement of Eyes

You've seen how eye structure determines the way a species sees an image. But something else about the eye is important to a species' vision—eye placement. Where an animal's eyes are located influences what it sees. To survive, species need eyes located where they can see what is most important to them, such as food and **predators**—animals that hunt other animals.

Animals that eat plants don't have to worry about their food running away from them. But plant eaters are often **prey**—animals that are eaten by predators. To survive, prey need to spot predators. Prey animals with a wider range of vision are more likely to escape predators. As a result, many prey species, such as the rabbit to the left, have eyes on the sides of their heads. They can see almost full circle, as in the picture above.

Vision has evolved differently in predators. Predators chase their food. They need to be able to see the prey, see how far away it is, and recognize it when it is close enough to catch. As a result, predators, such as the owl below, have eyes in the fronts of their heads. This kind of eye placement enables an animal to judge how far away something is.

▲ *The rabbit's eyes are placed so far apart that the only place it can't see is directly in front.*

➤ *The placement of this owl's eyes makes it better adapted to catching its prey.*

The dragonfly is a predator. But it is also prey for larger species. The evolution of large, bulging eyes enables the dragonfly to see sideways, as well as straight ahead.

Some animals, like the crab below, have their eyes on stalks. Because the stalks are movable, the animals can turn their eyes in all directions. Having eyes on stalks also enables some animals to see when they bury their bodies in mud while hiding from predators or waiting for prey.

Can you imagine what it would be like to have eyes on stalks that you could swivel around? Those eyes are very vulnerable. What if one of the stalks broke off? Your eyes are much more protected from damage by your skull bones.

The eye structure of many animals may seem strange. But each structure is an adaptation that helps the organism survive in its environment.

The rabbit sees this range when it looks straight ahead. Compare that to how much you would see, which is shown between the red lines.

Checkpoint

1. How are your eyes different from a bee's eyes?
2. What evidence do scientists have that bees can see color?
3. Describe some differences in what animals see.
4. How does the placement of eyes on an animal's head aid its survival?
5. **Take Action!** Design an experiment to test which colors a pet might see.

The eyes of this crab can be turned in all directions.

Are You Seeing Double?

You have two eyes, so why don't you see double? Try this activity to see how your eyes work together.

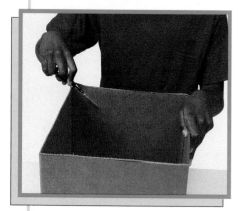

Picture A

Picture B

Picture C

Gather These Materials

cover goggles
cardboard box
scissors
masking tape

string
2 different objects
index card

Follow This Procedure

1 Make a chart like the one on the next page. Record your observations in your chart.

2 Put on your cover goggles.

3 Cut a cardboard box in half on the diagonal. (Picture A) *CAUTION: Be careful when using the scissors.*

4 Mark 2 holes near the upper edge of the box. You will look through these holes, so they should be as far apart as your eyes. Then, cut out the holes. (Picture B)

5 Place the box at one end of a long table. Tape the end of a 1-meter piece of string to the bottom of the box, directly below the space between the 2 eye holes. Run the string straight out from the box, in a line perpendicular to the side with the eye holes. Tape the other end of the string to the table to keep it in place.

6 Place the larger object on the string close to the edge of the box. Be sure you can see the whole object when looking through the holes in the box. Place the smaller object at the far end of the string. (Picture C)

7 Cover the left eye hole with an index card and some tape. Look through the other hole with your right eye. What do you see? Make a drawing, and record what you see.

> **Predict: *Will you see the same thing when you look with your other eye?***

8 Remove the index card and tape from the left eye hole, and place it on the right eye hole. Now look through the left hole with your left eye. Describe and draw what you see.

9 Remove the index card and tape, and look at the objects with both eyes. Make a third drawing, and describe what you see.

State Your Conclusions

1. How did the objects look when you looked with your right eye? your left eye? both eyes?
2. Do each of your eyes see things the same way at the same time?
3. Why do you see only one picture when both eyes are open?

Record Your Results

	Description and drawing
Right eye	
Left eye	
Both eyes	

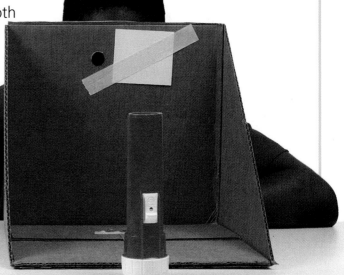

Let's Experiment

Now that you have seen how your eyes work together, see if you can judge distance better using one or two eyes. Use the box you made for this activity and what you know about scientific methods to find out.

1.3 *Traits for Survival*

What are some adaptations?

You've seen how a variety of visual adaptations have evolved that enable organisms to survive in their environments. But organisms need more than the right kind of vision to survive. What other adaptations have evolved that help species survive in their environments?

Behaviors

Have you ever heard someone say you were "playing possum?" If you did, you probably know they meant you were pretending to be asleep. This phrase comes from a trick that is often used by opossums when they're attacked by other animals. To protect itself an opossum will lie down and pretend it is dead, like the opossum in the picture. When the attacking animal leaves, the opossum suddenly comes to life again!

This behavior of the opossum that aids its survival is a **behavioral adaptation.** The spider in the picture is spinning a web. The spider's web-spinning behavior is the result of a behavioral adaptation. How does this action aid survival?

The spider inherited its web-spinning behavior from its parents. All young are born with inherited behaviors called **instincts**. Instincts are not learned. As a newborn you were able to suck because of instinct.

Instinct almost completely decides the behaviors of some species. For example, instinct allows a female digger-wasp to carry out all necessary activities for reproduction. Within its short life span, the female will mate, build a nest in the ground, lay eggs, and seal the nest. Then the wasp dies. In the spring young digger wasps hatch, and the females instinctively begin the process again.

▲ *This spider is spinning a web that is similar in design to the web of its parents.*

▼ *Is this opossum dead or just trying to fool a predator?*

⋀ *This young cheetah will learn many behaviors from observing its parents.*

Many animal behaviors are learned behaviors. Young animals learn behaviors that aid survival from their parents: how to care for themselves, how to catch food, and how to behave with others. What behavior is this young cheetah learning from its parent?

Some behaviors are a combination of instinct and learning. For example, baby gorillas instinctively know how to cling to their mothers when they are born. They continue this instinctive action for more than a year. But as they grow older, gorillas combine this instinctive behavior with trial and error to learn how to climb.

Control of Life Processes

Physiological adaptations involve the jobs of body parts that control the life processes that aid survival. You learned about one physiological adaptation when you learned how visual pigments detect color. Another example of a physiological adaptation is the making of chemicals by the poison glands of snakes.

Plants have physiological adaptations too. *Spartina* is a species of grass that lives in salty soil. Most land plants could not survive in soil as salty as the soil *Spartina* grows in. In *Spartina* water enters the plant through a membrane on the roots. The membrane removes most of the salt from the water before it enters the plant. This adaptation prevents salts from building up in plant tissues and killing the plant.

Adapting to Changes

If you were asked to draw a picture showing raccoons in their habitat, what would your picture include? Did you think of woodlands? Or did your picture include busy streets, houses, and lots of people? You might be surprised to find that either picture is correct.

Woodlands were the original habitat of these animals. But many woodlands have been cleared for farms and housing. As a result, some raccoons have been forced to live in urban areas. The chart shows some adaptations that enable raccoons to survive in both environments. Study the chart below. Use the information to answer questions.

Feet	Five toes with long claws; can open doors
Diet	Fish, mice, birds, berries, nuts, garbage, worms, insects
Shelter	Hollow trees, high grass, abandoned buildings
Defense	Attack with teeth and claws

What Did You Find Out?
1. *Which adaptations of the raccoon enable it to survive in populated areas?*
2. *Which adaptations are behavioral?*

Structural Adaptations

An organism's structure helps it survive in its environment.

What does the foot of a tarantula have in common with your face? You may find it hard to believe, but they both have "noses." On the spider's first pair of walking legs it has organs that are used for sensing odors. These organs enable the male tarantula to smell the trail left behind by a female tarantula. Many other spiders and insects smell with their feet too.

These special sense organs of the spider are called **structural adaptations**—or adaptations that involve body shape or color. You can see different kinds of structural adaptations on these pages. Observe each picture carefully.

Structural adaptations do many kinds of jobs. They protect as well as aid in food-getting and in reproduction. As you study each picture, think about how each adaptation helps the organism survive.

Protection

A

Reproduction

C

Getting Food

E

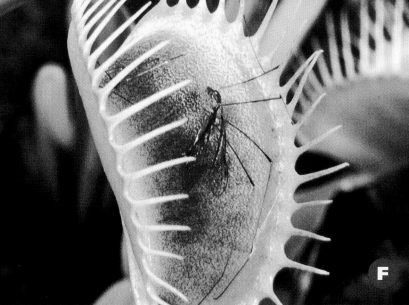

A. Under normal conditions, puffer fish look only slightly spiky. But when alarmed, they suck in water to blow themselves up. As a result, their spikes become very dangerous.
B. The spines of a cactus protect the plant from being eaten by animals.
C. Female mountain goats use their horns to challenge other females. The winner will have the best pasture for herself and her young.
D. The fluffy structure attached to each dandelion seed helps scatter the seed. Because the seeds are spread out, competition for food and water is reduced among growing plants.
E. Houseflies taste with hairs around their mouths. They also taste with their feet. Flies test food first by walking all over it. That's why they clean their feet so often.
F. Venus's-flytraps grow in soils that lack nitrogen—an essential plant nutrient. So the plant captures insects as a source of nitrogen. When an insect lands on a leaf, sensitive hairs on the leaf cause the leaves to close, trapping the insect, which is then digested.

Members of a species have variations and are not identical.

Variations are caused by sexual reproduction and mutations.

The earth's plates shift around the globe causing continents to break apart and collide and climate to change.

The natural selection of individuals best adapted to their environments enables only certain organisms to reproduce.

Adaptation and Evolution

How did all these adaptations develop? The answer lies in the interaction of some processes you already know about. Look at the chart to refresh your memory.

Now let's explore how the adaptation and evolution of a species such as the polar bear might have occurred. The diagram on the next page shows a cave bear that lived in Europe and North America about 2.5 million years ago. The fossil record shows cave bears were ancestors of the grizzly bears of today.

The diagram also shows a typical brown grizzly. Grizzly coat colors naturally range from dark browns to light browns. While many grizzly bears live in the forested mountains of the western United States, some live on the barren ground of northern Canada. Their feeding areas extend to the Arctic circle. Plants make up most of their diet, and their teeth are flattened for grinding. But some groups feed on salmon from rivers, and others have even been seen eating seals on the ice. So you can see that variations within this species exist.

How, then, do polar bears fit into this picture? Scientists think that polar bears began to separate from the grizzly bear line about 250,000 years ago.

You probably know that glaciers covered much of the Northern Hemisphere at various times. In between ice ages, life flourished in these areas. During one period between glaciers, large brown grizzly populations lived on the arctic coast of Siberia. As the next glacier covered much of the Arctic Ocean, individuals from these grizzly bear populations began to catch and eat arctic seals.

Perhaps the lighter brown grizzlies caught seals more often because their light color didn't show up as well against the white ice. As these lighter brown bears tended to survive more often than the darker-coated bears, they passed on the traits for a lighter coat color. Over time through natural selection their coats became as creamy white as polar bear coats are today.

As the glacier expanded, the lighter-coated bears could survive on the ice. They became separated from the darker-coated members of the species. Individuals of the two groups no longer reproduced together. During the last Ice Age—about 125,000 years ago—polar bears seemed to be a separate species from the grizzly bears.

Many factors influence how a species becomes adapted to its environment. But variations in the traits controlled by their genes are most important. Because if the variations aren't there to begin with, the individual will not be able to survive in the new conditions long enough to reproduce. So "survival of the fittest" means being already equipped for whatever comes along. And you'll see how that has resulted in the evolution of species adapted to some of the most extreme environments on the earth.

Polar bear

▼ *The fossil record provides evidence that cave bears were ancestors of today's grizzly bears.*

Grizzly bear

Cave bears

Checkpoint

1. Explain how physiological and behavioral adaptations are alike and different.
2. Explain how structural adaptations aid survival.
3. How did variations in coat color make brown grizzly bears better adapted to their arctic environment?
4. **Take Action!** Make a collage showing how animal feet are adapted for survival.

Chapter Review

Reviewing Words and Concepts

Write the letter of the word or phrase that best completes each sentence.

1. An _____ trait that enables a species to survive is an adaptation.
2. Chlorophyll is a _____ present in plants.
3. The cells of the eye that receive light are called _____.
4. The making of chemicals by the poison glands of snakes is an example of a _____.
5. A lion is a _____ because it hunts other animals.
6. Web-spinning of spiders is an example of a _____.
7. Inherited behaviors are _____.
8. An adaptation involving body shape or color is a _____.
9. When an owl eats a mouse, the mouse is the _____.
10. The color of light made up of all wavelengths of light is _____.

a. receptors
b. instincts
c. inherited
d. white
e. pigment
f. prey
g. behavioral adaptation
h. predator
i. physiological adaptation
j. structural adaptation

Connecting Ideas

1. Copy the concept map. Use the terms at the right to complete the map about the evolution of polar bears from grizzly bears.

polar bears   grizzly bears
Ice Age   survival of the fittest

A. _____ + B. _____ → C. natural selection → D. _____ → E. _____

2. Write a sentence or two that summarizes the ideas shown in the concept map.

Interpreting What You Learned

1. How is the bee's ability to detect ultraviolet light an adaptation for survival?
2. Why does chlorophyll appear green?
3. What kind of receptors might a person who is color-blind be lacking?
4. Why did Dr. von Frisch infer that bees were seeing their way to food?
5. State whether each of the following examples is either an instinct or a learned behavior: a person reading a book, a bird building a nest.
6. What is the most important factor that helps a species survive when changes occur in its environment?

Performance Assessment

How does distance affect your vision?

Materials • cardboard box (from Activity on page D20) • short cardboard tube • 3 pieces of string (1 meter, 2 meters, and 3 meters long) • masking tape • flashlight with batteries • metric ruler

Collecting Data

1. Place the box on the floor. Tape one end of the 1-meter-long piece of string to the bottom of the box, directly below the space between the two eye holes. Run the string out from the box so it is perpendicular to the side with the eye holes. Tape the end of the string to the floor.
2. Stand the flashlight on the string 30 centimeters from the edge of the box. Check to make sure you can see the entire object through the holes. Stand the short cardboard tube at the far end of the string.
3. Tape a piece of paper to the box so it covers the left eye hole. Look through the right eye hole with your right eye. Draw and describe what you see.
4. Remove the paper and tape from the left eye hole and tape the paper so it covers the right eye hole. Look through the left hole with your left eye. Draw and describe what you see.
5. Remove the paper and tape. Look at the objects with both eyes. Draw and describe what you see.
6. Replace the 1-meter-long piece of string with the 2-meter-long piece. Repeat steps 2 through 5. Record all your observations.
7. Replace the 2-meter-long piece of string with the 3-meter-long piece. Repeat steps 2 through 5. Record all your observations.

Analyzing Data

How does distance affect the way you see objects when you use your eyes separately?

2

Rainforest to Arctic

How low do you think it will go?

Where's the coolest place in your schoolyard?

Walk around your schoolyard. Try to find the coolest spot. Then find out if you are correct. Place a thermometer in that spot for a few minutes. Compare the temperature of your spot with those of your classmates'.

For Discussion

1. Where is the coolest spot in your schoolyard?

2. What factors affect temperatures in your schoolyard?

2.1 *Color Everywhere*

▶ *Is green the only color in a rainforest?*

Imagine you're exploring a world millions of people have never seen: the rainforest. In your first look you see nothing but green in every shade you can imagine.

Low-lying plants hug the forest floor. Pale and dark green leaves mix with reddish-green leaves. Fringed leaves of ferns overhang lower plants. Vines, some as thick as your thigh, circle tree trunks and draw your eyes up to giant ferns whose ancestors grew in the forests of the dinosaurs. It's hot, sticky, and dim here.

A little higher up, you can see more light, but just as much green. Low trees spread a layer of leaves, some pale green and small, others dark green and large. Fat, branchless trunks poke through the layer. These larger trees form the ceiling—or canopy—20 to 30 meters overhead.
—The canopy is lighter yet and provides a roof of leaves over the rainforest. Smaller plants grow everywhere—ferns, mosses, and orchids. They climb tree trunks, grow from bark crevices, and sit atop branches. You almost feel that a plant will wind around your leg if you stand still long enough.

You smell the sweet scent of ripe fruit mixed with the musty odor of rotting leaves and damp earth. Eerie wails rise and fall. Loud cries cut through the trills, whistles, and warbles. Something screeches. Leaves rustle as something moves unseen in the thick foliage.

Suddenly you see a flash of fiery red! What was that? What else will a closer look at the rainforest show?

Layers Within the Rainforest

A closer look at the rainforest shows that millions of species live there—about 50 percent of all the earth's species, in fact. How can so many species live there? The sun shines directly overhead, and the forest gets a lot of rain. Recall from the Discover Activity how temperatures varied around your school. Rainforest temperatures vary too. These varying temperatures, as well as varying amounts of light and moisture, provide many different habitats.

Because so many species are crowded into such a small fraction of the earth's surface, competition is keen for light, food, water, and mates. Many adaptations result from that competition. In some cases species have evolved in ways that enable them to live in the very specific conditions present in different layers of the forest. The pictures show some of those organisms.

On the forest floor much of the available food is dead material—leaves, blossoms, fruit, and animals. As a result, many decomposers, such as fungi, live there. Few plants bloom on the forest floor. Blooming requires much energy, and little light reaches this dim world. Occasionally, falling trees or branches create gaps, and shafts of sunlight brighten the forest floor. Very quickly seedling trees compete to fill the gap.

Leaves in the middle layer—or understory—filter out sunlight. But they are too thin to provide hiding places for most prey. So mostly small animals, such as lizards, insects, and birds, live there. However, many species, such as the gibbon, come to feed.

Organisms living on the rainforest floor, including this macaw and the brightly colored fungus, differ from those living at other levels.

Most rainforest species live in the canopy, the site of the most light and food. Competition in the canopy is so fierce that species adapt to more specialized conditions. An example of such specialization is the relationship between the hermit hummingbird and a species of passion flower. As the hummingbird sips nectar from the passion flower, the anthers of the flower deposit pollen on the back of the bird's head. Then the bird carries the pollen to the next flower. The plant feeds the bird and the bird pollinates the plant— adaptations that benefit both species. The bird and flower each evolved over millions of years resulting in a perfect fit between the shape of the hummingbird's head and that of the flower.

Specialized habitats exist within each layer of the rainforest. One group of plants called epiphytes (ep′ə fīts)—or air plants—have adapted to a specialized habitat. Epiphytes, such as the orchids in the picture, don't live in the soil. They live up in the air on a tree branch! Epiphytes can live there because microscopic spores of ferns and mosses sprout in bark crevices. The spores grow, die, and decay, leaving a compost in the tree branch. The compost contains nutrients that support orchids and other epiphytes. The epiphytes have developed two root systems. One holds the plant firmly to the tree. The other system hangs free, drawing moisture from the air.

In this dense, leafy green world, it's hard to be seen. For this reason, loud cries and bright colors are vital when recognition is important. How might the bright colors of the macaw in the picture help it compete?

The gibbon and orchid are two organisms that dwell in the rainforest canopy.

Living Color

Colors help organisms survive in tropical rainforests.

So many organisms inhabit the rainforest. The differences are amazing! Yet, what similarities can you see in how rainforest species have adapted to their environment? One important way rainforest species have adapted is through the use of color.
A. These two brightly colored birds are scarlet and blue-gold macaws. These largest members of the parrot family live in Central and South American rainforests. Macaws choose lifelong mates from their flocks of twenty or more birds. Coloration helps the macaws recognize their mates and other members of their own flock.
B. The hammock plant has red berries that are available on the plant for nearly a full year. In the dense, dark understory of the rainforest, the berries attract birds. The berries are eaten by the birds. The birds spread the seeds of the berries around the forest floor where they might germinate.

C. Can you guess how coloration helps protect this insect? The coloration of the owl butterfly of the South American rainforest is both soft and startling. The soft brown of the wings enables the butterfly to blend in with the bark of the tree branches that it rests on. But the pattern on its wings resembles eyes. These eyespots frighten the butterfly's natural predators, such as birds and lizards. The predators mistake the butterfly for a larger animal. As a result, they move away from the butterfly thinking they might become prey themselves!

D. The male mandrill of the Central African rainforest is perhaps unique among mammals for its vivid facial coloration. The elongated striped face with the bright red nose and blue cheeks is easily recognized by other members of the species. When the mandrill gets excited, its face color deepens and the skin under its chest hair turns blue. Red dots appear on its wrists and ankles. Other threatening males are likely to run off—usually without a fight!

A World Within A Plant

Over millions of years, rainforest species have evolved relationships with one another that help them survive. One example is the relationship between the hummingbird and passion flower that you learned about earlier. Another example is the interaction between a tree and one kind of epiphyte shown to the left. This epiphyte—called a bromeliad (brō mē′lē ad′)— furnishes the tree with nutrients, and the tree provides support and shelter for the bromeliad. This interaction is called **mutualism**. In a mutualistic relationship each member benefits from the other.

Bromeliads have extra nutrients because of the way the species has evolved. The spiky leaves of the bromeliad channel water into its center. Some plants hold as much as ten liters of water in this center tank. Falling leaves and other debris fall into the water, releasing nutrients. Roots from the tree branches grow into the plant's tank, tapping into the nutrients.

Other species have evolved relationships with the bromeliad. For example, one species of tree frog—so tiny it could sit on a penny—uses the bromeliad tank as a nursery. The tiny frog's tadpole is born on the forest floor and crawls onto its mother's back. The mother carries the newborn up the tree to the bromeliad. The frog backs into the water and the tadpole wriggles free. There it feeds on mosquito larvae.

The bromeliad is a popular place. Biologist Claudio Picado counted as many as 250 species living in a single plant's tank! These species include organisms as small as bacteria and as large as the mouse opossum.

Into The Field

How do plants and animals help one another?
Look in a pile of leaves or under some ground cover. Observe the living organisms you find there. Describe how they help each other.

◄ *Many organisms inhabit this bromeliad, including the mouse opossum, the blue damselfly, and the poison dart frog.*

Checkpoint

1. Why do most rainforest species live in the canopy?
2. How do color adaptations aid survival in the rainforest?
3. Explain the relationship between the bromeliad and its host tree.
4. **Take Action!** Design a travel poster for the rainforest. Include information about some unusual organisms living there.

Activity

Color
Their World

How does color help animals survive? Make a model of animals and their environment. See how well your "animals" survive.

Picture A

Picture B

Picture C

Gather These Materials

paper punch
5 sheets of different
  brightly colored paper

1 square meter of
  patterned cloth

Follow This Procedure

1 Make a chart like the one on the next page. Record your observations on your chart.

2 Use the paper punch to cut out 20 paper dots from each sheet of colored paper. (Picture A) Each dot represents an animal.

3 Spread the cloth on the floor. The cloth represents the habitat where the animals live.

4 Scatter all the dots on the cloth. Make sure that the dots are spread out. (Picture B)

5 Four students will work as a team. Each student will be a "predator," catching the paper dot "animals" by picking them up one at a time. Students should begin picking up the dots at the same time. When removing the dots, pick one up, turn away from the cloth, then turn back to the cloth and pick up the next one. Always pick up the first dot you see. (Picture C)

Predict: *Which colors are likely to be spotted and picked up first?*

6 Stop removing dots when each member of your team has removed 15 dot "animals."

7 Count the number of dots of each color that remain. These dots are the "animals" that survived. Record the number of animals that survived and the number that were caught. Then make a graph using your data.

Color	Number caught	Number of survivors

State Your Conclusions

1. Which colors were the first to be spotted?
2. Do you think the color of the "animal" and the color of the "environment" made a difference in the animal's survival? Explain.
3. If your cloth had the colors of the rain forest, and another cloth had colors of the grassland, would the same colors protect animals in both environments?

Let's Experiment

Now that you have seen how color helps animals survive, what do you think would happen if the "animals" lived in a different "environment?" Use what you know about scientific methods to find out.

2.2 *White on White*

▶ *Is color important everywhere?*

In the Arctic, white stretches over the earth as far as you can see. A biting wind whips snow around, piling it into drifts. The only sound is the howling wind. You might see a gyrfalcon (jėr′ fôl′ kən) circling the sky looking for a rabbit. But few organisms are visible in this white land. How do the arctic organisms below differ from those of the rainforest? How can color be important in this harsh, white land?

Harsh Environment

The arctic environment is harsh. During the winter the sun stays below the horizon for weeks, sometimes months at a time. In the arctic tundra, which is located south of the glacial ice cap surrounding the North Pole, winter is about nine months long. For weeks the sun may shine only minutes a day. With so little sunlight, the temperature may drop to –57°C. That's cold! If you went out in that temperature unprotected, your skin could freeze in a few minutes.

▼ *In the arctic climate, white coloring camouflages many animals, including the arctic hare, the arctic fox, and the ptarmigan.*

Because the harsh climate provides few habitats, only a few thousand species can survive in the arctic tundra. That's not many species, compared to the millions that inhabit the rainforest. How do species survive the arctic cold?

An important adaptation of some species is the way they find shelter. Insects bury themselves in the mud and spend the winter under the snow. Plants grow close to the ground where a blanket of snow insulates them from the cold. Birds grow a double layer of feathers.

During winter some animals hibernate in dens under the snow. Others, like the ptarmigan (tär′mə gən) below, find sheltered spots near rocks or snow drifts. Many animals come out of their shelters only to eat. Ptarmigans and other plant eaters dig for frozen vegetation. But this gyrfalcon, looking for prey, might not see them. Arctic animals are protected by white coats that are hard to see.

Ptarmigans are particularly well protected. White feathers grow in gradually to replace brown ones as the early snows cover part of the landscape. As a result, when the environment is brown and white, so are the ptarmigans. As more snow falls, more white feathers grow. Ptarmigans become practically invisible against the snow. Even their legs and feet are covered with white feathers. Other animals, such as the arctic fox and the arctic hare, grow white coats too.

▼ *This gyrfalcon has keen eyesight that enables it to see camouflaged prey in the snow.*

Adaptations of Polar Bears

Polar bears are adapted to frigid temperatures.

Imagine having to walk on snow and ice, swim through icy water, and hunt for food in sub-zero temperatures. Polar bears that live in the polar regions of the Northern Hemisphere do just that! They rarely venture inland, but live most of the year on ice and in water. An adult male has a mass of more than 450 kilograms. Its sleek head and body help it glide through the icy water.

A polar bear only goes into a winter sleep when food is extremely scarce. Ordinarily, it hunts all winter, hopping from ice floe to ice floe, as it kills seals and young walruses with blows from its large paws. A keen sense of smell helps locate prey. A polar bear can smell food as much as 16 kilometers away.

Most organisms could not survive in the harsh conditions of the polar bear's habitat. How does the polar bear survive?

Fur and Skin

Thick, white fur keeps the polar bear warm and camouflaged against the ice and snow. The hairs are colorless, which allows them to transfer light to the bear's dark skin. The black skin of the bear absorbs the light. As a result, the skin is heated.

Tail and Ears

Blood travels to the tail and ears of animals to keep them warm. As a result, much heat is lost to the cold air. The small size of the polar bear's tail and ears reduces the loss of body heat.

Blubber

A thick layer of fat, called blubber, lies under the bear's skin and over its muscles. This layer provides excellent insulation. It keeps the bear's body heat from escaping.

Paws

The polar bear has large, broad paws. The soles are covered with stiff hairs that serve two purposes. They keep the bear from slipping on the ice. And they act as insulation —keeping the polar bear's body heat from escaping through its feet.

➤ Saxifrage in bloom

▲ Ptarmigan with summer feathers

Color Comes To The Arctic

The arctic summer is short, but the summer days are long. For the six to eight weeks of summer, the sun stays above the horizon all day. It can be seen plainly even at midnight. With summer comes a change in the landscape. As snow melts, the color of the landscape changes. The sand, gravel, and rocks give the ground a spotted gray-brown appearance. If species are to survive, they must be able to adapt to the change. Arctic foxes, arctic hares, and ermines grow new coats in various shades of brown that blend into the background. Compare the picture of the ptarmigan on the left to the one on page 41. How has it changed for the summer season?

➤ Hoary marmots reproduce during the arctic summers.

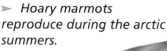

Only about a thousand species of plants grow in the arctic tundra. Soon after the snow is gone, saxifrage, seen to the left, and other plants are in bloom. Orange, purple, green, red, and yellow flowers compete for insect pollinators.

Although the arctic plants compete with bright colors for pollinators just as the rainforest plants do, arctic plants compete for a different reason. The large number of competitors doesn't threaten the arctic species' survival. Instead, time threatens arctic plants—summer is so short! They barely have time to flower and reproduce.

Summer brings millions of migrating birds—swans, ducks, loons, puffins and others. They come to breed. Long summer days of food-gathering enable the birds to have larger broods. Other animals, including the hoary marmot you see in the picture, also reproduce during this short warm period in the Arctic.

In August, species of the arctic tundra begin to prepare for winter. The ground squirrel—one of the few Arctic hibernators—is already in its nest, where it will stay until the following May. Other animals are feasting on summer's last bounty—red cranberries, yellow cloudberries, and purple bilberries. Plants end their summer growth by producing buds that will bloom the following spring. Migrators are on their way south. Only a few hardy arctic species remain, each preparing in its own way for the next long, cold winter.

Checkpoint

1. How are the white coats of ptarmigans and other species adaptations to their arctic environment?
2. In what other ways have species adapted to the arctic environment?
3. What adaptations enable organisms to respond to seasonal changes in the Arctic?
4. **Take Action!** Several cultures make their home in the Arctic. Construct a map showing where those cultures live and how they have adapted to living in the arctic environment.

An Absorbing Activity

 Wear cover goggles for this activity.

Will black materials absorb heat faster than white ones? Let's investigate.

What To Do
A. Prepare two metal cans as shown.

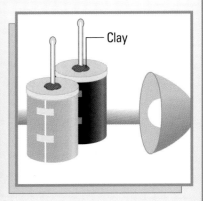
Clay

B. Record the temperature from each thermometer.
C. Turn on the light. Wait ten minutes. Then read and record the temperatures for both cans.
D. Record the differences in the starting and final temperatures.

Record Your Results

	Temperature	
	White can	Black can
Begin		
End		

What Did You Find Out?
1. *Which color absorbs heat better?*
2. *How does a polar bear's black skin help warm it?*

Activity

Fatty Insulators

To see how to keep warm, take a clue from the polar bear. In this activity, you'll make a model of the fat of an arctic animal.

Picture A

Gather These Materials

cover goggles

4 sandwich-sized plastic bags

2 rubber bands

shortening

large container of cold water

spoon

Follow This Procedure

1 Make a chart like the one on the next page. Record your observations in your chart.

2 Put on your cover goggles.

3 Use a spoon to fill a plastic bag about half full of shortening.

4 Make a fist with one hand. Place this hand in a second plastic bag, and have a team member use a rubber band to secure it to your wrist. (Picture A)

5 Insert your bag-covered fist into the shortening-filled bag. (Picture B) Adjust the rubber band so that it secures both plastic bags to your wrist.

6 Have a team member work through the outer bag to push the shortening around so that it covers your entire fist inside the bag. (Picture C)

7 Make a fist with your other hand. Have a team member cover this fist with two plastic bags and secure the bag with a rubber band.

Picture B

Picture C

Record Your Results

Time	Hand with shortening	Hand without shortening
Start		
30 seconds		
1 minute		

Predict: *Which fist will feel warmer when immersed in cold water?*

8 Immerse both of your bag-covered fists into cold water. Make observations about how warm each feels. Record your observations in your chart.

9 Keep your fists immersed for 1 minute. Record your observation at 30 seconds and at 1 minute.

State Your Conclusions

1. Which hand stayed warm longer? Explain why.
2. Compare the function of the shortening in this activity with that of the blubber of an arctic animal such as the polar bear.

Let's Experiment

How do you think the amount of fat affects how warm an animal stays? Use what you know about scientific methods to find out.

Chapter Review

Reviewing Words and Concepts

Write the letter of the word or phrase that best completes each sentence.

1. The middle layer of the rainforest is the _____.
2. During winter, some arctic animals _____ under the snow.
3. Varying amounts of light and moisture and differences in temperature in a rainforest provide many different _____.
4. The many species of the rainforest are always in _____ with each other for resources.
5. The relationship between a bromeliad and the tree on which it lives is an example of _____ because both species benefit.
6. Few plants bloom on the _____ of the rainforest.
7. Most rainforest species live in the top layer, called the _____.
8. A polar bear has a layer of _____ beneath its skin to help keep body heat from escaping.
9. The _____ of the arctic hare helps this animal blend in with its environment.
10. The large, flat paws of a polar bear are an _____ that helps prevent the bear from slipping on ice and snow.

a. blubber
b. floor
c. habitats
d. adaptation
e. understory
f. canopy
g. competition
h. color
i. hibernate
j. mutualism

Connecting Ideas

1. Copy the concept map. Use the terms at the right to complete the map to show how species evolve.

adaptations   competition

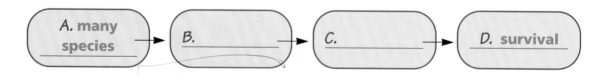

A. many species → B. _____ → C. _____ → D. survival

2. Write a sentence or two that summarizes the ideas shown in the concept map about the survival of species.

Interpreting What You Learned

1. Why do many more species live in the rainforest than in the arctic tundra?
2. Describe how rainforest organisms differ, moving upward from the floor to the canopy of the rainforest.
3. Why are bright colors and loud noises more important to species living in the rainforest than to species living in the Arctic?
4. Describe an adaptation of the ptarmigan that protects it from predators all year long.
5. How is color important to plants living in the Arctic?
6. Explain how mutualism is an adaptation for the survival of a species.

Performance Assessment

How do organisms help each other survive?

Materials • cover goggles • cutout flower • white paper • scissors • black construction paper • tape • dropper • flour • 2 pipe cleaners • small cup • water • sharpened pencil

Collecting Data

1. Put on your cover goggles. Using the cutout flower your teacher gives you, trace the flower on white paper. Use scissors to cut out the flower you draw. Use a sharpened pencil to poke two holes in the center of the flower.
2. Dip one end of each pipe cleaner in the flour. The flour represents pollen. Then poke the clean end of each pipe cleaner down through the two holes you poked in the flower. The pipe cleaners represent the flower's anthers.
3. Lay the flower flat on the tabletop. Place a small cup of water in the middle of the flower. The water in the cup represents nectar.
4. Cut the outline of a hummingbird from the black paper. Tape the dropper to the bird's head to represent the long beak of a hummingbird.
5. Position the anthers so they will touch the head of your hummingbird when it visits the flower. Adjust the pipe cleaners so they bend around the top of the cup of water.
6. Move the hummingbird toward the flower. Place the beak of your hummingbird into the nectar. Squeeze the bulb of the dropper so the hummingbird takes a drink.
7. Observe the hummingbird. Look for evidence that the hummingbird is carrying pollen from the flower.

Analyzing Data

What might happen if your hummingbird visits another flower of the same kind?

CHAPTER 3

Light in the Ocean

Discover Activity

What happens to the water pressure?

A manometer measures water pressure. You can make a manometer using a piece of cardboard, twist ties, rubber tubing, a balloon, and a funnel. The picture shows how to connect the pieces. Put colored water in the U-shaped tube. Press on the balloon. What happens to the colored water? Insert the funnel into a container of water. Move the funnel up and down.

Wear cover goggles for this activity.

For Discussion

1. What happens to the colored water as you move the funnel in the container of water?

2. How does this show that water exerts pressure?

3.1 *Fading Light*

▶ **How is living in the ocean different?**

Travel back in time to the first century B.C. You're standing on the shore of the Mediterranean Sea. You see a young man, a Greek, probably not much older than yourself. The owners of a sunken ship want him to salvage goods from that ship. He's in a small boat not far off shore. He picks up a big stone, takes a deep breath, and jumps in. The weight of the stone makes his descent quicker. And he wants to save time. He'll have only minutes under water and he's paid according to the depth at which he works. For an eight-meter dive he keeps half of what he salvages. For four meters he keeps one-third, and for one meter he keeps only one-tenth. The ship owners know that the deeper the dive, the harder it is. But they don't know why.

Today divers know how conditions in the ocean change as it gets deeper. So they use equipment like this to explore shallow waters, and more sophisticated equipment, such as air tanks and wet suits, to protect themselves from deeper ocean conditions. Let's look at some of those conditions.

Ocean Factors

You and most species around you are adapted to life on land. You've seen some of the harsh conditions on the earth in which organisms survive. But the conditions in the ocean are different from those on land. How does the ocean environment vary?

First, water pressure changes as you go deeper in the ocean. Temperature and light levels change at different depths too. Over millions of years marine species have adapted to live in the different conditions created by the changes in pressure, light, and temperature at different ocean levels.

▼ *How is each of these items used by sea divers?*

The depth to which light penetrates the ocean depends on how clear the water is. The graph on the next page is based on data for relatively clear ocean water. Compare the ocean depths reached by various wavelengths of visible light to that reached by divers, whales, and research submarines. A sport diver can safely descend to approximately 60 meters using an air tank and a wet suit. Sperm whales can dive to depths greater than 1.5 kilometers. Alvin can explore areas of the ocean more than 2.5 kilometers deep.

First, let's think about the pressure in the ocean. In the Discover Activity, you saw that deeper water has greater pressure. But you conducted your experiment with only centimeters of water. Imagine how much more pressure water has at greater depths such as those you find in the ocean! If you were down only 30 meters in the water, the water pressure would push your eyeballs inward and distort your vision—unless you were wearing a face mask. And some areas of the ocean are thousands of meters deep! The water pressure is so great at such depths that it's difficult to imagine that anything could live there.

Now, let's look at ocean temperatures. The water also gets colder as you go deeper. If the surface water is 21°C,—the temperature of an autumn day—water temperature at 4000 meters deep is close to 0°C, which is the freezing point of water.

The deeper the water, the less light penetrates. And not all of the sunlight reaches the same depths. As light travels through the water, different depths absorb different wavelengths of the visible spectrum.

Follow the diagram through the depths of the ocean. At 10 meters, water absorbs red light, the longest wavelengths of visible light. If you were to spear a fish below 10 meters, its blood would look black because no red wavelengths of light penetrate below that level for the blood to reflect. As light travels deeper, other wavelengths filter out—one at a time. At 100 meters the light isn't strong enough for photosynthesis to occur. Below 240 meters no light penetrates. The environment is completely black.

These changes in water pressure, temperature, and light create three different zones in the ocean: the upper level zone, the mid-level zone, and the bottom level zone. Let's take a look at how marine species have adapted to these different ocean environments.

Just as in the rainforest, most organisms in the ocean live in the upper level—the photosynthesis zone—because the food is most plentiful there. The brightly lit surface waters are rich with plankton—microscopic organisms that serve as food for larger organisms. Because conditions are so favorable at the upper level, more species live there than at any other level.

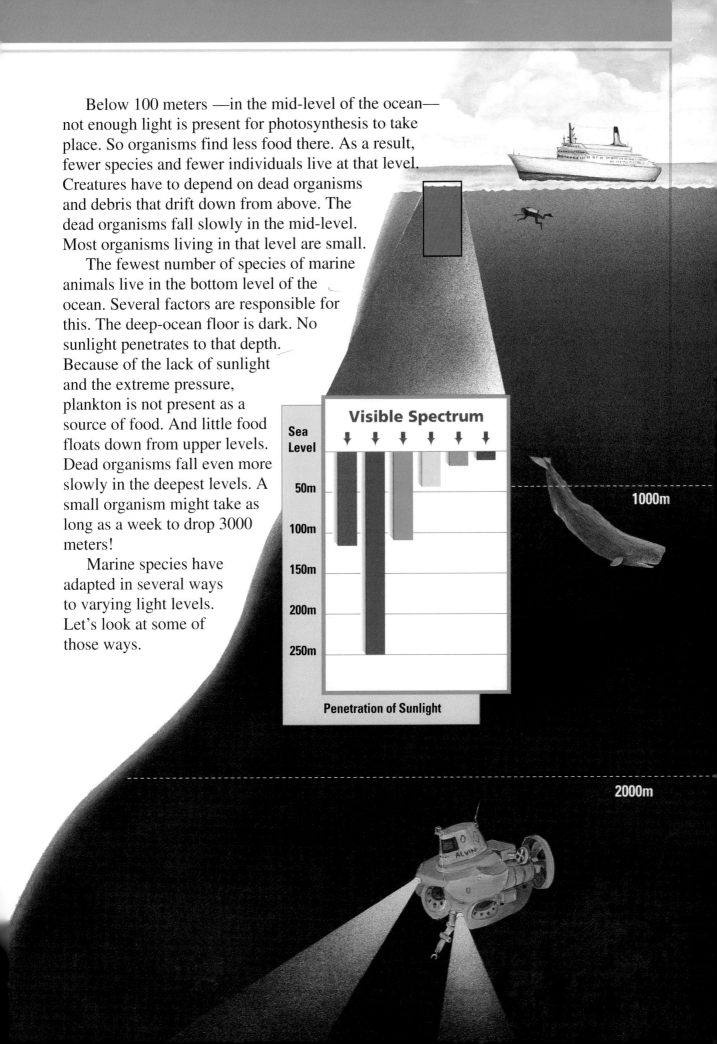

Below 100 meters —in the mid-level of the ocean— not enough light is present for photosynthesis to take place. So organisms find less food there. As a result, fewer species and fewer individuals live at that level. Creatures have to depend on dead organisms and debris that drift down from above. The dead organisms fall slowly in the mid-level. Most organisms living in that level are small.

The fewest number of species of marine animals live in the bottom level of the ocean. Several factors are responsible for this. The deep-ocean floor is dark. No sunlight penetrates to that depth. Because of the lack of sunlight and the extreme pressure, plankton is not present as a source of food. And little food floats down from upper levels. Dead organisms fall even more slowly in the deepest levels. A small organism might take as long as a week to drop 3000 meters!

Marine species have adapted in several ways to varying light levels. Let's look at some of those ways.

Visible Spectrum

Sea Level

50m

100m

150m

200m

250m

Penetration of Sunlight

1000m

2000m

Color and Light Levels

Like species in the rainforest, ocean species have evolved colors that protect them. Camouflage helps disguise both the hunter and the hunted. Camouflaged hunters succeed because their prey can't see them. Camouflaged prey don't get eaten—as often. Study the picture to see how color adaptations enable species to survive at different levels.

In the upper waters where it's so easy to be seen, some species have evolved almost transparent skins, which make them almost invisible. The body of the sea gooseberry reflects light that must be as blinding to fish as sunlight on water is to you. So the gooseberry passes by the hunter unseen.

Some larger fish species have evolved bi-colored bodies. Their blue backs blend with the blue surface water protecting them from seabird hunters overhead. Notice how the white bellies of the fish to the right can't be seen easily from below against sunlight filtering through the water.

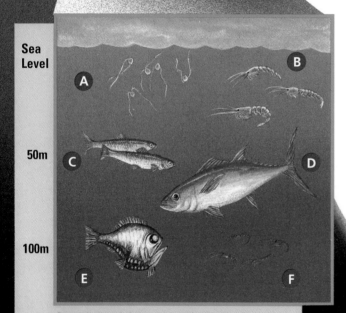

Sea Level

50m

100m

A B C D E F

Organisms of the upper and mid-level zone

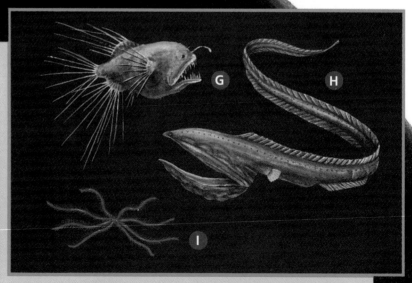

G H I

Organisms of the bottom-level zone

Prawn species living in the upper waters have also evolved a transparent blue skin, making them almost invisible. However, some prawn species in middle levels have developed a bright red shell. Because red wavelengths of light don't penetrate to deeper levels, the prawn's shell appears black and blends with the darker waters of the mid-level. Other animals at this level are silver. The little light that penetrates the area reflects off the mirror-like surface of fish such as the sardine.

Some mid-level fish species have evolved bi-colored bodies too. Hatchet fish and other fishes that live near the bottom of the mid-level zone have developed large eyes—some on the tops of their heads—that allow them to see enemies or prey overhead.

At the dark ocean bottom, some marine animals are black. Others are a sooty brown. The dark colors camouflage them in the dark water. How does the red coloring of the feather star camouflage it?

Many organisms are adapted to the lack of light in other ways. Because little can be seen in the dark waters, some organisms are blind; others have tiny eyes. Notice the sensor on the angler fish. These sensors detect movement in the water. Fish use the sensors to find food or detect predators. Some animals use sound to find mates. Other fish use smell to find food.

Marine species have adapted in many ways to life in the different light levels in the ocean. While many of these adaptations might seem unusual, all help the organism survive. But if you lived in the dark bottom zone, you'd probably think a flashlight would be the most helpful. And that's what many species have!

◄ *Use this key to identify the organisms on page 54.*
Ⓐ Gooseberry
Ⓑ Shrimp
Ⓒ Sardine
Ⓓ Tuna
Ⓔ Hatchet fish
Ⓕ Shrimp
Ⓖ Angler fish
Ⓗ Gulper eel
Ⓘ Feather star

◄ *These fish appear almost invisible against the bright sunlight filtering through the surface water.*

Bioluminescence

Many marine organisms are **bioluminescent** (bī′ō lü′mə nes′nt)—they create their own light. Organisms with bioluminescence use it for protection, courtship, food-getting, and in other ways that are not yet understood. Bioluminescent organisms can be found at all levels in the ocean. A few live in the lighter upper levels, but below 3000 meters, more than half are bioluminescent.

Bioluminescent organisms can emit light because they have cells that contain "light carrier" molecules. When atoms within those molecules become "excited," the molecules emit light. The emitted light ranges from blue to blue-green, possibly because blue-green wavelengths penetrate farthest in water.

In the upper levels, food is plentiful and courtship rituals are visible, so bioluminescence is probably mostly camouflage. These glowing bodies are hard to see in brightly lit waters.

In the mid-level, light levels vary. As a result, some bioluminescent species have evolved "dimmer switches"— ways of brightening and dimming their lights according to the amount of light in the water around them. Squid, like the one in the picture, excrete bioluminescent fluid into the water, leaving a glowing trail that confuses their enemies.

▼ How does this squid use bioluminescence to protect itself?

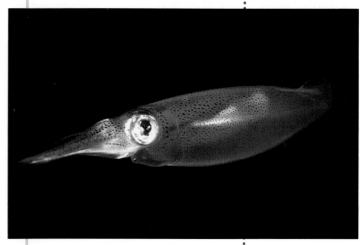

➤ The bioluminescent lure of the angler fish is flexible and moves in many directions. Its movement attracts prey that the fish then gulps into its mouth.

At the bottom level, food is hard to find in the dark. Locating a mate is even more difficult. There, more than half the species are bioluminescent. Their light helps them in more ways than it helps fish in upper levels.

At these depths a mutualistic relationship has evolved between certain bacteria and certain animals. Bacteria are the "batteries" that produce the light. Colonies of bioluminescent bacteria live in pouches at different places on the animals' bodies.

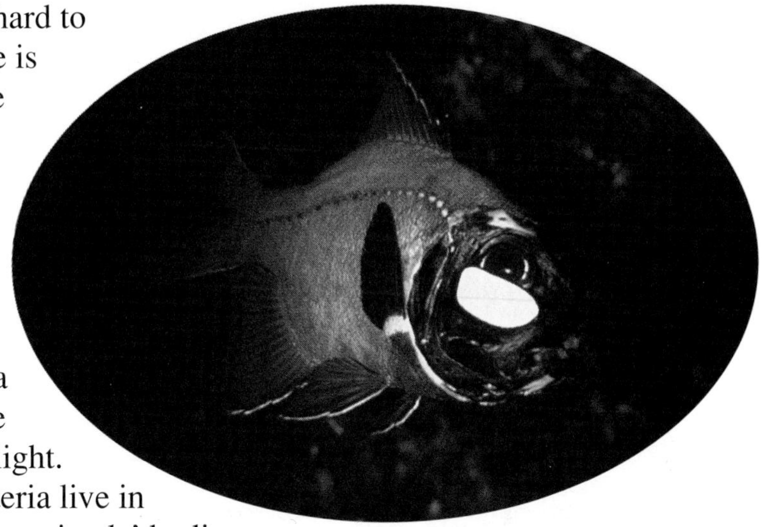

The bacteria shine continuously, so one species of fish—the flashlight fish—has evolved eyelid-like coverings of tissue that blot out the light. You can see the pouches of bioluminescent bacteria below the eyes of the flashlight fish in the picture above. Flashlight fish swim in schools, raising and lowering the coverings to turn the lights off and on. The signals seem to have two main functions: They keep the schools together and they enable males to attract females. Fish with these bacterial spotlights also flash light suddenly to frighten their enemies or startle prey.

But the mutualistic relationship between the bioluminescent bacteria and angler fish to the left helps the anglers in a different way. The membrane that dangles from a rod-like spine over its head contains bioluminescent bacteria. The light lures small fish close enough for the angler to suck them in.

▲ *The flashlight fish has pouches containing bioluminescent bacteria that it uses to attract mates and startle prey.*

Checkpoint

1. Why is it dark at the bottom of the ocean?
2. How does color help ocean species survive in their environment?
3. Explain how organisms use bioluminescence for survival.
4. **Take Action!** Make a collage of unusual fish eyes—both their structure and position—and describe how each is an adaptation.

Make It Disappear

Can you use light to make something disappear? The way the colors are filtered can affect what we see. Try this activity to find out how.

Picture A

Picture B

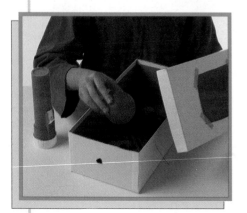

Picture C

Gather These Materials

cover goggles

small index card

shoebox with lid

scissors

tape

red cellophane

red object

flashlight

Follow This Procedure

1 Make a chart like the one on the next page. Record your observations in your chart.

2 Put on your cover goggles.

3 Center a small index card on the lid of a shoebox. Trace its outline with a pencil, and then cut out the rectangle with the scissors. (Picture A)

4 Tape a piece of red cellophane over the opening you made. (Picture B)

5 Cut a small viewing hole in one end of the shoebox.

6 Place red objects into the shoebox. (Picture C) Place the lid on the box.

Predict: *When you look through the viewing hole, how will the red objects appear?*

7 Shine a flashlight through the cellophane at the top of the box. Look through the viewing hole. Describe what you see.

Red light on red objects: observations

State Your Conclusions

1. What color light came into the box?
2. What color light does a red object usually reflect?
3. Could you see the red object in the box easily? Explain why or why not.
4. What would you see if the object inside the box were green?

Let's Experiment

Now that you have seen what appears to happen to a red object under red light, how do you think a red object would look if it were lit by other colors of light, but not red light? Use what you know about scientific methods to find out.

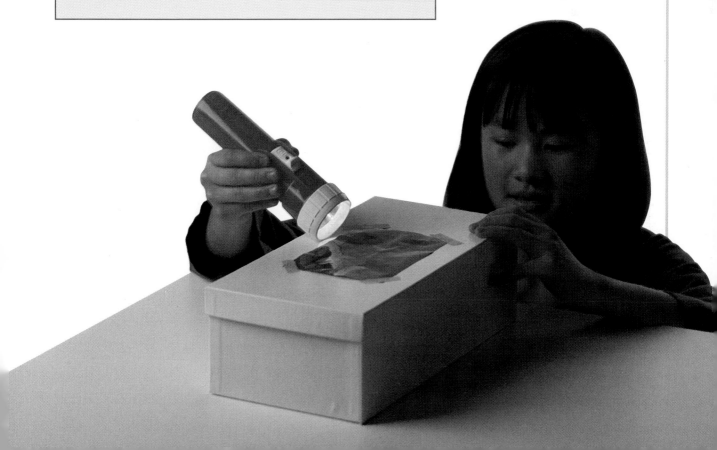

3.2 *Life in the Dark*

▶ *Is there something weird on the ocean floor?*

The day started out just like any other day for geologists mapping the ocean floor in 1977. From a ship on the surface, the scientists were using instruments to record temperatures on the ocean floor. Suddenly, the instruments showed the temperatures were warmer than the geologists expected. "Hydrothermal activity going on," they speculated, as they planned further investigation of the "hot-water" spot. They had no idea then how exciting that area of the ocean floor was going to be!

Hot-Water Vents

The map shows the area in which the geologists were working, a point midway between the Galápagos Islands and the South American continent. Scientists already knew that they were in the area of a spreading center. When tectonic plates move, they cause a deep crack in the earth's crust. As molten rock comes through the crack, it is cooled by the ocean water, forming new ocean floor.

Molten rock is not the only substance that flows from the ocean floor in the area of the cracks. Often hot-water springs, found under the surface of the ocean floor, vent their water into the ocean.

▼ Scientists discovered the first hot-water vents in an area east of the Galápagos Islands, shown in the box.

▼ A surface ship pulled Deep Tow at the end of a cable. The surface ship carried television cameras, sonar, pressure sensors, and probes to measure water temperature.

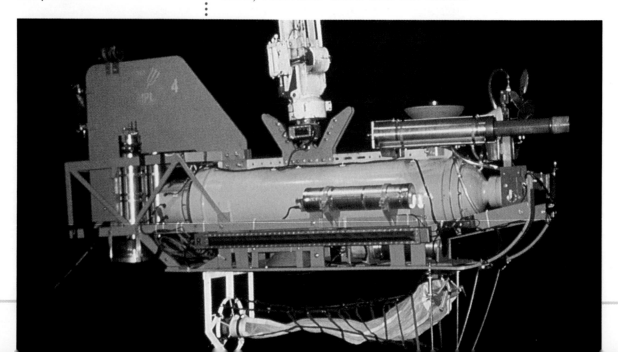

When geologists investigated the Galápagos area, they found the hot-water vents they expected. But they found more than that—a thriving community of organisms living in the vent area. These organisms were very different from those in other areas. The discovery excited biologists who immediately wanted to investigate. Science history was about to be made!

For the first investigation of the hot-water vent area, geologists remotely guided a tiny submarine called Deep Tow. Deep Tow was designed to map the ocean floor. It was equipped with a specially designed camera called Angus. As a surface ship pulled Deep Tow along the ocean floor, Angus snapped pictures. Among the 3000 photographs taken by Angus, 13 showed large clams and mussels at depths below 2500 meters. The sight was startling. Scientists were eager to take a closer look.

▲ These giant white clams were among the first photographs taken by Angus.

Next scientists went down to the site in a small submarine called *Alvin*. When *Alvin* neared the ocean floor, the scientists saw something that not even the Angus photographs had prepared them for. As *Alvin's* spotlights shone out across the ocean floor, scientists didn't see the empty gray expanse of ocean floor they had expected. Instead, they saw a sight that was hard to believe: Out of great cracks in the ocean floor spewed large volumes of hot, murky water.

What surrounded the cracks surprised the geologists even more. There, in the dark environment where no sunlight reaches and photosynthesis can't occur, scientists saw a thriving community of organisms. Clusters of large yellow mussels sprawled near the vents, while farther away lay the large white clams you see in the picture. But as scientists took a closer look, another surprise was waiting.

Usually only a few creatures struggle for life on the bleak ocean floor where food is so scarce. Typically you might find only a single organism in an area of several square meters. But here in the area of the hot-water vents was an oasis of life. What kinds of organisms did those scientists find?

An Oasis of Life

An abundance and variety of life exists around the hot-water vents.

Scientists exploring the hot-water vents near the Galápagos Islands found a scene even they were unprepared for. Hot water streamed from every crack in the sea floor over a circular area of about 100 meters. Reefs of huge, yellow mussels clustered closest to the vents. Nearby, colonies of giant tube worms waved in the current. Many were nearly 1.5 meters high, although some reached as high as 3 meters.

A little farther from the cracks, fields of huge, white clams—some of them up to 30 centimeters in diameter—could be seen. That's as big as a dinner plate! Some areas around the vents were covered with milky clouds. Further study revealed that at least 200 species of bacteria made up the clouds.

With every look, scientists found more exciting species. What were some of those organisms? Let's look!

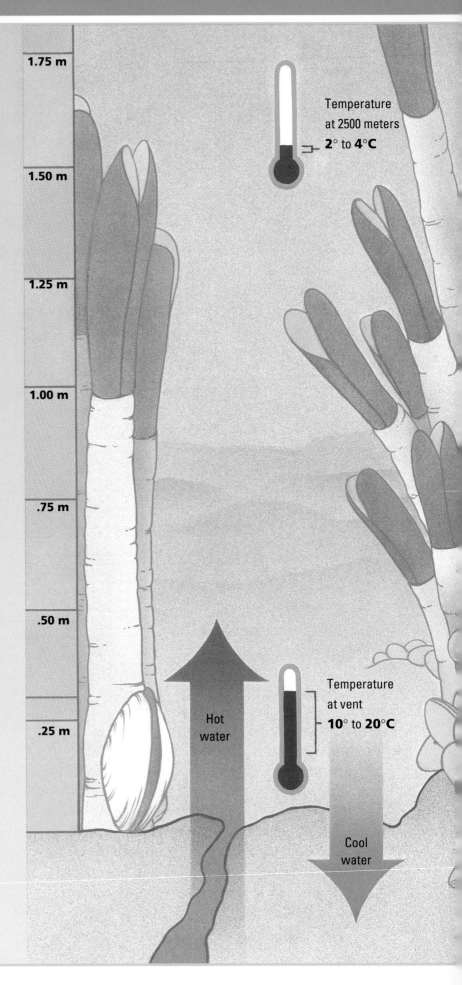

1.75 m

1.50 m

1.25 m

1.00 m

.75 m

.50 m

.25 m

Temperature at 2500 meters
2° to 4°C

Temperature at vent
10° to 20°C

Hot water

Cool water

A Giant tube worms   G Spider crab
B Giant white clams   H Brachyuran crab
C Mussels   I Dandelion
D Pink fish   J Brittle star
E Anemone   K Shrimp
F Spaghetti worms

▲ *Scientists who discovered the vent communities were startled at the large number of organisms they found.*

▼ *Few organisms live on the typical ocean floor.*

Vent Characteristics

Recall that scientists were first amazed by the hot-water vents because of the number and kinds of organisms they found there. To understand how scientists might have felt, compare the photos. Scientists were expecting to see a vast empty area—something like a Sahara Desert under water. Instead they encountered an oasis teeming with life—clams, tube worms, crabs—even pink fish!

The size of the organisms was especially startling. On the previous page you learned that the tube worms measured as much as 3 meters long. Clams measured up to 30 centimeters across the shell. If you are wondering why these measurements are unusual, compare them to those of ordinary clams. Most clams have shells between 2 to 8 centimeters, although a few species, such as the giant clams, grow to a diameter of 1 meter or more.

As scientists further studied these vent organisms, they discovered even more interesting facts. Some of the large vent organisms seem to be the same species as smaller forms in colder water. And some vent organisms grow at a much faster rate than other ocean organisms of the same species. For example, vent clams grow to adult size five times faster than other deep ocean clams.

As unusual as this vent life is, the vent areas can support such life because these areas are different from other ocean-floor areas. The vents occur only in the areas where movement of tectonic plates creates cracks. Molten rock lies within the deep cracks created by plate movement. Thus, the intense heat from inside the earth—geothermal energy—affects the ocean floor. As sea water seeps down through the cracks, geothermal energy heats the sea water. As the water is heated under the ocean floor, pressure increases. When the pressure becomes great enough, the hot water shoots up through the vents into the ocean. So temperatures around the vents are higher than elsewhere in the ocean.

As the hot water is spewing from the deep-sea vents, something else is happening. Minerals from the hot rock dissolve into the water. As a result, the water gushing out of the vents is thick with chemical compounds called sulfides. But sulfides are toxic, or poisonous, to most creatures. So how can life flourish in such a toxic environment where no light penetrates to support photosynthesis?

Checkpoint

1. What processes create the unique conditions at the hot-water vents?
2. Describe some organisms scientists found around the hot-water vents.
3. How do conditions around the hot-water vents differ from the conditions at other areas of the ocean floor?
4. Take Action! Make life-size models of the tube worms and giant clams from both the vents and other ocean areas and compare them.

Brrrrr, That's Cold!

Away from the hot-water vents, the deep ocean can be a very cold place. In general, as you go deeper in the ocean, the temperature gets colder.

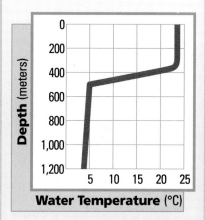

Water Temperature (°C)

Sunlight heats the surface water of the oceans, but can't reach deep into the ocean. The warm surface water mixes with the cooler water to a depth of about 200 meters. Below that depth the temperature drops sharply. The depth where temperature changes quickly is called a thermocline. Below the thermocline, water temperatures continue to drop gradually.

What Did You Find Out?
1. *What is the temperature at 200 meters?*
2. *At what depth is the thermocline?*
3. *What is the difference in temperature between the surface and the deepest part of the ocean?*

Activity

What's So Hot About a Vent?

What makes the warm water near ocean vents a likely home for animals? Try this activity to learn more about conditions at a vent.

Picture A

Picture B

Picture C

Gather These Materials

cover goggles
2 jars
hot water
cold water

thermometer
spoon
Epsom salts

Follow This Procedure

1 Make a chart like the one on the next page. Record your observations in your chart.

2 Put on your cover goggles.

3 Fill a jar halfway full with hot water. Fill another jar with the same amount of cold water. (Picture A) *CAUTION: Be careful when pouring the hot water.*

4 Use a thermometer to measure the temperature of the water in each jar. Record your results.

5 Add a level spoonful of Epsom salts to the hot water. Stir until it dissolves. (Picture B)

6 Add a second level spoonful of Epsom salts, and stir.

7 Continue adding Epsom salts by the spoonful until no more will dissolve. (Picture C) Record the total number of spoonfuls of Epsom salts added to the jar.

Predict: *Will cold water hold more or less Epsom salts than hot water?*

8 Repeat steps 5 through 7 with the jar of cold water.

Record Your Results

	Temperature of water	Number of spoonfuls added
Hot water		
Cold water		

State Your Conclusions

1. How did your prediction compare to your results?

2. Which area do you think would have more minerals dissolved in the water: the area around the ocean vents or the cold regions of the deep ocean? Explain why you think so.

3. Why are there large mineral deposits near old vent sites?

Let's Experiment

Now that you have found out about how minerals dissolve in hot and cold water, what do you think would happen to the dissolved minerals in hot water as the water cools? Use what you know about scientific methods to find out.

3.3 *Light—Who Needs It?*

▶ *How can organisms live in such a place?*

One question scientists began asking after the discovery of the vent community in 1977 was: Do other communities exist such as those found at the Galápagos vent? To their surprise scientists found more vent communities. And they all had similar conditions—large, numerous organisms, no sunlight, toxic hydrogen sulfide, and no plankton. In each case where organisms should have been dying, they were thriving. Scientists seemed to have a puzzle: How could so many organisms live where conditions seemed to be so unfavorable?

▼ *These chemosynthetic bacteria use energy stored in hydrogen sulfide to make sugars.*

A New Energy Source

As biologists investigated the vent communities, they discovered something amazing. Sugars were being created in the dark! In a process called chemosynthesis (kem′ō sin′thə sis), bacteria, such as those to the left, produce sugars similar to those produced by green plants during photosynthesis. But the bacteria use chemical energy from hydrogen sulfide instead of the energy of sunlight. The process is summarized in the diagram below.

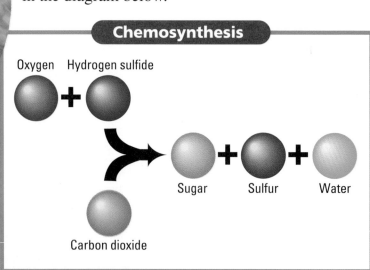

Chemosynthesis

Oxygen   Hydrogen sulfide

+

Sugar + Sulfur + Water

Carbon dioxide

Chemosynthesis and photosynthesis both produce sugars. After that the food chain works the same. In a community that depends on photosynthesis, animals either eat producers directly or they eat other animals that eat the producers. In the dark vent community the bacteria are the producers. All other animals depend on the bacteria either directly or indirectly for food.

Scientists studying the vent organisms learned that the large tube worms living in the vent communities have no mouths or digestive systems. But they're filled with a special core that provides a home for the chemosynthetic bacteria. In this mutualistic relationship, the bacteria provide the tube worms with food, and the tube worms protect the bacteria. Other vent organisms, such as the large white clams and yellow mussels, also have mutualistic relationships with the bacteria.

Not all vent organisms obtain their nutrients through a mutualistic relationship with the bacteria. Some filter the bacteria from the water. Others feed on animals that contain the bacteria. For example, vent crabs, like those below, have been observed feeding on tube worms.

But what about the toxic effect of hydrogen sulfide? Because many organisms live in the vent communities, biologists know the species have adapted in some way to the toxic hydrogen sulfide. Species have adapted to toxic conditions before. Oxygen was toxic to most species millions of years ago when oxygen first developed in the earth's atmosphere. Variations within species enabled some individuals to survive by getting rid of the toxic oxygen.

For most animals sulfides are toxic because they prevent the hemoglobin in the bloodstream from carrying oxygen molecules necessary for respiration. Vent species have evolved a variety of ways for dealing with toxic hydrogen sulfide. For example, the vent clam has a special protein to carry hydrogen sulfide to the chemosynthetic bacteria that live in its gills. And the hemoglobin of the vent tube worms binds to both oxygen and hydrogen sulfide at the same time.

▼ Vent crabs might feed on giant tube worms.

Into The Field

Do different areas around your home get different amounts of light?

Go outside and observe the same type of plants growing in areas with varying amounts of sunlight.

▼ *Discovery of a thriving community on the ocean floor caused scientists to change their hypothesis about food chain energy sources.*

Changing Theories

Scientists studying the vents already knew about chemosynthesis. For example, scientists knew that chemosynthetic bacteria lived in some hot sulfur springs. But these hot spring bacteria were not considered the primary producers of the community food chains. Until the discovery of the vent community, scientists thought the source of energy for all major food chains was the sun. So scientists developed a hypothesis: All communities depend directly or indirectly on sunlight.

When the vent community was discovered, the hypothesis was proved wrong because the vent community depended on hydrogen sulfide, not sunlight. That's why the discovery of flourishing life in the vent communities was so important. Other scientists all over the world added this discovery to their thinking. And as you know, when new discoveries are made, the ideas of science change and become more correct as the new facts are added to the "big picture."

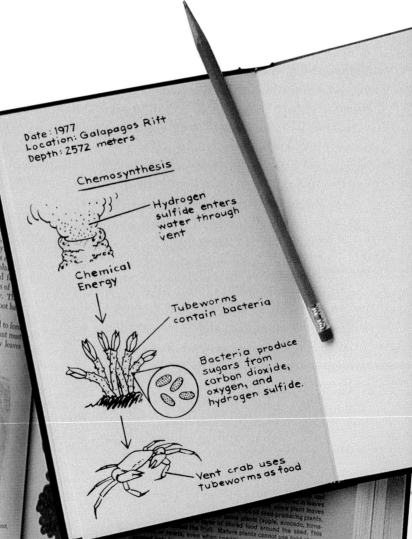

PROBLEM **3**

What happens to the food made in a green plant?

Some of the food made in the leaves of green plants is stored by the plants. Do you know where? Think about such plants as apple trees, wheat plants, and potato plants. Where do these plants store food? What other things do you think plants do with the food they make?

You have already learned that the cells of your body use energy whenever you work or play and even when you are resting or sleeping. Your cells need energy

to carry on digestion and keep your heart and lungs going. Your body uses energy to produce the heat you need for growth and for repair of injured or worn-out parts. Your body needs because you are alive. Anything that is alive needs energy to live.

Because plants are living things, they also need energy. For example, the process of food-making requires energy. In this way, a plant's need for energy is similar to an animal's need. But in plants, as in animals, energy is needed for the replacement of cells. Some kinds of plant cells must be replaced constantly. This is especially true of the cells with root hairs, which live only for a short time.

In plants, energy is also needed to form chlorophyll. A growing green plant must keep making chlorophyll for new leaves

Energy from the sun transforms water and carbon dioxide into sugar which is stored and used for food.

Date: 1977
Location: Galapagos Rift
Depth: 2572 meters

Chemosynthesis

Hydrogen sulfide enters water through vent

Chemical Energy

Tubeworms contain bacteria

Bacteria produce sugars from carbon dioxide, oxygen, and hydrogen sulfide.

Vent crab uses tubeworms as food

Vent Shrimp

The discovery of the chemosynthetic bacteria wasn't the only new bit of information to come from exploration of vent communities. In 1985 scientists discovered a species of shrimp swarming around a hot-water vent. Scientists named the species *Rimicaris exoculata*, meaning "without eyes" because the shrimp didn't have the usual eyestalks other shrimp had.

Several years later a biologist studying the vent shrimp noticed strange patches on their backs. Further study revealed that those patches are actually eyes. The eyes have no lenses, so the shrimp can't see images. But they can see brightness and direction of light. Actually the shrimp's eyes have at least five times more of a light-sensing molecule than other shrimp have. As a result, this shrimp is able to detect very weak light.

Scientists began to question: What are those eyes seeing in the darkness? At first, researchers thought that the vent glowed. Maybe the glow led the shrimp to their food. Or maybe the eyes helped them avoid the vent water that is so hot that it would cook them!

Tests proved that the vents do glow and the plumes of hot water emit light—light humans can't see. But further tests gave the researchers another puzzle. The tests showed that the light from the vents was at the red end of the color spectrum. But the shrimp's unusual eyes are not sensitive to red light. Their eyes sense light at the blue end of the spectrum. Could there be another source of light at the blue end that the shrimp see?

Scientists don't know yet. Perhaps the shrimp see some unknown source of light that humans cannot see. Only future research will answer the question.

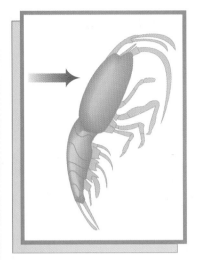

▲ *The arrow shows the unusual location of this species' eyes.*

Checkpoint

1. How are photosynthesis and chemosynthesis alike and different?
2. When do scientists change hypotheses?
3. Why are scientists studying the vent shrimp?
4. **Take Action!** Write a news bulletin based on information you find in science magazines about how a current science idea is changing.

Chapter Review

Reviewing Words and Concepts

Write the letter of the word or phrase that best completes each sentence.

1. Microscopic organisms called _____ serve as food for larger ocean organisms.
2. A _____ organism creates its own light.
3. The heat emitted at ocean vents results from _____.
4. During chemosynthesis, bacteria use chemical energy from _____ instead of energy from sunlight.
5. The bioluminescence of some fish is produced by _____ living in different areas on the fish's bodies.
6. Bacteria living near ocean vents produce sugars in a process called _____.
7. Hot-water vents emit _____ but humans cannot see it.
8. The upper level of the ocean is the _____ zone, where light penetrates the water.
9. In a vent community, bacteria are the _____ of the food chain.
10. The color of many ocean fish helps _____ them in the water.

a. bioluminescent
b. photosynthesis
c. plankton
d. camouflage
e. bacteria
f. hydrogen sulfide
g. producers
h. chemosynthesis
i. geothermal energy
j. light

Connecting Ideas

1. Copy the concept map. Use the terms at the right to complete the map about the process of chemosynthesis.

sugars   hydrogen sulfide
carbon dioxide   water

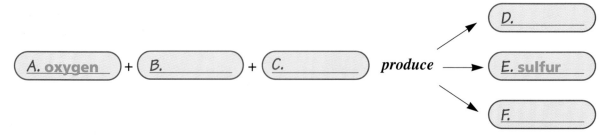

2. Write a sentence or two that summarizes the ideas shown in the concept map.

Interpreting What You Learned

1. Why is a transparent body a useful adaptation for some species that live in water?
2. Why do most marine organisms live in the upper level of the ocean?
3. Why were scientists surprised to find so many organisms in the vent areas of the ocean floor?
4. Explain why temperatures around ocean vents are different from temperatures of other areas of the ocean floor.
5. How did the discovery of the chemosynthetic community of hot-water vents change the hypotheses of many scientists?

Performance Assessment

How can sunlight in ocean water be modeled?

Materials • graduated cup • water • vegetable oil • light corn syrup • food coloring (red, green, and blue) • 2 paper cups • plastic jar • 2 sheets of paper • colored pencils (red, green, and blue) • 3 straws • dropper

Collecting Data

1. Use the graduated cup to measure 100 milliliters of water. Pour the water into one of the cups. Use a dropper to add two drops of green food coloring to the water. Using a straw, gently stir the coloring through the liquid.
2. Pour 100 milliliters of vegetable oil into a second cup. Use a dropper to add two drops of red food coloring to the vegetable oil. Rinse the graduated cup. Using another straw, gently stir the coloring through the liquid.
3. Pour 100 milliliters of corn syrup into the plastic jar. Use a dropper to add two drops of blue food coloring. Using the third straw, gently stir the coloring through the liquid.
4. Roll one sheet of paper into a funnel shape. Hold the end of the funnel against the inside of the jar. Slowly pour the colored water into the funnel so it runs down the inside of the jar. Try not to disturb the layer of colored corn syrup.
5. Make a second paper funnel. Slowly pour the colored vegetable oil into the funnel. Hold the funnel against the inside of the jar. Try not to disturb the other layers of liquid.
6. Use colored pencils to draw a side view of the jar. Color in the different levels of liquid.

Analyzing Data

Compare your colored diagram to the chart showing sunlight in ocean water on page D53. Identify places on your diagram where the colors in the chart that are not shown in your diagram would appear.

Kids, Light, and Color

Young people have been responsible for some interesting inventions that involve light and color. Here are two stories of such inventions.

On a car trip one day, nine-year-old Rebecca Schroeder found that there wasn't enough light for her to see to write. That experience sparked her bright idea—a glow-in-the-dark board to write on.

Rebecca experimented with a type of glowing paint. Soon, she was able to fasten a sheet of special glowing paper into a plastic clipboard. When a piece of plain paper was placed on the clipboard, the paper would glow, making it possible to write in the dark.

The clipboard's glow faded quickly. To improve her invention, Rebecca added a battery to the clipboard. It provided the clipboard with enough power to make the glow last a long time.

When a piece of plain paper was placed on the clipboard, the paper would glow.

Rebecca, now in her mid-20s, has her own "Glow Sheet" business. The company began with a bright idea. But unlike Rebecca's glow sheet, another invention did not come about so easily. In fact, two young people needed about 20 years to perfect the first usable color film.

Early photographers could only take pictures in black and white like those on the next page. A process for producing color film was invented in 1865, but it produced a very blurry picture. By the early 1900s, when the two men to the left— Leo Godowsky and Leo Mannes—were in high school, this process was still the only one around.

Godowsky and Mannes conducted experiments in the school physics lab, trying to come up with a better color process. In 1916, their first efforts just duplicated the existing method. They continued experimenting and soon improved the method enough to patent their version of the process. However, even their improved method still resulted in a fuzzy photograph.

Then Godowsky and Mannes came up with a new approach to color-film photography, using chemicals instead of light. The two Leos thought that if they could layer light-sensitive chemicals on film so that each layer would turn a particular color, they would produce a clear photograph. Early in their research, they almost had to stop because they couldn't afford the chemicals and other materials they needed. Then an investment firm gave them money to pay for their work. At about the same time, Dr. Mees, the director of research at Eastman Kodak, the world's biggest film company, gave them equipment and their needed light-sensitive chemicals.

Besides being interested in physics, Godowsky and Mannes were also musicians. For a few years, their research slowed down while Mannes was studying music in Europe. In 1930, at the invitation of Dr. Mees, Godowsky and Mannes continued their research at the Eastman Kodak laboratory. Even there, the two Leos used their musical talents. Since no electronic timing devices existed in those days, the musician-scientists precisely timed chemical reactions by singing musical passages.

By 1935, Godowsky and Mannes had perfected clear color photography. At a press conference, they displayed the world's first color slides. Afterward, they entertained the audience by playing a violin and piano sonata. In time, this team earned over 40 patents before returning to full-time music careers. They were the talk of the world of photography and the world of music.

On Your Own

Interview a professional photographer. Find out which kinds of photographs she or he prefers to use black and white film for, and which photographs she or he uses color film for.

An Underwater Designer

LeRoy Winbush

Occupation: Underwater photographer, designer
Hobbies: Tennis, bowling, and jazz guitar

Who says life has to follow a straight path—grow up, choose a profession, work at that profession until you retire, and then settle down and take it easy? Not LeRoy Winbush. At an age when most people have retired, Mr. Winbush is busy doing more. One of the many things Mr. Winbush does now is underwater photography.

Mr. Winbush only learned to swim when he was 49 years old. Then he learned skin diving and went on to scuba diving. "Now I'm really hooked on it. Once you're really comfortable underwater, you can start thinking about what you're seeing."

What do you see underwater?
"It depends on where you're diving, whether it's the Caribbean, the Red Sea, or the coast of Mexico. I've been 24 times to Jamaica— it's like a paradise island. In all those places you'll find different kinds of fish. And you'll also see many kinds of coral—finger coral, brain coral, plate coral, stag-horn coral, or fire coral. You have to watch out for fire coral. It causes an infection if you cut your hand on it."

Is there anything special about taking underwater photographs?
"One difference is that the water magnifies objects. But in some ways, it's just like any other photography. I'm a designer, so I use a design approach in my photography. I don't make snapshots. The ocean colors are my palette and the fish are the composition. I'm designing with the elements of the ocean."

Are there dangers in the water?
"Lion fish and stone fish have a venom that can paralyze you. Sea wasps can also paralyze. It's best to wear a wet suit and gloves, and to not touch anything you don't know. You also need to dive with an experienced guide and to always keep the boat's anchor line in sight."

What do you like best about diving?
"Being in the ocean is relaxing. It's floating in inner space, like an astronaut floating in outer space. Suspended in the water, you see a totally different kind of life."

Compound Eyes: Seeing a Daisy

Have you ever tried to swat a fly? Were you successful? Nine chances out of ten, you were not! A fly has thousands of tiny lenses in each of its compound eyes. Each lens captures your slightest motion in every direction.

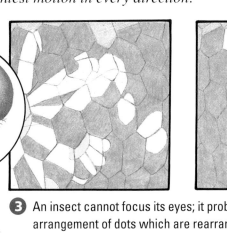

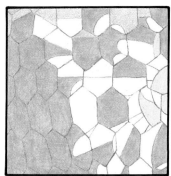

❸ An insect cannot focus its eyes; it probably sees an arrangement of dots which are rearranged by motion. Here, even the slightest movement of the daisy causes a different image to fall on each lens.

❷ Each unit of the eye looks like a cone with a lens at the surface; it narrows down to a nerve fiber that leads to the brain.

❶ An insect's compound eyes look like curved honeycombs, with row after row of six-sided lenses.

Find Out On Your Own

Look at a picture in the newspaper through a magnifier and notice the mosaic of dots. Draw a portion of the picture as "seen through insect eyes."

Module Performance Assessment

Nature Awareness Day

Using what you learned in this module, help prepare exhibitions to be used at a Nature Awareness Day celebration to be held at your school. Complete one or more of the following activities. You may work by yourself or with others in a group.

Art

Make one or more drawings to show several animals camouflaged in their environment. See if your classmates can locate the animals in your drawings.

Biology

Use two identical pieces of elodea with growing tips, two identical large test tubes, a meter stick, and water to compare the rate of growth of plants in dark and light environments. Write a report to summarize your observations.

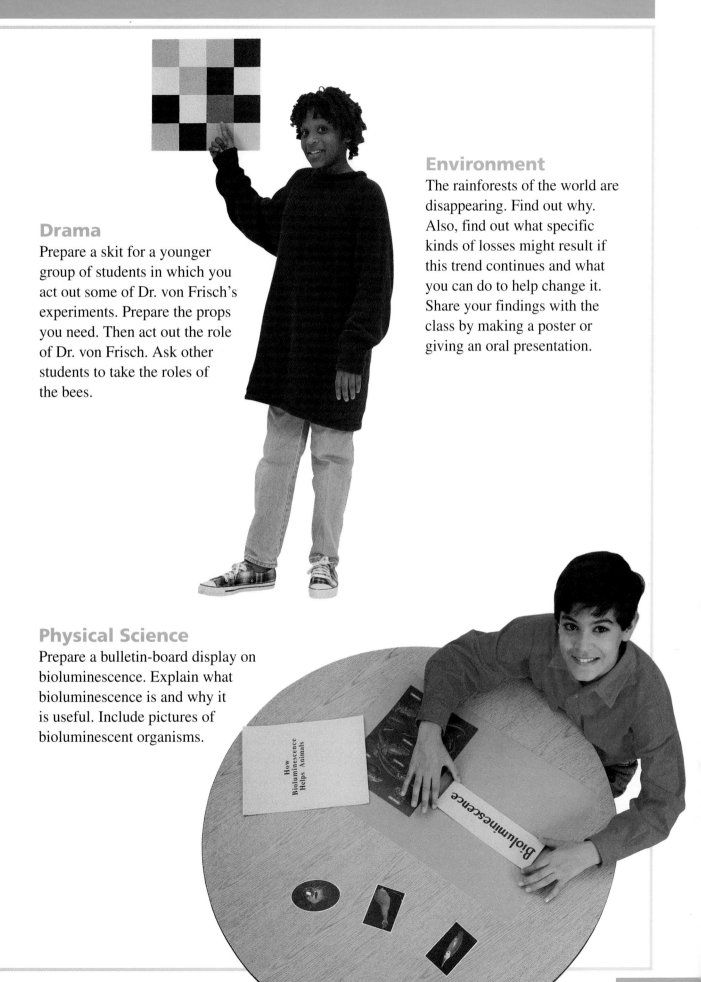

Drama

Prepare a skit for a younger group of students in which you act out some of Dr. von Frisch's experiments. Prepare the props you need. Then act out the role of Dr. von Frisch. Ask other students to take the roles of the bees.

Environment

The rainforests of the world are disappearing. Find out why. Also, find out what specific kinds of losses might result if this trend continues and what you can do to help change it. Share your findings with the class by making a poster or giving an oral presentation.

Physical Science

Prepare a bulletin-board display on bioluminescence. Explain what bioluminescence is and why it is useful. Include pictures of bioluminescent organisms.

How Bioluminescence Helps Animals

Bioluminescence

Module Review

Reviewing Words and Concepts

Write the letter of the word or phrase that best completes each sentence.

1. The spines of a cactus are an example of a _____.
2. Adaptations that control the life processes that aid survival are called _____.
3. The cells of the eye that receive light are _____.
4. An animal eaten by a lion is called _____.
5. An inherited _____ that enables a species to survive in its environment is an adaptation.
6. Chlorophyll is a _____ that gives plants their color.
7. An interaction in which two organisms benefit from each other is called _____.
8. An opossum that plays dead is using a _____.
9. Owls act as _____ when they hunt other animals.
10. Deep ocean fish that create their own light are _____.

a. bioluminescent
b. mutualism
c. trait
d. pigment
e. receptors
f. physiological adaptations
g. predators
h. prey
i. behavioral adaptation
j. structural adaptation

Interpreting What You Learned

1. Why is camouflage an important adaptation among many species?
2. How can environmental changes bring about the existence of new species?
3. How are the eye structures of insects and humans adapted to the lifestyle and environment of each organism?
4. Name an organism that does not rely on the sun as its source of energy. How does this organism get energy?
5. Why does an object with blue pigments appear blue?
6. How are polar bears adapted to absorbing and converting the sun's energy and conserving thermal energy?
7. Why do rainforests and oceans have a greater number of species at their upper levels than at their lower levels?

Applying What You Learned

1. Arrange the following according to how deep they penetrate ocean water: red light, green light, yellow light.
2. Imagine you are a biologist on the crew of the *Alvin* on the first day it investigated hot-water vents. Write a journal entry for that day.
3. Develop a skit to show how light reflected from black and white objects differs.
4. How do colors of arctic organisms in summer compare with their colors in winter?
5. Identify two traits that would lead you to classify a plant as an epiphyte.
6. Explain how Dr. von Frisch knew bees could see shades of blue.

High-Tech, Low-Tech

High-Tech, Low-Tech

What are the most successful modern inventions? Cars? Cameras? Computers? How about sneakers? They're only lowly footwear, but today's sneakers are high-flying examples of modern technology at work. In this module, you'll learn how science and technology work together in systems that bring water to your faucet, electricity to your light switch, and sneakers to your closet.

CHAPTER 2 Turning on the Power

This place is wired! Buildings of all sorts are linked into a vast electrical system of generators, transformers, switches, and wires.

CHAPTER 1 Technology and You

You can tap into technology with a twist of the wrist. Modern water systems deliver clear, pure drinking water right to your tap. They also clean up watery wastes.

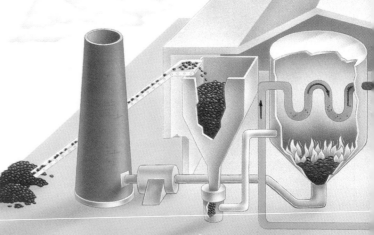

3 Science and Industry

Can you follow the bouncing ball?

Manufacturing sneakers is a complex process that begins with computer-aided design, continues through long assembly lines, and ends in your local shoe store.

In this module

At the end of the book

Technology and You

I think this will do in a pinch . . . get it?

Discover Activity

Of what use is a clothespin?

An important part of technology is using tools and materials in inventive ways. Examine a pinch-type clothespin. How does this tool work? Now look at this tool from a different point of view. How might the clothespin be useful for something other than hanging out the wash? Design a useful tool using one or more clothespins and any other materials you may need.

For Discussion

1. How did you construct your tool?

2. How does your tool work?

1.1 *A Day Without Sneakers*

▶ *How can you get through a day without technology?*

Imagine that one morning you wake up and notice your room is strangely quiet. That's funny, you think, the clock-radio alarm didn't go off. You wonder what happened—it was working last night. Yikes! What time is it? You can't be late for school! You stare at the blank black front of the radio, waiting for the digital display to suddenly flash the green light showing you the time. No help there, you think.

"Lights! I need light!" you say, and fumble for the light switch on the wall. You flip the switch, but nothing happens. Oh, the electricity must have gone off, but that's okay, you think. You figure you can get dressed easily enough in the dark. Actually, it's kind of fun when the power goes out. Maybe you'll get to eat breakfast by candlelight.

You feel your way into the bathroom to wash your face. You yank up on the handle of the bathroom faucet and wait for the sound of splashing water, but you hear only more eerie silence. You touch the opening under the faucet—totally dry. You twist and pull the handle this way and that, but not a drop comes out. This is weird, you think. Can the water be out too? Did I sleep through an earthquake or something?

▲ *What problems might cause no electricity or no running water?*

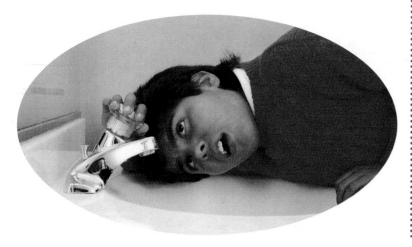

You rush to your closet and throw open the door. Your brand new sneakers—where are they? You left them right here on the floor. Aha, you spot the shoe box. You grab it, tear off the lid, and thrust your hand inside. All you come up with is a fistful of air. "What's going on around here?" you demand. Maybe you can get through a day without water and electricity, but sneakers—that's the last straw! Without sneakers, how can you get help, get to school, or get anywhere?

Surrounded by Technology

Say the word *technology* out loud. Can you almost hear the word "know-how" hidden inside? **Technology** is the know-how that puts the knowledge of science into practice. Science is knowledge of the world around us—both living and nonliving—that tries to explain how and why things happen. On the other hand, technology puts scientific knowledge to work to meet people's needs and wants. Technology depends on scientific knowledge for inventions of new tools, machines, materials, and methods, or ways of doing things. When you found a new use for the clothespin in the Discover Activity, you were putting *your* knowledge to work. Technology results in products or processes that simplify life or make life more enjoyable by making work easier.

A bicycle is a good example of technology. It's a machine that can take you places more easily than walking. Bicycle makers use special materials, such as strong and lightweight metals, to make the parts. They design special tools to build the frame, and they have a special way of putting the pieces together. Bicycle making involves all kinds of technology—tools, machines, materials, and methods.

In fact, almost everything you use is a product of modern technology, which depends greatly on science. Just look around. You've probably heard the word *high-tech*. Maybe that word makes you think of electronic equipment such as computers, compact disc players, cordless telephones, and video cameras. However, much technology has gone into producing the everyday things you use, too. Toothbrushes, pens and pencils, plastic bags, glue, cans and bottles, lamps, clothing, and even this book are products of technology.

◄ *This closet is full of products of technology. Which of these items are high-tech?*

where - does electricity come from.
how - does it work
when - was it invented
what - does it need

▼ *Give an example of how one of these systems depends on another system to work.*

water supply system

electric power supply system

manufacturing system

You were born in the Age of Technology. But life wasn't always the way you know it. Throughout most of human history, indoor toilets, indoor running water, and electrical service were unknown. To get water, people went to a well or river and carried the water home in buckets. For light, people burned oil lamps or candles. A little more than 100 years ago there were no telephones, automobiles, airplanes, refrigerators, light bulbs, televisions, motion pictures, or many of the other items you use every day. And bicycles had barely been invented.

In the past 100 years, an incredibly large number of inventions based on scientific knowledge were developed. Industries that make, or manufacture, these inventions on a large scale were also developed. As technology provided industry with new tools, machines, materials, and methods, technology grew and grew.

Here's an example that shows how technology grows. Suppose you decide to use your knowledge of rechargeable batteries to invent something new and helpful. Let's say it's an invention to light a dangerous mountain road at night. You invent a photoelectric cell that can recharge batteries used to power bright lights. Congratulations! Your invention, the *Super Light Cell,* has added to the technology of the world!

You don't expect your Super Light Cell to be very popular, but now everyone who lives anywhere near the mountains needs your invention. You want a factory to build many thousands of cells. Suddenly you need more technology. Special machines, tools, materials, and methods have to be invented just to make and put together your Super Light Cell. That's how industry multiplies the world's technology!

Systems of Technology

A **system** is a set of parts that work together as a whole. Remember the bicycle? It has a frame, gears, wheels, handlebars, a crank with pedals, brakes, and a seat. The parts work together to get you where you want to go. A system is also a way of doing things, such as the step-by-step assembly of bicycles in a factory.

Once you know what a system is, you can find systems all around you. Remember the imaginary day when you woke up without electricity, water, or sneakers? You had to do without some high-tech systems that you normally depend on—electric power, public water, and manufacturing.

Your faucet is a smaller system called a subsystem. It has parts that work together—a handle, a spigot, and some parts hidden inside. It also connects to a larger system of pipes and a huge facility—the public water supply system.

Your light switch is another subsystem. It's one tiny part of a complex system of electrical technology—the power-supply system that brings electricity to your home. And don't forget your sneakers, which were produced by a manufacturing system. High-tech machines prepared high-tech parts and materials in a high-tech system to make your shoes.

As you can see in the diagram at left, technology is like a giant web surrounding you. Strands of the web connect you with all the tools, machines, and systems that you use and enjoy daily. Other strands connect the tools, machines, and systems with one another. One system often depends on other systems to work. You just can't do without technology, or escape it!

Checkpoint

1. How is technology more than just knowledge of science?
2. Describe how each of the following is a system or subsystem: (a) a faucet (b) a bicycle (c) bicycle production.
3. **Take Action!** Use your knowledge of science to design and build a new machine—the Super Room Cleaner.

1.2 *Piping Water*

Where does your water come from? Where does it go?

Imagine life 100 years ago. You carried water by hand from a nearby river, lake, or spring. You just hoped it was free from anything that might make you sick. Today many more people live on the earth and use more water. But technology brings clean water right to your door.

Piping Fresh Water

Four out of five families in the United States receive water from a public water supply system similar to this one. The system brings water free from harmful bacteria and chemicals to your home. The fifth family draws its water from a private well or spring, which can be just as clean. Many public water supply systems get water from lakes, rivers, or reservoirs. A **reservoir** is an artificial lake that collects and stores water. It's usually in the hills or mountains, fed by a large river, and formed by a dam. Gravity pulls the water downhill toward the city.

▼ *Follow the path of water from the reservoir to the purification plant. Then use the key to trace the steps in water purification.*

Ⓐ Reservoir
Ⓑ Water purification plant
  ❶ Chemicals added
  ❷ Mixing tanks
  ❸ Settling tank
  ❹ Filtration tank

If you live in Chicago, your water comes from Lake Michigan. Offshore, a deep shaft leads to a tunnel under the lake bed. Water fills the shaft and passes through the tunnel toward the water purification plant. There it is cleaned, treated, and tested to make sure it's pure and safe for drinking. Now pretend that you can ride inside a tiny bubble through the water purification plant. Your journey is about to begin!

You pass through the first of four treatment steps—purifying by chemicals. A machine bubbles chlorine compounds through the water. The chlorine disinfects the water by killing harmful microorganisms. Other machines add fluoride, which protects your teeth, and alum. Alum attracts dirt and other particles, forming little globs called flocculence (flok′yə lens), or floc.

Now you pass through the second and third steps in water purification—mixing and settling. You flow up and down through mixing basins, then into a large tank where the water stands still. The floc slowly settles to the bottom, leaving you in a top layer of clear water. Several hours later, you pass into a filtering basin, the fourth step of purification. The water seeps slowly through a large bed of sand and gravel. At last, you're surrounded by crystal clear water.

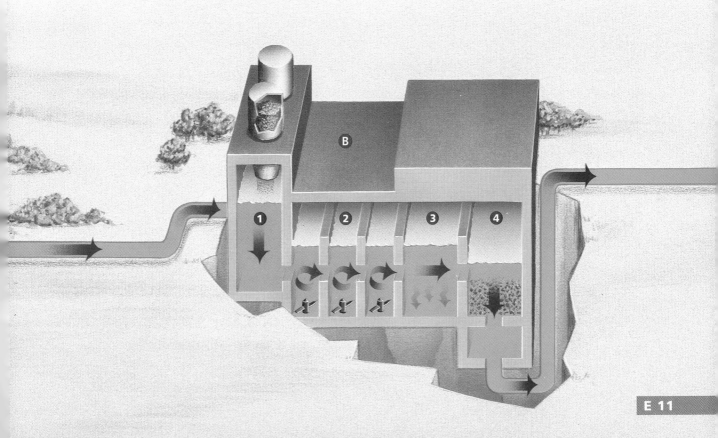

Suddenly you're pulled swiftly into a tunnel and through the pumping station. Huge electric pumps give the water a big push that provides the water pressure to keep the water moving through the city water mains. Water mains are large pipes that run in a maze beneath the streets. You move to a smaller main that branches off to another area of the city. Then you float into a much smaller main that passes near an apartment building. The different sizes of mains help maintain the water pressure until you reach your destination—the faucet! The water pressure pushes you quickly up pipes inside the walls of a house. The water pressure pushes strongly against your bubble and the pipes around you. Will someone *please* turn on the faucet? Relief! Your air bubble gushes through the faucet and into a bathroom sink. Plop!

You've been on quite a journey! Think of all the people in all the large cities in the United States that get their water in this way. They don't need to carry water from the nearest river! And the water contains no disease-causing bacteria. People can get a tall, cool glass of clean water whenever they want it.

▼ *Follow the path of water from the pumping station to the sewage treatment plant. Then use the key to trace the steps in sewage treatment.*

© Pumping station
Ⓓ Sewage treatment plant
   ❶ Screen house
   ❷ Settling tanks
   ❸ Sludge tanks
   ❹ Air and bacteria tanks
   ❺ Settling tanks

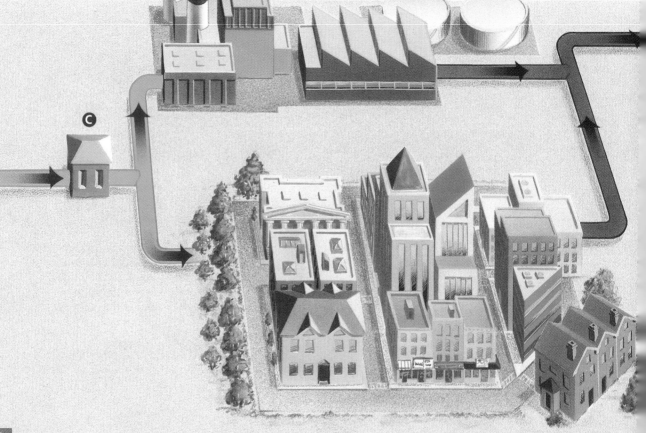

Removing Waste Water

Most of the water you use goes down the drain with other wastes. Ever wonder where it goes? It might enter a septic tank, but in many homes each sink, toilet, bathtub, and shower connects to a drain pipe, or sewer. The mixed water and waste, called sewage, drains into a larger system—the sewage system. The mixture then passes to a sewage treatment plant for cleaning.

Touch each step of the diagram as you follow the main steps of sewage treatment. First, sewage passes through large screens that trap branches, rags, and other solid wastes. The rest slips easily through into a large settling tank. About half the solids slowly settle, forming a thick sludge. Pumps draw the sludge into tanks where, over a few months, bacteria digest it. Meanwhile, partly clean sewage enters the next tank for mixing with air and helpful bacteria. The more air, the faster these bacteria break down harmful wastes into harmless particles. In the next tank, tiny particles settle to the bottom. The nearly clean water passes through a filter, and chlorine kills any remaining harmful bacteria. Then the cleaned water is piped into a waterway.

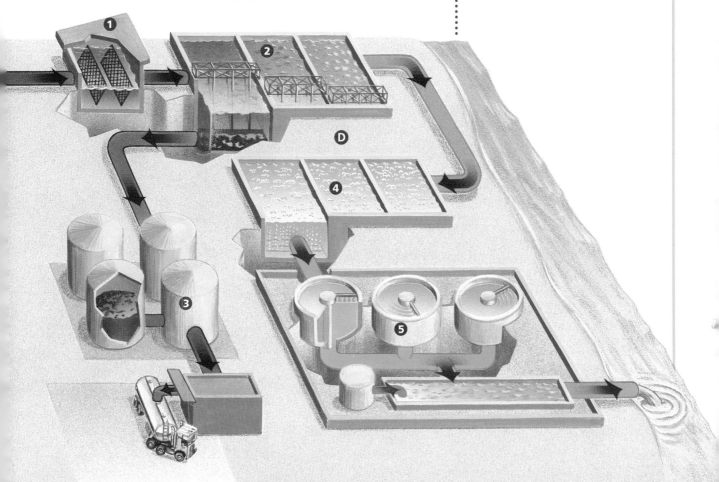

Hidden Pipes

A plumbing system supplies hot and cold water and gets rid of wastes.

Inside the walls of a house or an apartment building, water moves through a system of pipes, valves, and drains.

Water mains carry cold, clean water under the streets. Smaller pipes connect the water mains to individual houses and apartment buildings.

Inside the walls, the water moves through a system of pipes. Some pipes deliver water directly to cold-water taps. Other pipes carry water into a tank to be heated and then carried to hot-water taps.

After water is used, it flows into drain and sewer pipes. These pipes carry the waste water back to the public sewage treatment plant.

One empty pipe, called a vent, leads from the drain pipes up through the roof. The vent allows sewer gases and odors to escape, preventing the gas from building up in the pipes.

1. Water main
2. Sewer pipe
3. Water heater
4. Hot-water pipe
5. Cold-water pipe
6. Drain pipe
7. Faucet
8. Vent

► *A faucet is a subsystem of the plumbing system in a bathroom.*

▼ *Study the parts of a single-handle faucet. Then follow the path of water through the system.*

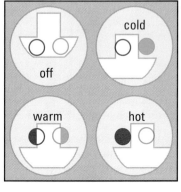

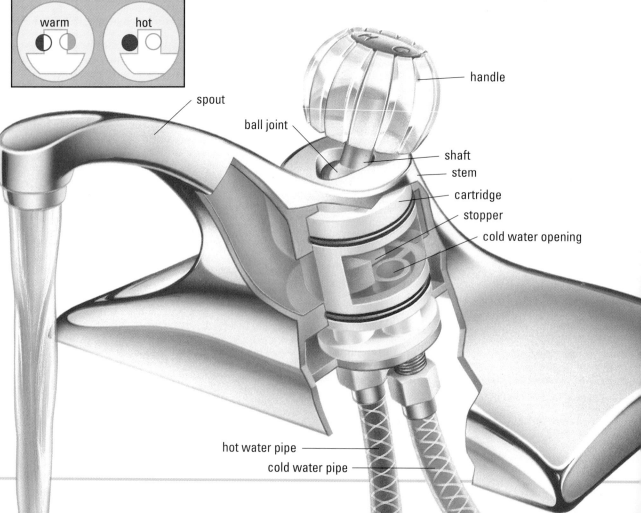

spout

handle

ball joint

shaft

stem

cartridge

stopper

cold water opening

hot water pipe

cold water pipe

Inside a Water Faucet

After traveling from the reservoir to the pipes in your home, water finally reaches your faucet, which does several important things. Your faucet lets you turn on hot or cold water. It lets you mix cold and hot water to make warm water. And it lets you shut off the water so it doesn't flood your house. Remember those pumps and all that water pressure! Your faucet is a subsystem of that greater water system. It marks the end of the water supply system and the start of the sewage system.

A faucet is a subsystem of technology with many parts that work together. Look at the faucet in the drawing. The parts you normally see include a handle, a stem, and a spout. Find the cartridge hidden inside the stem. It contains parts that turn the water on and off and control the water temperature. Notice that the handle connects to a stopper by a shaft and a ball joint. The ball joint allows the shaft to move back and forth and sideways within an opening shaped like a triangle.

When you pull the handle forward, the stopper covers two holes—one for hot water and one for cold water. No water flows out of the spout. Move the handle to the left, and the stopper covers the cold water hole. Only hot water flows through. In the drawing, the handle is moved to the right. Which hole is covered? What is the temperature of the water flowing out of the spout? But how do you get warm water to wash your hands? Move the handle to a center position so that the stopper partially covers both holes. Cold and hot water mix and warm water flows out of the spout and onto your hands.

Into The Field

How does a toilet work?

Ask an adult to help you remove the top of a toilet tank cover. Flush the toilet. Observe what happens to the water in the tank. Record what you find out.

Checkpoint

1. What are the four most common steps in purifying a public water supply?
2. How are bacteria used in sewage treatment?
3. What kinds of pipes make up the plumbing system of a building?
4. How do the parts of a single-handle faucet work to let water flow through?
5. **Take Action!** Build a model of a public water supply system.

1.3 *Underground and Far Away*

A Pumping station
B Chemicals
C Water table
D Aquifer
E Water main
F Water tower
G Sewage pipe

▼ *The water storage tower below holds almost 2 million liters. Water storage towers are part of most small town water systems.*

▶ **What systems do other people use for getting water?**

Millions of people live in areas, such as the Great Plains, that have little rainfall and few rivers or lakes. And sometimes the lakes or rivers are too small to serve the number of people who live nearby. How do these people get the water they need? How are their water supply systems different?

Pumping Groundwater

If you live in a town or small city, your water supply probably comes from groundwater. In fact, groundwater supplies the water systems in many communities in the United States. Groundwater comes mostly from rain that soaks into the earth. It seeps down until it hits a layer of rock that doesn't let the water through. Water collects there, soaking into soil layers and a zone of porous rock called an aquifer. The top of this underground water is called the water table, and its depth varies. In some areas, the water table lies near the surface. But in other areas, it may lie 1 kilometer below the surface! The amount of rainfall in an area can cause the water table to rise and fall.

Groundwater systems like this one differ from the reservoir system you just learned about in three ways. First, wells are drilled below the ground into the water table. Pumps bring the water to the surface. Second, the water is pumped up into a water tower. You might have seen these towers before, especially in the Midwest. A water tower is a tall structure that stores water. It's like an "in-town" reservoir. You might wonder why anyone would go to all the trouble of lifting the water so high. Remember, *something* has to push the water through the water mains and out your faucet. Instead of a pumping station, the force of gravity pulls the water downward out of the tower and provides the water pressure needed to deliver the water to your faucet.

Third, the purification system usually is simpler because groundwater usually is cleaner than lake or river water. Soil and sand layers are a natural filter, so dirt particles are left behind as water seeps through the layers. Many harmful bacteria can't live in the dark and nearly airless aquifer. So most towns using groundwater just add chlorine to kill the few bacteria that survive in the water. The sewage systems in towns and small cities are usually similar to those in larger cities. Waste water drains into public sewers and the sewage is cleaned at a sewage treatment plant.

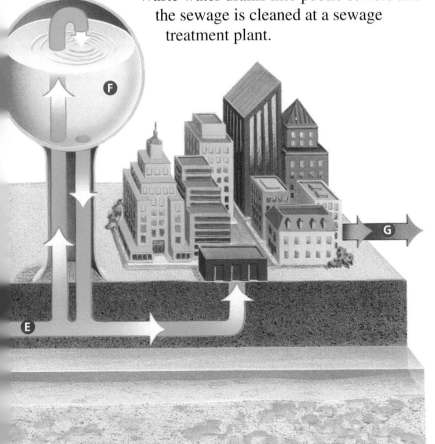

Water Watch

In parts of the United States, water shortages may occur at certain times of the year. During a water shortage, laws may require people to cut back on the amount of water they use every day. Some experts believe that unless everyone starts to conserve daily water usage, people may not have enough water in the future.

According to one survey, the average American uses 380 liters each day. The chart shows about how much water is used for certain everyday activities.

Activity	Normal Water Usage Per Person (Liters)
Showering	95
Brushing teeth (with tap running)	38
Tub bathing	136
Dishwashing (by hand or machine)	114
Washing hands	8
Flushing toilet	23
Washing clothes	227

What Did You Find Out?
1. *Based on the data in the chart, how much water do you use each day?*
2. *Do you use more or less water than the average American?*
3. *Suppose your community had a water shortage. You must cut back on daily water usage by 10%. Calculate how much water you must save each day.*

Oroville reservoir

Aqueduct

Edmunton pumping station

California's Water System

Suppose you live near Los Angeles, California. When you turn on your faucet, the water you use has traveled hundreds of kilometers. Why? The Los Angeles area is desertlike and has no lakes of any size. Its rivers are dry much of the year. And the groundwater supply is far too small for the number of people. Seventy percent of all water use in California is south of Sacramento, while seventy percent of the state's water is north of it. How would you get water to the people who use it?

In fact, water is piped from one end of the state to the other. California's water system includes around 1200 dams and reservoirs and about 5120 kilometers of aqueducts (ak′wə dukts), a kind of "ancient technology." An **aqueduct** is a large pipe or channel that carries water a long distance. The first aqueduct may have been built in the Middle East. The people of Athens built one in about 500 B.C. A few centuries later aqueducts carried water to the city of Rome!

In California, aqueducts carry water from reservoirs in the mountains. Gravity provides part of the force to push the water through the aqueducts. The system also has 20 pumping stations, including one that pushes water 610 meters over the Tehachapi Mountains!

Many California coastal cities use groundwater. But the supply isn't large enough. Some coastal cities have turned to **desalination** (dē sal′ə nā′shən), a process that removes salt from ocean water to make fresh water. A new desalination plant in Santa Barbara can provide over 12 billion liters of water a year. However, desalination is costly. Desalinated water from the Santa Barbara plant costs almost 50 times more than the same amount of water from a reservoir. Scientists are working to develop technology that will lower the cost.

◄ Locate the dams, reservoirs, and aqueducts that are part of California's water supply system. How is Los Angeles's water supply system different from Chicago's?

Checkpoint

1. How does a groundwater system get water from an aquifer?
2. How is California's water carried over long distances?
3. **Take Action!** Design and carry out an experiment to desalinate salt water.

Activity

Under Pressure

Water can have a great deal of "pushing power." How does water pressure affect how fast and how far a stream of water will leak from holes in a container of water?

Picture A

Picture B

Picture C

Gather These Materials

cover goggles   masking tape
three 2-liter milk cartons   water
scissors   tray
pencil   meter stick

Follow This Procedure

1 Make a chart like the one on the next page. Record your observations in the chart.

2 Put on your cover goggles.

3 Cut the top and bottom off 2 milk cartons. Cut only the top off the third carton. (Picture A)

4 Use a pencil to poke 3 holes, spaced equally apart, down the sides of the third carton. (Picture B) Cover the 3 holes with tape.

5 Fill the milk carton with water. Set the filled carton near one end of the tray.

6 Remove the tape from one of the holes. Measure the initial distance the stream travels and record. (Picture C)

7 Tape this hole again, refill the carton, and repeat the procedure for each of the remaining 2 holes. Record your findings in the chart.

8 Place one of the milk cartons with both ends removed inside the top edge of the milk carton containing the holes. Overlap the cartons by about 2 cm. Tape the cartons together.

Record Your Results

Hole position	Distance water travels with		
	1 carton	2 cartons	3 cartons
Top			
Middle			
Bottom			

Predict: *How far will the water stream travel compared to when you used 1 carton?*

9 Fill the stacked cartons and measure the initial distance the water travels from each hole. Be sure to fill the stacked carton to the top for each trial.

10 Add a third milk carton to the stacked cartons. Tape it securely. Fill the cartons with water. Measure the initial distance the water travels from each of the holes.

State Your Conclusions

1. How does the height of the water column affect the initial distance the water travels?

2. How is the height of the water column related to water pressure?

3. How might you go about getting the water to shoot out of the hole even farther?

Let's Experiment

Use what you know about scientific methods to determine whether the height of the cartons or the diameter of the cartons has a greater effect on the distance the stream of water travels.

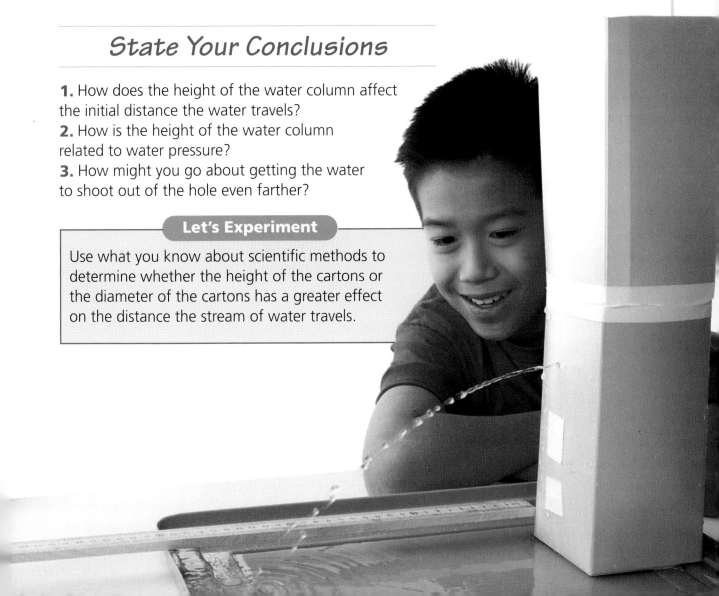

1.4 *To Drink or Not to Drink*

▶ *Does technology make water safe to drink?*

Recall that cities add chlorine to drinking water to kill disease-causing bacteria. But back in the early 1800s that didn't happen. Many people died of diseases such as typhoid, cholera, and dysentery. At that time, the rivers, lakes, oceans, and streams were used freely as dumps for human, farm, and industry wastes.

In the mid-1800s, scientists discovered bacteria, and learned that many bacteria carried by water caused diseases. Communities realized that diseases were being spread when sewage mixed with the water supply. As a first step toward preventing this harmful mixing, communities began filtering their water. By the 1900s, cities began to test water supplies, but still found harmful bacteria. Finally, in the 1930s, many communities began adding chlorine to their water supply to kill harmful bacteria.

Today, most communities rely on chlorine and filtering to purify their water. However, even these careful steps do not remove certain harmful chemicals dissolved in the water. Some water supplies have become polluted with these chemicals, mostly through human activities.

▼ *When water pressure is too low, only a trickle of water may flow from a faucet.*

Water Pressure Problems

Besides pollution, the growing population has led to overuse of the water supply. Farms and ranches use great amounts of water for irrigation when producing food for the growing number of people. In homes, washing machines, dishwashers, and lawn sprinklers use large amounts of water. Some industries also use huge amounts of water as they produce the things you use every day.

Sometimes the demand for water becomes larger than the supply. This situation can happen when many people suddenly use water at the same time. On the first hot weekend of June, 1988, thousands of people in Oak Brook, Illinois, began washing cars, filling swimming pools, and watering lawns. Normally the town uses 16 million liters of water a day. On that weekend, the demand jumped to 36 million liters a day and drained the town's three storage tanks nearly dry!

When people use more water than the system can supply, the amount of water in the pipes falls and the water pressure drops. In 1977, a fire raged in Sycamore Canyon near Santa Barbara, California. People there began watering their roofs, trying to protect their homes from flying embers. When firefighters arrived and hooked their hoses up to nearby hydrants, no water came out because the water pressure had dropped drastically.

In a drought, demand may use up stored supplies. The water table can fall, and reservoirs can dry up. The drought of 1988 caused water shortages in many parts of the country. In much of the West, the drought continued until 1992. Many communities asked people to cut back on water use. Some towns passed laws against watering lawns, and green lawns turned brown. In 1991, Goleta, California, ran so short of water that it decided to buy water, shipped in ocean tankers, from Canada. In a drought, people must learn to conserve, or save, water.

▲ The top picture shows children playing in an open fire hydrant on a hot day. The second picture shows firefighters controlling a fire. How do these activities cause water pressure problems?

Pollution Flows

Factory, farm, and home wastes can enter water supplies.

What do you think is responsible for water pollution? Are factories responsible? Factories bury wastes produced in manufacturing. But can these wastes get into water supplies?

Are farmers responsible for water pollution? Farmers spread chemicals on their land to produce your food. But can these chemicals get into the water supplies?

Are *you* responsible for water pollution? People use chemicals in their homes and gardens. But how can these chemicals get into water supplies?

As a matter of fact *everyone* is responsible for water pollution. Farms, factories, and homes use chemicals that can find their way into water supplies. But how do these chemicals get into water? To answer this question, you need to learn about pathways by which chemicals find their way into the water supply system.

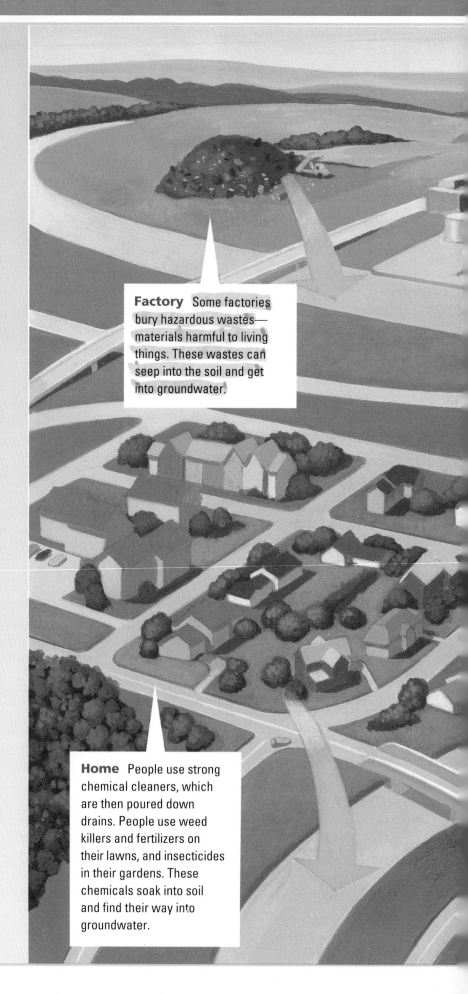

Factory Some factories bury hazardous wastes—materials harmful to living things. These wastes can seep into the soil and get into groundwater.

Home People use strong chemical cleaners, which are then poured down drains. People use weed killers and fertilizers on their lawns, and insecticides in their gardens. These chemicals soak into soil and find their way into groundwater.

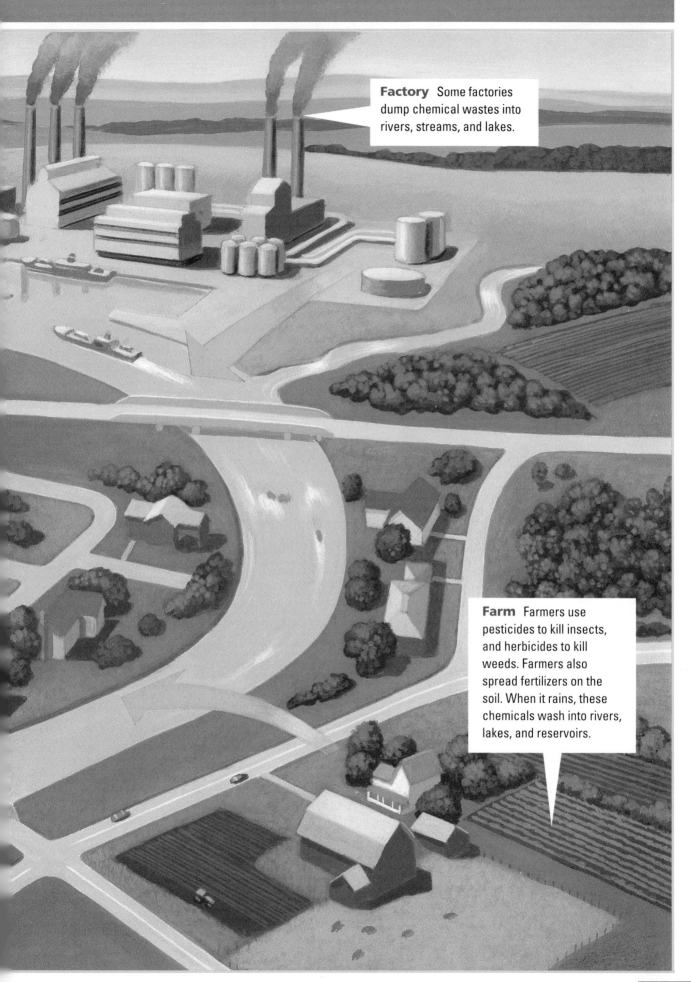

Factory Some factories dump chemical wastes into rivers, streams, and lakes.

Farm Farmers use pesticides to kill insects, and herbicides to kill weeds. Farmers also spread fertilizers on the soil. When it rains, these chemicals wash into rivers, lakes, and reservoirs.

What steps are taken to make sure that this drinking water is free of harmful bacteria?

Protecting Water Supplies

Does the water bubbling from this fountain look cool, clean, and refreshing? Like most people, you're used to going to a faucet or a drinking fountain whenever you're thirsty. You probably don't think about whether or not the water is safe. Actually, the United States has very safe water supplies. But sometimes problems can happen.

You already know how most communities purify water. But in recent years, water testing shows that some kinds of harmful chemicals have entered water supplies. And chlorine and filtering alone cannot remove these substances. Drinking or breathing even tiny amounts of the chemicals can harm you.

One dangerous chemical found in water supplies is TCE, which causes cancer. TCE is an ingredient in degreasing products. You may have seen someone use such a spray or dip to clean grease from oily engines or parts. These wastes seep into the groundwater along with the rain. Laws now control the release of TCE and other hazardous wastes from industry. Unfortunately, TCE is now widespread in the groundwater supply.

Another dangerous group of chemicals, THMs, come from chlorine. In fact, the same system that protects you from disease creates this problem. When chlorine is added to water at the purification plant, it breaks down into THMs. One type of THM is called chloroform. Breathing chloroform can cause cancer.

The United States government has regulations that control the amounts of many potentially dangerous chemicals in drinking water. These regulations set maximum contaminant levels (MCLs). MCLs are the maximum amounts of these chemicals permitted in drinking water. The MCLs are based on knowledge about health problems that may result if higher amounts of these chemicals are present. The MCLs and health problems caused by certain metals are listed in the chart. Your water company tests drinking water to make sure that the amounts of these and other chemicals do not go above the MCLs.

Scientists are developing new technologies to remove TCE, chloroform, metals, and other chemicals from the water supply. Complex filters, such as those made of activated carbon, can remove materials such as chloroform. But adding new filtration systems to city water purification plants is costly. The best solution is to keep harmful chemicals out of landfills, waste water, and water supplies—it costs much less in the long run!

Metal	MCL (in mg of metal / L of water)	Organ or system affected by the metal
Arsenic	0.050	1,4,5
Barium	1.000	3
Cadmium	0.010	5
Chromium	0.050	2,4,5
Copper	0.200	4
Lead	0.050	1,5
Mercury	0.002	1,5

❶ Brain and Nerves   ❸ Heart   ❺ Kidneys
❷ Lungs   ❹ Liver

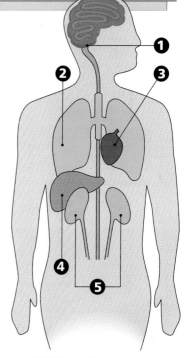

▲ Some of the metals found in water supplies are listed in the chart. What parts of the body would be affected by unsafe amounts of these metals in drinking water?

Checkpoint

1. How can water usage cause water pressure to fall?
2. Describe two ways that pollutants can get into water supplies.
3. What is an MCL, and what do MCLs tell about the purity of drinking water supplies?
4. **Take Action!** Imagine that your town discovers dangerous chemicals in your drinking water. Organize a mock town meeting in your classroom and debate solutions to the problem.

Activity

Is Dilution a Solution to Water Pollution?

When small amounts of chemicals are dissolved in large bodies of water, the water is a dilute solution. When harmful chemicals are diluted in water, do they disappear?

Picture A

Picture B

Picture C

Gather These Materials

6 plastic cups
100 mL graduated cylinder
water

food coloring
dropper
spoon

Follow This Procedure

1 Make a chart like the one on the next page. Record your observations in the chart.

2 Number the plastic cups by writing the numbers 1 through 6 on the outside of each cup. (Picture A)

3 Use the graduated cylinder to place 100 mL of water into cup 1 and 50 mL of water into each of cups 2–6.

4 Add 1 drop of food coloring to cup 1. (Picture B) This represents the pollutant. Use the spoon to mix well.

5 Place 50 mL of the "polluted water" from cup 1 into cup 2. Remember to use the graduated cylinder when measuring liquids. Mix well. Is this water a lot less polluted?

Predict: *How dark will the color be in cups 3 through 6 if you repeat the procedure?*

6 Now add 50 mL of the polluted water from cup 2 into cup 3. Mix well. Is this water still polluted or does it look clean?

7 Repeat the procedure for cups 4–6.

8 Place the cups on a sheet of white paper. Observe the color of the solution in each cup.

9 Record the color of the solution in each cup.

State Your Conclusions

1. Were there any signs that the pollution still remained after it was watered down so many times?

2. How many times do you think the polluted water in cup 1 would need to be diluted so the color of pollution could no longer be seen?

3. Do you think that dilution is a good way to deal with pollution?

Record Your Results

Cup number	Description of color

Let's Experiment

Use what you know about scientific methods to determine whether filtering water can be used to remove dissolved pollutants.

Chapter Review

Reviewing Words and Concepts

Write the letter of the word or phrase that best completes each sentence.

1. A faucet is a ____ of the plumbing system in a house.
2. A large pipe or channel that carries water a long distance is an ____.
3. A set of parts that work together as a whole is a ____.
4. When alum is added to water, it causes globs called ____ to form.
5. Science put to use is ____.
6. Fertilizers and pesticides that enter water cause ____.
7. A ____ is an artificial lake that collects and stores water.
8. The purification process for ____ is simpler than for lake or river water.
9. The top of a layer of groundwater is the ____.
10. The removal of salt from ocean water to make fresh water is ____.

a. pollution
b. water table
c. desalination
d. flocculence
e. technology
f. aqueduct
g. reservoir
h. subsystem
i. groundwater
j. system

Connecting Ideas

1. Copy the concept map. Use the terms at the right to complete the map about water.

water purification plant
sewage treatment plant
reservoir
waterway

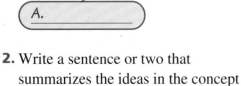
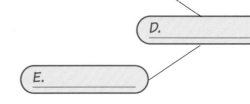

2. Write a sentence or two that summarizes the ideas in the concept map.

Interpreting What You Learned

1. Explain why understanding water pressure is science, but building a shower is technology.
2. List three items in your school that are part of the water-supply system.
3. State the purpose of each of these chemicals in water: chlorine, fluoride, and alum.
4. What happens to water when it goes down the drain?
5. Why would a city need to be near an ocean to benefit from desalination?
6. What are two things that might cause low water pressure?
7. Describe activities in your home that might cause water pollution.

Performance Assessment

How can an aqueduct be modeled?

Materials • cover goggles • 2 long cardboard tubes • scissors • tape • water • graduated cup • plastic bowl • 6 thick books

Collecting Data

1. Put on your cover goggles. Use scissors to cut each cardboard tube in half lengthwise.
2. Lay the cut cardboard tubes end to end. At the places where two tubes meet, overlap the tubes slightly. Use tape to fasten the tubes together. The taped tubes represent an aqueduct.
3. Fill a graduated cup with 200 milliliters of water.
4. Place one end of the aqueduct you made so it rests on top of the opening of a bowl. Place the other end of the aqueduct on top of a stack of books so that the aqueduct slopes downward.
5. Slowly pour the water from the graduated cup into the highest end of the aqueduct. Continue pouring water until the cup is empty.
6. Carefully pour the water you collected in the bowl back into the graduated cup. Measure the amount of water collected and record this amount. Compare the amount of water collected to the amount you started with.

Analyzing Data

How is the model you built like a real aqueduct? How is it different from an aqueduct?

Turning On The Power

Hey, look at this. I've got 10 paper clips already!

Wear cover goggles for this activity.

Discover Activity

Can you make a stronger electromagnet?

Remove about one centimeter of the insulation from each end of some insulated copper wire. Wind the wire around a nail. Connect the ends of the wire to the battery holder. Then put the battery in the holder. See how many paper clips you can pick up with the nail. Find out what you can do to your electromagnet to pick up even more paper clips. Be sure to wear your cover goggles.

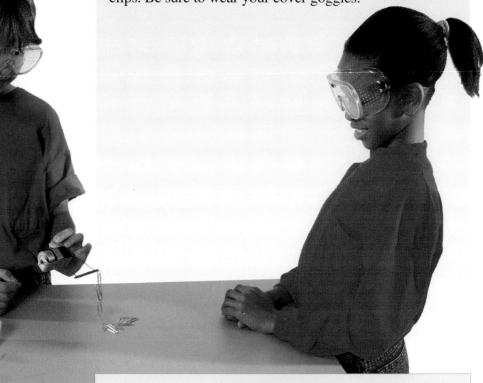

For Discussion

1. How does the size of the nail affect the magnet?
2. How does the length of the wire affect the magnet?

2.1 *Charged Up!*

What do you know about electricity?

Try listing ten things you use daily that run on electricity. If you could not use any of these things for one week, how would you get along? You can see how important electricity is to you. But what *is* electricity? Electricity is a form of energy. Electricity results from the flow of electrons in a wire or other conductor. You may remember that electrons are tiny negative particles in an atom. In certain substances, like copper wire, electrons flow easily. This flow of charged particles is electric current. The electric current flowing through wires lights lamps and runs your blow dryer and other appliances.

People didn't always depend on electricity. For thousands of years people lit candles or built fires to get light. They made clothes and furniture by hand. Only in the past few hundred years did scientists make discoveries about electricity and how it works. These discoveries led to a supply of electricity to light cities, run factories, and make possible watching television!

In 1820, Danish scientist Hans Oërsted discovered that if electric current flows through a wire, it can move a nearby compass needle. Oërsted's finding showed that electric currents generate magnetic fields. When you did the Discover Activity, you observed how this happens. About ten years later, the English scientist Michael Faraday and the American scientist Joseph Henry each showed that a magnet can be used to produce electric current. By moving a magnet around and through a loop of wire, they produced electric current in the wire loop. They also produced current by moving the wire instead of the magnet. At first, people didn't know what to do with this knowledge. But without this discovery, life would be very different.

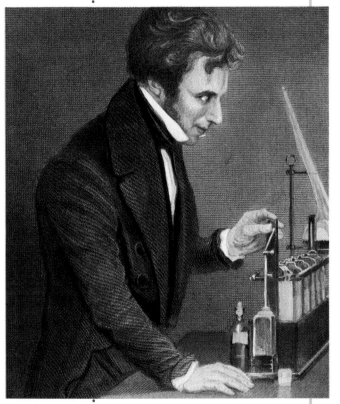

▲ *Michael Faraday at work in his laboratory*

➤ *Study the picture of the inside of this generator. Compare the picture to the diagram to learn how a bicycle generator works.*

Producing Electricity

The discovery that magnetism can produce an electric current led to the invention of the generator (jən′ ə rā′ tər). A **generator** is a machine that uses a magnet to change mechanical energy, or motion, into electrical energy. In Faraday's and Henry's experiments, the movement of a wire near a magnet—mechanical energy—produced an electric current in the wire.

You might wonder how magnets produce electricity. If you have ever used a magnet, you know that a magnetic field surrounds a magnet. Try sliding a paper clip toward a magnet. As the paper clip passes into the magnetic field, the clip is pulled toward the magnet.

A generator magnet also has a magnetic field. In a generator, a wire coil passes into the magnet's magnetic field. The magnetic field forces electrons to move, or flow, through the wire coil.

A bicycle generator, like the one shown, is a simple generator. It changes mechanical energy to electrical energy to power the lamp on this bicycle. When you pedal, your legs turn a crank and some gears. This mechanical energy turns the wheels. Turning the wheel rotates a magnet in the generator next to the wheel. Coils of wire surround, but do not touch, the magnet. When the magnet rotates within the coils, electrons flow through the wires to a filament inside the lamp. Resistance to this flow heats the filament, and the lamp lights.

A bicycle generator can fit in your hand and generates just enough electricity to light the lamp. The electricity that lights your home is produced in a similar way by a huge generator at an electric power plant. This generator may be 9 meters across and 9 meters long—as big as some houses—and provides enormous amounts of electricity for homes and businesses.

Like a bicycle generator, most power plant generators have a magnet that spins inside a coil of wire, but the magnet and coil are huge. The coil contains hundreds of windings of wire. The more windings, the more current the generator can produce. In some power plant generators, the wire coil itself spins between two large magnets that form the field. The result is the same—electric current.

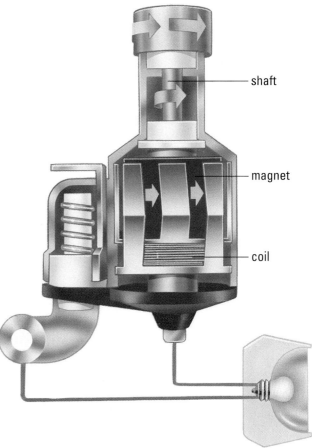

shaft

magnet

coil

Characteristics of electricity are measured in several ways. The force that causes electrons to move through a wire is **voltage.** Voltage is measured in units called volts. The amount of current that flows through a wire is measured in amperes, or amps. One amp is a certain number of electrons that move past a point in one second. The amount of energy given up every second by a current is called power. Power is measured in watts. If one volt is required to push one amp through a wire, the power would equal one watt.

A bicycle lamp often has a three-watt bulb. When you pedal a bicycle, you and the bicycle generator produce enough watts to light the bulb. But a power plant generator may produce over 500 megawatts—500 million watts—of power. That's enough power to light 166 million three-watt bicycle lamps. And each power plant might have four or more such generators!

Most houses and apartment buildings have an electric meter that measures the amount of energy a family uses. The meter measures kilowatt-hours—the amount of energy supplied in one hour by one kilowatt of power. A kilowatt is equal to 1000 watts. Electric companies use the meter readings to charge their customers for each kilowatt-hour used.

▼ *Follow the path of water as it flows through a hydroelectric power plant.*

Ⓐ Dam
Ⓑ Hydroelectric power plant
  ❶ Generator
  ❷ Turbine

Ⓐ

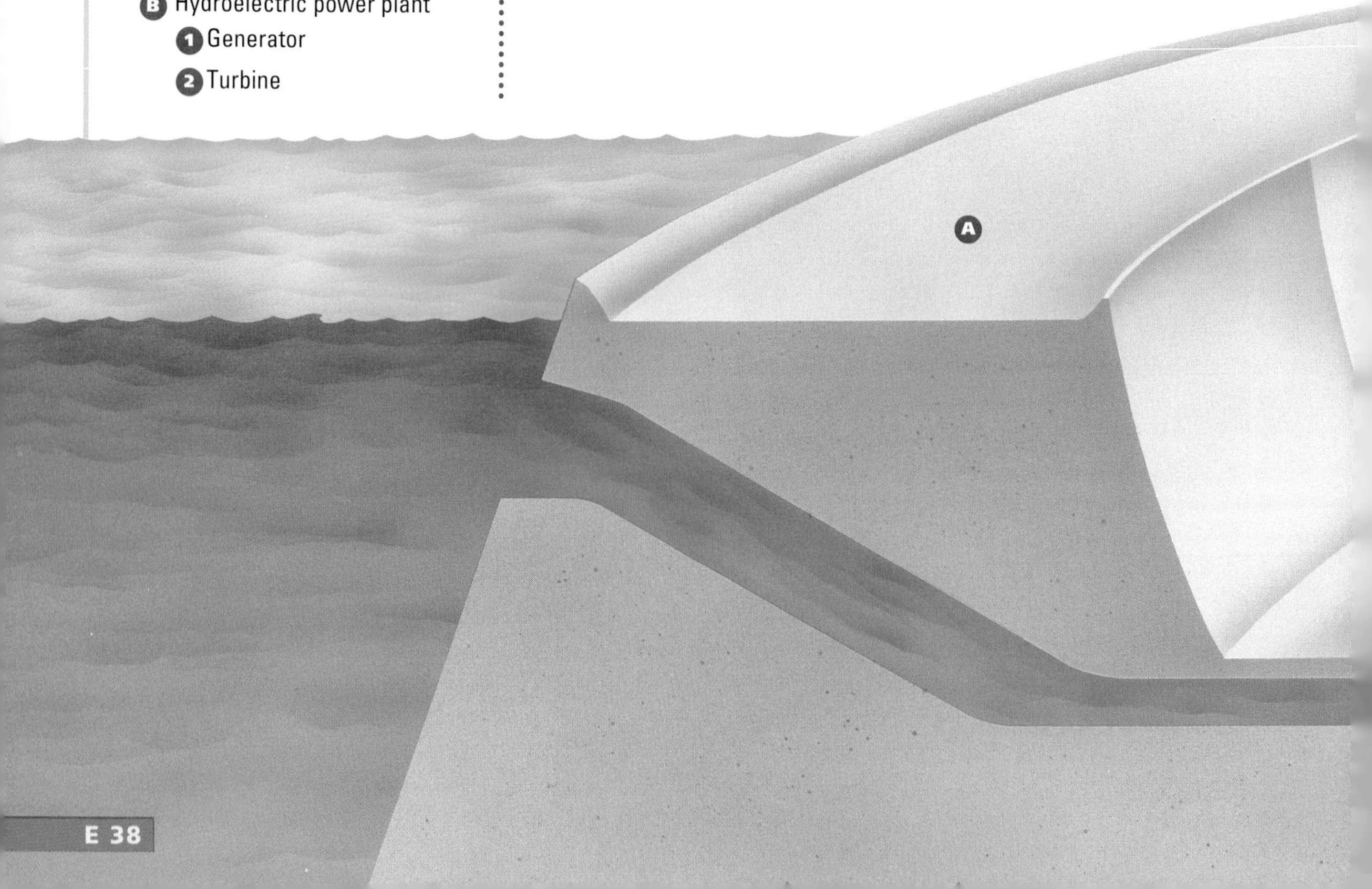

Electric Power from Falling Water

Some power plants are built next to a river. Others, like the one below, are built into a dam that forms a reservoir. Others are built next to a waterfall. These hydroelectric power plants use the mechanical energy of falling water to generate electricity.

Remember that a bicycle generator depends on your legs giving a push of mechanical energy to the wheel. In a hydroelectric plant, falling water gives a mechanical push to the blades of a giant turbine. A **turbine** (tėr′ bən) is a machine that can be turned by flowing gas or liquid. A pinwheel is a kind of turbine. What happens when you hold a pinwheel up to the wind? The flowing air, or wind, pushes the blades of the pinwheel, making the pinwheel spin. In the same way, the falling water pushes the blades of a water turbine, making the turbine spin. A turbine may measure 22 meters across—about six or seven times the size of your bedroom!

A rod connects the turbine blades to the enormous magnet inside the generator. As the turbine rotates, the magnet spins, producing electric current in the coil. The current flows out of the power plant through thick wires.

▼ *Inside view of a power plant generator*

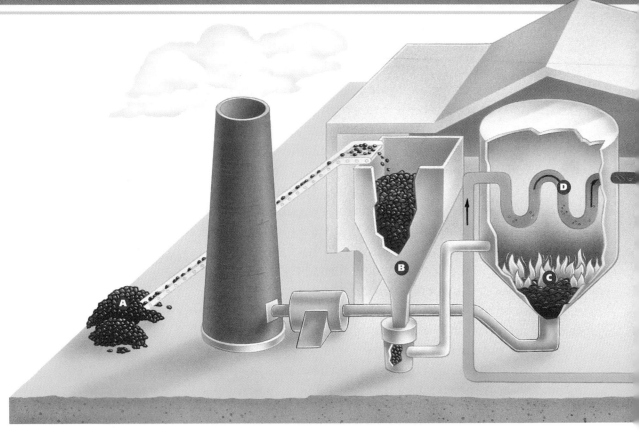

▲ Study the diagram to
learn how electricity is
generated in a coal-burning
power plant.

Ⓐ Pile of coal
Ⓑ Grinder
Ⓒ Furnace
Ⓓ Steam
Ⓔ Turbine
Ⓕ Generator
Ⓖ Condenser
Ⓗ Hot water
Ⓘ Cool water
Ⓙ Air
Ⓚ Cooling tower

Electric Power from Fuels

Many power plants use fuels, instead of falling water, to generate electricity. Some power plants use nuclear fuels. But most power plants burn fossil fuels—coal, oil, or natural gas. Both fossil fuel and nuclear power plants use heat energy to produce steam. The moving steam gives the mechanical push to the turbine, which turns the magnet inside the generator.

What's it like inside this coal-burning power plant? Follow the coal as it enters the power plant on a conveyor belt. First, a grinder smashes the coal into dust and a fan blows the dust into a furnace, where it is burned. Smoke from the burning coal goes into the air through a smokestack. Heat from the burning coal changes water into steam, which is piped to a turbine. The steam pushes the turbine's blades, which spin the generator magnet. Now follow the steam to the condenser. There, cold water in pipes cools and condenses the steam to liquid water. The liquid water is recycled to the furnace. Notice that the condenser pipes absorb heat from steam. Pipes carry this hot water to a cooling tower, where the water is sprayed out and cooled by air flowing into the tower. Cool water collects at the bottom and is recycled in the condenser or released into a river or lake.

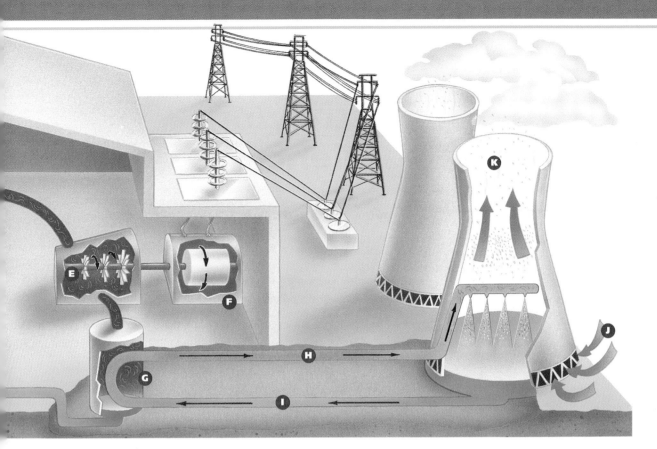

Like coal-burning plants, nuclear power plants produce steam to drive turbines that turn the generator magnets. But nuclear plants produce heat by splitting atoms, such as uranium, in a process called nuclear fission. In nuclear fission, tiny amounts of fuel produce tremendous amounts of heat to boil the water. Nuclear power plants have no smokestacks, because nothing is burned. But they do have cooling towers for cooling the water used in the condenser. The cool water is recycled in the condenser or released into a river or lake.

Checkpoint

1. How does a generator produce electric current?
2. How does a hydroelectric power plant change mechanical energy into electrical energy?
3. How does a turbine work in a coal-burning or nuclear power plant?
4. **Take Action!** Make a pinwheel and observe what happens when you blow on it. How could this be used to power a generator?

Activity

An Electrifying Experience

You've read about how a generator produces electricity. Now try this activity and see for yourself.

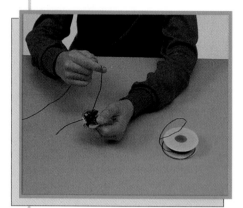
Picture A

Picture B

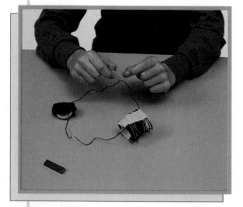
Picture C

Gather These Materials

cover goggles

7 meters of insulated copper wire

wire cutters

masking tape

directional compass

D-cell battery

empty bathroom tissue tube

bar magnet

Follow This Procedure

1 Make a chart like the one on the next page. Record your observations in your chart.

2 Put on your cover goggles.

3 Use wire cutters to cut your long piece of wire in half. Remove the insulation from the last 3 cm of both ends of the 2 wires.

4 Construct a current detector by wrapping one piece of wire around the N-S ends of a compass. (Picture A) Leave about 10 cm of wire unwrapped at both ends of the compass.

5 To test your current detector, touch both wire ends to the opposite ends of the battery. What happens to the compass needle? This shows that electric current is passing through the wire.

6 Wrap the other piece of wire around the bathroom tissue tube. Leave about 10 cm of the wire at both ends uncoiled. Hold the coil in place as you remove the tube. (Picture B) Have a teammate place strips of tape across the top and bottom of the coil of wire to hold the coil in place.

Record Your Results

Magnet movement	Movement of the compass needle
Moved outside of coil	
South end moved in coil	
North end moved in coil	

7 Attach the wires of the coil to the wires of the current detector. (Picture C)

8 Slide the magnet quickly back and forth inside the coil. Look at the compass as you do this. Does the compass needle move? In which direction does it move?

9 Experiment with the magnet. Does the needle move when the magnet is moved above the coil? Record how the movement of the compass needle is affected.

10 Does it matter if the north or south end of the magnet is moved in the coil? Try this. Record your findings in your chart. Be sure to notice the direction in which the needle moves.

State Your Conclusions

1. Why does the compass needle move when you slide the magnet through the coiled wire?

2. What can you do to the coil to increase the electric current produced?

Let's Experiment

How does the strength of the magnet affect the strength of the current produced? Use what you know about scientific methods to find out.

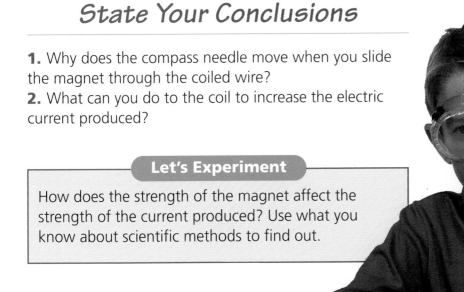

2.2 *Turning It On*

▶ *How does electricity get to your home?*

Just as the faucet in your home connects to a huge water and sewer system, so does your light switch connect to a huge electrical supply system. The path of electricity toward your home begins at the power plant. Electricity reaches nearly all homes, businesses, and industries. Best of all, electricity arrives in a way that is safe for everyone to use.

Transmitting Electricity

Somewhere near your town you may have seen giant steel towers called pylons. These pylons carry high-voltage, bare-wire, transmission lines high above the ground. The pylons and lines may cross the land in paths quite different from roads, because high-voltage electricity is dangerous. This power-line network carries electricity from the generator to you! Now look at the diagram and follow the path of electric current as it leaves the electric power plant.

▼ *Follow the path of electricity as it leaves the power plant and is transmitted over long distances.*

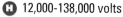

A Electric power plant
B Step-up transformer
C Pylon
D High voltage electricity (750,000 volts)
E Step-down transformer
F Large factory
G Step-down transformer
H 12,000-138,000 volts

A power plant generator produces current that moves through wires and may provide electricity at about 22,000 volts. This is plenty of electrical force to reach nearby areas, but your home might be 600 kilometers from the power plant! The electricity needs more volts to push it that far. So, when electricity leaves the power plant it first goes through a step-up transformer. A **transformer** is a device that increases or decreases voltage. The step-up transformer increases the voltage to at least 60,000 volts and possibly to more than 700,000 volts.

A step-up transformer usually has an iron core with two separate wires coiled around it. Current from the generator enters one coil, creating a magnetic field that starts a current flowing in the second coil. The second coil has many more windings than the first coil, which raises the voltage. The second coil connects to transmission wires that run out from the transformer.

The high-voltage electricity from the transformer can travel long distances. Now it travels in thick, bare wire transmission lines. Large factories, such as those that make airplanes or cars, use this high-voltage current. A connection line may lead directly from the transmission lines into these factories.

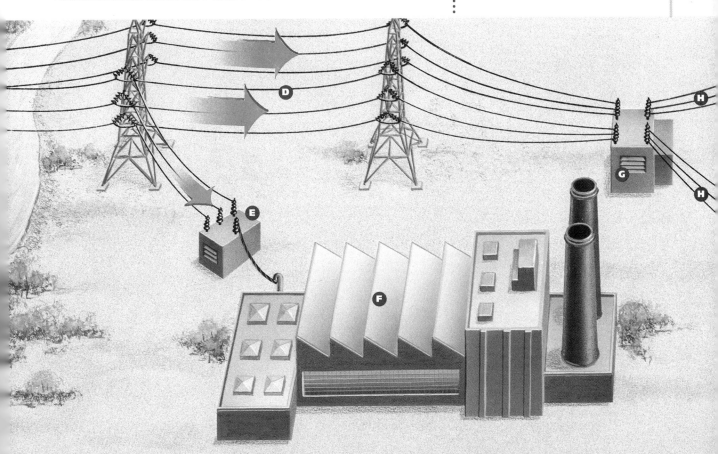

Distributing Electricity

As you can see in the diagram, the high-voltage electricity has now reached your city or town. The next step is to distribute, or deliver, electric power to all the customers of the power supply company. But first, the voltage has to be reduced. High-voltage electricity is not safe for most factories, businesses, and homes. To bring down the voltage, the electricity passes through one or more substations. The substations have step-down transformers. These transformers change high voltages into lower voltages.

A step-down transformer is the exact opposite of a step-up transformer. Current flows from the high-voltage lines into one coil of the step-down transformer. The second coil has far fewer windings of wire. So the current from the second coil leaves the transformer at reduced voltage.

The electrical wires from this first, or primary, substation carry electricity at 12,000 to 138,000 volts. These wires are hung on smaller pylons or tall poles. Individual power leads connect the power lines to factories or businesses that use high-voltage electricity. Electric trains also use high voltage in this range. Some factories have their own substations.

▼ *Follow the path of electricity as it is distributed to farms, factories, homes, and businesses.*

I Substation
J Underground wires
K 2000-34,000 volts
L Transformer
M Small factory
N 110-220 volts

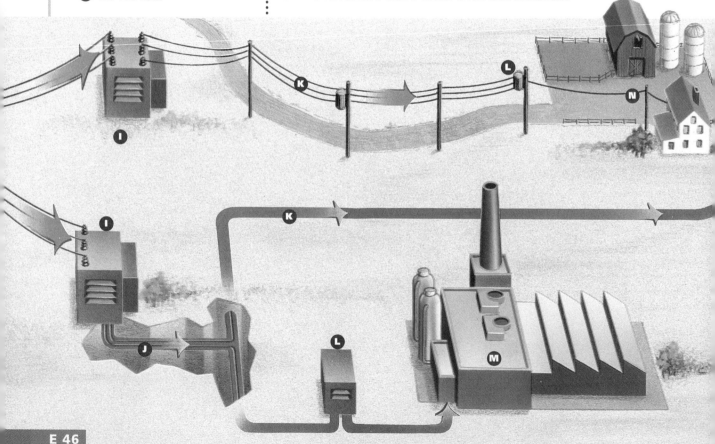

After the high-voltage electricity leaves the primary substation, it fans out in a grid to smaller, secondary substations in various communities. At the secondary substation, another transformer changes the voltage again, to anywhere from 2000 to 34,000 volts. Factories often use voltages at this level. You've probably seen a substation surrounded by fences for your protection.

From the second substation, the electricity travels underground or overhead to neighborhoods. Usually the power lines are strung between tall wooden poles. The lowest wires are wrapped with insulation—material that blocks the flow of electricity. In cities the lines may be underground. If you could see under the ground, you would see cables laid inside metal or plastic pipes. The pipes—surrounded by heavy insulation—snake this way and that through passageways under the streets. Workers reach the passageways through holes in the streets.

From these overhead or underground lines, a power line leads to one more step-down transformer. You may have seen one of these transformers on nearby power poles. The transformers lower the voltage to 110-220 volts, a level that homes and businesses can use safely. A final set of wires connects the transformers to homes and businesses.

Into The Field

Where can you find transformers at home?
Find transformers on the ends of electric cords of electronic devices. These transformers step down the voltage from 110 volts to 6 volts.

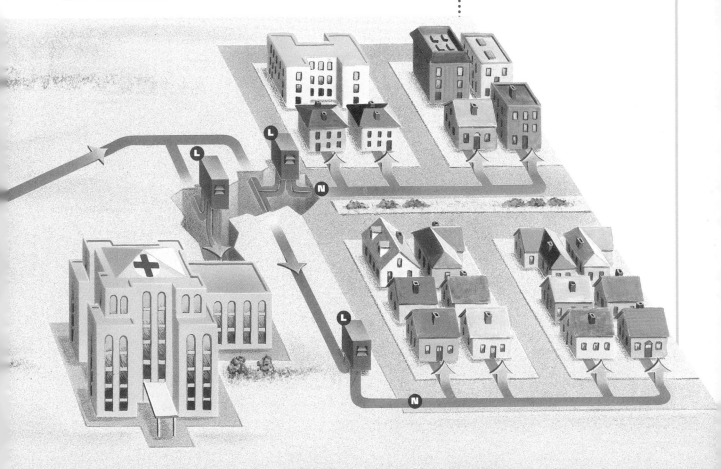

Hidden Wires

Electric current travels around the house through a system of circuits.

After traveling from the power plant where it is generated, electricity arrives at a house or an apartment building. There it keeps traveling—through wires inside the building's walls!

An electric current travels in a circuit, or closed path. If a break occurs in the circuit, the current stops flowing through the circuit.

An electrical system inside an apartment building contains many circuits that lead to and from appliances and lights. Fuses, plugs, and switches create breaks in these circuits. The switches allow you to turn the electricity on and off.

Fuses and switches called circuit breakers automatically turn off during a power surge or other emergency. These fuses and switches interrupt the flow of electricity through the circuits and protect the entire electrical system.

1 Circuit breaker box
This box contains switches that protect wires and appliances from surges of electric current. When a circuit overloads, the circuit breaker cuts off the current.

2 Electric meter
This device measures the electrical energy that enters the building, so that the residents can be billed for the use of the electricity.

3 220-volt wire
This wire carries current at 220 volts to major electrical appliances such as the stove and dryer.

4 110-volt wire
This wire carries current at 110 volts to most outlets and switches.

5 Outlet
An outlet has holes that represent breaks in the circuit. When you plug in an appliance, the metal prongs allow current to flow through the plug and into the cord when you turn on the appliance.

6 Switch
This device is used to break or complete the circuit.

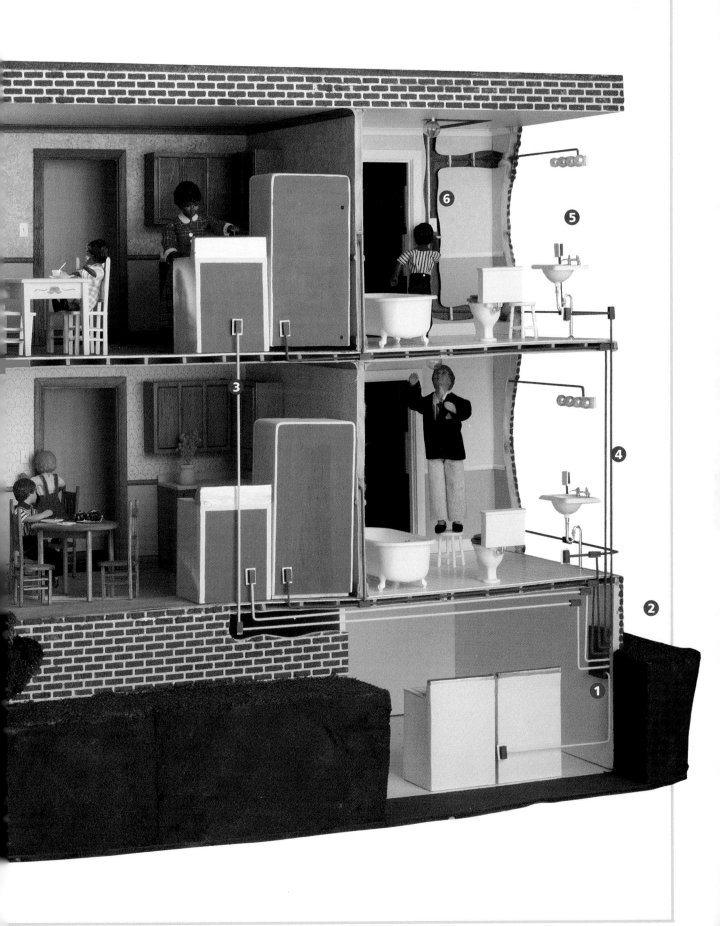

➤ A light switch is a subsystem within the electrical system of a bathroom.

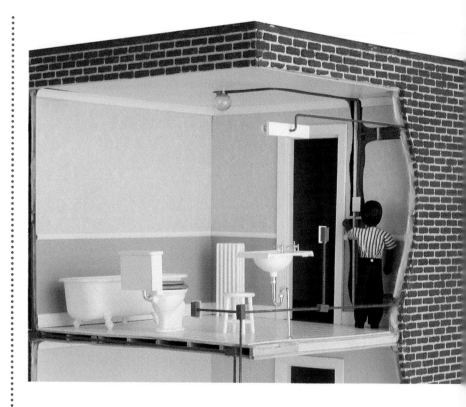

▼ Study the parts of a light switch. Then trace the path of electric current through the switch and through the light bulb.

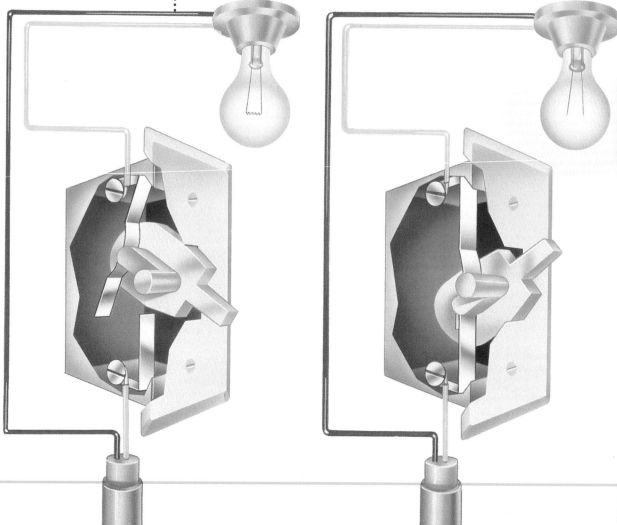

Inside a Light Switch

After traveling from the power plant to the circuits in your home, electricity, at 110 volts, finally reaches your light switch! Take a close look at the diagram as you read about how a light switch works.

Your light switch is a subsystem within the larger electrical supply system. Like all systems, it has parts that work together. Notice the flat plate, which covers a small hole in the wall. In the center of the plate is a handle that moves up and down. If you look closely, you may see the word *OFF* printed on the top of the handle when the handle is pushed down. When the handle is pushed up, you see the word *ON* printed beneath it. The handle is actually a lever. It pushes another metal lever or spring that bridges a small gap in the circuit.

When the switch is *off*, the gap opens between the wires. No current can flow because the circuit is not complete. Electricity cannot get to the light bulb. When the switch is *on*, the metal lever presses against a metal contact. The gap is closed, and current flows through to the light bulb. You have light! That is, you do if your light bulb works!

The light bulb is another circuit within the wiring circuit. Current flows into the bulb through a metal base, through a tiny wire called a filament, and back out through the base. Look closely at the light bulb in the diagram. Notice the filament wire, coiled like a tiny spring. If the filament breaks, the circuit breaks. Also, if you don't screw in the bulb tightly, the circuit stays broken and your light bulb won't light.

Checkpoint

1. How is electricity transmitted over long distances?
2. How does high-voltage electricity change to the 110-220 volts used in homes?
3. Where are the breaks in circuits in a building?
4. How does a light switch open and close an electric circuit?
5. **Take Action!** Draw a diagram that shows how electric current flows through a light switch.

Power For Thought

The average American uses 11 kilowatts of power each day. What does it cost to use this power? The electric company charges customers for each kilowatt-hour used. A kilowatt-hour (kwh) is the amount of energy supplied in one hour by one kilowatt of power. The power used by some common electrical appliances is listed in the chart below. Use the data in the chart to answer the following questions.

Appliance	Kw/hr
Light bulb (average)	0.075
Clothes dryer	5.50
Clothes washer	0.50
Electric oven	3.00
Dishwasher	1.30
Water heater	3.80
Refrigerator	0.60
Stereo	0.12
Color TV	0.10

What did you find out?
1. *At a cost of 8 cents per kwh, what would it cost to use an oven for two hours?*
2. *At a cost of 10 cents per kwh, what would it cost to use a stereo for one hour?*
3. *Make a list of ways that you can decrease the amount of electricity you use at home.*

LESSON

2.3 Power at a Price

▶ *Have you ever been in a power brownout?*

It's a sizzling hot afternoon in August. Every air conditioner in the city is on full blast. Suddenly the lights flicker for a moment. The normally bright, white glow dims to a pale, yellow haze. Refrigerator motors shudder; some TVs blink off suddenly. The enormous demand for electricity has caused a power brownout—a reduction of electric power that can dim lights.

Supplying Enough Power

Just as the demand for water has grown, the demand for electricity has also grown. At certain times, such as in a heat wave, people use more electricity than the power company can supply. Then the power company may be forced to reduce the electric power going out. Everyone gets a little less power, lights dim, and a brownout occurs. Brownouts cause problems, because electrical equipment, such as computers, can be damaged by changes in the power supply.

▼ This map shows a portion of the power pool in the northeastern United States. The colored lines represent transmission lines of different voltages. The squares show power plants.

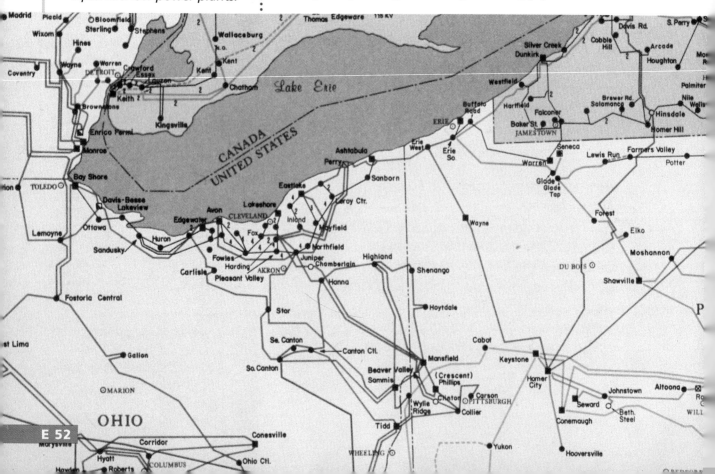

But, most power companies have a plan that prevents brownouts and meets demands for power during emergencies. Electric companies are now linked with one another in regional power pools, such as the one shown on the map below. These power pools allow a power company to "borrow" electricity from another area in an emergency. In March, 1989, high-voltage lines at the James Bay hydroelectric plant in Canada shorted out. All of Quebec went dark. New England, which gets some power from Canada, suddenly fell short of supply. Minutes later, with the help of computer technology, power flowed east from as far west as the Rocky Mountains. The system worked, and the lights stayed on in Massachusetts.

A second way to meet demands for power is by storing energy for future use. Certain hydroelectric plants—called pumped-storage plants—pump water from the river below back up into the reservoir. Water is pumped during non-peak hours, or times when people use less electricity. Later, the energy in the stored water is used to generate electricity. When demand for electricity is at its peak, the power company lets the stored water flow downhill through the turbines to generate electricity.

water converts mechanical energy to electrical energy

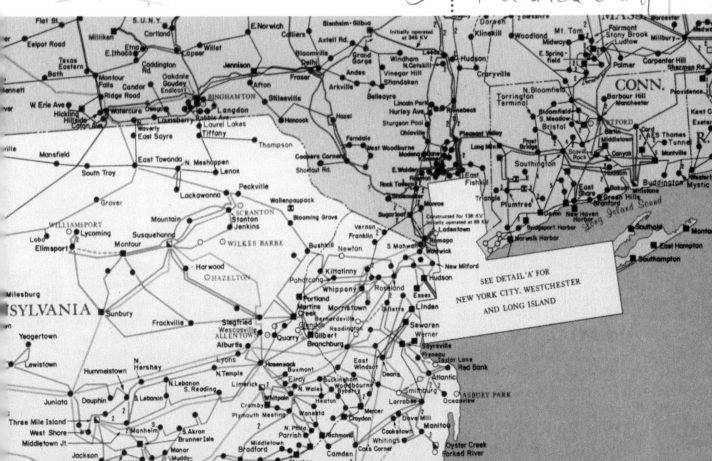

Power Plants That Burn Coal

Coal-burning power plants provide inexpensive electricity but also cause pollution.

If you're like most people in the United States, you get your electricity from a power plant that burns fossil fuels, mainly coal. Compared with some other energy sources, coal is inexpensive and plentiful.

But burning coal causes one big problem—pollution. Coal smoke contains harmful gases, such as oxides of sulfur and nitrogen. These gases mix with water in the air, causing acid rain. Another gas, carbon dioxide, may contribute to **global warming**—a warming of the earth's atmosphere.

Some coal-burning power plants also release hot water into rivers and lakes, causing **thermal pollution**—a heating of water that is harmful to living things.

Global warming Carbon dioxide in the air acts like a blanket, trapping heat near the earth's surface. This extra heat could cause climate changes.

Thermal pollution Hot water released into rivers affects animals. Warm water holds less oxygen, making breathing difficult for fish.

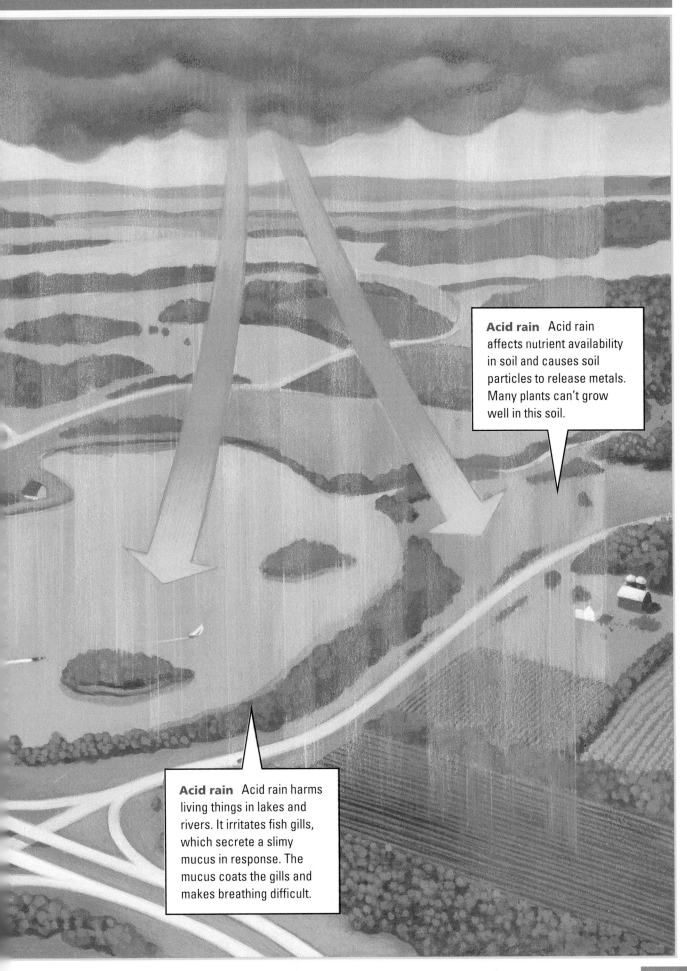

A nuclear power plant in France

The Nuclear Power Debate

Nuclear power plants have many advantages over coal-burning power plants. For one thing, they don't produce carbon dioxide or smoke. So nuclear power doesn't cause global warming or acid rain. Another benefit is that they produce tremendous amounts of electricity and thousands of megawatts of power! Finally, the nuclear fuel supply can be used for several years, while coal and oil can be burned only once.

But nuclear power plants, like all other kinds of power plants, have problems. Remember, nuclear plants use water as a coolant. Some nuclear plants do not have cooling towers and may discharge heated water into lakes and rivers. So nuclear power plants, like coal-burning plants, can cause thermal pollution.

The main challenge with nuclear power is radioactive waste. Nuclear fuel is mostly uranium, a radioactive element. Radioactive elements give off radiation, some of which is harmful to living things. Radiation destroys or changes living tissues.

The uranium used in power plants is pressed into pellets and loaded into thin rods, 2 or 3 meters long. After several years, the fuel rods can no longer be used to produce electricity. These spent fuel rods, which contain radioactive wastes, are stored for a few years in pools of water at the power plant.

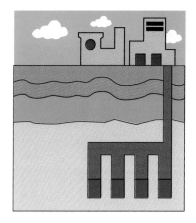

◄ *In the future, radioactive wastes may be buried in tunnels like the one in the picture. The diagram shows where the waste containers would be stored. Find these blue containers at the bottom of the chambers.*

Most of the fuel's radioactivity disappears after several years. But enough remains to be dangerous for tens of thousands of years. So the problem becomes, what to do with the used fuel? Because of real and imagined dangers of radiation, people don't want a nuclear waste dump near their homes. So nuclear scientists and engineers are developing technologies for getting rid of radioactive wastes.

One idea being tested is to bury the wastes in salt or rock tunnels at least 600 meters underground. The fuel may be fused inside glass blocks and placed in sealed containers. These burial places must be chosen carefully so that no leaks occur for thousands of years. Scientists do not agree about whether this storage method is best.

Some scientists think the radioactive wastes will leak into soil and groundwater. For now, spent fuel rods will be stored on the surface.

Checkpoint

1. How do power pools help meet emergency power shortages?
2. How do coal-burning power plants contribute to global warming? acid rain?
3. Why is nuclear waste dangerous?
4. **Take Action!** Design a plan to conserve electrical energy at home. Then carry out your plan for one week.

The Acid Test

Have you had problems with acid indigestion? Are your shampoos "pH balanced"? These are phrases you frequently hear on TV, but what do they mean?

Picture A

Picture B

Picture C

Gather These Materials

cover goggles

dropper

vinegar

lemon juice

shampoo solutions

water

baking soda solution

soap solution

food samples

pH paper

Follow This Procedure

1 Make a chart like the one on the next page. Record your observations in your chart.

2 Put on your cover goggles.

3 The pH of a substance tells whether the substance is an acid, a base, or a neutral substance. The pH of a substance is measured by a scale of numbers from 0 to 14. Acids have pH values less than 7. If the pH is above 7, the substance is a base. If the pH equals 7, the substance is neutral. That means it is neither an acid nor a base. The strongest acids have the lowest pH values. The strongest bases have the highest pH values.

4 A liquid can be tested for pH by placing 1 drop of the liquid on a clean piece of pH paper. (Picture A)

5 Compare the color of the tested strip with the color code on the outside of the container. Each color on the container represents a certain pH value. (Picture B)

6 Test each sample with pieces of pH paper. Record the pH value of each substance tested. (Picture C)

Record Your Results

Sample tested	pH	Acid, base, or neutral?

7 Use what you know about the pH scale to determine which of the substances are acids, which are bases, and which are neutral.

State Your Conclusions

1. Lemon juice is a citrus juice. Predict the pH of other citrus juices, such as grapefruit juice or orange juice.
2. Think about the kinds of solutions that are acids and bases. Based on your knowledge of the substances in this activity, what general statement can you make about how acids and bases taste or feel? *CAUTION: Do not taste or touch substances to determine if they are acids or bases.*

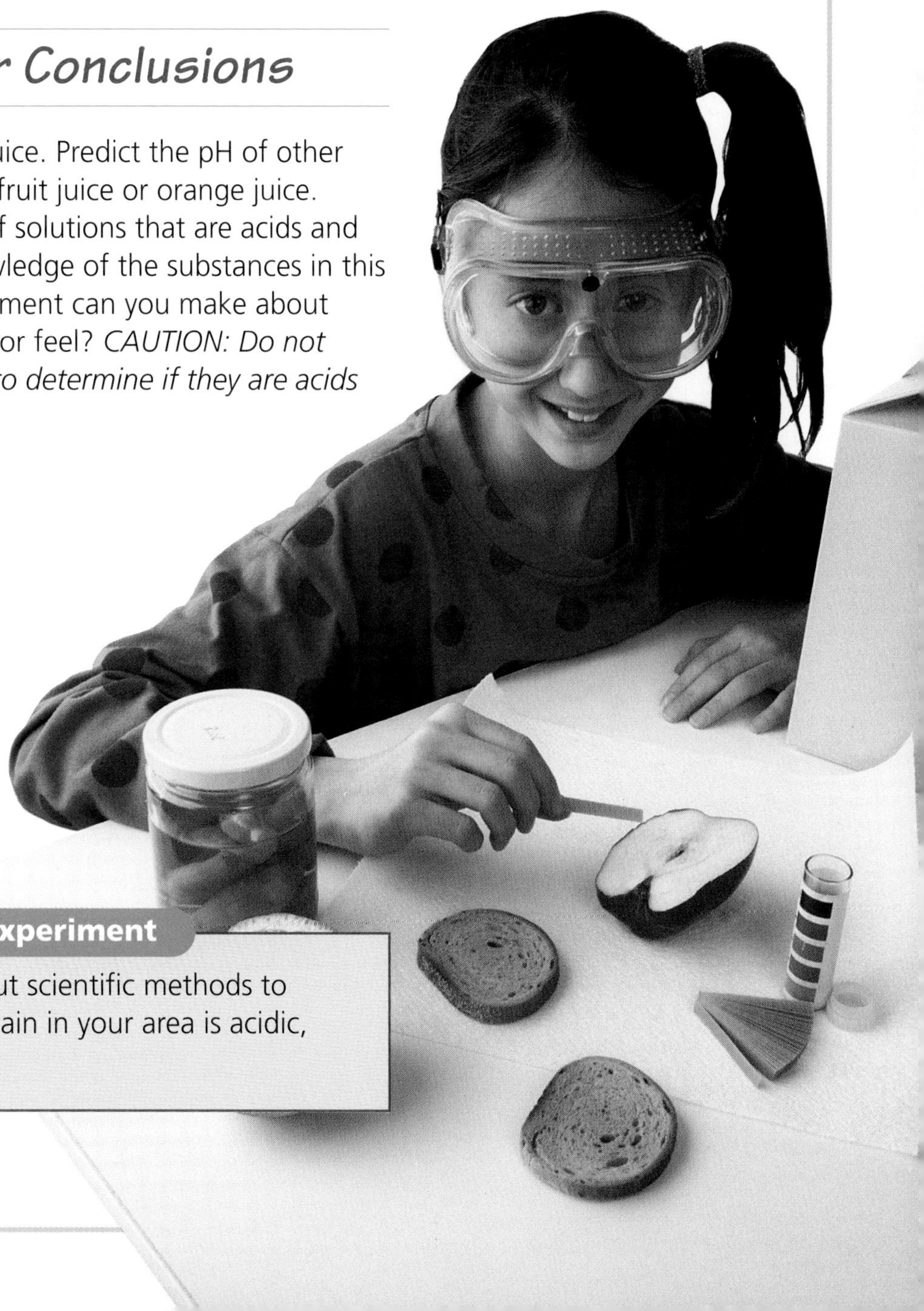

Let's Experiment

Use what you know about scientific methods to investigate whether the rain in your area is acidic, basic, or neutral.

Chapter Review

Reviewing Words and Concepts

Write the letter of the word or phrase that best completes each sentence.

1. In soil, _____ causes soil particles to release metals.
2. A flowing gas or liquid pushes the blades of a _____, which helps produce electricity.
3. In a _____, a magnet is used to change mechanical energy into electrical energy.
4. Increased carbon dioxide levels in the atmosphere may lead to _____.
5. Electrons are forced through a wire by _____.
6. Voltage is increased or decreased by a device called a _____.
7. The fuel for a nuclear power plant is usually _____.
8. Oil, coal, and natural gas are _____.
9. Heated water released from power plants into lakes and streams is a cause of _____.
10. A transformer that reduces the voltage passing through it is a _____ transformer.

a. fossil fuels
b. step-down
c. acid rain
d. uranium
e. thermal pollution
f. global warming
g. transformer
h. turbine
i. voltage
j. generator

Connecting Ideas

1. Copy the concept map. Use the terms at the right to complete the map about pollution caused by power plants.

acid rain   thermal pollution
sulfur and nitrogen oxides
global warming

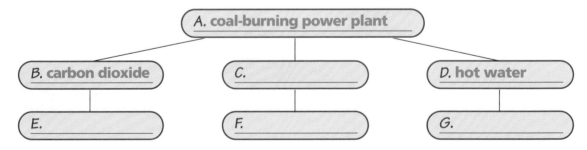

2. Write a sentence or two that summarizes the ideas shown in the concept map.

Interpreting What You Learned

1. How are a bicycle generator and a generator in a large electric power plant similar?
2. What is voltage and how is it measured?
3. Describe some forms of energy that can be used to move the blades of a turbine.
4. How does a step-up transformer increase voltage?
5. Describe the path of electricity from a power plant to a home.
6. Describe the path of electricity from a main power line to a lamp in your room.
7. Why won't a light bulb work if it is not screwed in tightly enough?
8. Describe two strategies power companies use to avoid power shortages.
9. How do power plants cause thermal pollution?
10. List the advantages and disadvantages of nuclear power plants.

Performance Assessment

How can acid rain be neutralized?

Materials • cover goggles • "acid rain" solution • blue litmus paper • baking soda • water • graduated cup • plastic cup • spoon • straw • dropper

Collecting Data

1. Put on your cover goggles. Use blue litmus paper to determine whether the "acid rain" solution is acidic. If the sample is acidic, the blue litmus paper will turn red. Dip the end of a piece of litmus paper in the "acid rain" solution. Record your results.
2. Using a graduated cup, measure 20 milliliters of water. Pour the water into a plastic cup. Place one spoonful of baking soda into the water and stir for 1 minute.
3. Using a dropper, add five drops of the baking soda solution to the "acid rain" solution. Stir the "acid rain" solution with a straw.
4. Use litmus paper to determine whether the "acid rain" solution is still acidic. If the "acid rain" solution is no longer acidic, the litmus paper will not change color.
5. Repeat steps 3 and 4 until the "acid rain" solution is no longer acidic. Record how many drops of the baking soda solution are needed to neutralize the "acid rain" solution.

Analyzing Data

What might be done to change the acid level of a lake or pond that has been polluted by acid rain?

3

Science and Industry

Whose shoes are these?
These are cool!

What are the qualities of a good sneaker?

You might buy a new pair of sneakers every year. What things do you look for in a sneaker? Examine an assortment of sneakers. How do they compare? Forget about name brands for a moment. Decide which qualities *really* make one sneaker different from another.

For Discussion

1. Which qualities of a sneaker can you test?
2. Is testing a good way to judge qualities of sneakers?

3.1 A Manufacturing System

Did you know that rubber gives sneakers their bounce?

Suppose you could collect sap from a rubber tree. You find you can make water bags, tires, or balloons, because rubber holds water and air without leaks. You even try to make waterproof "booties" the way the ancient South and Central Americans did. But in hot weather, your booties get soft and sticky. In cold weather, they get hard and crack easily. If only you could discover a way to solve the problems of rubber!

Charles Goodyear's Discovery

Charles Goodyear, an inventor from the United States, searched for a solution to the problems with rubber. One freezing February evening in 1839, he accidentally spilled a mixture of sulfur and rubber on top of his hot stove. Later he noticed the rubber was firm and dry instead of soft and sticky. He left the rubber outside all night in the cold. The next day, it still had its bounce! He had discovered a simple way to make rubber more useful.

Goodyear's process, called curing or vulcanizing, works like this. Rubber is made of polymers. A **polymer** is a long molecule made up of many smaller units strung together like beads on a chain. At rest, rubber polymers look like crumpled pieces of string. Look at the polymers—the red "strings"—in the diagram. When you stretch rubber, the polymers straighten. But when you release the rubber, the polymers crumple back up. This gives rubber that elastic, bouncy quality. By heating sulfur with rubber, a chemical reaction happens. Sulfur atoms join the long-chain polymers, forming bridges between the polymers. This makes them stable during temperature changes. Because of Goodyear's discovery, rubber can even be used to make rubber-soled shoes!

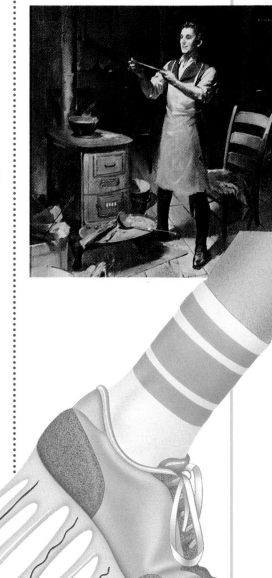

Charles Goodyear accidentally discovered a way to cure rubber. Without this discovery, the soles of your shoes would stretch like the shoe in the diagram.

Stepping Onward

The design of athletic shoes has changed as new technologies have developed.

A quick glance at these pages should convince you that athletic shoes have changed quite a bit over 150 years! Many improvements are the result of advances in technology, such as the development of new materials and better construction methods.

Today's sneakers are designed to keep up with the latest fashions. But many of today's sneakers are also designed with anatomy and the physics of motion in mind.

More than ever before, people are participating in activities such as jogging, aerobics, and tennis. Shoe designers are developing features that improve an athlete's performance and help prevent injuries. These features include soles that cushion and support the leg and foot. Recent designs have featured air pumps for improved fit, and springs and gel-filled soles for higher jumps!

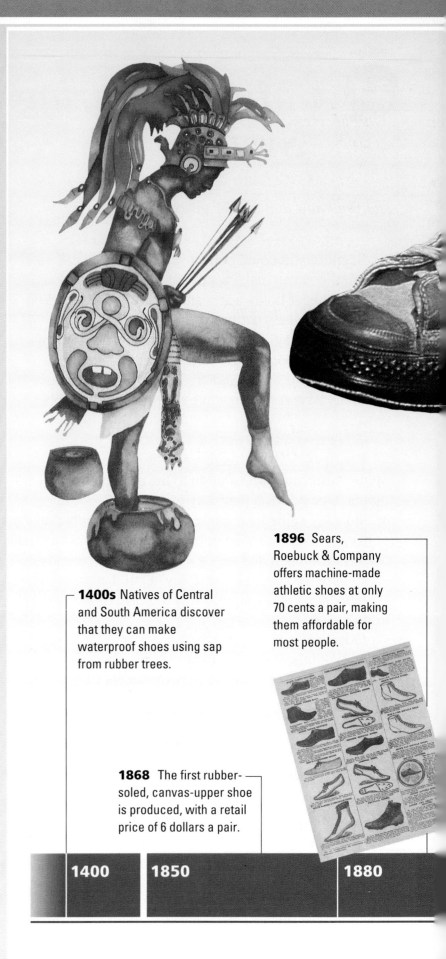

1400s Natives of Central and South America discover that they can make waterproof shoes using sap from rubber trees.

1896 Sears, Roebuck & Company offers machine-made athletic shoes at only 70 cents a pair, making them affordable for most people.

1868 The first rubber-soled, canvas-upper shoe is produced, with a retail price of 6 dollars a pair.

| 1400 | 1850 | 1880 |

1917 Manufacturers introduce high-top basketball shoes.

1990s Manufacturers produce many different styles of athletic shoes designed for a variety of activities.

1962 The first modern running shoes are introduced.

1942 Scientists develop synthetic rubber during World War II.

| 1910 | 1940 | 1970 | 2000 |

upper

sole

▲ *Sneaker cut lengthwise to show how the parts fit together*

Manufacturing System

Your sneakers are the product of a system—a system of manufacturing. Manufacturing is making finished products from raw materials using technology. Many shoes just like yours were made by the manufacturer. The technology used is based on the science of machines, computers, electricity, and water. People interact with this technology to make a manufacturing system that produces your shoes. The three main steps are: designing the product, getting raw materials and making them into parts, and then putting together the parts. These three steps are used to make most products, whether they are shoes, bicycles, or toothbrushes.

You know that sneaker design has changed quite a bit over the years. New designs often result from new technology, such as computers. Sneaker designers use computer drawings to create an imaginary foot walking in a shoe. They see how the bones and muscles move, run, and jump, in slow motion. Then they design shoes that perform better with the foot. The result is high-tech designs including honeycombed soles and air cushions.

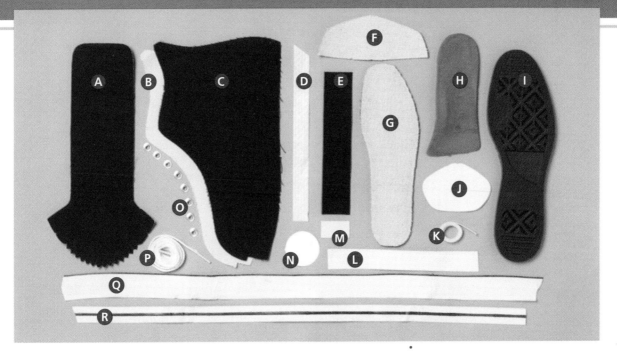

The raw materials in your shoes—rubber, canvas, and metal—were gathered from all over the world. The rubber, for example, comes from rubber tree plantations in tropical countries, such as Malaysia and Indonesia. The parts made from the raw materials are put together in a certain order at the factory.

As the picture shows, a sneaker has two main parts. The upper covers your foot, and the sole is under your foot. A sneaker sole usually has two parts: an insole that your foot rests on, and a hard rubber outsole that touches the ground. The upper has more parts. Two quarters and two linings make up the upper's sides. In the picture, find the tongue, the back stay, and the eyelet stay, which are also parts of the upper. The back stay holds the quarters together at the heel. The eyelet stay is material that holds the metal eyelets securely in place.

A	Tongue	**J**	Toe cap
B	Lining	**K**	Counter tape
C	Quarter	**L**	Bumper strip
D	Eyelet stay	**M**	Heel label
E	Back stay	**N**	Ankle patch
F	Counter	**O**	Eyelets
G	Insole	**P**	Shoe laces
H	Arch cushion	**Q**	Gum foxing
I	Outsole	**R**	Friction piping

▲ *Use the key to identify the parts of a sneaker.*

Checkpoint

1. What is vulcanizing and how does it make rubber more useful?
2. Give some reasons why the design of athletic shoes has changed over the years.
3. How are computer technology and the science of foot movement used to design sneakers?
4. **Take Action!** Trace the outline of your shoe sole on centimeter-square graph paper. Count the squares to estimate the area of your foot.

Gobs of Glop

Even though individual polymer molecules are too small to see, you can experiment with the giant chains of polymers.

Picture A

Picture B

Gather These Materials

cover goggles	2 spoons
2 plastic cups	borax
100 mL graduated cup	white glue
water	wax paper

Follow This Procedure

1 Make a chart like the one on the next page. Record your observations in your chart.

2 Put on your cover goggles.

3 Place 2 spoonfuls of glue in a cup. Add one spoon of water. Stir. (Picture A)

4 Place 60 mL of water into a cup. Use a graduated cup to measure the water.

5 Using a second spoon, add 1/2 spoonful of borax to the water. Mix well. This is your borax solution. (Picture B)

6 Observe the properties of the glue solution. Record your observations in your chart.

7 Add 3 spoonfuls of the borax solution to the glue solution. Stir for 1 minute.

8 Place your "glop" onto the wax paper for 2 minutes. (Picture C)

9 Closely examine your polymer. What happens as you stretch the material?

Picture C

Record Your Results

How the glue and glop feel, look, and stretch	
Glue properties	Glop properties

10 Experiment with the polymer to find some of the unusual properties of the substance. Be sure to wash your hands when you are finished experimenting with your polymer. Do not taste it.

State Your Conclusions

1. Did your polymer have the same properties or different properties from the glue that was used to make it?

2. Can you think of any other substances that might be made with long chains like those in your glop?

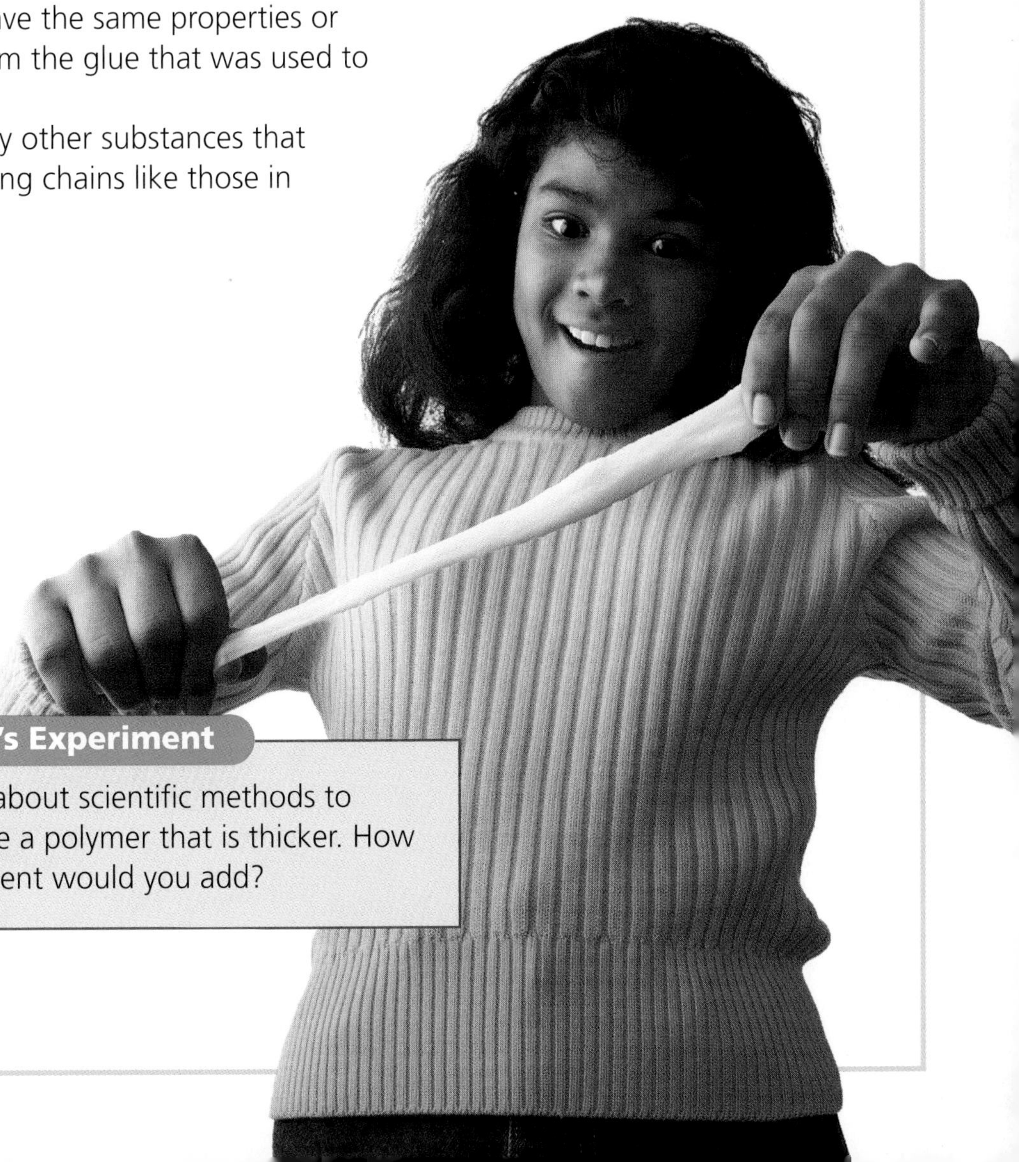

Let's Experiment

Use what you know about scientific methods to discover how to make a polymer that is thicker. How much of each ingredient would you add?

3.2 *Visit to a Sneaker Factory*

▼ *Use the key to identify the steps in the manufacturing of sneakers.*

- **A** Raw materials
- **B** Water supply system
- **1** Automated knife cuts uppers
- **2** Water jet cuts insoles
- **3** Presses mold outsoles
- **4** Upper parts are sewn
- **5** Upper, insole, and outsole are placed on last
- **6** Last is dipped in latex

What's it like inside a sneaker factory?

Imagine what you might see and hear if you visited a factory where sneakers are made. What kinds of machines are used? How are the parts of shoes made and put together? How many people work on a pair of shoes before it's finished? Well, the next tour leaves now. Step right this way—into brand new sneakers!

Inside a Sneaker Factory

If you could look through a glass wall into a sneaker factory, you'd see a view like this drawing. The factory is so huge that ten or more football fields could fit inside it. Over 1000 people work there. One end of the factory has loading docks, where workers receive raw materials from trucks. Here bundles of rubber and leather, bolts of flat canvas and nylon cloth, boxes of laces, and eyelets come into the factory. From there the raw materials go into different areas where parts are made or assembled.

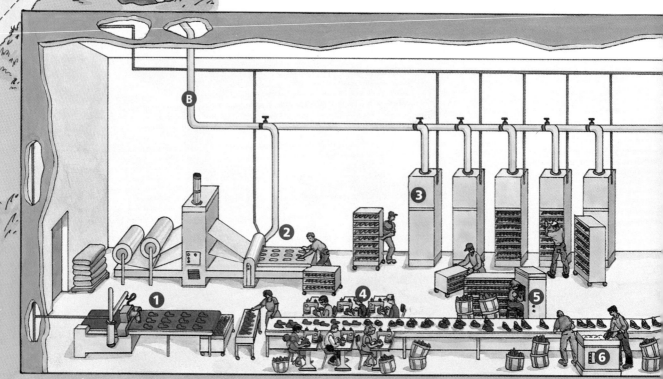

This factory is set up for mass production—making thousands of shoes very quickly. It's laid out so materials move from one end of the factory to the other as they pass through the three main steps of making the shoes. First, the parts of shoes are made. Rubber is made into outsoles. Powerful machines cut uppers and insoles. Next, the parts go to areas where workers stitch the upper pieces together using sewing machines. Then the uppers, insoles, and outsoles are glued together. Finally, the shoes go through finishing, where they're inspected, matched into pairs, and packaged.

Huge amounts of electricity are needed to run the machines. The factory uses five electrical substations with transformers to adjust the voltage to the levels needed by different machines. Use your finger to trace the orange pathways of electrical supply to various machines. The highest voltage—over 400,000 volts—is needed to make steam to vulcanize rubber.

The factory also needs a large water supply. Remember, water is used to produce steam to vulcanize rubber. One machine even uses high-pressure jets of water as a knife to cut certain shoe parts. Trace the blue path of water supply pipes leading to machines. Finally, at the far end of the factory, workers load boxes of shoes onto trucks. From there they will be shipped to market.

7 Rubber trim is attached

8 Sneakers are vulcanized

9 Sneakers are inspected, put into boxes, and placed on a truck for distribution

C Electrical supply system

Making the Parts

Imagine walking through the various areas of the factory and seeing each step in making your shoes. Notice how each step shows ways that technology uses the principles of science and mathematics. The sound is awesome—you hear the hiss of steam and the roar of motors, the noise of moving parts, and the stamp of heavy presses. These complex machines use systems of simple machines—levers, wheels and axles, and screws. These simple machines combine with gears to do work.

Follow the pictures to see the machines that make the parts of a sneaker. First you watch the uppers being cut from cotton canvas by a computer-controlled, automatic knife. Each piece has its own pattern. The person who operates the machine chooses the correct pattern and enters it into the computer's memory. The computer program guides the knife that cuts the selected pattern. The computer calculates the placement of each cut so that barely any material is left over. This uses 14 percent less material than cutting by hand.

▼ *The pictures show the automated knife cutting through many layers of canvas, and a worker removing the cutout pieces of the uppers.*

◀ The picture shows a machine using a water jet to cut insoles.

Next you see a machine that cuts insoles. This technology was first used to make aircraft parts. The machine shoots a jet of water under super-high pressure through a tiny hole drilled in a diamond. By forcing the water through the tiny hole, the speed of the water is increased. The water jet becomes a knife that cuts shapes from the layers of rubber and fabric making up the insole.

The outsole is made from chopped up natural rubber and other ingredients, such as clay, called fillers. The fillers help strengthen the rubber. Different machines chop and mix the ingredients together, until it looks like modeling clay. The clay-like material is cut into oblong bars called slugs. The slugs are loaded into sole-shaped molds, like muffin holders. When the shoe design calls for a certain tread on the bottom of the shoe, the molds will have that tread in their bottoms. A press comes down on the slug and squeezes the slug to fill the mold. High temperature—178°C —and very high pressure are applied for three minutes to cure, or vulcanize, the outsole. When the molds are cooled and then opened, you see a set of cured, fully formed outsoles. It's a bit like baking bread. You bake some mixed ingredients in a hot oven for a certain time, and the dough changes into spongy bread!

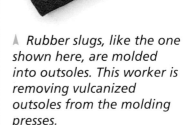

Rubber slugs, like the one shown here, are molded into outsoles. This worker is removing vulcanized outsoles from the molding presses.

Assembling the Parts

Next you enter an area that has hundreds of sewing machines. It's part of the assembly line—a rapid system for putting parts together. In an assembly line, each person does one step or more of a product's assembly. The unfinished product from one person is then given to another worker. For example, you and your friends might set up an assembly line to make sandwiches for a picnic. One person gets out two slices of bread. The next spreads mustard. The next person adds cheese. The next adds lettuce. The last person wraps each sandwich. Each sandwich passes from person to person until it's completed.

An assembly line makes sense in sneaker manufacturing. It takes one person a long time to make a shoe, even with high-tech machines. However, an assembly line of 70 people can finish over 1900 pairs of shoes a day. First the parts of the sneaker upper have to be sewn together, as the picture shows. You walk along the rows of sewing machines and watch each operator sewing together all the pieces that make up the sneaker's upper. After all of the upper's pieces are assembled, it's moved to another area.

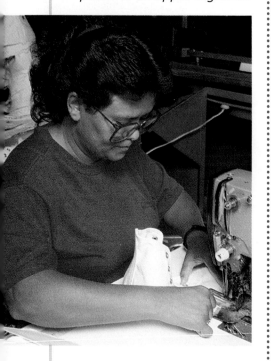

▼ This operator sews the pieces of an upper together.

➤ The stamp shows Jan Matzeliger, who invented the lasting machine in 1882. A worker glues the upper and insole together around a last.

Jan E. Matzeliger
Shoe Lasting Machine No.274,207
Patented March 20,1893
29
Black Heritage USA

The upper is then taken to the operator of a hole-punching machine, who punches eyelet holes in it. The assembled parts are just starting to look like a sneaker. Next you head for the lasting area. The smell of latex, a kind of rubber cement, fills your nose. Ugh! You hope this part doesn't "last" too long.

In the lasting area, another assembly line system joins together the uppers, the insoles, and the outsoles. How are these parts joined together? The upper, insole, and outsole are joined around a last. Invented in 1882, a last is an aluminum mold shaped like a foot.

The lasting area has lasts for every size and shape of foot. Canvas uppers are made from flat fabrics, but the shape of your foot is partly round. The lasting process shapes the fabric around the foot. First, someone heats the uppers to help stretch the material. Then the worker lays the insole on the sole of the last. The lasting worker then glues the insole to the upper. Sometimes spongy arch pads, known as "cookies," are inserted with the insole. Next, as you can see in the picture, a worker dips the sole of the last into a shallow pan of latex. Another worker then attaches the outsole to the insole.

▲ *A worker dips the last, with the upper and insole attached, into a pan of latex.*

Finally, rubber trim, such as a toe cap and side strips, are placed on the shoe. Still wearing the shoe, the last goes into another vulcanizer, called an autoclave. The autoclave uses steam to cure the rubber trim. It has to "cook" for exactly 88 minutes at 146°C and extremely high pressure. Again, it's like baking bread. The ingredients have to reach a certain temperature before the chemical reaction happens and turns the dough into bread. The vulcanizing holds the parts onto the shoe. And without vulcanizing, the rubber around the sides and toes wouldn't be much good if temperatures were very hot or cold.

A technician operates the mainframe computer that keeps track of the production process.

Checklist
- ☑ Color
- ☑ Size
- ☑ Right Shoe
- ☐ Left Shoe
- ☐ Loose Parts
- ☐ Dirt ☐ Laces
- ☐ Height ☐ Stains
- ☐ Threads

Finishing the Job

The final steps include adding the "findings," or small parts that are made elsewhere and brought in to be added to the sneakers. The findings added at the finish include aluminum eyelet vents and shoelaces. One person cleans away excess glue and dirt. Another trims off extra threads, fabric, or rubber pieces. The finished sneakers are then put onto a conveyor belt, where each sneaker is examined by a quality control inspector.

As you can see in the picture, the quality control inspector has a checklist of points that each shoe has to pass. Just as you listed good sneaker qualities in the Discover Activity, the inspector makes sure each shoe shows a high quality of good looks, strength, and fit. Each pair must be the same size, color, and height. You wouldn't like it very much if you opened a new box of sneakers to find one size 8 and another size 9 shoe in the box. The inspector also looks for thread ends, dirt, loose parts, and rubber cement stains.

If the sneakers pass inspection, they go into boxes—the ones that you see them in at a shoe store. The boxes are packed for shipping in trucks to various stores.

The pictures show a quality control inspector examining a sneaker, and a worker putting sneakers into a shoe box.

Next you see the mainframe computer room. Large mainframe computers like this one perform complex mathematical calculations almost instantly. This computer tracks all the production steps, from raw materials to finished product.

Skilled computer operators program the computer. They write instructions for it using complex computer languages. They enter and analyze facts about each step of the production process. A major responsibility of computer operators is to make sure that all the systems in the factory work together smoothly.

For example, a computer can be programmed to calculate the amount of raw materials used in each shoe. If rubber is being wasted, this will show up in the computer reports. Many production facts go into the computer, such as how many sizes, colors, and styles of shoes are made each day. The computer also tracks orders for sneakers, and whether enough raw materials are there to fill the orders quickly. And sometimes orders need to be filled quickly!

Checkpoint

1. How are water and electrical power used in sneaker manufacturing?
2. How is water pressure used by the insole cutting machine?
3. How are assembly lines useful in making sneakers?
4. Name two uses for a mainframe computer in the process of manufacturing sneakers.
5. **Take Action!** Think of how items other than sneakers might be made using an assembly line process. Design and diagram the process.

Sticky Business

Some children's shoes fasten with hook and loop fasteners instead of with shoe laces. How do these fasteners work? Let's investigate.

What To Do
A. Look at the separate hard and soft halves of a hook and loop fastener. Pick at the hard loops with a fingernail. Diagram what you see.
B. Look at the halves when pressed together. Draw a diagram of what you see.
C. *Softly* press both sides together and pull them apart five times.
D. *Firmly* press both sides together and pull them apart five times.

Record Your Results

	Diagram
Soft half	
Hard half	
Together	

What Did You Find Out?
1. *Describe each half of a hook and loop fastener.*
2. *Explain what happens when the halves stick together.*
3. *Explain why softly pressing together the halves doesn't work.*

3.3 *Sneaker Snags*

> **Can the manufacturer make enough sneakers for everyone who wants them?**

Imagine that all of a sudden everyone wants to buy a new high-tech design sneaker. How does the factory meet the skyrocketing demand? Production must increase to get shoes to all the new customers. Suddenly, the manufacturer needs more raw materials, people, electricity, and water. What if the manufacturer can't get enough of one of those key things?

Problems at the Factory

Practically all the machinery in the sneaker factory operates on electricity. The cutting machines, vulcanizing machines, outsole presses, sewing machines, and conveyer belts use tremendous amounts of electricity. Also, large amounts of water are used to make steam for high-pressure vulcanizing and to run other machines. And, of course, water is used as a knife to cut insoles. Production depends on materials moving steadily from one end of the factory to the other.

▼ *What might happen if a power failure shuts down the insole cutting machine in a sneaker factory?*

"It's that break in the electrical system that's holding everything up."

Now, suppose one afternoon something interrupts the electric power supply to the water-jet insole cutting machine, or the water pressure drops suddenly. A shout goes up, "Insole cutter is down!" Uppers and outsoles start to pile up in the lasting area. Find the piles in the drawing. Workers begin to stand around with nothing to do. Inspectors watch empty conveyer belts, and trucks with empty trailers wait in the shipping area.

In other words, a break in the power or water supply in one part of a factory can affect the whole factory. All the systems have to work together. If one key system breaks, such as the water supply or the electrical supply, all the other systems may stop too.

Sometimes a failure in one system causes a failure in another. If the power supply failed, the electric pumps that push water through the factory to all the machinery wouldn't work. Water pressure would fall. The factory has an emergency water supply in its water tower. But the tower can't supply enough water to keep the machinery running. Emergency electrical generators can also be used to supply power. But these provide only enough power to safely light the place for people trapped inside when the power goes out. These generators do not produce enough electricity to run the high-power machinery.

"We'll never get all of those shoes out to the stores today."

Into The Field

What is recycled paper like?

Compare recycled and nonrecycled types of paper. Describe how the papers are alike and how they are different.

Disposing of Wastes

Do manufacturers have other problems? Well, what do they do about wastes? The computerized cutting machine and the water-jet insole cutting machine save great amounts of fabric. Pieces are cut so that very little material has to be thrown away. But all manufacturing systems produce wastes. These wastes have to be disposed of without polluting the environment.

The pictures show some waste scraps produced by sneaker manufacturing. At which step do you think each of the scraps was produced? Try to identify trimmings of rubber and small scraps of fabric. The making of one pair of shoes does not produce much scrap, but the production of hundreds and thousands of shoes makes mountains of it.

Sometimes manufacturing wastes are taken to landfills and buried. If these wastes contain dangerous chemicals, they might seep out and pollute the soil and water supply. Even if solid wastes don't contain dangerous chemicals, they often do not decompose, or break down into soil. This is a problem, because landfills in the United States are filling up rapidly.

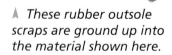
▲ These rubber outsole scraps are ground up into the material shown here.

Some manufacturers burn their wastes, but this often causes air pollution. Just like people in homes, manufacturers are having to develop new technologies to reduce or recycle their solid wastes. Fortunately, in a sneaker factory many wastes can be recycled. This factory recycles both rubber scraps and fabric.

Rubber scraps from the making of outsoles are sent to another factory. Here they are ground up and returned to the sneaker factory in batches. The batches of material are recycled in the outsole mixture.

The fabric scraps in the picture come from the cutting of quarters and linings. These scraps are put through shredders and then made into a material called rag. The rag becomes filler in the mixture that is used to make insoles. Recycling saves the manufacturer money, because the manufacturer has to buy fewer raw materials. Recycling also helps the environment, because fewer solid wastes go into landfills.

▲ *Canvas scraps on a conveyer belt are chopped into pieces. Then they are shredded to make rag, which is recycled in sneaker insoles.*

Checkpoint

1. How can a power failure affect other systems in a sneaker factory and interrupt production?
2. How are solid wastes recycled by some sneaker manufacturers?
3. **Take Action!** Make a list of products that use packaging made from recycled materials.

Activity

Waste Not,
Want Not

Waste in manufacturing causes disposal problems. How can you arrange a shoe sole pattern on a sheet of rubber to get the most soles with the least amount of waste?

Picture A

Picture B

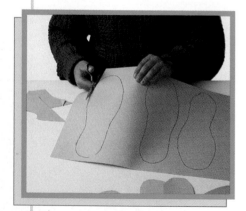

Picture C

Gather These Materials

28 X 43 cm sheet of paper   scissors
gram masses   small shoe
metric balance

Follow This Procedure

1 Make a chart like the one on the next page. Record your observations in your chart.

2 Imagine that the sheet of paper is a big piece of rubber. You will cut out shoe soles from this sheet.

Predict: *How many shoe soles will you be able to cut from your sheet of rubber?*

3 Begin by measuring the starting mass of the paper using a metric balance. Roll up the paper to make measuring easier. (Picture A)

4 Record the mass of the paper in your chart.

5 Arrange and trace the sole on the paper to get as many patterns as you can. (Picture B)

6 Cut out the sole patterns. How many soles were you able to get from one sheet of paper? Save all of the paper scraps. (Picture C)

7 Measure the mass of the paper scraps. Record this value in your chart.

8 Use the data in the chart to figure the percentage of waste.

Record Your Results

Mass of paper	
Mass of paper scraps	
Percentage of waste $\dfrac{\text{mass of scraps}}{\text{mass of paper}} \times 100$	

9 Compare your results with those of your classmates.

State Your Conclusions

1. Did everyone get the same percentage of waste?
2. Which pattern arrangement produces the least waste?
3. What are some ways in which the waste scraps could be reused?

Let's Experiment

Use what you know about scientific methods to figure out how to reduce waste even further while not affecting the comfort of the shoe. How can you adjust the sole pattern to reduce the percentage of waste?

3.4 *Looking Back, Looking Ahead*

What happened during the 1988 drought?

Where were you in the summer of 1988? Across the United States—in 37 states from California to Vermont—people lived through the driest year since 1934. Many farmers had withered crops. Even the Mississippi River ran low, stranding barges filled with raw materials used in power plants and manufacturing plants. Some power plants had to cut back on output.

Systems Working Together

You've seen that a system failure in one part of a factory can affect the whole factory. In the same way, a shortage in one technological supply system can affect other supply systems. The drought in 1988 affected the water supply greatly. As the dry, hot summer months dragged on, water levels in rivers and lakes fell drastically in many parts of the United States.

As you know from visiting the sneaker factory, manufacturing can use lots of water. Products that use the most water in manufacturing include paper, iron, chemicals, and steel. One paper factory had to stop production for short periods during the drought because a nearby river was too low. But the drought also affected the production of electrical power. The low water supply caused hydroelectric power production to fall sharply.

▼ *Newspapers reported the effects of the 1988 drought in the midwest.*

Chicago Tribune 35¢ Wednesday, June 22, 1988   Sports Final

Another day, another sizzler

2d straight 100-degree day for city

By John Lucadamo and Jerry Shnay

Temperatures of 100 degrees scorched Chicago and its suburbs for the second straight day Tuesday, hitting 101 at 4 p.m.

It was so hot that the pavement buckled on some highways, and people seeking relief at the beach risked burning their feet on sun-baked sand.

Suburbanites flocked to air-conditioned shopping malls, nor

Summer's drought had its roots in winter Page

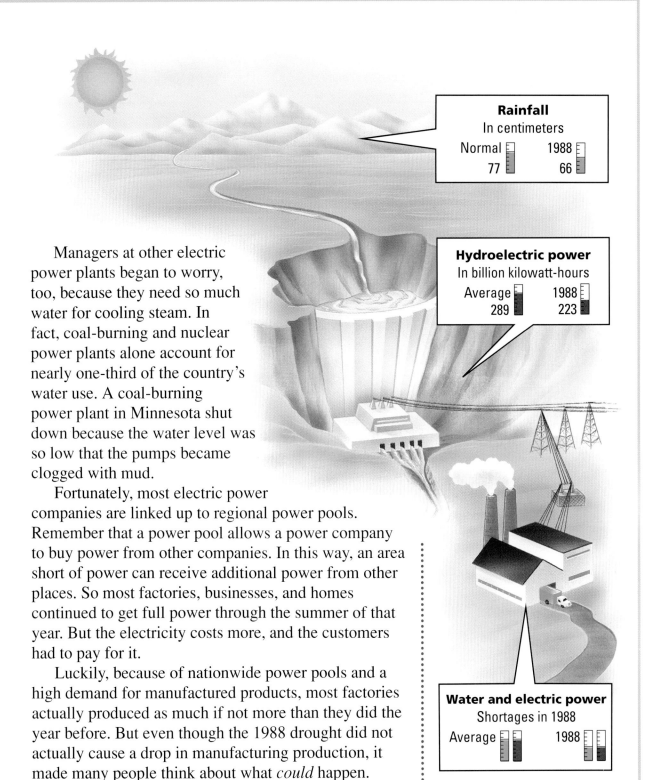

Rainfall
In centimeters
Normal 1988
77 66

Managers at other electric power plants began to worry, too, because they need so much water for cooling steam. In fact, coal-burning and nuclear power plants alone account for nearly one-third of the country's water use. A coal-burning power plant in Minnesota shut down because the water level was so low that the pumps became clogged with mud.

Hydroelectric power
In billion kilowatt-hours
Average 1988
289 223

Fortunately, most electric power companies are linked up to regional power pools. Remember that a power pool allows a power company to buy power from other companies. In this way, an area short of power can receive additional power from other places. So most factories, businesses, and homes continued to get full power through the summer of that year. But the electricity costs more, and the customers had to pay for it.

Luckily, because of nationwide power pools and a high demand for manufactured products, most factories actually produced as much if not more than they did the year before. But even though the 1988 drought did not actually cause a drop in manufacturing production, it made many people think about what *could* happen.

Manufacturers began developing ways to save water, such as by building cooling equipment that recirculates water. A recirculating system is one that pumps the same water through the system over and over again. Many factories built larger reservoirs, fixed leaks, and encouraged workers to save water.

Water and electric power
Shortages in 1988
Average 1988

▲ Study the data in the boxes. Explain how the 1988 drought affected hydroelectric power plants.

Late 1800s Scientists identify the bacterium that causes cholera, a disease that comes from contaminated water.

1938 Scientists split the uranium atom and show that nuclear fission releases energy.

| 1900 | 1920 | 1940 |

▲ *The bottom of this time line shows three important new technologies of this century. The top shows the advances in science that led to the development of the technologies.*

1912 Chlorine, which kills cholera bacteria, is first used in water purification plants.

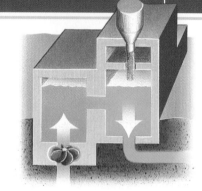

Technology's Benefits and Costs

Have you heard the saying, "Necessity is the mother of invention"? Just think about the numerous helpful inventions since the 1800s! As the time line shows, you could also say, "Science is the mother of technology." You have the use and benefit of many modern inventions only because of advances in science.

For example, the discovery of nuclear fission led to producing power from fission—nuclear power plants. Knowledge of mathematics, chemistry, and physics led to the invention of the computer. Scientists studied the properties of substances called semiconductors, which led to the development of computer chips. Computers now direct machines that cut sneaker parts. Chemical experiments led to the development of plastics, which can be lightweight, strong, and inexpensive. Today plastic pipes are widely used in water supply systems.

Technology is often wonderful and beneficial. But technology has costs as well as benefits. Technology has changed rapidly, and now many people's daily lives depend greatly on it. If a major technological system— water supply, electric supply, or manufacturing—breaks down, well, you know what can happen! Practically everything connected to it stops.

1970s The science of biomechanics is developed. This science studies how the leg and foot move during different kinds of athletic activities.

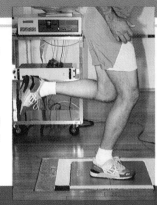

| 1960 | 1980 | 2000 |

1956 The first nuclear power plant begins operating at Calder Hall in England.

1980s Biomechanics makes it possible to design athletic shoes that provide better support for the leg and foot.

Unfortunately, the increased use of technology has also become a major cause of pollution. A growing population—most of whom use many products of technology—has polluted and overused all three parts of the biosphere—air, water, and soil. Some electric power plants pollute the air with smoke. Others produce radioactive wastes that can be harmful to living things. Some factories release wastes into the air and water. Landfills overflow with solid wastes that do not break down into soil easily. Now scientists and engineers are working on developing new technologies to solve these pollution problems. If you stay mindful of the costs of technology, perhaps you will never wake up to a day without water, electricity, or sneakers.

Checkpoint

1. How did the drought of 1988 affect the electric power supply system?
2. Describe one benefit and one cost of modern technology.
3. **Take Action!** Make a poster urging other people to conserve water or electricity.

Chapter Review

Reviewing Words and Concepts

Write the letter of the word or phrase that best completes each sentence.

1. Electrical power companies are often linked in _____ to keep electricity running when resources are scarce.
2. To prevent water shortages, many factories use a _____ to use water over and over again.
3. Factories use _____ to make many products in a short time.
4. Increased use of technology has led to an increase in the _____ of air, water, and soil.
5. Nuclear power plants produce energy through _____.
6. By _____, fewer raw materials are used to make new products and fewer solid wastes go in landfills.
7. Sneakers are made in a system of _____.
8. A long molecule made up of many smaller units is called a _____.
9. A water shortage can reduce the availability of energy from _____.
10. A landfill is a place used to dispose of _____.

a. manufacturing
b. mass production
c. recycling
d. polymer
e. power pools
f. pollution
g. hydroelectric power
h. recirculating system
i. nuclear fission
j. solid wastes

Connecting Ideas

1. Copy the concept map. Use the terms at the right to complete the map about the steps in a manufacturing system.

assembling parts   making parts
gathering raw materials
designing the product

A. _____ B. _____ C. _____ D. _____

2. Write a sentence or two that summarizes the ideas shown in the concept map.

Interpreting What You Learned

1. Why are rubber polymers more stable after vulcanizing?
2. How did the natives of Central and South America make waterproof shoes?
3. Name five items that are produced by manufacturing systems.
4. How can failure of the electric supply in one part of a factory affect other parts of the factory?

Performance Assessment

How can mass production be modeled?

Materials
- 20 pieces of square white paper
- 10 pieces of square green paper
- 20 pieces of square yellow paper
- 10 pieces of yellow yarn
- 10 circles of red paper
- stopwatch or clock with second hand

Collecting Data

1. The materials represent the different parts of a cheese sandwich: white paper is bread; yarn is mustard; green paper is lettuce; red paper is tomato; yellow paper is cheese. Arrange the materials so materials that are alike are together.
2. Time yourself as you complete this step of the activity. Make one cheese sandwich as follows: Place a slice of bread on your desk. Add a stripe of mustard to the bread. Place two pieces of cheese on the bread slice. Add one tomato slice and one piece of lettuce. Cover with a second slice of bread. Record the time it took to make one sandwich.
3. Make a second sandwich by repeating step 2. Record the time it took.
4. Make eight more sandwiches, repeating step 2. Record the time needed to make each sandwich. Then add to find the total time needed to make complete sandwiches separately.
5. Take apart the sandwiches and return the materials to separate piles.
6. Devise a plan to make ten sandwiches, exactly like those you've made, as quickly as possible.
7. Use your plan to make ten sandwiches. Record the time needed to make all the sandwiches. Compare the time using your plan with the time needed to make complete sandwiches separately.

Analyzing Data

How was your plan for making sandwiches quickly different from making sandwiches separately? What ideas from mass production does your plan use?

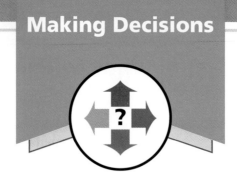

The Right Energy for the Job

Most of the world's electricity is produced by the burning of fossil fuels—coal, oil, and natural gas. Fossil fuels are nonrenewable energy sources. So, it's important to try to save fossil fuels whenever possible.

A good way to cut down on the use of fossil fuels is to use alternatives—energy sources such as the sun, wind, and heat inside the earth. These energy sources can't be used up easily. And unlike fossil fuels, renewable energy sources don't pollute the atmosphere.

Needs and Goals
Renewable energy sources have benefits, but people don't have the technology to use renewable energy sources to meet *all* their energy needs. The biggest problem is that each of these energy sources is useful only in certain parts of the country. Why? Only certain regions have the conditions needed to use the energy source.

Gathering Information
Suppose you're on the committee that's in charge of choosing an alternative energy source for your community. What would

Unlike fossil fuels, renewable energy sources don't pollute the atmosphere.

you need to know to make the best decision? You would need to know such things as where the energy source is found and how it is used. Read the following information about each energy source. Then use it to make your decision.

1. Solar energy is trapped and stored in devices called solar collectors and solar cells. Solar collectors change solar energy to thermal energy that can be used to heat water and air in homes. Solar cells change solar energy to electrical energy. The amount of solar energy reaching the earth is much more than would be needed to generate electricity for the entire world! But people don't yet have the technology to use this solar energy. With present technology, only places that get a certain minimum amount of sunlight every day can depend on solar energy as the main energy source.

2. Wind energy can be used to generate electricity. In certain places, wind is used to turn windmills. The windmills act on turbines—they power generators that produce electricity. For wind power to be useful, a region must have strong, steady winds.

3. Geothermal energy is produced when underground water is heated by hot rocks deep inside the earth. Wells drilled into the ground allow the heated water to be carried to the surface as steam. Pipes carry the steam to turbines inside geothermal energy plants. There, the steam is used to generate electricity. Geothermal energy is useful only in places where heated water is close to the surface, because drilling is expensive.

Possible Alternatives

Building the equipment to collect and use renewable energy sources can be expensive. For this reason, it's important to be quite sure that a particular region can depend on a constant supply of this alternative energy. The three maps on this page can help you decide whether an energy source can be used in a particular region of the country.

Evaluating Alternatives

On each of the maps, locate a region in one state. Evaluate that region as a possible site for collecting and using wind, solar, or geothermal energy.

Making the Best Choice

Is one alternative source the best choice for that region? Or is the region a good site for more than one alternative form of energy?

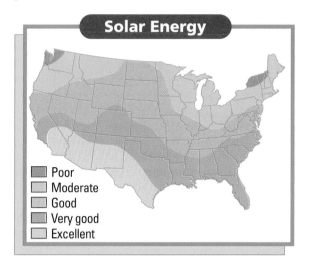

Solar Energy

- Poor
- Moderate
- Good
- Very good
- Excellent

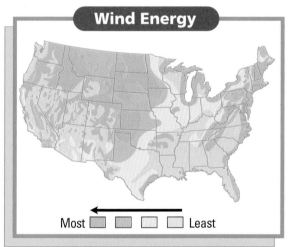

Wind Energy

Most ◼ ◼ ◻ ◻ Least

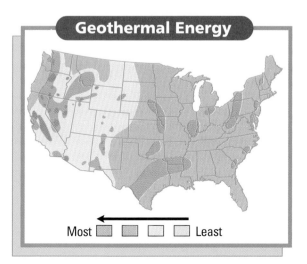

Geothermal Energy

Most ◼ ◼ ◻ ◻ Least

Now You Do It

1. What source of alternative energy would you recommend for the region you chose?
2. Are any regions possible sites for all three of these alternative energy sources?
3. *On Your Own* Choose one energy source. Find out about an area of the world that uses it. What machinery must be built to collect and use it?
4. *Critical Thinking* How would you persuade people that it's worth spending the money to research and develop alternative energy sources?

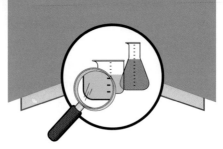

Technology in Medicine

Occupation: Biomedical engineer
Other activities: gives talks to students about their career possibilities

I t might have been because she wanted to feel a tie to her great grandmother, a Yurok Indian medicine woman. Tianna's not sure why, but she always knew she wanted to do something with medicine. Tianna Fletcher is a biomedical engineer. She works at a NASA research center.

What do biomedical engineers do?

"They use technology that puts scientific knowledge to work. Biomedical engineers use their knowledge of medicine to design equipment that is used to help the human body. This could be equipment that measures functions of the body, or that treats a problem. From thermometers to X-ray machines, many types of equipment measure functions of the body."

What do you design?

"One project I'm working on is designing equipment that would record measurements of astronauts while they're in space. Think about measuring heart rate over many days. When everything is normal, most of the data would look just about the same. A doctor would only be interested in looking at the parts of the data that showed something unusual happening. Storing that normal background data would waste space. We're working on developing a system that would store only those parts of the data that are different."

Are there other uses for your designs?

"Yes. One of NASA's goals is to do basic research that is helpful to the public. Many products that came from NASA research are part of our everyday world. A program that would allow equipment to store only the most important data could have many uses in medicine and in business."

How did you pick bioengineering?

"If it had not been for a program called Expanding Your Horizons, I would have never thought of it. This program gets girls interested in careers in science. I went to a small high school on an Indian reservation and had never thought of the possibility of being an engineer."

Electric Water Heater

Can you imagine having only cold water for your shower or bath? Hot water is a convenience that you may take for granted. But many in the world consider hot water a luxury.

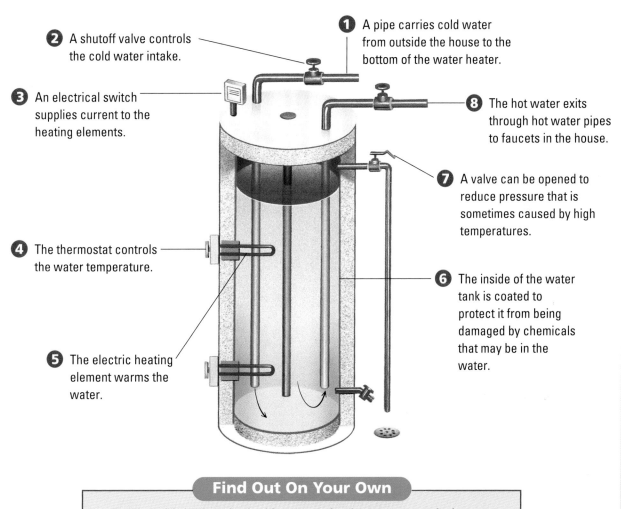

2 A shutoff valve controls the cold water intake.

3 An electrical switch supplies current to the heating elements.

1 A pipe carries cold water from outside the house to the bottom of the water heater.

8 The hot water exits through hot water pipes to faucets in the house.

7 A valve can be opened to reduce pressure that is sometimes caused by high temperatures.

4 The thermostat controls the water temperature.

5 The electric heating element warms the water.

6 The inside of the water tank is coated to protect it from being damaged by chemicals that may be in the water.

Find Out On Your Own

Learn which chemicals, if any, are in the water supply in your community. Make a list of chemicals that are added to the water and write the purpose of each.

Module Performance Assessment

Energy Awareness Day

Using what you learned in this module, help prepare exhibitions to be used at an Energy Awareness Day conference to be held at your school. Complete one or more of the following activities. You may work by yourself or with others in a group.

Social Studies

Investigate the Morse code system to find out what it is, when it was developed, and how it is used. Use a battery, insulated wire, a light bulb, a light socket, and a switch to send messages based on Morse code. Your system will use light instead of sound to communicate messages.

Hydrology

Make a bulletin-board display showing how your town receives its water. Decide how to find out this information and gather the information you need. Make diagrams and charts to illustrate your display.

Drama

Survey adults and other students to find out whether they think nuclear power plants are better or worse than coal-burning power plants. Ask each person to explain his or her opinion. Then create a presentation or skit to show the viewpoints you gathered.

Art

Use three sheets of paper to draw pictures of yourself using the following:
1. a subsystem of the power-supply system
2. a subsystem of the water-supply system
3. something produced by a manufacturing system

Environment

In the future, the supply of electricity may not be large enough to meet people's needs. Find out what individuals and families can do to conserve electric power. Prepare a list of actions. Design a flyer for everyone to take home.

Ways to Conserve Energy

Module Review

Reviewing Words and Concepts

Write the letter of the word or phrase that best completes each sentence.

j **1.** Rubber is made up of chains of molecules called ____.
c **2.** A pipe that carries water is one kind of ____.
A **3.** Salt is removed from water in a process called ____.
i **4.** In a ____, a magnet changes mechanical energy into electrical energy.
g **5.** In a power plant, a ____ rotates to spin a magnet, producing electricity.
f **6.** Voltage can be increased or decreased by a ____.
d **7.** Releasing heated water into a river may cause ____.
H **8.** The force that moves electrons through a wire is ____.
B **9.** An artificial lake that stores water is a ____.
e **10.** Excess carbon dioxide in the atmosphere may contribute to ____.

a. desalination
b. reservoir
c. aqueduct
d. thermal pollution
e. global warming
f. transformer
g. turbine
h. voltage
i. generator
j. polymers

Interpreting What You Learned

1. A high-pressure jet of water is used as a knife to cut shoe parts. Is the water jet an example of mechanical, chemical, or electrical energy?
2. What energy conversions must occur to bring electricity from a hydroelectric power plant to your home?
3. How might shortages in the supply of natural resources affect manufacturing?
4. How might the amount of rainfall in an area affect each of the following?
   (a) your home water supply
   (b) the amount of electricity available
   (c) the supply of sneakers

Applying What You Learned

1. City X is in a desert but has no water shortage. What does this tell you about its water supply?
2. Why should you let tap water stand a few days before adding it to an aquarium?
3. Place the following in order from most acidic to most basic: plain water, grapefruit juice, soapy water.
4. What discovery in the mid-1800s led to laws requiring cities to purify water?
5. Of the following, which would you classify as examples of technology: an apple, a car, a lake, the sap of a rubber tree, a turbine, a sneaker?

Wetlands: Making Decisions

Wetlands: Making Decisions

It's time for you to make up your mind. Do you want old wetlands or new jobs? In this module, you'll get a firsthand look at how people's needs can come into conflict with the needs of nature. It's a complicated conflict, but it has to be resolved. Every vote counts!

CHAPTER 1 A Sample Ecosystem

Can you balance an ecosystem? To make an ecosystem, you need to balance the needs of every member.

CHAPTER 2 Wetland Ecosystems

Let's be fair to the fowl. Ducks and other waterfowl depend on wetlands for their food, homes, and lives.

CHAPTER 3 Applying Science

According to the NEPA, the EIS needs an OK. The National Environmental Policy Act requires Environmental Impact Statements for projects that affect the environment.

1

A Sample Ecosystem

You've got to be kidding!

Wear cover goggles
for this activity.

How difficult is it to make a balanced system?

Put on your cover goggles. Place a large nail in a lump of clay so that the head is standing upward. Obtain eleven other flat-headed nails. Your task is to balance all eleven nails on the nail that is standing. You cannot use anything except the nails. Describe your balanced system to the class.

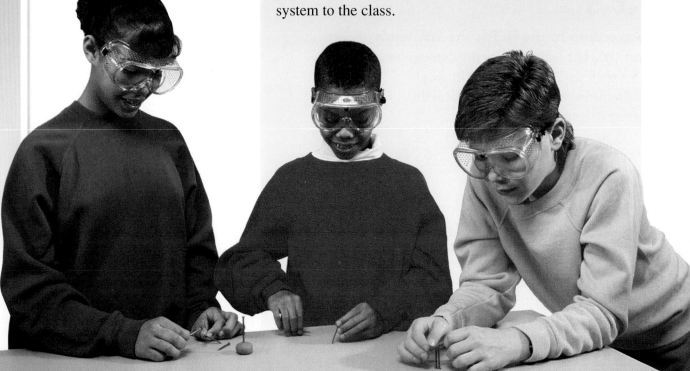

For Discussion

1. *Why was it difficult to balance your system?*
2. *What happens when you add or subtract one nail from the balanced system?*

1·1 *Life In the Tank*

▶ *Would your aquarium welcome a new fish?*

Suppose you keep an aquarium as a hobby. During the past two years you have slowly added different kinds of animals to your tank. Now you have a California newt, two marble hatchetfish, two swordtail fish, two angelfish, and three orange-and-black striped clown loaches. You are proud of your healthy fish community, and your friends help you care for it.

One day a friend gives you a beautiful red Siamese fighting fish. You like the idea of owning one, but you know you can't just add a new fish to your tank without finding out more about it. Should you add this beauty to your tank? If you do, what will happen to your community? Will the new fish attack or upset the other fish? Will the other fish attack the new one? What do you need to know about your aquarium and about Siamese fighting fish in order to decide?

▼ *You wonder, "It's a neat fish, but what will it do to the community I've made over the last two years?"*

Every Fish Has a Niche

To decide whether to add a new fish to your tank, you must first know what each fish does.

So how do you find out what each fish does in your tank? The most obvious way is just to observe the fish. Then you can look in books to see what other people know about your fish.

The aquarium is a balanced system. Each species of fish in it has a specific role, or **niche,** (nich) in the community. Notice in the notebook that each species does something different, such as eating different foods. Imagine if all the fish ate algae. Some fish would starve because there wouldn't be enough algae to go around. What if there were no plants? Where would the fish get their oxygen?

As you can see, the different parts within the system are balanced in ways that support one another. Look at the data collected by one student. Notice how the species of this aquarium help one another.

Angel fish:
large fins, calm, can only eat things smaller than its small mouth, slow moving and graceful

Clown loach:
eats leftovers that fall to bottom of tank, active but calm, has spikes by each gill that protect it from predators (can't be swallowed by larger fish)

California newt:
amphibian, calm, not a predator, eats worms and krill

Silver hatchet:
calm, surface dweller, eats flake food

Swordtail fish:
will chase other fish away from food, will eat whatever it's fed (flake food, the newt's food)

O₂

CO₂

O₂

Waste

► Nutrients and energy
constantly flow through an
ecosystem.

Waste

CO₂

Aquarium Interactions

After considering the niche of each animal in your aquarium, you have to think about the whole community as a system. A system is something made of many parts that work together. An ecosystem is made up of living organisms and nonliving things that interact.

When you look at your tank, you see living things— your newt resting on a branch above the water's surface, plants floating in the water, and fish swimming around quietly. You see the nonliving water and rocks, and air is at the top. The ecosystem appears to be a **stable system**—or a system that is in balance. You built a balanced system in the Discover Activity. But unlike that system, a stable ecosystem depends on a constant flow of chemical nutrients and energy passing through the system.

For example, carbon dioxide and oxygen are nonliving chemical compounds that living plants and animals take in and give off. Use your finger to trace the pathways of oxygen and carbon dioxide through the ecosystem. The fish breathes in oxygen and breathes out carbon dioxide as it carries on respiration. At the bottom of the tank, tiny bacteria called decomposers also take in oxygen. The decomposers break down the wastes and dead parts of plants and animals into simpler chemicals that become nutrients, or fertilizers, for the plants. The decomposers also give off carbon dioxide.

The plants in the tank also use oxygen during respiration and give off carbon dioxide. But during the process of photosynthesis, they take in carbon dioxide from the water and give off oxygen. The oxygen the plants give off is not enough for the fish to live on. So you have a pump that pumps air bubbles through the water. The water picks up oxygen from the air bubbles. When the larger bubbles break at the surface, they make ripples. This rippling helps even more oxygen enter the water, because more water surface touches the air.

Now, where do the animals get *their* nutrients? Small fish may nibble on aquarium plants, especially if no other food is available. However, most of your animals get their nutrients and energy from the small amounts of food you add every day to the aquarium. Usually, you feed the fish some flakes made of a mixture of fish, meat, shrimp, egg, and grains. For variety, you give the fish some live food—water fleas, brine shrimp, or tiny tubifex worms. The newt gets shrimp or worms.

Also, you maintain the environment by heating the water to the right temperature, by adding clear water, and by cleaning the water and tank of excess fish wastes and other debris. The aquarium ecosystem depends on your help for its stability.

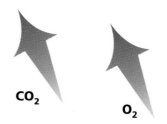

▼ *Plants take in and give off both oxygen and carbon dioxide.*

CO_2

O_2

Nutrients

CO_2

O_2

Checkpoint

1. Choose a member of the aquarium community and describe its niche.
2. Briefly explain how living and nonliving things work together in an ecosystem.
3. **Take Action!** Your school is a balanced system. Draw a floor plan of the school. Show how energy and nutrients move into and out of the system.

It's a Small World

By making a freshwater habitat, you can learn about the conditions plants and animals need to survive and how they interact.

Picture A

Gather These Materials

two 2- or 3-liter clear, plastic bottles
scissors
sand
ruler
kitchen strainer
aquarium gravel
masking tape

marker
water
elodea plants
thermometer
fish net
goldfish or guppies
fish food

Follow This Procedure

1 Make a chart like the one on the next page. Record your observations in your chart.

2 Rinse out one plastic bottle with water. Cut off the bottle top carefully with the scissors. (Picture A)

3 Rinse the sand in a strainer, and place about 10 cm of the sand into the bottom of the bottle.

4 Fill the bottle and the second bottle about three-quarters full of water, and let them age for 2 days. This time allows chlorine and other gases to escape.

5 Plant the elodea in the sand. (Picture B)

6 Now add 2 cm of gravel to anchor the plants securely. (Picture C)

7 After the water clears, add one or two small fish.

8 Mark the water level with a marker. Add more aged water to maintain this level as water evaporates.

Picture B

Picture C

Record Your Results

	Day 1	Day 2	Day 3	Day 4	Day 5
Temperature					
Water level					
Light level					
No. of fish					
No. of plants					

9 Feed the fish a tiny pinch of fish food each day.

10 Record the water temperature, water level, and level of light (bright, moderate, or dim) each day for a week.

11 Change the water when it gets cloudy. Place the fish in a container of clean water while changing the dirty water.

State Your Conclusions

1. All environments go through changes. How did your freshwater habitat change?
2. How did the changes in the habitat affect the fish? How did the changes affect the plants?

Let's Experiment

What conditions are important in keeping a habitat healthy? Make another habitat, using a green-tinted bottle. Include only the plants in both habitats. Does the color of the container affect the plants?

Into The Field

What would life be like at your home if twice as many people lived there?

Write about the short-term and long-term effects of doubling the number of people living in your home.

LESSON

1.2 *Making Changes*

▶ *How do changes affect the aquarium ecosystem?*

You've worked many months to create your aquarium with its community of different animals and plants. As long as everything stays healthy, you figure you're doing a good job of keeping the system stable. But what would happen if you changed the system?

Increasing the Population

Each population—a group of individuals of the same species living in an ecosystem—has certain needs that must be met in order for the individuals to continue living. They need space where they can find nutrients, light, and oxygen. They need space for leaving waste products. They need space to find mates and to lay eggs or give birth to offspring. If not enough space, nutrients, light, and

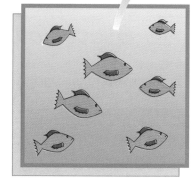

other factors are available to meet the needs of each population, some of the organisms will become ill or die. Eventually, if enough plants and animals die, the remaining individuals can survive. The system becomes stable again.

Your tank's ecosystem is balanced now. But every change you make can affect the tank's stability. What if you were to add seven more fish—three Siamese algae eaters and four zebra danios—to your tank? What parts of the ecosystem would be affected?

First of all, the seven additional fish will increase the demand for food and oxygen in the system. Do the plants plus your air pump provide enough oxygen for that many new fish? Is there enough algae for that many algae-eating fish? If not, they might starve. You might have to feed them spinach every day, or find out what else they can eat.

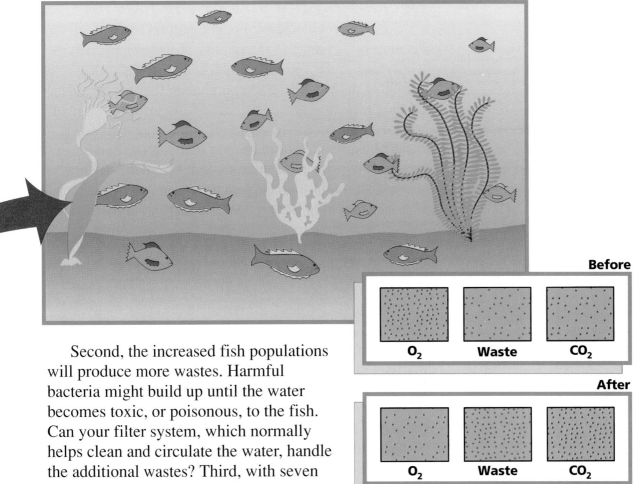

O_2	**Waste**	CO_2

After

O_2	**Waste**	CO_2

Second, the increased fish populations will produce more wastes. Harmful bacteria might build up until the water becomes toxic, or poisonous, to the fish. Can your filter system, which normally helps clean and circulate the water, handle the additional wastes? Third, with seven more fish, less space is available for each fish. They might fight over space or even eat each other!

The boxes show the levels of oxygen, waste, and carbon dioxide you could expect before and after adding the seven new fish. How will each substance change?

How much clean, oxygen-rich water is needed for a stable, healthy fish community? Most aquariums require 2 liters of water for every centimeter of fish length. Suppose you have a 100-liter tank and these fish:
• two 7.5-centimeter angelfish
• three 5-centimeter clown loaches
• two 5-centimeter swordtail fish
• two 2.5-centimeter marble hatchetfish

Your total fish length is 45 centimeters. At 2 liters per centimeter, you need 90 liters for healthy fish. The new Siamese algae eaters are each 3.75 centimeters long, and the zebra danios are each 2.5 centimeters. That adds over 20 centimeters of fish to the tank. Will the aquarium support the population increase?

▲ *More fish use up more oxygen and produce more wastes and carbon dioxide.*

Decreasing the Size of the Habitat

Sometimes change occurs in a natural ecosystem because of a change in the quality of its habitat, such as a decrease in the amount of space, air, or water. A habitat is the place where an organism lives. It includes all the places it roams, eats, sleeps, or carries out any of its activities. All the resources that the organism needs must be available within or near that habitat. Some habitats are natural, such as a pond, marsh, or stream where fish might live. Other habitats are artificial, such as your aquarium. Because your aquarium is an artificial habitat, you have to work to maintain good living conditions. You have tried to make your aquarium as natural an environment as possible for your animals and plants.

One day you think, "Maybe I should add more gravel or big rocks to make more hiding places for my fish, or another big rock for my newt to climb on." How will this change affect the ecosystem?

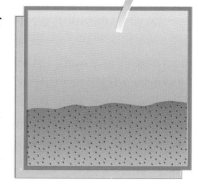

First, the amount of space taken up by gravel or rock increases. This change increases the amount of hiding space. But space for other resources—such as living space, water, air—will decrease. The result may be the same as adding too many fish to the population. The diagram shows the amount of gravel to be added to the tank. The boxes on the next page show the levels of oxygen, waste, and carbon dioxide before and after the added gravel. Will the levels rise or fall?

The decrease in habitat means the fish have to share a smaller living space. This change upsets the stability, so the whole system will likely undergo more change. Some members of the community will probably die.

Two other important nonliving parts of the aquarium ecosystem are temperature and light. If the aquarium does not get enough light, the plants will turn yellow and die. An aquarium needs about three hours of sunlight or eight to ten hours of artificial light a day to keep fish and plants healthy.

> ➤ *How will adding gravel affect your tank ecosystem?*

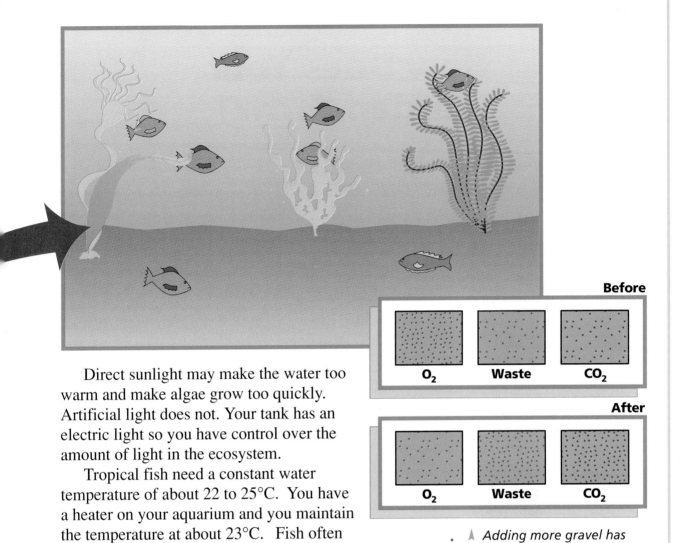

Before

O$_2$	Waste	CO$_2$

After

O$_2$	Waste	CO$_2$

Direct sunlight may make the water too warm and make algae grow too quickly. Artificial light does not. Your tank has an electric light so you have control over the amount of light in the ecosystem.

Tropical fish need a constant water temperature of about 22 to 25°C. You have a heater on your aquarium and you maintain the temperature at about 23°C. Fish often get sick from sudden temperature changes.

Knowing how changes can affect your ecosystem helps you decide whether or not to make certain changes. And, speaking of decisions, what about that Siamese fighting fish? You still have to decide whether or not to add that fish to your tank.

▲ *Adding more gravel has much the same effect as adding more fish.*

Checkpoint

1. List three ways that an increase in population can affect an aquarium ecosystem.
2. How is adding gravel to an aquarium tank like adding fish to the population?
3. **Take Action!** Design and conduct an experiment to show how sunlight affects the temperature of a bowl of water.

Activity

How Does Your Garden Grow?

Many factors affect ecosystems. You can see the effect of pollution by observing duckweed, a tiny plant that grows on the surface of water.

Picture A

Picture B

Picture C

Gather These Materials

cover goggles	masking tape
duckweed plants	salt
4 petri dishes	liquid soap
water	spoon
vinegar	2 droppers

Follow This Procedure

1 Make a chart like the one on the next page. Record your observations in your chart.

2 Put on your cover goggles.

3 Place several duckweed plants in each of 4 petri dishes. (Picture A)

4 Half-fill each petri dish with water.

5 Add 2 drops of vinegar to one petri dish. Label the dish. (Picture B)

6 Add the remaining 2 environmental pollutants to 2 of the remaining petri dishes. Add a pinch of salt to one and 2 drops of soap to the other. Label each dish. (Picture C)

7 The fourth petri dish will contain only duckweed and water and serve as a control.

Predict: *How will the duckweed grow in the polluted and control dishes?*

Record Your Results

Pollutant	Day 1	Day 2	Day 3	Day 4	Day 5
Vinegar					
Salt					
Soap					
Control					

8 Place the petri dishes in a warm, bright place for several days. Observe the growth of the duckweed.

9 Measure the rate of growth of each population of duckweed over one week or more. Record your observations in your chart.

State Your Conclusions

1. What is the effect of vinegar, salt, and soap on duckweed populations?

2. How might these pollutants affect other plant growth?

Let's Experiment

Use the procedures you have learned and what you know about scientific methods to investigate the effect of different levels of light and temperature on the growth of duckweed.

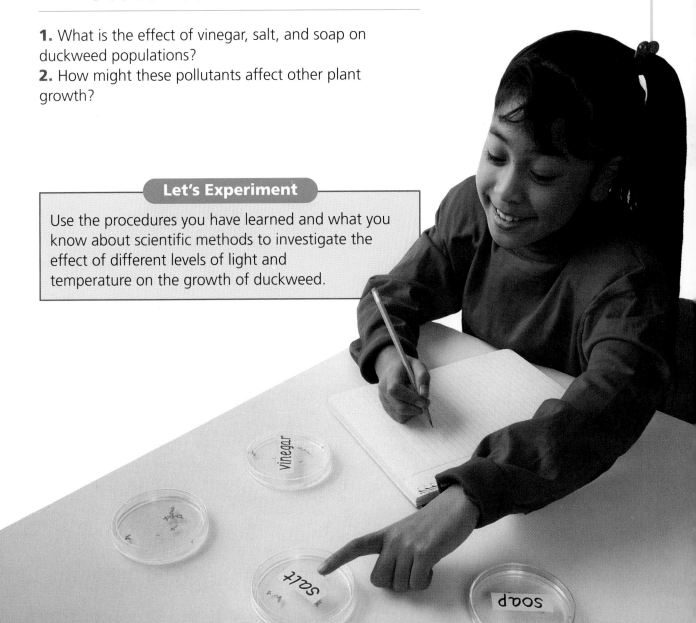

1.3 *You Decide*

▶ ***How badly do you want the Siamese fighting fish?***

Now you're alone—just you and your fish. The Siamese fighting fish sits in its little bowl on the table next to you. Your other fish happily swim around in their safe habitat. What do you need to know about this fish in order to decide whether it joins the others or not? Suppose it tries to bite or eat the other fish? Do you care if some fish die? Only you can decide.

New Betta on the Block

When biologists study animals, they try to make predictions about their behavior. You know that you have to predict what could happen if you add this fish to your tank. In order to predict, you have to gather some information. You have to know the characteristics of the animals you already have and the characteristics of the new fish. You especially want to know how each fish gets along with other species. To learn these things, you have to do research. You've probably done research before. It includes looking up information and taking notes.

▶ *Should you add your new fish to the ecosystem?*

Researching the characteristics of *your* fish is easy. You can look back at your notes about each species on pages 6 and 7. The animals in your tank that eat other fish are the angelfish and the swordtails, and they will only eat very small fish. The Siamese fighting fish is over 2.5 centimeters long, so you draw a conclusion: it is too big to be eaten.

Now you have to find out about Siamese fighting fish. You bring home some books from the library about tropical fish. In the index of one you find this listing: *Siamese fighting fish*, 54.

You turn to page 54 and see a brilliant color photograph that looks just like your new fish! Reading the caption under the picture, you discover that this species is also called a betta, short for its scientific name, *Betta splendens*. You also learn that you have a male betta.

You make the following notes about male bettas:
• grows to about 6 centimeters long.
• fights other males and sometimes females.
• eats smaller fish and fish with long fins.
• usually raised in its own tank or bowl.
• not friendly to other fish.
• sometimes gets along in a community tank.

So, what can you predict? Probably, the male betta will try to eat some of your other fish. Your research seemed to hint that sometimes a betta can get along in a community. Do you want to experiment with your other fish and take the chance of losing them?

Making Environmental Decisions

For many questions there is no single right or wrong answer. The right answer depends upon the results you want. If you don't care about possibly losing some fish, you might decide to place the betta in your tank as an experiment. If you want to keep all your fish and also have the betta, you might decide to keep it in a separate tank. Or perhaps you will give it back to your friend. You have many possible decisions.

Now, what have you learned about ecosystems by studying your aquarium? You know that making a change in the ecosystem sets other changes into motion. By introducing a betta into your aquarium, you endanger other fish. Even if some fish die, you know that eventually the ecosystem might become stable again—but with fewer fish. Or you might end up with one very large betta! Your choice will determine the results.

The world has many, many habitats where all the various species of plants and animals live and interact. In each ecosystem, changes in the habitat or population create other changes within that system or in neighboring ecosystems.

▼ *Environmental problems involve many factors and many points of view.*

1. *Why is the system important?*

2. *How will the system change?*

3. *Does it matter if it changes?*

4. *Why make the change?*

5. *What are the other options?*

Wetlands debate has old battle lines, but new ground rules

By Stevenson Swanson
Environment writer

The status of wetlands has been in doubt from the beginning.

On the third day, Genesis says, the Almighty gathered the waters together and called them seas. The dry land he called earth.

But what about swamps, marshes, fens, bogs and all the other places on Earth that are neither wholly wet nor wholly dry?

Through the centuries, wetlands have had their ups and downs—mainly downs—as societies have tried to figure out what to do with these tracts where water and land mingle.

In the most recent oscillation, President Bush decided that the federal government, having gone too far in trying to protect America's remaining wetlands, needed to be reined in with a tighter wetlands policy.

In the Chicago area, environmentalists say the stricter definition of a wetland in Bush's new policy could lead to greater flooding through loss of flood plains, and a state official estimates that 66 percent of what the state currently classifies as wetland would fail to meet the new standard.

Ecologists value wetlands because they are rich wildlife habitats, store storm water that would otherwise flood homes and businesses, and purify polluted water. However, the vast majority of America's wetlands have already been lost to agriculture and development. In 1818, when Illinois became a state, wetlands

Wetland acres
By county; in percent of total county acreage

County	Acres
Lake	30,487
Du Page	8,229
Will	14,881
Kane	8,564
Cook	15,177
Kendall	2,186
Kankakee	4,801
McHenry	3,665

according to propo... new policy, because set forth in some small type an... language, was onl... week in the Fe... Figuring out how plies in the field they say. Also, could be forthco... gress, where a ... ported by devel... is pending, or ... Assembly, wh... varying wetla... pending.

Everyone a... The changes mean that fe... as wetlands ment collap... real-estate the change... ment res... rights; en... Bush for final ren... pledge t... presiden...

"To ...

Humans have many different habitats, all of which are part of the earth. The human population is enormous and still growing. Today human activities often crowd and endanger other species as well as the physical environment. Because of these effects, every citizen needs to know how to make environmental decisions. Each person should know how to get information, how to do research, and how to make scientific predictions about the environment and our future needs.

Look at the process you went through to make an informed decision about your aquarium. You gathered information about the various species. You studied the effects of different changes in the ecosystem. People use this same process to make decisions that affect the environment and its living inhabitants.

One area of decisions facing people today concerns wetlands. Wetlands are marshy or swampy areas of shallow water or soggy soil. They include a variety of living organisms. Read the newspaper headlines on page 20. What concerns about wetlands do they raise?

Because of the growing human population, many wetlands have disappeared—drained and converted to farmfields and land for buildings. However, many species depend on wetlands, and these areas are important for humans too. You can already see a problem shaping up. Important decisions about wetlands will be made by citizens in the coming years. The next chapters will look further at this issue and help you prepare to make decisions about the environment.

Checkpoint

1. What characteristics of a male betta would be important to know when deciding whether to add it to the aquarium?
2. What things does a person need to do or know in order to make an informed decision about the environment?
3. **Take Action!** Suppose you decide to add the male betta to your aquarium. Make diagrams showing three events that might happen as a result of your decision.

INVESTIGATE

Changing Habitats

 Wear cover goggles for this activity.

How might the size of a habitat affect life within it? Investigate by comparing the concentration of carbon dioxide in two different volumes of water.

What To Do
A. With your cover goggles on, mix 0.1 g of bromothymol blue dye in 2000 mL of water.
B. Fill a jar with 100 mL of this solution. Use a colored pencil to match and record the liquid's color in the *Before* box of a chart like the one shown.
C. Using 4 straws, exhale 40 times into the liquid.
D. Record the color in the *After* box.
E. Repeat steps B–D using 1000 mL of the blue liquid.

	Color	
	Before	After
In 100 mL		
In 1000 mL		

What Did You Find Out?
1. *Carbon dioxide makes the blue indicator change color. In which volume of water was the carbon dioxide most concentrated?*
2. *Why might the same number of organisms in a large habitat have trouble surviving in a small habitat?*

Chapter Review

Reviewing Words and Concepts

Write the letter of the word or phrase that best completes each sentence.

j **1.** The role of an organism in its environment is its _____.

H **2.** When an ecosystem is balanced, it is considered a _____.

e **3.** Organisms that break down wastes into simpler chemicals that become nutrients are called _____.

g **4.** All the organisms in a community and the nonliving things with which they interact make up an _____.

F **5.** All the frogs living in a pond make up a _____.

b **6.** A stable system must have a constant flow of _____ and nutrients passing through it.

c **7.** Plants in an aquarium take in _____ during respiration and give off carbon dioxide.

D **8.** Ponds, marshes, and streams are _____ habitats of fish.

A **9.** The activities of humans sometimes _____ other species.

I **10.** An aquarium is a _____ for fish.

a. endanger
b. energy
c. oxygen
d. natural
e. decomposers
f. habitat
g. ecosystem
h. stable system
i. niche
j. population

Connecting Ideas

1. Copy the concept map. Use the terms at the right to complete the map about how a change in a population affects the ecosystem.

~~less oxygen~~   ~~more fish~~
~~less space~~   ~~more wastes~~
~~more carbon dioxide~~

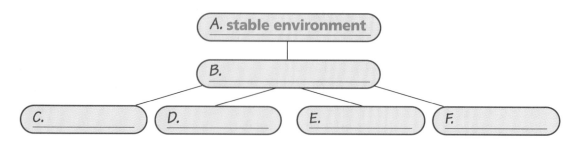

A. stable environment

B. _____

C. _____   D. _____   E. _____   F. _____

2. Write a sentence or two that summarizes the ideas shown in the concept map.

Interpreting What You Learned

1. Explain what would happen if several kinds of fish in an aquarium had the same niche.
2. Describe the ways an aquarium ecosystem depends on human help to remain a stable system.
3. What is the role of decomposers in an aquarium ecosystem?
4. Give an example of how a change in the size of an organism's habitat affects that organism.
5. What information might you find that would lead you to decide not to add a certain fish to your aquarium?
6. Explain why people should know how to make environmental decisions.

 Performance Assessment

How can you create a stable system?

Materials • 20 dark seeds • 20 light seeds • sheet of paper • metric ruler • plastic cup • pencil

Collecting Data

1. Use a metric ruler and a pencil to draw a large square measuring 20 centimeters on each side on a sheet of paper.
2. Divide the square in half by drawing a line straight across the center from one side to the other. Draw a second line straight down from the top of the square to the bottom to divide the large square into four equal-sized smaller squares. Each small square represents a different aquarium. Label the small squares *1, 2, 3,* and *4.*
3. Place all of the seeds in the cup and shake the cup to mix the seeds. The dark seeds represent fish. The light seeds represent plants. Spill the seeds from the cup onto the large square.
4. Pick up any seeds that fall outside the large square and place them back in the cup. Spill the seeds again so all the seeds are on the large square.
5. Observe where the seeds fall on each small square. Draw a diagram that shows where the seeds fell. Record on your diagram the total number of different seeds that landed in each numbered square.
6. A stable system in each aquarium consists of five fish and five plants. Write about changes you would need to make to each aquarium for it to become a stable system.

Analyzing Data

Describe one of the aquariums that is not a stable system. What would happen to the fish and plants in this aquarium if no changes were made?

2 Wetland Ecosystems

Tah dah. . . let me introduce you to Mr. Boat Foot!

How would you design a "wetland critter"?

If you ever visit a marsh in a state park, you'll probably walk on wooden boards that float on the water or rest on the spongy grass. Think about what it would be like for an animal to live there. Design and build a model of an animal that is adapted to life in a wetland.

For Discussion

1. *How is your animal adapted for survival?*
2. *What would happen to your animal if the wetland became dry?*

2.1 *Looking at Wetlands*

▶ *Can a wetland share space with an airport?*

Suppose your class goes on a field trip to a soggy flatland a few kilometers outside of town. Your teacher explains that some citizens want to build an airport on this land. You have studied an artificial ecosystem—your fish tank—and know that you can disrupt its stability by making changes. You also understand how your tank might eventually reach stability after a change. But the new stable system might be different from the original system. Natural ecosystems also might find stability after disruption. If the airport is built, what changes will happen? Your assignment is to decide if the airport is worth the changes. First you must gather information, just as you did for your aquarium.

Kinds of Wetlands

The first thing to find out is what, exactly, is a wetland. A **wetland** is an area that is at or near the water table for at least part of the year. Over 32 million hectares of wetlands exist across the United States. Some are just tiny wet places along the highway fringed with a few cattails. Others seem vast and endless.

▼ *The great Okefenokee Swamp in Georgia and this small pool fringed with cattails in Michigan are both wetlands.*

So, put on your waders, get out your binoculars, and come along for a closer look at some wetlands. The first thing you look for is water. It must be near ground level during at least part of the year, making the ground mushy, wet, or flooded. When you study wetlands, you have to look for certain kinds of soil along with certain kinds of plants and animals. Wetland soils are rich with decayed parts of plants and animals. The kinds of plants and animals found in a wetland depend upon the kind of wetland—whether it's a bog, a marsh, a swamp, or some other kind of wetland.

Watch your step around a bog! The thick moss looks like solid ground, but it quakes and bounces with every step. The "ground" is really a mat of moss floating on water. The bog was once a hole left by a glacier about 11,000 years ago. The hole became a pond that slowly filled up with thick sphagnum moss, which soaks up water like a sponge. The bog's soil and water are so acid that few species of plants and animals can survive there. However, you do see spruce and pine trees, insect-eating plants, cranberry bushes, and orchids, as well as insects, frogs, and birds.

▼ *The long legs of these birds are adapted to life in the wetlands.*

➤ *Salt marshes occur along the ocean and Gulf coasts.*

The Native Americans called marshes "betweenlands"—not exactly bodies of water and not exactly dry land. Here you often see soft-stemmed plants that stick partly out of the water—grasses, bulrushes, cattails, reeds, and wild rice. The water in marshes can be as shallow as a few centimeters or as deep as a meter. Marshes form along the shallow edges of lakes, rivers, and oceans. Some marshes began as lakes that gradually filled up with decomposed plant matter. In some parts of the inland plains, water collects in marshes called prairie potholes and dries up later in the year. In marshes, you find many species of plants and animals. Have your binoculars ready! How many different plants and animals can you find in this picture of a salt marsh?

In a swamp you find yourself under tall trees such as cypress or tupelo, and surrounded by large shrubs. Some swamps have wisps of grey Spanish moss hanging from tree branches. This organism takes nutrients from the air alone. A swamp has more kinds of plants, insects, birds, fish, and other living things than any other kind of wetland.

Life in a Salt Marsh

Many species have adapted to the harsh environment of a salt marsh.

For many people, living right along the ocean coast would be a dream come true. Actually, the salt water and the daily action of tides in a coastal salt marsh form a difficult environment in which most species could not survive. Those that have adapted depend on each other like organisms in any other community.

Snails and mollusks live on the marsh bottom, where they eat decaying plant matter. Insects and amphibians make their homes among the plants on the muddy banks, or under the broad leaves of floating plants, which have adapted to the salty conditions.

Many birds stop to rest and feed on their way to other areas. They eat worms, fish, and insects. The birds use gravel and plants to line their nests.

Think of how each of these organisms fits into the community.

Pickleweed
This plant grows in shallow, quiet water and on muddy banks. It is bright red in the fall and green in the spring. Because the plant stores salt, people named it after salty pickles!

Purple Shorecrab
This small crab lives under stones and among seaweeds. It feeds mostly on algae, which it scrapes from rocks with its claws.

Shellfish
While most mollusks live in the sea, species such as these oysters, cockles, and jacknife clams are adapted to salt marsh conditions.

Birds
These feathers were left by killdeer and willet, birds that come to the marsh to bathe and feed.

Salt Grass
Stiff, smooth salt grass grows in dense clumps in and around the water.

▼ *Muskrats eat a variety of foods including stems, leaves, berries, and snails.*

Marsh Species

Do all marshes have the same species? No, different kinds of marshes have different inhabitants. The kind of marsh is determined by many factors—water and air temperature, salt and nutrient content of the water, depth of the water, and even on what species are in the marsh. You have seen some of the members of a salt marsh community. In a freshwater marsh you are more likely to see cattails than salt grass. Red-winged blackbirds, ducks, and muskrats, like the one shown here, like to live among cattails, so you can expect to find these species where you find cattails.

When you think of marshes, it's hard not to think of ducks. They go together. Over half the ducks in North America were hatched in prairie pothole marshes. On their migration routes—or flyways—they rest, feed, and hide in marshes across the land. In shallow marshes, you see "dabbling" ducks such as pintails, mallards, and northern shovelers. These ducks stick their heads down in the water to feed on plants and animals along the marsh bottom. Deeper marshes attract "diving" ducks such as the canvasback, redhead, and ruddy duck. These ducks have short legs, set far back on their bodies, which they use to steer underwater. What features did your critter in the Discover Activity have that would help it in a wetland?

▼ *Marshes are homes to many kinds of ducks including the mallard, at right, and canvasback, below.*

The species in a marsh can change because of human activities. Among these activities are building dams and canals, draining or filling the land, and changing the supply of nutrients that enters the marsh. The photograph shows what often happens when extra fertilizer from nearby farmfields drain into a marsh. The same nutrients in fertilizer that help crops grow also increase the growth of bacteria and algae. A marsh can become clogged with these organisms, which block sunlight for other forms of life. When the bacteria and algae die and decay, their decomposers use up much of the water's oxygen. Just as with the aquarium, one change can upset an ecosystem.

▲ Fertilizers from nearby fields add extra nutrients to the marsh, causing the growth of bacteria and algae.

Checkpoint

1. What are some characteristics of all wetlands?
2. What factors make a salt marsh a difficult environment for most organisms?
3. How do human activities change the species that live in a marsh ecosystem?
4. **Take Action!** Design and set up an experiment to show how building a dam or canal can affect a wetland.

Activity

Plants Need
Their Space Too

All living things compete for energy and space. Find out what happens to two plant species when space and sunlight are limited.

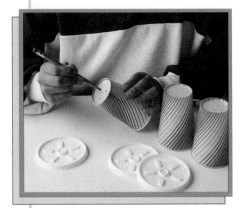

Picture A

Picture B

Picture C

Gather These Materials

sharp pencil   water
3 paper cups   wheat seeds
vermiculite   clover seeds
newspaper

Follow This Procedure

1 Make a chart like the one on the next page. Record your observations in your chart.

2 Use the sharpened pencil to punch several small holes in the bottom of the 3 paper cups. (Picture A)

3 Fill each cup with vermiculite. (Picture B)

4 Add water to completely moisten the vermiculite.

5 Label the cups 1, 2, and 3.

6 Gently press 10 wheat seeds and 10 clover seeds into each cup. (Picture C) Record these numbers.

Predict: *How many of the plants will sprout? How many will survive and grow?*

7 Place the cups in a sunny place. Add water daily to keep the vermiculite moist.

8 When the plants are 3 cm high, uproot the plants in Cup 1.

9 Count the number of each kind of plant that sprouted. Record your data in the appropriate boxes in your table.

Record Your Results

Cup and Time	Seeds	Number of seeds planted	Number of seeds sprouted	Number of plants growing
Cup 1	Wheat			
at 3 cm	Clover			
Cup 2	Wheat			
at 2 weeks	Clover			
Cup 3	Wheat			
at 1 month	Clover			

10 After 2 weeks have passed, uproot and examine the plants in Cup 2. Count the number of each kind of plant that sprouted and grew. Record your data.

11 After 1 month has passed, uproot the plants in Cup 3. Count the number of each kind that is still growing. Record your data.

State Your Conclusions

1. What happens when these 2 species of plants compete for soil, water, and sunlight?

2. What do you infer about the plants that survived in Cup 3?

Let's Experiment

Sometimes a species becomes overcrowded. What will happen then? Use what you know about scientific methods to find out.

2.2 *Interactions in a Marsh*

How does a marsh work as an ecosystem?

You've seen how a fish aquarium ecosystem works. The plants and animals interact. Nutrients and energy flow between the living and nonliving parts of the system. A marsh ecosystem has the same kinds of interactions, but they are more complex. Energy and nutrients flow through the entire system.

Energy Flow in the Marsh

How do food and energy pass through the system? You know producers trap the energy of sunlight and serve as the first level of food chains. The producers in this marsh include grasses and algae. Other basic sources of food in marshes are decaying plants and animals. The producers and the decaying plants and animals are eaten by consumers—animals. Find the first level consumers—animals that eat either producers or decaying plants and animals. What are some first level consumers in this system?

These first level consumers become the prey of larger animals like ducks, fish, and raccoons. Animals that eat first level consumers are called second level consumers. Second level consumers may be eaten by third level consumers, such as ospreys or people. As you can see in the chart, some consumers eat foods at different levels. Through this food chain, chemical energy passes from producer to consumer.

When you try to draw the whole ecosystem with organisms in their niches, it ends up looking like a web with arrows connecting all the inhabitants. Some insects and shrimp eat algae and other producers. Use your finger to trace the arrows that connect those organisms. Insects are eaten by ducks and fish. Fish may be eaten by ospreys or people. Trace those connections too. Because the food interactions are complex and web-like, the system is called a food web.

▼ *Follow the connections among organisms in this food web.*

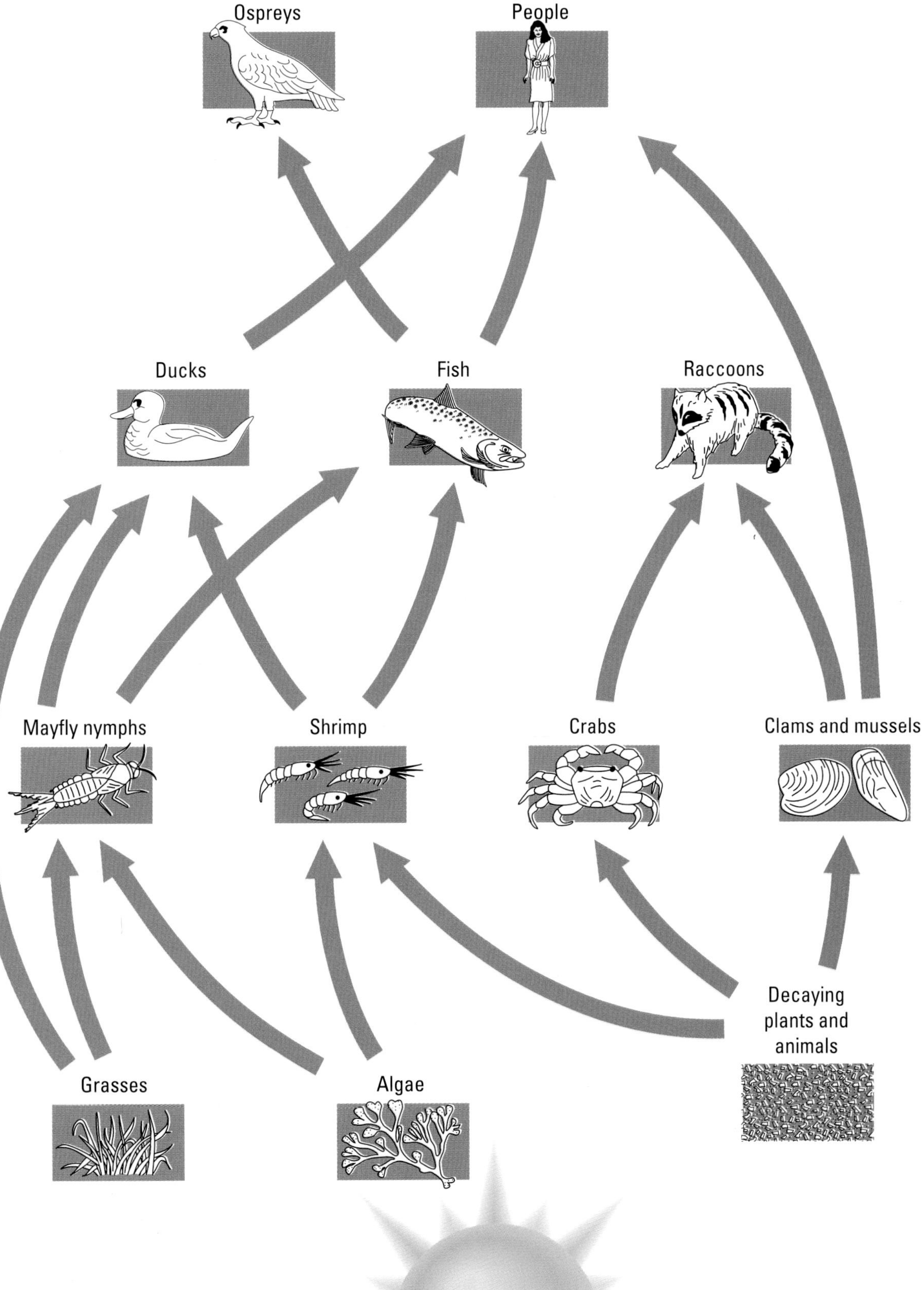

Ospreys

People

Ducks

Fish

Raccoons

Mayfly nymphs

Shrimp

Crabs

Clams and mussels

Grasses

Algae

Decaying plants and animals

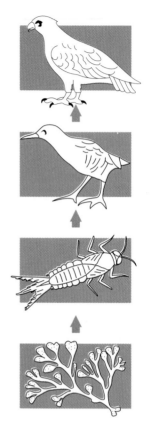

Energy is lost at each level of the energy pyramid.

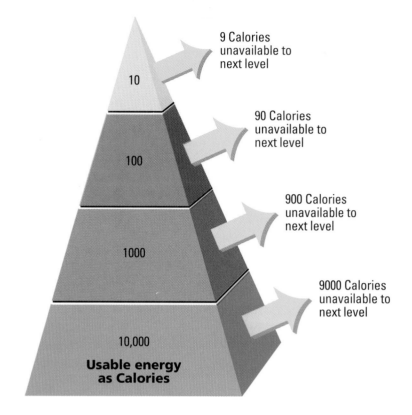

9 Calories unavailable to next level

90 Calories unavailable to next level

900 Calories unavailable to next level

9000 Calories unavailable to next level

10
100
1000
10,000

Usable energy as Calories

How does energy flow through the marsh? The energy of sunlight floods the marsh. Imagine that you're riding a sunbeam as it enters a tiny cell in a large strand of green algae. You could watch and see how the algae use light energy to make molecules of sugars.

Along comes a mayfly nymph—a small insect that gobbles up algae. As the mayfly digests the algae, the energy stored as sugars in the algae is released. The mayfly uses some of the energy for digestion and movement. Some is used to make new cells for mayfly body parts. But about 90 percent of the energy in the algae is used, undigested, or released into the environment as heat. This energy is "lost" from the ecosystem—it cannot move through the food chain.

Later, a clapper rail eats the mayfly, and more energy is released. The energy pyramid above shows the relationship between a food chain and available energy. Again, notice that 90 percent of the energy is lost at each level. Only about 10 percent gets passed on at each step as stored chemical energy for use by organisms of the next level. You can see that the osprey population has much less energy available to it than first level consumers, such as the populations of insects.

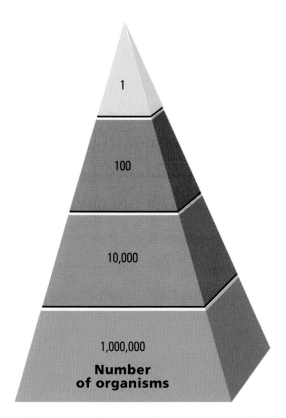

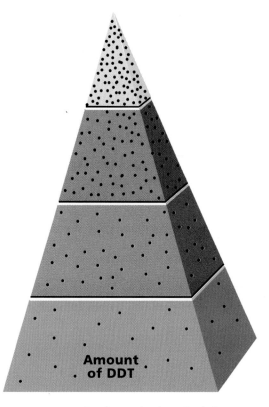

1
100
10,000
1,000,000
**Number
of organisms**

**Amount
of DDT**

Chemicals and the Food Chain

The large base of the energy pyramid shows that energy from producers supports the whole ecosystem. So plants have large populations, while consumers are fewer in number, as shown above. How does the number of consumers compare as you go up the food chain? You find very few ospreys compared to plants and algae.

Unfortunately, toxic chemicals sometimes enter the food web and go up the food chain too. The second pyramid shows how at each consumer level the concentrations of those toxic chemicals retained in living tissue increase. At the top of the food chain, the concentrations can be deadly. Which organism in the food chain on page 36 will end up with the most DDT?

Recall that before DDT was made illegal, it was a popular pesticide. Salt marshes on Long Island, New York, were sometimes sprayed with DDT to help control mosquitoes and other insects. A small amount of DDT ended up in the water. Blue crab and fiddler crab populations died off as DDT poisoned the ecosystem. Animals that ate the crabs were also affected. Biologists noticed falling populations among shrimp, fish, small birds, ospreys, and bald eagles.

The Nitrogen Cycle

Living and nonliving parts of the environment interact as nutrients continually cycle through an ecosystem.

Among the most important nutrients is nitrogen. It is a main component of protein, a building-block molecule.

Nitrogen is a common element. In fact, the atmosphere is about 78 percent nitrogen gas. But most organisms can't use nitrogen in its pure form. They can only take in nitrogen when it's combined with other elements. The actions of bacteria and lightning combine nitrogen with other elements to form the compounds that living things can use.

Trace the path of nitrogen into the tree's roots. Animals get their nitrogen from eating plants or other animals. When an organism dies, the nitrogen in its remains returns to the ecosystem. Bacteria release nitrogen as they break down proteins. And the cycle continues.

A. Bacteria called nitrogen fixers combine nitrogen gas with oxygen.
B. In a flash of lightning, nitrogen and oxygen combine and wash into the soil with the rain.
C. Plants take in nitrogen compounds that are dissolved in water in the soil.
D. Bacteria decompose plant and animal material and release the nitrogen from their proteins into the soil.
E. The bacteria release nitrogen into the air, too.
F. Wetlands are rich in nitrogen. Bacteria feast on the abundant plant material rotting at the bottom of a marsh.

Wetland

Bacteria

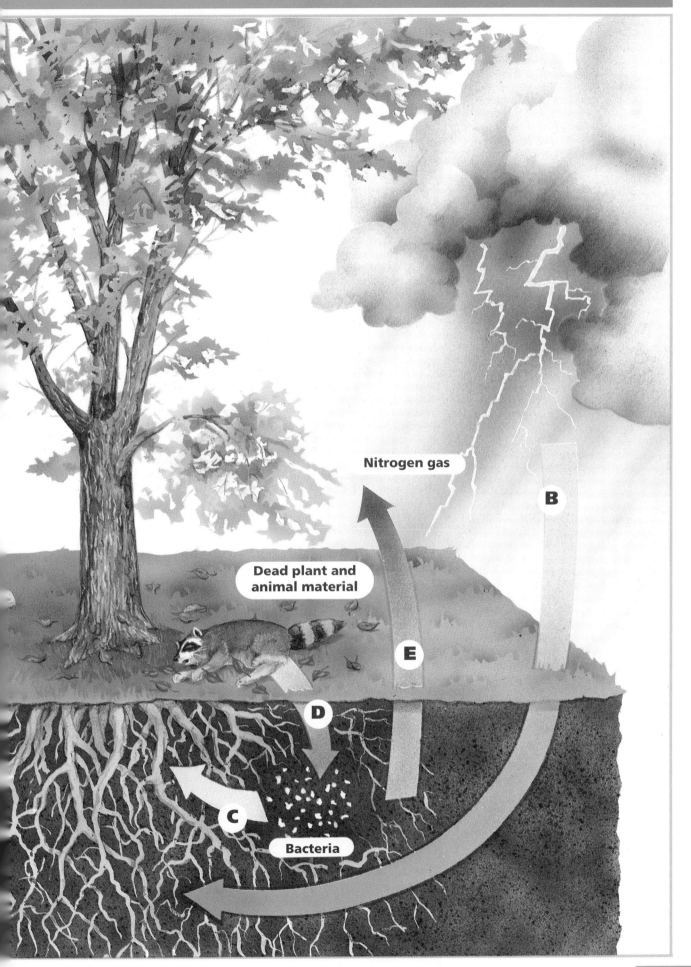

Nitrogen gas

B

Dead plant and
animal material

E

D

C

Bacteria

A great blue heron uses its bill to catch a fish.

Community Relationships

You have seen how energy, food, and chemicals pass through the marsh ecosystem. Now, how do the living things interact with each other? One way is through **competition**—the struggle among organisms for the things they need to live and reproduce. Species and individuals compete with each other for limited resources—food, oxygen, water, nesting space, light, and mates. Those individuals and species who "win the competition" get more food, water, light, and so on. The winners will continue to live in the ecosystem and have the largest populations.

In a marsh, ducks, geese, clapper rails, and fish all compete to eat insects. If fewer insects are born during a dry year, competition for food might mean that some members of the duck, goose, clapper rail, and fish populations die.

The three pictures on these pages show that animals also interact with each other through **predation**—the eating of one consumer by another. When a mink eats a muskrat, the mink is the predator and the muskrat is the prey. The numbers of predators and prey may vary from year to year, as the chart on the next page shows. But the numbers tend to reach a balance over time. One year might have more mink, while another year might have more muskrats. Minks tend to catch very young, old, or weak muskrats. So predation doesn't really hurt the muskrat population since healthy adult muskrats survive.

The spider is the predator; the dragonfly is the prey.

◄ Fish make up most of this otter's diet.

Predation also benefits the whole ecosystem. Minks limit the muskrat population. Too many muskrats might overgraze the plants, upsetting the energy base for the ecosystem.

Human activities can increase the risk to prey. For instance, many prairie potholes have been filled or drained to plant crops. As nesting spaces disappeared, many ducks had to build their nests in less protected cover. Many were preyed upon by foxes, skunks, and raccoons, and duck populations decreased.

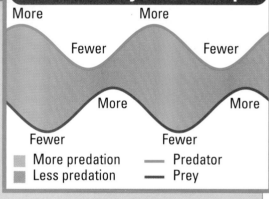

Predator-Prey Relationships

More		More
	Fewer	Fewer
	More	More
Fewer	Fewer	

  ■ More predation   — Predator
  ■ Less predation   — Prey

▲ Predation helps balance population sizes.

Checkpoint

1. Describe a marsh food chain from producer through third level consumer.
2. What happens to toxic chemicals as they pass through the food chain?
3. How are bacteria important in the nitrogen cycle?
4. How do competition and predation benefit an ecosystem?
5. **Take Action!** Make a poster showing a food web for organisms in your area.

Activity

The Case of the Poisonous Plankton

You can use a model to find out how some toxic chemicals build up in the food chain.

Picture A

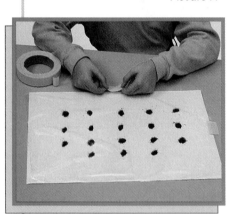

Picture B

Picture C

Gather These Materials

cover goggles

tape

large sheet of paper

iron filings

3 magnets

plastic wrap

Follow This Procedure

1 Make a chart like the one on the next page. Record your observations in your chart.

2 Put on your cover goggles.

3 Tape a large sheet of paper flat on a desk. Place a pinch of iron filings on it.

4 Make 18 such piles of iron filings scattered all over the paper. (Picture A) Record this number under "Plankton" in your data table.

5 Each pile represents a toxic chemical stored in the body of a tiny organism—part of the plankton community that lives in water. Cover the piles with plastic wrap and tape it in place. (Picture B)

6 Imagine that one magnet is a small fish. Move this magnet over a pile of iron filings. The small fish has eaten plankton full of toxins. Repeat this move 2 more times, dragging the 3 small "plankton" piles together to form a larger "small fish" pile. (Picture C)

7 Make 5 more of these "small fish" piles of filings for a total of 6. Record this number in your data table.

Record Your Results

Number of piles			
Plankton	Small fish	Medium fish	Large fish

8 Connect 2 magnets. Imagine this is a medium-sized fish. Drag the magnets together over 2 of the piles, making a larger pile. Repeat this move 2 more times making 3 piles. Record your data.

9 The 3 piles of "medium fish" iron filings represent the toxic chemical in 3 medium-sized fish.

Predict: *What happens to the amount of toxic chemicals as you go higher in the food chain?*

10 Connect 3 magnets to represent a large fish. Drag the filings to represent the large fish eating the 3 medium fish. All of the iron filings in the single "large fish" pile represent the toxic chemicals in its body. Record your data.

State Your Conclusions

1. In this model, what eventually happened to the toxic chemicals that were in the 18 plankton?

2. What happens to the toxic chemicals when a fish-eating bird, such as an osprey, feeds on several large fish?

3. Draw a model of this activity. Start with 18 small circles on a sheet of paper. Use different colored pencils to group the circles, showing how toxic chemicals concentrate in animals higher up the food chain.

Let's Experiment

Now that you have modeled one food chain, show a similar process for other food chains and then for a food web.

2.3 *Value of Wetlands*

▶ *Why are wetlands so valuable?*

Still on your field trip, you hike along the mushy edge of the marsh. A heron stands in the water, half-hidden in the misty fog that rises over the grasses and cattails. You wonder, why are wetlands so important? Why should they be protected?

Wetlands as a Wildlife Habitat

Biologists recognize how necessary wetlands are to the balance of life. First, they contain an astonishing number of producers, forming the base of a complex food web. Salt marshes alone produce more green material per hectare than the best-managed farms.

Second, migratory birds need wetlands for feeding and resting areas along their flyways. The snow geese shown here migrate from northern Canada to southern California each year.

Third, a wide variety of wetlands is necessary for the many species of waterfowl to survive. Shallow marshes are preferred by some; deeper marshes by others. The small prairie pothole marshes in Minnesota, Montana, Nebraska, Iowa, and the Dakotas are the most important breeding grounds for waterfowl in the United States.

➤ *Wetlands are important for these snow geese.*

Fourth, more wetland species are endangered or threatened than any others. Just one example is the whooping crane. Whooping cranes nest in wetlands in the Northwest Territories of Canada in spring and summer. In the fall they migrate to Texas, stopping off in marshes along the migration route. Overhunting and loss of wetland habitat have severely reduced the numbers of this species. In 1941 the wild population of whooping cranes had just 13 adults and 2 young. With protection, the population has grown to about 200 birds. Other endangered or threatened species include the bald eagle, egret, salt water otter, and snail kite.

Fifth, salt marshes are the nurseries and farms of the ocean. Ocean food webs begin in salt marshes where outgoing tides carry bits of living and dead material from the marsh into the ocean. This "tidal soup" feeds many of the ocean animals. The incoming tides bring minerals and salts that help the marsh plants grow.

Sixth, most fish and shellfish that people eat live in wetlands when young. Shrimp, salmon, oysters, crabs, flounder, and clams depend on the salt marsh for food and shelter. They are born in marshes and may live there for a good part of their lives. Two-thirds of the fish taken from the Atlantic and Gulf coasts and one-third of those taken from the Pacific depend on coastal wetlands for breeding. The federal government controls the fishing industry to help keep balance in the fish populations.

Into The Field

How do birds in your area get the food, water, and shelter that they need to survive?
Go outside and observe how birds are able to survive in your neighborhood.

Controlling Pollution and Flooding

Besides being important to wildlife, wetlands also help the environment. They are natural water treatment and flood control systems. And, as you know from studying the water supply, clean water and flood control are both important to the human population.

How do wetlands clean the water? Recall the processes used in a water treatment plant: settling, filtering, and chemical treatment. All three processes occur naturally in wetlands. As water enters a wetland from a stream it moves very slowly, allowing sediments and other solids to settle out or cling to the vegetation. Plants continually add oxygen to the water, which keeps alive the populations of decomposers. Harmful nitrogen compounds that enter the water from farmland runoff are broken down by decomposers. Harmless nitrogen gas then escapes into the air.

The picture below is a powerful reminder of another value of wetlands—they reduce the danger of flooding. Wetlands soak up rain like a sponge, keeping rivers from filling and spilling over their banks. Then, as if gently squeezing the sponge, wetlands slowly release the stored water over a safe period of time.

➤ *When wetlands are destroyed, the danger of flooding becomes greater.*

The storing ability of wetlands also helps replenish the groundwater supply. Many areas face water shortages partly because wetlands were destroyed.

Wetlands along the coasts help protect places inland. As storms hit the coast, marshes absorb much of the energy of high waves that would otherwise batter against buildings and beach areas.

Wetlands also have a greater importance to the whole earth than most people realize. Because of the large number of producers that give off oxygen, absorb carbon dioxide, and utilize nitrogen compounds, wetlands contribute to the balanced cycles of carbon dioxide, oxygen, and nitrogen worldwide.

Checkpoint

1. In what ways do wildlife species depend on wetlands?
2. How do wetlands help protect communities from flooding?
3. **Take Action!** Make a map showing the route migrating birds might take when stopping over in wetlands near you.

DATAFILE

MATH

Disappearing Wetlands

Every year more and more wetlands disappear in the United States. These ecosystems are drained and filled in to make room for housing developments, shopping centers, highways, and other construction projects. The conversion of wetlands to farmlands has also taken its toll on these ecosystems.

Laws have been passed that protect the unchecked destruction of the remaining wetlands. But the chart gives you an idea of how much of this valuable resource has already disappeared, mostly in this century.

State	Hectares of Wetlands	
	Original	Today
California	2 mil	182,000
Connecticut	12,000	6,000
Iowa	945,000	10,700
Louisiana	4.5 mil	2.3 mil
Michigan	4.5 mil	1.3 mil
Nebraska	38,000	3,400
N. Dakota	2 mil	810,000
Wisconsin	4 mil	2.7 mil

What Did You Find Out?
1. *Which state has the least amount of wetlands? the greatest amount?*
2. *Which state has the greatest percentage of its original wetlands remaining? the smallest percentage?*

Chapter Review

Reviewing Words and Concepts

Write the letter of the word or phrase that best completes each sentence.

1. The concentration of toxic chemicals _____ at each higher level of the energy pyramid.

2. Organisms that struggle with each other for the things they need to live are involved in _____.

3. A _____ has more kinds of organisms than any other wetland.

4. Swamps, marshes, and bogs are examples of _____.

5. The eating of one consumer by another is an interaction called _____.

6. An organism that obtains energy by eating other organisms is a _____.

7. Cattails and ducks are likely to live in a _____ marsh.

8. Osprey and bald eagle populations became threatened because of poisoning by a chemical called _____.

9. Grasses and algae are two kinds of _____.

10. The relationship between a food chain and available energy in an ecosystem can be shown in an _____.

a. competition
b. energy pyramid
c. producers
d. wetlands
e. DDT
f. consumer
g. predation
h. increases
i. swamp
j. freshwater

Connecting Ideas

1. Copy the concept map. Use the terms at the right to complete the map about how energy flows through food chains.

third level consumers
first level consumers   producers
second level consumers

A. sunlight

E. _____

B. _____

D. _____   C. _____

2. Write a sentence or two that summarizes the ideas shown in the concept map.

Interpreting What You Learned

1. Describe three kinds of wetlands.
2. Describe an example in which the kinds of species in a marsh have changed because of human actions.
3. What happens to the energy that is "lost" at each level of a food chain?
4. How does a plant get its nitrogen?
5. What are some of the resources that species compete for?
6. Why is a toxic chemical in the food chain more likely to be dangerous for an osprey than for a species of grass?
7. Explain how wetlands are similar to water treatment plants.

Performance Assessment

How can a predator-prey relationship be modeled?

Materials • 4 sheets of construction paper • masking tape • 20 counting chips • 10 index cards

Collecting Data

1. Tape four sheets of construction paper together to make a large rectangle. The paper rectangle represents a field. Place the field on the floor.
2. Each chip represents a mouse. Evenly spread 10 mouse chips on the field.
3. Stand two steps away from the field. The index cards represent owls, which are predators of mice. Toss three index cards onto the field, trying to touch one or more of the mouse chips.
4. Remove any mouse chips that were touched by owl cards. These mice were caught by owls. Record how many mice remain.
5. Owls that do not catch any mice die. Remove cards that do not touch any chips on the field and place those cards in a pile off to the side. If an owl catches a mouse, it survives. Record how many owls remain.
6. If an owl catches two or more mice, it will reproduce. Place another card next to each owl that reproduces. Then gather all the cards from the field so you can toss them again.
7. Assume each mouse left in the field has one offspring. Add one chip to the field for each mouse not caught by an owl.
8. Toss the owl cards at the mouse chips as you did in step 3. Then repeat steps 4 through 7. Continue to record how many chips and cards remain. Keep repeating until you run out of chips or cards.

Analyzing Data

Explain how the changing number of cards and chips in the owl-mouse game models a predator-prey relationship.

CHAPTER

3

Applying Science

Hey! I was here first. Find your own land!

Discover Activity

How should we use the land?

Draw a map with mountains, a forest, and a lake. Assign a role to each person: lumber executive, gas station owner, golf course developer, mining executive, and an executive of a land preservation organization. Ask each member to mark on the map the land they want for their project.

For Discussion

1. What happened when people marked off their land?

2. What is the best way you found to divide the land?

3.1 *Preparing to Decide*

▶ *Should flyways be turned into runways?*

As your class tramps through the black mud at the edge of the salt marsh, your teacher reminds you that the city council is close to deciding whether to build an airport here. She explains that a law helps protect wetlands from being needlessly destroyed by certain projects. Before anyone builds an airport on a wetland, the builder must get a permit from the United States government.

Your class project is to make a decision about the airport, then present your group opinion to the city council. Is it more important to leave the wetlands alone or to use the land for an airport? What do you need to know to decide?

You've visited the marsh and studied wetland habitats. As a result, you know how marshes are important in a general way. But how will *this* airport change *this* marsh? In order to make predictions about the effect of building an airport, you need more specific information. Where can you get enough information— and the *right* information—to make an informed decision? Fortunately, the federal government gathers information about the project and makes this information available to the public.

▼ *The proposal for the airport is reviewed by the federal government.*

How the Government Gets Involved

From your teacher and from studying newspaper articles about the project, you learn many things. You learn that *federal* refers to the United States government, not your state or city government. Also, you learn that local governments often must use federal money to help pay for airports.

You also learn that the federal government has a policy—or plan—to help protect the environment. This policy was stated in a major law, the National Environmental Policy Act of 1969 (NEPA).

NEPA was passed as a result of the increasing damage to the environment across the country. Biologists and other scientists discovered that major construction projects often caused damage to the environment that could not be repaired. More and more citizens complained about the damage and insisted that the federal government do something. Finally, laws to help protect the environment were passed. NEPA and the other laws support the idea that the government must help lessen the harmful effect human activities can have on the environment.

NEPA has three major parts: First, it declares that each person in the United States has the right to enjoy a healthful environment. It also says that government has a responsibility to protect that right.

▼ To gather information about the marsh, scientists collect soil and water samples.

Second, NEPA requires that a special council be formed to advise the president about environmental issues. The council members might be scientists, teachers, or other experts on the environment.

Third, NEPA requires all federal agencies to study the effects on the environment of any action that involves the agencies. The results of the study must be written into a report called an Environmental Impact Statement (EIS). An impact is the effect of an action. In other words, the EIS predicts the environmental effects of any action that involves federal agencies or federal money.

To make changes to a salt marsh, such as the airport will do, builders must get a federal permit. The airport project also involves federal money. Because the project requires a federal permit and involves federal money, the project has to be reviewed by the government. The government makes its review using the EIS, which is submitted by the people who want to build the airport.

As part of the EIS review, scientists visit the wetland to collect data. They list all the species present in the marsh. They estimate populations of the plant and animal species. And they take samples of the soil and water, as shown here.

The EIS

Your class decides to visit a city council member, Flora Mendoza. You ask Councilwoman Mendoza whether an EIS has been written about the airport project. She says yes, and that you can see a copy of it at the city hall. She explains that a federal agency called the Army Corps of Engineers issues all permits having to do with construction in wetland areas.

The first step in the EIS process is for the Army Corps of Engineers to decide whether the possible effects of the airport project are serious enough to require that an EIS be done. In this case, the agency found that the airport could have major environmental effects. So the agency decided to require an EIS on the project. By law, the EIS must do the following.

1. Describe the project and land that will be affected.
2. List the benefits and harmful effects to the environment that will probably occur if the project is done. This includes any possible air, water, and soil pollution or any possible dangers to human health.
3. List other possible alternatives to the airport project, such as building the airport elsewhere, or not at all.
4. Predict what the short-term and long-term effects might be of the project.
5. List any resources that would be used up or destroyed by the project that cannot be recovered.
6. Show the methods and research that the agency used to make its predictions.

Councilwoman Mendoza explains that the EIS had to be reviewed by a federal agency called the Environmental Protection Agency—the EPA. The agency's review is printed in a publication called the *Federal Register*. The Army Corps of Engineers then sent copies of the EPA report to all the citizens and groups who had voiced any interest in the project.

Copies of the EPA report are also at the city hall, the Chamber of Commerce, local businesses, the League of Women Voters office, and the U.S. Fish and Wildlife Service. In this way, all citizens have the opportunity to read the report. Public hearings may also be held. Some citizens strongly want the airport. Others fiercely want to protect the wetlands. The EIS process, including the public hearings, gives citizens the chance to present additional facts and opinions.

All citizens, including students, can get involved with the EIS process. First, they can read the EPA's opinion. Second, they can do what the people in the picture are doing—making their concerns known at the public hearings and meetings. The EPA, the Army Corps of Engineers, and the City Council depend on citizens to raise all their concerns. However, if few or no citizens attend the meetings, all the public concerns may not be considered in the report.

▼ *At public hearings, all citizens can voice their concerns.*

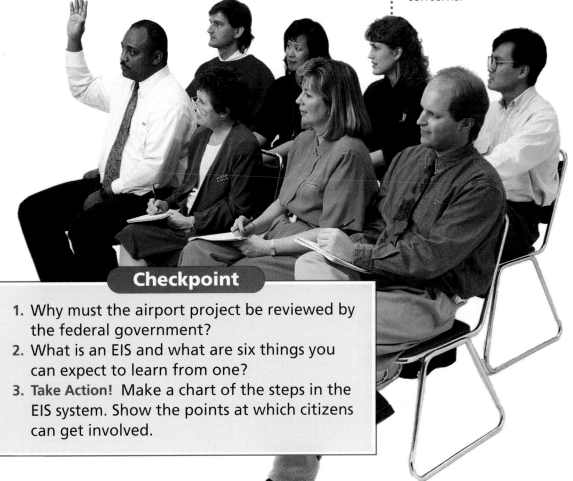

Checkpoint

1. Why must the airport project be reviewed by the federal government?
2. What is an EIS and what are six things you can expect to learn from one?
3. **Take Action!** Make a chart of the steps in the EIS system. Show the points at which citizens can get involved.

Activity

Draining a Wetland

How does a wetland change as it dries out? Try this activity to find out.

Picture A

Picture B

Picture C

Gather These Materials

colored markers: red, green, and blue

15 seeds

plastic container

soil

water

duckweed

Follow This Procedure

1. Make a chart like the one on the next page. Record your observations in your chart.

2. With colored markers, color 5 seeds red, 5 green, and 5 blue.

3. Fill the plastic container with soil so that the soil makes a ramp from one side of the container to the other. (Picture A)

4. Half-fill the plastic container with water so that the water covers the soil about halfway up the ramp. (Picture B)

5. Sprinkle the soil with the 5 red seeds. Make sure some seeds fall on land and some on water. (Picture C)

6. Add some duckweed to the water.

7. Set your model wetland in a sunny place.

Predict: *How will your model wetland change with time?*

Record Your Results

Date	Water level	Plant growth

8 After one day, record any changes in water level and plant growth in your model wetland.

9 On Day 5, sprinkle the 5 green seeds on the soil and water. Do the same with the blue seeds on Day 10.

10 Continue to record any changes that occur in your wetland.

State Your Conclusions

1. The environment constantly changes. What changes did you notice occurring in your wetland?

2. How might the kind of changes that occurred in your model be different in an actual wetland?

Let's Experiment

How might a pollutant such as oil, salt, or soap affect your drying wetland model? Use what you know about scientific methods to find out.

3.2 *Considering the Impact*

▶ *Is the total impact helpful or harmful?*

Your class discusses the marsh property. You all feel that you understand how the wetlands are important and how the species interact and depend on one another. You have located the EIS, a report about how the project will affect the environment. What kinds of effects should you look for as you read through the EIS? What else do you need to do before making a decision?

Impact on Society

When you read the EIS, you look for the list of benefits and costs to the environment if the airport is built. The list of helpful effects is short: By filling the marsh, some mosquito breeding grounds would

▼ *The airport would provide many jobs for people in the community.*

disappear, thus helping to eliminate a pest.

On the other hand, you find the list of costs to the environment is rather long: The project may eliminate some plant species. It would eliminate a large area of breeding ground for fish, birds, and mammals. The loss of breeding ground would most likely result in smaller populations of commercial ocean fish. The airport would greatly reduce the flood control ability of the marsh, which may cause flooding in surrounding areas. Increased air and ground traffic will add to air pollution. Spilled fuels, oils, and cleaning liquids may cause water and soil pollution. Planes will add noise pollution to nearby housing and business developments.

But what about the non-environmental benefits of the airport? That information is not in the EIS. So you ask Councilwoman Mendoza why the city wants to build the airport. She points out how the airport could help the citizens of the area.

First, the community has many people without jobs. The project will provide construction jobs for workers who help build the airport. Then just think of all the people who work at or around an airport: ticketing and boarding agents, baggage handlers, cooks, foodservers, mechanics, bus and cab drivers, and many others. The photographs show just some of the jobs. Airports also attract other businesses: hotels, shops, restaurants, rental car agencies, and so on. And an airport makes it easier for people to come to the area.

Which choice holds the greatest benefits to society? On one hand, the airport helps a lot of people and the whole community. On the other hand, the benefits to society might be greater by protecting the wetlands as a natural water purifier and flood controller. Each decision has benefits and costs. When making environmental decisions, you have to balance the benefits and costs of all sides. Sometimes, neither decision is the best answer and you have to look for other choices. For example, could the airport be built somewhere else?

Disappearing Wetlands

Past decisions have significantly reduced the area of wetlands in the United States.

1. About two-thirds of the original pothole wetlands in the Midwest are now farmlands. Most of these wetlands were drained before the Clean Water Act of 1972 helped protect them. But draining has continued, partly because many potholes are not considered wetlands— many of them are dry during much of the year. Also, many potholes are relatively small—from the size of a house to the size of a football field— and are easily overlooked for protection.

2. About 95 percent of the Central Valley wetlands of California is gone. These areas have been drained so the land could be used for farmland and buildings. Central Valley wetlands were not protected as much as others because people didn't realize that these are important resting and feeding areas for migrating birds.

❶ Midwest

Pothole wetlands

67% Lost

❷ West Coast

California wetlands

95% Lost

❸ Northeast
Connecticut wetlands

50% Lost

❹ Everglades
Wading birds

300,000

50,000

1930   1990

3. Wetlands are disappearing all over the Northeast because of shore erosion and expanding cities. For example, Connecticut has lost 50 percent of its wetlands. Many people want to take action to protect what's left. But their plans have to be approved by the federal government. One of the drawbacks of the system that was set up to protect wetlands is that the process takes time.

4. In 1947 part of the Florida Everglades became a national park. But the boundaries did not include the northern part of the Shark River Slough, which is the main source of water into the Everglades. In the 1960s and 1970s, a system of dikes and canals was built along the river to make the swampland suitable for homes and farms. The system has decreased the amount of water that flows into the area. Also, fertilizers and pesticides from surrounding farms drain into the Everglades. These factors have led to a decline of wildlife, especially wading birds such as storks, egrets, and herons.

Future Impact

Because so much wetland area has been lost, predicting the future effects of human actions becomes especially important. The EIS tries to predict both short-term and long-range effects of the project. In the past, before NEPA and the EPA existed, many decisions were made without considering future environmental effects.

For example, the plant in the picture—called purple loosestrife—was brought to the eastern United States from Europe because it has beautiful purple blossoms. However, very few American animals eat or build cover using this plant. Therefore, since the loosestrife has no natural controls on its population, it grows very easily and crowds out native plants. As a result, some native plants have almost disappeared in places. Two examples are a species of bulrush in Massachusetts and a rare group of dwarf spike rush plants in New York.

When plant species—or any species—disappear from an ecosystem, the food web is disrupted. Animals that feed on native plants crowded out by the loosestrife no longer have a source of food. Many animals may die. The loosestrife also eliminates places where canvasback ducks and black terns make their nests.

▼ The purple loosestrife, though beautiful, has crowded out native species.

The Pacific yew tree is used for making a medicine to treat cancer.

Some human actions, such as introducing a new species to an area, can cause extinction of species. Why does extinction matter? One reason is that we still have much to learn about many species on the earth. We will never know how extinct species affected other organisms.

For example, humans use plant and animal substances to make almost half of all medicines. One medicine, taxol, is an experimental cancer treatment made from the Pacific yew tree. The bark is stripped from the tree, as shown here, and a chemical is extracted from the bark to make taxol. However, in the Pacific forests, yew trees have been treated as giant forest weeds. People cut and burned them by the thousands. Since 1991, the Forest Service has stopped burning cut yews.

Checkpoint

1. How might a community benefit from a new airport built on the salt marsh?
2. List as many reasons as you can for the disappearance of wetlands.
3. Why are some plants valuable for their possible future uses? Give an example.
4. **Take Action!** Make a chart with four columns: *Environmental costs, Environmental benefits, Social costs, Social benefits.* Fill in the columns using the airport example. Compare the lists. Rate the importance of each item.

Into The Field

How does new construction affect your community?

Observe a newly constructed area. Write about the positive and negative impact of the construction.

Activity

Planning Ahead

The way in which people use land affects every living thing. Plan a town that will use land with minimal damage to the environment.

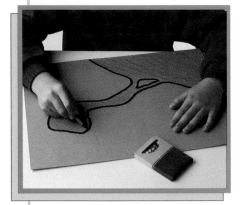

Picture A

Picture B

Picture C

Gather These Materials

large poster board   scissors
construction paper   glue

Follow This Procedure

1 Make a chart like the one on the next page.

2 Divide into groups so that each group has someone who will represent home owners, farmers, business owners, a parks department, a highway department, industry, and schools.

3 On posterboard, draw a map of a wetlands area. Include at least a river, a pond, and marshland. (Picture A)

4 In the chart, describe how each member of the group would like to use the land. List the pros and cons of each type of land use.

5 On construction paper, draw shapes that represent the buildings, fields, or parklands. Cut out the shapes. (Picture B)

6 Work with your group to arrange the development of the land so that it has as little impact as possible on the wetlands. There are 3 rules for development. (a) All types of land use must be included. (b) An area must be set aside for a wildlife preserve. (c) Everyone must agree.

7 When everyone agrees on the best plan, glue your cutouts on the map. (Picture C)

Record Your Results

	Proposed development	Pros	Cons
Home owners			
Farmers			
Business owners			
Parks dept.			
Highway dept.			
Factory reps.			
Schools			

Predict: *Which development will least affect the wetlands? Which will be most damaging?*

8 Compare and discuss your group's proposed development plan with other groups in your classroom. Solving some of the problems will not be easy. Even the best solution may not be perfect.

State Your Conclusions

1. How is the development for your group a compromise?
2. List all the things that community residents could do to minimize damage to the wetlands environment.

Let's Experiment

Think about the area where you live. Make a map showing what changes you would like to make to protect the environment or restore part of the land to the way it was before being developed. List the pros and cons of the changes you would make.

3.3 Deciding the Future

▶ *What kinds of decisions need to be made now?*

Environmental issues are in the news daily from almost every corner of the world. The total area of many kinds of natural habitats has shrunk worldwide. Wetlands in the United States alone have disappeared at the rate of 120,000 to 200,000 hectares per year.

Local environmental issues have contributed to worldwide issues. For example, the atmosphere contains a growing amount of carbon dioxide, which may trap enough heat to cause worldwide climate changes. One healthy tree can remove between 12 and 20 kilograms of carbon dioxide from the air each year. Everyone needs to know more about science and the environment than ever before, because finding the balance between the environment and other human needs is not a simple problem, and concerns everyone's well-being.

Past Decisions

Society is now faced with solving problems created in the past by people who did not understand the relationships in an ecosystem. In many places, natural predators were killed off because they were seen as nothing more than pests. As a result, populations of prey species increased to unfavorable levels.

For example, wolves were eliminated from Yellowstone National Park in Wyoming. Wolves are natural predators of moose. Without wolves, moose populations soared and overgrazed the meadow and wetland plants. The food supply was not great enough to support the high moose population. Many moose died of starvation. In an effort to restore the balance between predators and prey, wolves were reintroduced into the Yellowstone ecosystem in 1995.

The deer in the photograph look harmless, but their human neighbors are angry. Deer have become pests in many residential neighborhoods largely because their natural predators—bobcats, wolves, and mountain lions—have been eliminated from those areas. The deer population is rapidly increasing as they eat millions of dollars worth of garden plants, shrubs, and trees.

◄ *In addition to destroying vegetation, deer are linked with the spread of Lyme disease, an illness carried by deer ticks.*

➤ *Quarrying threatened the destruction of the prairie shown below. So volunteers actually moved the prairie to another place!*

Today's Decisions

Since 1969 many decisions have been made that helped the environment. A reason for this is education: People are learning more about the interactions between living things and the environment. This knowledge has been used to make decisions that lessen the impact of development on ecosystems.

You know that sometimes human activities such as building and development destroy the habitats of various plants and animals. Scientists have had some success with introducing such species into other new habitats.

What do you think the people in the picture are doing? They are moving a prairie! Recently this group transplanted a dry gravel prairie from one location to another. The prairie was one of the few remaining prairies of its type and was threatened by a gravel quarry. Gravel mining had already eliminated 4 of the 81 known plant species in the prairie.

Deer in Numbers

The two graphs show evidence of an increasing deer population in Illinois. Study and compare the data on the graphs.

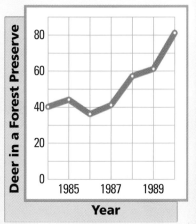

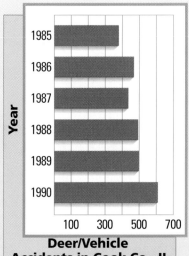

In 1990, over 400 people, including biologists and local citizens, helped move the prairie 10 kilometers away. One year later, 63 out of the 77 remaining species had survived the transplant. However, it will take decades for the ecosystem to fully recover.

Biologists have also used their scientific knowledge of **ecology**—the study of interactions between living things and the environment—to manage threatened ecosystems such as "old growth" forests. Old growth forests have been growing undisturbed for many years. They support healthy, complex food webs with many different species. In the past, many old growth forests were destroyed when all the trees were cut down. Often new trees—"new growth forests"—were planted in their place. These new growth forests have mainly one species of tree and are more susceptible to diseases.

Forest managers have begun to see the value in cutting forests in a selective way. In some cases, they cut a few trees in an area at a time. This practice allows new trees to grow naturally. In other areas, patches of trees are cut and then replaced with a variety of species.

What Did You Find Out?
1. *By how many deer did the population increase in the forest preserve from 1985 to 1990?*
2. *How might the graph of deer/vehicle accidents show the deer population is increasing?*

▲ *Young people have opinions, too.*

SAVE OUR WETLANDS!

Controversy and Compromise

Now, suppose your neighborhood is near the marsh where the airport might be. You attend a public meeting where citizens discuss the airport. Your parents say how unhappy they will be with the noise that the planes will make. They are afraid of flooding also. The water that would normally flow into the marsh would be forced into other low areas, such as your neighborhood. You are worried about whether the birds and other wildlife will survive the airport.

Your friend's parents own a hotel. An airport would bring many guests to the hotel. They want the airport to be built. You hear other people talking about the number of jobs the airport will bring. Some people carry signs to get support for each side. What is the best decision, you wonder.

For most environmental issues, no answer is "correct." Often either choice involves some costs and benefits. Even the best plan may have at least one harmful impact on either society or the natural ecosystem. Saving the marsh may affect the business growth of the community and cost many needed jobs. On the other hand, building the airport will endanger wildlife species and also may increase flooding and water supply problems, which will be costly to the community, too.

Your family cares most about protecting your home from flood damage. Other people care more about helping the town gain jobs and increase business. Everyone seems to care about the wildlife. But because people have different values, they want different results. Because people have strong feelings about their wants and needs, great controversy often results over environmental issues. A controversy is a public argument or debate. When each person believes he or she is "right," how can a good decision be made?

Sometimes the answer involves a compromise in which each side agrees to give up some of what they wanted, so that each can end up with a part of what they wanted. Did you compromise about land use in the Discover Activity? In the case of the airport, one solution might be to build the airport on the inland side of town. Perhaps wetland areas could be carefully "created" nearby, so that wildlife and flooding areas could be kept. Whatever the decision, not everyone will be completely happy with it.

So, you have gathered all the facts possible. You have read the EIS and understand what the environmental costs and benefits are if the airport gets built. You understand what the costs and benefits are to the community. You have thought about the impact that each decision can have. Now…what will you decide?

Checkpoint

1. How and why have deer become a problem in some residential areas?
2. How does the transplanted prairie show how scientific knowledge can be helpful?
3. Why are environmental issues likely to involve controversy and compromise?
4. Take Action! Organize two groups to debate the airport project.

Chapter Review

Reviewing Words and Concepts

Write the letter of the word or phrase that best completes each sentence.

1. The study of how organisms behave and interact with their environment is ____.

2. The ____ government is the government of the United States.

3. An impact is the effect of an ____.

4. A report that predicts the environmental effects of any action that involves federal agencies or federal money is called an ____.

5. Some species that become extinct may have great ____ for humans.

6. A plant that grows naturally in a region is a ____ plant.

7. If natural predators in an area are killed off, populations of species that are their ____ may grow out of control.

8. The populations of many native plants are threatened by ____ species.

9. In a ____, each side gets part of what it wanted.

10. In 1969, the federal government passed a major law called ____ to help protect the environment.

a. benefits
b. federal
c. compromise
d. introduced
e. action
f. prey
g. NEPA
h. ecology
i. native
j. Environmental Impact Statement

Connecting Ideas

1. Copy the concept map. Use the terms at the right to complete the map about the factors in the decision to build the airport on the marsh.

new businesses   decision
lost breeding grounds   new jobs
reduced flood control
air pollution
ease of travel

A. airport

B. advantages

C. disadvantages

D. ____
E. ____
F. ____
G. ____
H. ____
I. ____
J. ____

2. Write a sentence or two that summarizes the ideas shown in the concept map.

Interpreting What You Learned

1. What are the three major parts of the National Environmental Policy Act?
2. How can you acquire information about a project that might have an impact on your environment?
3. What should be considered before making decisions affecting the environment?
4. State three costs to the environment of building an airport on a marsh.
5. List reasons why the areas of wetlands in the United States have been reduced.
6. Give an example of a human action that resulted in the disruption of a natural food chain. Explain what kind of disruption occurred.

 ## Performance Assessment

How can new species affect an area over time?

Materials 20 paper circles • marker • plastic cup

Collecting Data

1. Using the marker, write *PL* on one side of each paper circle. *PL* stands for *purple loosestrife*. Write *NP* on the other side of each circle. *NP* stands for *native plant*.
2. Place all of the paper circles in a cup and shake the cup to mix the circles.
3. The table top represents a wetland. Spill the paper circle plants onto the wetland. Count how many circles landed with *PL* facing up and how many landed with *NP* facing up. Record the numbers.
4. Pick up the circles that landed with *NP* facing up and place them back in the cup. Leave the circles that landed with *PL* facing up in the wetland.
5. Shake the cup, then spill the circles onto the wetland. Again, count and record the total number of circles with *PL* facing up and the total number with *NP* facing up.

6. Repeat steps 4 and 5 until all circles in the wetland land with *PL* facing up. Record the total number of circles with *PL* facing up and the total number with *NP* facing up each time you spill the circles.
7. Each time you spill the circles represents one year. Determine how many years were required for purple loosestrife to crowd out all the native plants in your wetland.

Analyzing Data

How much time was needed for purple loosestrife to crowd out half the native plants in your wetland?

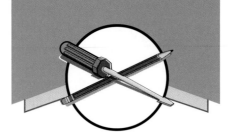

Kids Care for Wetlands

What do you picture when you hear the words *marsh, swamp,* and *bog*? Does an image of a worthless, mosquito-infested pool of water filled with rotted plants come to mind?

Not so long ago many people thought just that way about such wetlands. Companies often polluted the water with factory wastes. Some developers drained and cleared the areas to use as building sites. But you know that not only do wetlands support life for a variety of plants and animals, they act as pollution filters and

> *Some kids are taking action to protect the wetlands where they live.*

flood controllers, and they add oxygen to the atmosphere. Other people too have now come to learn that wetlands are definitely not worthless places.

Kevin Ryan Bell, a sixth-grader from Nevada, is one such person. Kevin did a special study on water contamination in the Nevada Stillwater Wildlife Refuge, an endangered wetland. When he saw birds and fish dying in this area, he tested organisms to determine how much clean water it would take to maintain life in the wetland. Kevin's efforts brought the area to the attention of the Nature Conservancy, a conservation organization. This organization provided the needed water to restore the wetland.

The efforts of these kids show that even ecosystems that are disrupted and polluted can be helped. They also prove that people of all ages do make a difference.

In another case, two sixteen-year-olds helped to preserve the vegetation in Biscayne Bay, Florida. Christian Swift and John Arana spent one summer doing some underwater landscaping. When pollution killed the sea grasses that once grew in the bay, the boys put on their diving gear and swam to the bottom of the bay. There they replanted young sea grasses into the sand. The sea grasses are part of the bay's food web and support a variety of sea life. "We're helping to bring back the environment of the bay," says John.

On Your Own

The first step in helping protect wetlands, and the environment in general, is to stay informed. Periodically, look through the newspaper for headlines that refer to wetlands or other environmental issues. Read the articles and bring them to class. If you have an opinion on one of these issues and would like to express it, write a letter to the newspaper editor. Most newspapers have a comment and opinion section where such letters are printed.

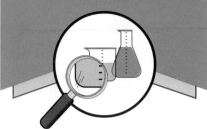

Exploring Careers

Saving the Wetlands

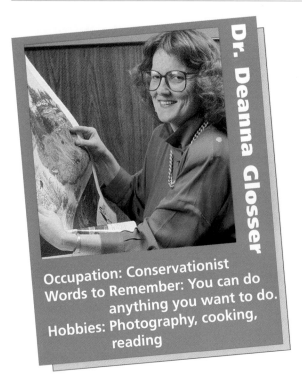

Dr. Deanna Glosser

Occupation: Conservationist
Words to Remember: You can do
anything you want to do.
Hobbies: Photography, cooking,
reading

Can you imagine getting people to destroy a valuable natural resource? That's exactly what's happened in the past. People used to think that wetlands were just a nuisance—a place where mosquitoes bred. So wetlands were given to anybody who would just promise to drain the land and "make something of it." Now that scientists have found how valuable wetlands are, people are working together to save them. One of these people is Deanna Glosser. She's a conservationist. Her job is to protect endangered species.

How are wetlands important to endangered species?

"In the state of Illinois, one-third of all endangered plants live in wetlands. And these plants are the food for many endangered animals. Other endangered animals eat the fish that live in wetlands."

What is being done to save wetlands?

"The Swamp Act of 1849 gave land away if people promised to drain it. Now we're trying to get laws passed that will preserve the wetlands. 'No net loss' laws would require that any wetland area that is drained must be replaced. Replacing a wetland is not always easy. About half of the newly created wetland areas fail. So there's a ratio for replacement. For example, if a developer drains one square kilometer of cattail marsh, it would need to be replaced with one and a half square kilometers of new marsh. But if the developer drained a cypress swamp, the ratio would be about one to five—five square kilometers to replace each square kilometer drained. This type of wetland is so complex that most new areas fail. When the ratio gets that high, developers can't afford to drain wetlands.

What's the best part of your job?

"I love my job. What I do makes a difference. Because of what I do, animals and plants that might otherwise disappear will be here fifty years from now."

Outdoor Laboratory

Wetlands often occur naturally on either side of a river. Once the wetlands are drained, soil and nutrients that would have been trapped in the wetlands now flow into the river. Some scientists are conducting experiments by building wetlands near a river and finding out how the wetlands act as filters to keep rivers clean.

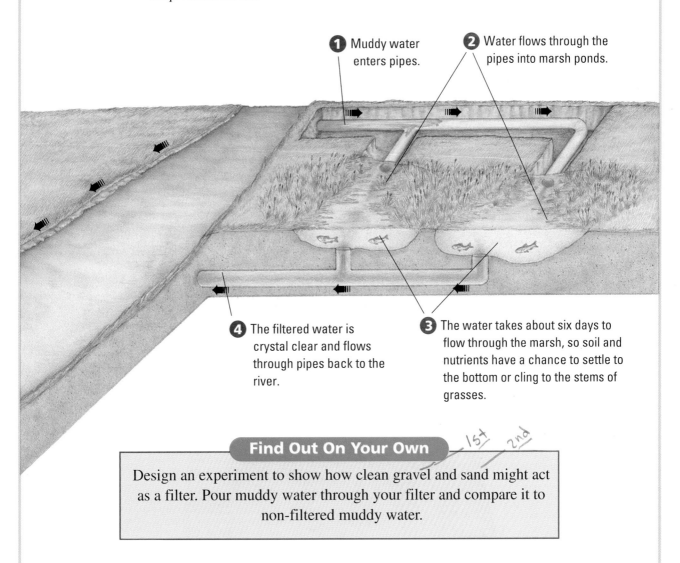

1 Muddy water enters pipes.

2 Water flows through the pipes into marsh ponds.

4 The filtered water is crystal clear and flows through pipes back to the river.

3 The water takes about six days to flow through the marsh, so soil and nutrients have a chance to settle to the bottom or cling to the stems of grasses.

Find Out On Your Own

Design an experiment to show how clean gravel and sand might act as a filter. Pour muddy water through your filter and compare it to non-filtered muddy water.

Module Performance Assessment

Environmental Convention

Using what you learned in this module, help prepare exhibitions to be used at a convention about environmental awareness to be held at your school. Complete one or more of the following activities. You may work by yourself or with others in a group.

Drama

Find out about an animal or plant species that is threatened by human activity. Then write a script for a play in which the group responsible for threatening the species is taken to court. Be sure your script includes parts for the defendant, the defense attorney, the prosecuting attorneys, the judge, witnesses, and a jury.

Art

Make drawings depicting one negative effect and one positive effect of building an airport on a wetland.

Civics

Find out what projects in your area are under review by the federal government. Obtain a copy of the EPA reports and a schedule of public hearings. If you feel strongly about an issue, make a poster to publicize the meeting.

Earth Science

Make a bulletin-board or poster display showing photographs of different wetlands in the United States. Label each type, and tell where it is located.

Biology

Use three clear plastic containers, aquarium salt, water, brine shrimp eggs, and a hand lens to see how changes in the environment, such as the amount of salt in the water, affect the rate at which brine shrimp eggs hatch and grow.

Module Review

Reviewing Words and Concepts

Write the letter of the word or phrase that best completes each sentence.

1. An ____ is used to explain how an action involving the federal government might affect the environment.
2. Floating masses of moss are a characteristic of a ____.
3. The study of how organisms interact with their environments is called ____.
4. A spider eating an insect is an example of ____.
5. Any struggle between organisms for resources is ____.
6. Swamps, marshes, and bogs are all kinds of ____.
7. The role of an organism in the environment is its ____.
8. An oak tree is part of the ____ of a squirrel.
9. All the mushrooms on a log make up a ____.
10. A balanced ecosystem is one type of ____.

a. niche
b. habitat
c. stable system
d. population
e. wetlands
f. predation
g. competition
h. ecology
i. bog
j. Environmental Impact Statement

Interpreting What You Learned

1. Explain how predation helps keep the populations in an ecosystem in balance.
2. How do wetlands aid the worldwide balance of carbon dioxide and oxygen?
3. Explain why having many different kinds of organisms and habitats helps maintain stability in an ecosystem.
4. How do the interactions in an aquarium mimic the interactions in a wetland?
5. How can evaluating the causes and effects of past events concerning the environment help you make future decisions?
6. Give an example of how making a change in an ecosystem causes other changes.
7. What should an individual do before adding a new organism to an ecosystem?

Applying What You Learned

1. How have people's actions involving the environment changed over time?
2. Describe the difference between a swamp and other kinds of wetlands.
3. A huge new factory is being proposed for the community in which you live. What do you know about this project just by learning that a full EIS has been prepared?
4. Every spring you've seen a certain species of migratory bird in your area. This year you don't see any. What might have happened?
5. Which group of organisms recycle the raw materials plants use to produce sugars?
6. How might a sudden change in temperature affect a stable aquarium ecosystem?

Using Metric

About 1 centimeter

About 1 millimeter

About 1 meter

Water boils (100°C)

Normal body temperature (37°C)

Water freezes (0°C)

1 cm

1 cm

1 square centimeter

1 cm

1 cm

1 cm

1 cm

1 cubic centimeter

About 1 kilogram

Degrees Celsius

11 football fields end to end is about 1 kilometer

1 liter of milk

Using Scientific Methods

Scientists ask many questions. The answers cannot always be found in books. In fact, no one may know the answers. Then scientists use scientific methods to find answers. Scientific methods include steps like those described below. Sometimes the order of the steps changes. The experiments in this section give you a chance to use scientific methods to explore the world around you.

Identify Problem The problem is usually in the form of a question such as, "How acidic is the rain in your area?"

Make Observations Recorded observations become data and might include size, color, or shape.

State Hypothesis A hypothesis is a likely explanation of the problem. It may turn out to be incorrect; it must be tested.

Test Hypothesis If possible, experiments are done to test the hypothesis. Experiments should be repeated to double check the results.

Collect Data The information you gather from the experiment is your data.

Study Data The data collected during an experiment is better understood if it is organized into charts and graphs. Then you can easily see what it all means.

Make Conclusions The conclusion relates to the hypothesis. You might conclude your hypothesis is correct, or that it is incorrect.

Safety in Science

Scientists know they must work safely when doing experiments. You need to be careful when doing experiments too. Here are some safety tips to remember.

Safety Tips

- Read each experiment carefully.

- Wear cover goggles when needed.

- Clean up spills right away.

- Never taste or smell substances unless directed to do so by your teacher.

- Handle sharp items carefully.

- Tape sharp edges of materials.

- Handle thermometers carefully.

- Use chemicals carefully.

- Dispose of chemicals properly.

- Put materials away when you finish an experiment.

- Wash your hands after each experiment.

Using Models

Experimenting with Views of Galaxies

Tanita saw pictures of spiral galaxies in a book. The book said that our galaxy, the Milky Way Galaxy, is a spiral galaxy. That night, Tanita and her father went outside. Her father told her that nearly all the stars she could see were in the Milky Way Galaxy.

The night sky did not look like the spiral galaxies in the book, however. Those pictures were from outside each galaxy. Tanita thought of it as looking at a house. From the street, you can see the shape of the house. You cannot see the shape of the house while standing in one of the rooms. Tanita realized that she could not see the shape of the Milky Way Galaxy because she was inside it. She decided to make a model so that she could better understand what she saw in the sky.

Thinking About the Experiment
Scientists use models to help them understand how things work. Scientists have many reasons for using models.
1. Why did Tanita use a model in her experiment?

Many models, including Tanita's, do not look exactly like the real thing.
2. Look at Tanita's model on the next page. How is her model like a spiral galaxy?

3. How is Tanita's model different from a spiral galaxy?

4. If her model does not look exactly like a real spiral galaxy, how can it be useful?

Tanita collected information to make her model.
5. Where did Tanita get the information she needed to make her model?

Try It!

Try Tanita's experiment and see if you come to the same conclusion.

Problem

Why are there different views of a galaxy?

Hypothesis

The way a galaxy appears depends on the location of the observer.

Materials

24 paper cups   pencil
paper

Procedure

1 Arrange the paper cups upside down on a table. Arrange them in a spiral pattern. Some of the cups should be right on the edge of the table. The cups represent a spiral galaxy somewhere in the universe.

2 Look at the cups from above the table, as though you were looking at the galaxy from somewhere out in space. In the box labeled *View from outside,* draw a diagram of what you see.

3 Now kneel beside the cups that are right on the edge of the table. Look across the table at the other side of the cups. Your position is what it would be if you were on a planet near the edge of the galaxy. You are inside the galaxy looking through it.

4 In the box labeled *View from inside,* draw a diagram of what you see.

Data and Observations

Spiral Galaxy	
View from outside	View from inside

Conclusion

Write your conclusion based on your data and observations.

Practice

Using Models

1. Suppose you want to show how an elliptical galaxy looks from inside. How would you change the model?

2. How could you set up a galaxy model that would allow you to look at the edge of the galaxy from its center?

Setting Up an Experiment

Experimenting with Fish

Dan visited a pet store where he saw many kinds of fish. He noticed that some of the fish moved their gills more often than others. A fish's gills move when a fish "breathes." He wondered if the temperature of the water affected how fast a fish's gills moved. He did an experiment to find out.

Dan thought about how to set up his experiment. First, he set out a large jar of water overnight. The next day, he measured the temperature of the water and recorded it. Then he placed a goldfish in the jar. Dan recorded how many times the goldfish opened and closed its gills in one minute.

Next, Dan added one ice cube to the water in the jar. When the ice cube melted, he added another ice cube. He added several ice cubes until the water temperature had dropped a few degrees. Then, he recorded the number of times the goldfish opened and closed its gills. Dan concluded that fish "breathe" more slowly in cool water than in warmer water.

Thinking About the Experiment

Dan's idea about temperature affecting gill movement was his hypothesis. He set up the experiment to test his hypothesis. Something was different about the water in the jar before and after Dan added the ice cubes. This factor was the variable being tested.

1. What was the variable being tested in this experiment?

Dan used the data he had recorded to reach his conclusion.

2. What did Dan measure to get his data?

3. What did his data show him?

4. Did his conclusion show that his hypothesis was correct?

Note Dan's data table on the next page. Dan decided to count gill movement more than one time at each temperature.

5. How many times did he count gill movement at each temperature?

6. Why is it important that he count gill movement more than one time and take an average count?

Try It!

Try Dan's experiment and see if you come to the same conclusion.

Problem
Does temperature affect the rate at which fish "breathe?"

Hypothesis
The rate of gill movement increases with temperature.

Materials
fishnet
goldfish
ice cubes
large jar

stopwatch
thermometer
water

Procedure
1 Fill a large jar with water. Allow it to stand overnight.

2 Measure the water temperature in the jar. Record.

3 Place a goldfish in the jar. Let it adjust for a minute or so. Observe how it opens and closes its gills.

4 Set the stopwatch and count the number of times the fish breathes in one minute.

5 Repeat two more times. Take an average of your results.

6 Add one ice cube to the jar and let it melt. Check the water temperature.

7 Add several more ice cubes, one at a time. When the temperature has dropped a few degrees, stop adding ice cubes.

8 Allow the goldfish to adjust for a minute or so. Record the final water temperature in the jar.

9 Repeat steps 4 and 5.

10 Compare the results.

Data and Observations

Gill Movements Each Minute				
	Trial #1	Trial #2	Trial #3	Average
Warmer water				
Cooler water				

Conclusion
Write your conclusion based on your data and observations.

Practice

Setting Up an Experiment
Other factors affect the rate at which fish breathe. These factors might be the size or kind of fish, the purity of the water, or the amount of oxygen in the water.
1. Choose one factor. Write a hypothesis about how you think that factor affects the rate at which fish breathe.
2. Think of how you would set up an experiment to test your hypothesis. Which variable would you change? How would you collect data?

Making Observations

MODULE C

Experimenting with Imprints

Tina and Sue visited a museum of natural history where they bought a kit to make a dinosaur "skeleton." They read that the skeleton was designed after models of dinosaurs scientists had reconstructed from fossils. Some models were reconstructed from incomplete remains. Tina and Sue wondered how scientists could determine what a dinosaur looked like by observing only fragments. They identified their problem: *How can the complete structure of an object be determined from imprints of only part of it?*

Tina and Sue decided to try an experiment to find out. They asked several friends to help them. The friends acted like scientists; they tried to identify objects from imprints. Tina and Sue showed only one imprint of an object at a time. They wanted to get an idea of how much of an object must be observed before it can be identified.

Thinking About the Experiment

The problem is the question you want to answer. Observations are anything you notice about the problem. Making observations is the first step in solving the problem.

1. What did Tina and Sue ask their friends to observe?

2. What can you tell about an object by observing its imprints?

3. What can you not tell about an object by observing its imprints?

4. How might using an imprint as a mold be helpful in making better observations?

5. What information about the object that cannot be observed from the mold might be helpful in identifying the object?

....
Try It!
Try Tina and Sue's experiment
and see if you come to the
same conclusion.
....

Problem
How can the complete structure of an object
be determined from imprints of only part
of it?

Hypothesis
The structure of an object can be determined
by inferring—using knowledge of the object
or other objects like it.

Materials
4 lumps of modeling clay
a small object that will leave an imprint
   in the clay

Procedure
1 Ask a group of four friends or
   classmates to work with you.

2 Choose a small object that will leave an
   impression in the clay. Do not show it to
   the group.

3 Gently press part of the object against a
   lump of clay to make an imprint.

4 Repeat step 3 three times. Each time use
   a different part of the object to make the
   imprint.

5 Show one clay imprint to your friends.
   Ask them to observe the imprint. Then
   ask them to write down what they think
   the object is.

6 Repeat step 5 three times. Each time
   show another imprint of the object.

7 Record how many imprints each person
   needs to see before he or she can
   identify the object correctly.

Data and Observations

Person observing	Number of observations needed to identify object

Conclusion
Write your conclusion based on your data
and observations.

Practice

Making Observations
One of the most important skills a
scientist has is the ability to make careful
observations.
1. Choose a common object, such as a
   pencil or eraser, and describe it. Make
   as many observations about it as you
   can.
2. Trade descriptions with classmates
   and try to name the object being
   described.

Testing a Hypothesis

Experimenting with Colors

Jan and Gordon were walking home from school. It was getting dark. They noticed that some of their clothes were harder to see than others. They wondered if clothing of some colors is harder to see in dim light than clothing of other colors. They thought of this hypothesis to answer their question: *Against a dark background, dark colors are harder to see than bright colors.*

When they arrived home, Jan and Gordon decided to set up an experiment to test their hypothesis. They looked at different colored pieces of paper against a background of gray paper. The colored paper is a model of the clothing. Jan and Gordon used gray paper to model the conditions at nightfall.

Thinking About the Experiment
Anything in the experiment that changes is a variable. An experiment should have only one variable changed at a time. That way you can be fairly sure that the results of the experiment were caused by that variable.
1. What is the variable that changes in this experiment?

2. What is the function of the gray background?

Testing a hypothesis is done by collecting data. An experiment is an organized way to collect data about a problem.
3. Look at the experiment on the next page. Would it test the hypothesis better if teachers as well as students look at the colored paper? Explain your answer.

Try It!
Try Jan and Gordon's experiment and see if you come to the same conclusion.

Problem
Are some colors harder to see against a dark background?

Hypothesis
Against a dark background, dark colors are harder to see than bright colors.

Materials
large shoe box
1 sheet each of red, yellow, gray, and black construction paper
scissors
metric ruler
dark gray or black paper

Procedure
1 Cut out strips of red, yellow, gray, and black construction paper. The strips should be about 1.5 cm by 6 cm. Make at least 10 strips of each color.

2 Cover the inside of a large shoe box with dark gray or black paper.

3 Place a few strips of each color on the bottom of the shoe box. Try to scatter the colors so they are not clustered in any one place.

4 Ask a classmate to glance briefly into the box. Ask how many strips of each color appear to be in the box. Record the responses on a chart like the one shown.

5 Repeat step 4 with several other students. The amount of time students look into the box should be the same in all cases.

Data and Observations

	First Trial		Second trial	
Color of strips	Number in box	Student guess	Number in box	Student guess
Red				
Yellow				
Gray				
Black				

Conclusion
Write your conclusion based on your data and observations.

Practice

Testing a Hypothesis
Suppose you wanted to find out how different background colors affected how well colors could be seen.
1. What would your hypothesis be?
2. What experiment could you do to test your hypothesis?
3. How would your experiment be different from the experiment Jan and Gordon did?

Stating a Hypothesis

Experimenting with Oil Drops

Jeff noticed that a drop of water made the pattern on a bowl look bigger. In science class, Jeff had learned that light rays bend when they pass through water. He believed this bending caused the drop to act like a little magnifying glass. Jeff wondered if a drop of oil would also make something look bigger. Before doing an experiment to find out, Jeff needed to state a hypothesis. His hypothesis would be a possible answer to his question. His hypothesis was that a drop of oil would make things look bigger too.

Jeff did an experiment to test his hypothesis. Then he used his results to make a conclusion about whether his hypothesis was correct or incorrect.

Thinking About the Experiment

Jeff guessed that an oil drop might act just as a water drop does.

1. How did the water drop change the pattern on the bowl?

2. In Jeff's experiment on the next page, he used the letter *A*. What did Jeff think a drop of oil would do to the letter *A*?

Jeff has a control in his experiment. The control is a part of the experiment that does not have the tested variable.

3. What is the control in this experiment?

Jeff found that the oil drop spread out on the paper. It did not make the letter look bigger. He had made an incorrect hypothesis.

4. Write a hypothesis that Jeff might have used for his experiment.

5. Can Jeff apply what he learned about oil to all liquids? Explain.

Try It!

Try Jeff's experiment and see if you come to the same conclusion.

Problem

Does a drop of oil bend light in the same way that a water drop does?

Hypothesis

Jeff's hypothesis was incorrect. Write your own hypothesis for this experiment.

Materials

newspaper page
sheet of white paper
scissors
masking tape
1 piece of cardboard

plastic wrap
2 droppers
cooking oil
water

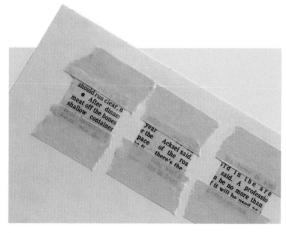

Procedure

1 Get a piece of newspaper that contains small, regular printing (not headlines).

2 Find three capital *A*'s that are the same size. If you cannot find three *A*'s, find three of another letter in the alphabet. Cut out three pieces of the newspaper so that an *A* is in the middle of each piece.

3 Tape the cutout letters to the white paper. Do not put tape over the *A*'s. Tape the paper to the cardboard.

4 Tape a piece of plastic wrap so that the letters are covered by plastic.

5 Place a large drop of water on one *A*. Place a large drop of cooking oil on another *A*. Do not put any drop on the third *A*.

6 Closely observe how the letters look through the drops. Compare their sizes to the letter with no drop.

Data and Observations

Is the size of the letter larger, smaller, or unchanged?

Conclusion

Liquid	Letter size
Water	
Oil	

Write your conclusion based on your data and observations.

Practice

Stating a Hypothesis

1. You could do an experiment to find out how drops of liquids, such as vinegar or lemon juice, affect the size of the letters. What might your hypothesis be?

2. Write a hypothesis for an experiment to find out how the number of drops of water changes a letter.

Collecting Data

Experimenting with Seeds

After a late afternoon rainstorm, David saw a rainbow. He remembered what he had learned in school about the many colors that make up white light. He also remembered that he had learned that plants need light to live. He wondered if the color of the light would affect how a plant grows. He thought of this hypothesis to answer his question: *Plants grow better in some colors of light than in others.*

David decided to do an experiment to test his hypothesis. The purpose of an experiment is to collect data about the problem you want to solve. Data are pieces of information. In David's experiment, he grew bean plants under light of five different colors and white light. He collected data on how the plants grew by measuring the height of each plant every day. Then he entered his data on a chart like the one on the next page. He wrote the height in millimeters in the column of the chart beneath the color of light used.

Thinking About the Experiment

David had to decide how to tell how well a plant was growing. He thought about describing the color of the plant or counting the number of leaves on each plant. He decided to measure how tall the plant grew.

1. What units of measure did David use in his data table?

2. Why are measurements better than counting leaves?

3. Why is it important to measure a plant in the same way each time?

Suppose one of the seeds in the experiment never germinates.

4. Should David use the data from *that* plant to make a conclusion about the color light that is best for plant growth? Explain your answer.

Try It!

Try David's experiment and see if you come to the same conclusion.

Problem

Does the color of light affect the growth of plants?

Hypothesis

Plants grow better in some colors of light than in others.

Materials

6 small milk cartons
clear plastic wrap
red, orange, yellow, green, and blue cellophane squares
6 kidney bean seeds, soaked overnight
plastic tray
potting soil to fill 6 milk cartons
scissors
water
6 straws
cover goggles
metric ruler

Procedure

1. Cut the tops off six small milk cartons. Wash the cartons thoroughly.

2. Cut small holes in the bottom of each carton for water drainage.

3. Fill each carton 2/3 full of potting soil. Plant a soaked bean in each carton. (Beans will not germinate unless they have been soaked.)

4. Place the cartons on a plastic tray. Water them well. Put the same amount of water in each carton.

5. Put a straw into the soil in each carton. Cover the straw and carton with one of the cellophane squares or with clear plastic wrap. Each carton should have a different color covering.

6. After the seeds germinate, measure their height each day. Enter the height of each plant in a chart like the one below.

Data and Observations

Day	Color of Cellophane					
	Clear	Red	Orange	Yellow	Green	Blue
1						
2						
3						
4						
5						

Conclusion

Write your conclusion based on your data and observations.

Practice

Collecting Data
Suppose you wanted to find out how much water each of the kidney beans absorbed when they were soaked overnight.

1. What data would you need to collect to find this out?
2. What equipment and materials would you need to use to collect these data?

Stating a Hypothesis

Experimenting with Water

Roberta read about hydroelectric dams in her science book. She noticed in the pictures that turbines were located near the bottoms of the dams. She also noticed that each dam was built so it was thickest at the bottom.

Roberta decided the dam probably was thickest where the weight of water—or water pressure—was greatest. Also, she knew that moving water was used to spin the blades in the turbines. She thought turbines probably were placed where water pressure is greatest.

These ideas caused Roberta to think that water pressure must be greatest near the bottom of the dam. She wanted to find out more about water pressure.

Roberta decided to do an experiment with water pressure. She discovered that she already had a hypothesis. All she had to do was find a way to test her hypothesis .

Thinking About the Experiment

Roberta's problem was to find out whether or not water pressure is different at different depths.

1. What is Roberta's hypothesis?

Roberta thought water presses against the walls of a container in the same way water presses against a dam. For her experiment, she decided to use a tall milk carton to hold water.

Note Roberta's set up on the next page.

2. What can Roberta learn about water pressure by watching water flowing from holes in the milk carton?

3. Why did Roberta make the holes in the milk carton at different levels?

Suppose that water comes out of the bottom hole harder than it comes out of the other two holes.

4. What does this tell you about Roberta's hypothesis?

Try It!

Try Roberta's experiment and see if you come to the same conclusion.

Problem

Is water pressure different at different depths?

Hypothesis

Write your own hypothesis for this experiment.

Materials

paper milk carton   masking tape
pencil   water
shallow baking pan

Procedure

1 Use a pencil to make three holes in one side of the milk carton. The bottom hole should be 8 cm from the bottom. The second hole should be about 12 cm from the bottom. The third hole should be about 16 cm from the bottom.

2 Cover the holes with a single piece of tape.

3 Fill the carton with water.

4 Place the carton in a shallow pan with the holes facing into the pan.

5 Pull the tape off quickly. Observe how water flows from each hole.

6 Record your observations.

Data and Observations

	Water pressure
Top hole	
Middle hole	
Bottom hole	

Conclusion

Write your conclusion based on your data and observations.

Practice

Stating a Hypothesis

Roberta wants to find out if oil pressure is different at different depths.

1. What might be her hypothesis for this experiment?

2. Describe how she could set up the experiment to test this hypothesis.

Identifying Variables

Experimenting with Brine Shrimp

In school, Mia learned about tiny animals called brine shrimp. She learned that they live in estuaries— places where salt water mixes with fresh water. She wondered how the salt in the water affects brine shrimp eggs.

Mia thought of this hypothesis to answer her question: *The amount of salt in the water affects how fast brine shrimp eggs hatch.*

Mia set up an experiment to test her hypothesis. She put 200 milliliters of tap water into one cup. She placed different amounts of salt into three other cups and added enough tap water to make 200 milliliters of salt water. Then she placed the same number of brine shrimp eggs in each cup. She put two of the cups on a shelf in a cool place.

She left the other two cups on a warm radiator. Every day for a week she checked all the cups to find out how many eggs had hatched.

Thinking About the Experiment

Anything in an experiment that can be changed is a variable. Only one variable should be changed at a time. Then you can be fairly sure that the results of the experiment were caused by that variable. Mia did not set up her experiment correctly. Her experiment had two variables that changed.

1. What were the two variables that changed?

2. What was the variable that Mia wanted to use to test her hypothesis?

3. What was the other variable in her experiment? What would this variable test?

Mia put the same amount of water in each cup. She added the same number of eggs. Read her experiment on the next page to see how she corrected her experiment.

4. Were the number of eggs in the cups and the amount of water in the cups variables? Explain your answer.

5. How did she change the experiment so that it tested only one variable?

Try It!
Try Mia's experiment and see if you come to the same conclusion.

Problem
Does the amount of salt in the water affect how brine shrimp eggs hatch?

Hypothesis
The amount of salt in the water affects how fast brine shrimp eggs hatch.

Materials
4 clear plastic cups	hand lens
brine shrimp eggs	paper towel
tap water that has	salt
sat out overnight	marker
(about 800 mL)	toothpick

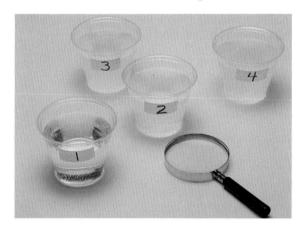

Procedure
1 Label the cups *1*, *2*, *3*, and *4*.

2 Fill cup *1* with 200 mL of water that has been sitting out overnight.

3 Place 2g of salt in cup *2*, 4g of salt in cup *3*, and 6g of salt in cup *4*. Add enough of the tap water to make 200 mL of solution in each cup. Your teacher may prefer to prepare the solutions for you.

4 Place some brine shrimp eggs on a paper towel. Use the flat end of a toothpick to place a small amount of eggs in cup *1*.

5 Place a similar amount of eggs in each of the other cups.

6 Place the cups together in a place where they will not be disturbed.

7 Observe the water in the cups each day through a hand lens. In cups where the eggs have hatched, you can see the brine shrimp swimming. Record on the chart each day whether you can see movement.

Data and Observations

	Movement in Each Cup			
Day	Cup 1	Cup 2	Cup 3	Cup 4
1				
2				
3				
4				
5				

Conclusion
Write your conclusion based on your data and observations.

Practice

Identifying Variables
Suppose you wanted to find out if temperature had an effect on how brine shrimp hatch.
1. What would be the variable in the experiment?
2. How would you change the experiment to test that variable?
3. What factors would you have to keep the same in order to test the variable?

Using Models

Experimenting with Salt Water

Kim lived close to the ocean. She knew that a river nearby emptied fresh water into the ocean. She wondered what happened when fresh water and salt water come together. Does fresh water mix immediately with salt water, float on salt water, or sink under salt water? She thought that the fresh water might float on the salt water. Kim decided to make models of fresh and salt water meeting to test her hypothesis. A model shows how something looks or works.

Thinking About the Experiment

Scientists often use models to stand for something they cannot see directly. Kim knew she could not see what was happening when fresh and salt water mixed. She added food coloring to one kind of water so she could see what happened when the two kinds of water mixed.

1. How are the parts of Kim's model like the river and the ocean?

2. Why did she need a model to help test her hypothesis?

Kim needed two models to show that the water being added did not always sink or float. Read her procedure on the next page.

3. What did Kim do for her first model?

4. How was her second model different from her first model?

Try It!

Try Kim's experiment and see if you come to the same conclusion.

Problem

What happens when fresh water and salt water come together?

Hypothesis

Fresh water floats on salt water.

Materials

measuring cup   food coloring
water   balance
plastic box or   metric ruler
  aquarium   plastic spoon
table salt

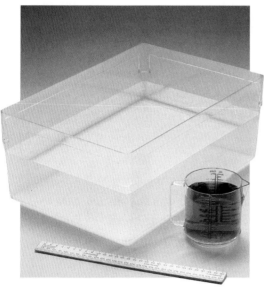

Procedure

1 Use the measuring cup to fill the plastic box with tap water to a depth of about 10 cm. Record how much water you put into the box.

2 Add 10 g of salt for every 100 mL of water you put into the box. Stir the water until the salt disappears.

3 Fill the measuring cup with tap water. Color the water with food coloring.

4 Slowly pour the colored tap water into the box of clear salt water. Try not to make water currents.

5 Let the water stand for a few minutes. Record what you observe in this model.

6 Repeat the experiment, but this time make a model by pouring colored salt water into a box of clear tap water. Record your observations.

Data and Observations

Procedure	Observations
Pouring fresh water into salt water	
Pouring salt water into fresh water	

Conclusion

Write your conclusion based on your data and observations.

Practice

Using Models
Suppose you wanted to find out what happens when water of one temperature flows into water of another temperature.
1. What would be your hypothesis?
2. How would you set up your model?
3. Would you use one or two models? Explain.

Making Conclusions

Experimenting with Cleaning Oil Spills

Pat was watching the evening news. She watched a report about an oil spill in the ocean. A ship carrying oil had hit a rock. Huge amounts of oil were leaking out of the ship. People were trying to clean up the oil using hoses to siphon the oil into tanks on another ship. However, they could not clean up the oil fast enough. Oil was leaking from the ship faster than the people could clean it up.

Pat wondered how she might remove a small amount of oil from a bowl of water in the shortest amount of time. She knew that oil floats on water. She thought that scooping the oil from the top of the water might be the fastest way to remove oil from water.

Pat decided to do an experiment and make observations to see if her hypothesis was correct. She decided to try three different methods to remove cooking oil from the surface of water.

Thinking About the Experiment

In order to make observations that would allow her to draw conclusions, Pat had to set up her experiment very carefully.

1. Why should Pat color the water first?

It took Pat more than seven minutes to remove oil by siphoning it. It took her more than two minutes to scoop the oil out. The cotton balls soaked up the oil in about one minute.

2. What conclusion about removing oil from water can you make using Pat's data?

3. Does this conclusion support Pat's hypothesis? Explain.

4. How might the conclusion have been affected if Pat had used different amounts of oil in each test?

5. Based on the results of this experiment, could Pat conclude that the fastest way to remove large oil spills from the ocean is by soaking them up? Explain.

Try It!

Try Pat's experiment and see
if you come to the
same conclusion.
....

Problem

How can oil be removed from water in the
shortest amount of time?

Hypothesis

*Pat's hypothesis was incorrect. Write your
own hypothesis for this experiment.*

Materials

4 jars of the same size   pen or pencil
water   1 dropper
food coloring   1 spoon
metric measuring cup   cotton balls
watch or clock with   cooking oil
   second hand

Procedure

1 Put 150 mL of water in each of 3 jars.
Add 5 drops of food coloring to the
water in each jar. Stir the water.

2 Add 50 mL of oil to each of the 3 jars.

3 Time yourself as you use the dropper to
siphon the oil from the water in one jar.
Squeeze the oil you siphon into the extra
jar. Continue siphoning the oil until you
cannot remove any more oil. Record
how much time it took to remove the oil
by siphoning it.

4 Repeat step 3, but use cotton balls to
soak up the oil from the water in the
second jar. Use each cotton ball only
once to soak up oil. Be sure to record the
time needed to soak up the oil.

5 Repeat step 3 using the spoon to scoop
oil from the water in the third jar. Empty
the spoon into the extra jar. Record the
time needed to scoop the oil from the
water.

Data and Observations

Method	Time needed to remove oil
Siphoning	
Soaking up	
Scooping	

Conclusion

Write your conclusion based on your data
and observations.

Practice

Making Conclusions
Detergent is sometimes used on oil
spills. Suppose Pat repeated the
experiment, adding detergent to each jar
before testing it.
1. What conclusion might you make if it
took less time to clean up the oil in all
three tests?
2. What conclusion would you make if
there was no difference in time when
siphoning or soaking up oil, but
scooping oil took less than 1 minute?

Glossary

A

acid rain, mixture of oxides of sulfur and nitrogen and water in the air.

adaptation (ad′ap tā′shən), an inherited trait within a species that increases the chances of survival and reproduction.

albinism (al′bə niz′əm), condition in which organisms cannot produce melanin, and are thus white or colorless.

albino (al bī′nō), an organism that has albinism.

amber (am′bər), a hard translucent, yellow or yellowish-brown fossil resin.

ampere (am′pir), measure of the amount of electricity that flows through a wire; the number of electrons that move past a point in one second; abbreviation: amp.

animal, one of a kingdom of multicellular organisms that have specialized sex cells and eat other organisms to obtain energy; eukaryotes.

aqueduct (ak′wə dukt), an artificial channel or large pipe for bringing water from a distance.

arctic (ärk′tik), at or near the North Pole.

artificial selection (är′tə fish′əl si lek′shən), practice of mating plants or animals with certain traits to produce offspring with those traits.

asexual (ā sek′shü əl) **reproduction,** reproduction by one parent.

assembly line (ə sem′blē līn), a rapid system for putting together parts.

astronomer (ə stron′ə mər), scientist who studies objects in space.

atom (at′əm), basic unit of all matter.

autoclave (ô′tə klāv), a strong, closed vessel that develops superheated steam under pressure.

B

bacteria (bak tir′ē ə), a group of one-celled microorganisms that reproduce by fission or by forming spores.

base (bās), one kind of molecule that makes up a DNA strand; four kinds of bases are represented by the letters A, C, T, and G.

behavioral (bi hā′vyər əl) **adaptation,** an action that aids survival.

big bang theory, explanation of how the universe formed 13 billion years ago.

bioluminescent (bī′ō lü mə nes′nt), creation and emission of light by living organisms.

biosphere (bī′ə sfir), total of all the communities on the earth and the environments in which they live.

black dwarf, small, dark, dense star that has no fuel for nuclear fusion and does not shine.

black hole, a region in space in which so much mass is concentrated that nothing, not even light, can escape its gravitational attraction.

bog, piece of wet, spongy ground, consisting mostly of decayed or decaying sphagnum moss.

brownout (broun′out′), situation in which people are using more electricity than the power company can supply; temporary reduction in power.

C

camouflage (kam′ə fläzh), characteristics that enable organisms to blend in with their surroundings.

canopy (kan′ə pē), the upper layer of a forest that receives the most sunlight.

carbohydrate (kär′bō hī′drāt), building-block molecule that provides energy.

carnivore (kär′nə vôr), a consumer that eats only other consumers.

carotene (kar′ə ten′), yellow-orange pigment in many plants.

cast (kast), fossil formed by sediments filling up a mold.

cell (sel), the basic living unit of an organism.

cell division (sel də vizh′ən), process by which a cell divides into two nearly equal-sized cells.

Cenozoic (sen′ə zō′ik) **Era,** the time in the history of the earth, about 65 million years ago to the present, when recent life evolved on the earth.

chemical (kem′ə kəl) **energy,** energy stored in the bonds of molecules.

chemosynthesis (kem′ō sin′thə sis), process in which bacteria produce sugars using chemical energy from hydrogen sulfide.

chlorophyll (klôr′ə fil), green substance in producers that absorbs light energy for photosynthesis.

chloroplast (klôr′ə plast), organelle in producers that contains chlorophyll.

chordate (kôr′dāt), any of a phylum of animals that have, at some stage of development, a backbone.

chromosome (krō′mə sōm), threadlike strands found in the nucleus of a cell and made mostly of DNA molecules.

circuit (sėr′kit), a closed path through which current flows.

classify (klas′ə fī), to sort into groups based on similarities and differences.

cold-blooded, organisms whose body temperatures change as the temperature of the environment changes.

community (kə myü′nə tē), two or more populations of different species living together and interacting with each other within a certain area.

competition (kom′pə tish′ən), the struggle among organisms for the things they need to live and reproduce.

compost (kom′pōst), mixture of decaying plant materials.

compound (kom′pound) **eye,** eye with many lenses characteristic of many insects.

concave (kon kāv′) **lens,** lens with the middle thinner than the edges.

cone (kōn), one of a group of microscopic sense organs in the retina of the eye that responds to light; enables color vision in humans.

constellation (kon′stə lā′shən), a group of stars that is named for an object or person or other animal.

consumer (kən sü′mər), an organism that gets its energy from the stored chemical energy in the food it eats.

control (kən trōl′), the part of an experiment that does not have the variable being tested.

convection (kən vek′shən) **current,** transfer of energy by the movement of a rather large amount of a gas or liquid; circulation of a gas or liquid in which the heated material rises, cools, and falls back down in a circular pattern.

convex (kon veks′) **lens,** lens with the middle part thicker than its edges.

core (kôr), center of the earth.

crust (krust), outer layer of the earth that varies from 8-65 kilometers in depth.

cytoplasm (sī′tə plaz′əm), clear, jellylike substance between the nuclear membrane and the cell membrane; contains the cell's organelles and aids in moving material.

D

DDT, abbreviation for dichloro-diphenyl-trichloro-ethane, a powerful insecticide.

decomposer (dē′kəm pō′zər), organism that helps to break down and decay dead organisms and the wastes of living organisms.

desalination (dē sal′ə nā shən), a process that removes salt from ocean water to make fresh water.

diversity (də vėr′sə tē), variety.

DNA, abbreviation for deoxyribonucleic acid, a building-block molecule that contains the instructions that control how an organism takes shape and grows.

dominant (dom′ə nənt) **gene,** a gene that prevents the expression of another gene.

E

ecology (ē kol′ə jē), the study of how organisms behave and interact with their environments.

ecosystem (ē′kō sis′təm), distinct community of species and the nonliving environment with which the community interacts.

egg (eg), female sex cell.

EIS, abbreviation for Environmental Impact Statement, a study of the effects on the environment of any action that involves federal agencies or federal money.

electric (i lek′trik) **current,** the flow of electric charge.

electrical (i lek′trə kəl) **energy,** kind of energy carried by moving charges.

electromagnetic (i lek′trō mag net′ik) **radiation,** energy moving in waves through space.

electromagnetic spectrum, scale of electromagnetic waves from shortest to longest or longest to shortest.

electromagnetic wave, energy that travels through space at a speed of 300,000,000 meters per second.

electron (i lek′tron), negatively charged particle that moves around the nucleus of an atom.

element (el′ə mənt), any substance made of only one kind of atom; one of 109 basic substances that cannot be broken down by chemical reactions.

elliptical (i lip′tə kəl) **galaxy,** galaxy shaped like a sphere that's been stretched out at the ends.

embryo (em′brē ō), organism in the early stage of development.

endangered (en dān′jərd) **species,** species that might die out because so few are left on the earth.

energy pyramid (en′ər jē pir′ə mid), graph that shows the relationship between a food chain and available energy.

EPA, abbreviation for the Environmental Protection Agency.

epiphyte (ep′ə fīt), any of various plants that grow on other plants for support, but draw nourishment from the air and rain instead of from their host; air plant.

eukaryote (yü′kar′ē ōt), organism made of cells that contain many different structures surrounded by thin coverings called membranes.

evolution (ev′ə lü′shən), process that results in changes in the genetic makeup of species over time.

extinct (ek stingkt′), term referring to species that no longer exist.

F

fertilizer (fėr′tl ī′zər), substance, either chemical or natural, spread over or put into the soil to supply missing nutrients.

first level consumer (kən sü′mər), animals that eat only producers.

flocculence (flok′yə ləns), little globs of dirt and other particles that collect around alum at a water purification plant; abbreviation: floc.

flyway (flī′wā′), migration route.

focal (fō′kəl) **point,** where light waves come together in a single point.

food chain, simple feeding pattern that shows the transfer of energy from one organism to another.

food web, system of food chains in an ecosystem that shows how energy flows through the ecosystem.

fossil (fos′əl), any remains or trace of a once-living thing.

fossil fuel, long chains of hydrogen and carbon atoms resulting from partially decomposed organisms from millions of years ago.

free mount, reconstruction of a skeleton.

frequency (frē′kwən sē), the number of waves passing a point in a given time; indicates how much energy a wave has.

fungus (fung′gəs), one of a kingdom of multicellular organisms that absorb food from dead or living organisms; reproduce by spores; eukaryotes.

G

galaxy (gal′ək sē), a group of hundreds of billions of stars, gas, and dust that is relatively close together in space and held together by gravity.

gene (jēn), a section of DNA that controls one or more traits.

generator (jen′ə rā′tər), machine that uses a magnet to change mechanical energy to electrical energy.

genus (jē′nəs), a group of closely related species.

geologic (jē′ə loj′ik) **time scale,** history of the earth divided into units of time based on fossil evidence and evidence of climatic changes.

geologist (jē ol′ə jist), scientist who studies the structure of the earth.

geothermal (jē′ō thėr′məl) **energy,** thermal energy from within the earth.

glacier (glā′shər), a large, slow-moving mass of ice.

global warming, a warming of the earth's atmosphere.

gravity (grav′ə tē), a force that pulls any two objects together.

groundwater (ground wô′tər), water in the ground that collects near the earth's surface.

H

habitat (hab′ə tat), the place where an organism lives.

herbivore (hėr′bə vôr), a consumer that eats only producers.

hibernator (hī′bər nāt ôr), animal that goes into an inactive state while outside temperatures are cold.

hybrid (hī′brid), organism that has a dominant and recessive gene for a trait.

hydroelectric (hī′drō i lek′trik) **power plant,** power plant that uses the mechanical energy of falling water to generate electricity.

hydrothermal (hī′drō thėr′məl), having to do with hot water.

hypothesis (hī poth′ə sis), a likely explanation of a problem.

I

Ice Age, a period of time when ice sheets covered large parts of the world.

index fossil (in′deks fos′əl), fossil of an organism that lived only during a certain time that can be used to date undisturbed rock layers.

inherit (in her′it), to receive from one's mother or father.

insecticide (in sek′tə sīd), poison that kills insects.

instinct (in′stingkt), complex, inborn behavior not dependent on experience.

invertebrate (in vėr′tə brit), an animal with no backbone.

irregular galaxy (i reg′yə lər gal′ək sē), galaxy that does not have a spiral or elliptical shape; contains many young stars.

K

karyotype (kar′ē ō tīp), picture of an organism's chromosomes that shows them paired according to size.

kingdom (king′dəm), the largest group into which an organism can be classified.

L

landfill (land′fil′), place where garbage and other refuse are buried and covered with dirt in order to build up low-lying or wet land.

larva (lär′və), immature stage of many animals.

lens, a piece of glass or other transparent material shaped so that it will bend light to form an image.

life processes, activities of living things including getting energy, using energy, growth, getting rid of wastes, response, and reproduction.

light-year (līt′yir′), the distance light travels in one year.

lithosphere (lith′ə sfir), rigid outer shell of the earth containing the crust.

Local Group, group of galaxies that includes the Milky Way Galaxy.

M

magma (mag′mə), hot, melted rock deep inside the earth.

magnetic (mag net′ik) **field,** the space around a magnet in which an object feels a magnetic force.

main, large pipe through which water moves from the source to the place of use.

mammal (mam′əl), warm-blooded vertebrate that has hair and feeds milk to its young.

mantle (man′tl), layer of the earth between the crust and the core.

manufacturing (man′yə fak′chər ing), making finished products from raw materials using technology.

marsh (märsh), a wetland area that contains soft-stemmed plants and decomposed plant matter.

marsupial (mär sü′pē əl), any of an order of mammals having a pouch covering the mammary glands on the abdomen in which the female nurses and carries her incompletely developed young.

mass production, the making of goods in large quantities, especially by machinery.

MCL, abbreviation for maximum contaminant level.

mechanical (mə kan′ə kəl) **energy,** energy an object has because of its motion and the forces acting upon it.

megawatt (meg′ə wot′), one-hundred thousand watts.

meiosis (mī ō′sis), process by which sex cells are produced; results in a cell with one-half the number of chromosomes of the original cell.

melanin (mel′ə nən), chemical that gives body coverings their color.

Mesozoic (mes′ə zō′ik) **Era,** the time in the history of the earth, about 250 to 65 million years ago, during which reptiles were the major life form.

Milky Way Galaxy, large star group to which our solar system belongs.

mitosis (mī tō′sis), process by which a cell's nucleus divides to form two identical nuclei with the same number of chromosomes as the original cell.

model (mod′l), a representation of how something looks or works; reconstruction of an organism that reflects the skin, bones, and muscles.

mold (mōld), hollow spot in the shape of an organism.

molecule (mol′ə kyül), the smallest bit of a compound that has the properties of that compound.

moneran (mə nir′ən), one of a kingdom of unicellular organisms made up of cells that lack nuclei and many other organelles; prokaryotes.

mutation (myü tā′shən), permanent change in DNA that occurs when DNA copies itself.

mutualism (myü′chü ə liz′əm), relationship between two different species where each member benefits from the relationship.

N

natural selection (nach′ər əl si lek′shən), the process by which organisms best suited to the environment survive and reproduce, thereby passing their genes to the next generation.

nebula (neb′yə lə), cloud of gas and dust in space.

NEPA, abbreviation for the National Environmental Policy Act, which is a major law that helps protect the environment.

niche (nich), the specific role of an organism in the community.

nocturnal (nok tėr′nl), active at night.

nova (nō′və), star that suddenly increases in brightness.

nuclear fusion (nü′klē ər fyü′zhən), process by which atoms of one element join together to form atoms of another element.

nucleic (nü klē′ik) **acid,** building-block molecule that controls the activities of a cell.

nucleus (nü′klē əs), central part of the atom; control center of the cell.

nutrient (nü′trē ənt), a substance needed for growth and survival.

O

organism (ôr′gə niz′əm), a living thing made up of one cell or more.

P

paleontologist (pā′lē on tol′ə jist), scientist who studies fossils.

Paleozoic (pā′lē ə zō′ik) **Era,** period of time from about 570 to 250 million years ago during which fish were the dominant life form.

Pangaea (pan jē′ə), supercontinent consisting of all the continents about 300 million years ago.

pesticide (pes′tə sīd), chemical that kills pests that damage crops.

petrify (pet′rə fī), act of dissolved minerals seeping into an organism and replacing the tissues of the organism, thus turning the organism to stone.

photosynthesis (fō′tō sin′thə sis), the process by which producers make sugars from sunlight, water, and carbon dioxide.

phycobilin (fī′kō bi′lin), pigment found in red algae and blue-green bacteria.

phylum (fī′ləm), subdivision of a kingdom.

physiological (fiz′ē ə loj′ə kəl) **adaptation,** adaptation that involves the jobs of body parts that control life processes that aid survival.

pigment (pig′mənt), chemical molecules that absorb light energy and thus appear the color of the light they reflect.

placental (plə sen′tl), mammal that carries its young inside the body in a uterus nourished by a placenta until the baby is fully developed.

plankton (plangk′tən), tiny, free-floating protists, plants, and animals that live near the surface of the water and form the basis of many food chains.

plant, one of a kingdom of multicellular organisms that undergo photosynthesis and reproduce by seeds, cones, or spores; eukaryotes.

plate (plāt), large section of the earth's surface made up of the crust and upper mantle.

plate boundary (plāt boun′dər ē), place where two plates meet.

plate tectonics (plāt tek ton′iks), theory stating that the earth's rocky outer skin, or lithosphere, is made of at least a dozen moving plates.

polymer (pol′ə mər), a long molecule made up of many smaller units strung together like beads on a chain.

population (pop′yə lā′shən), a group of individuals of the same species living in a certain area.

power (pou′ər), the rate at which work is done.

Precambrian (prē′kam′brē ən) **time,** time unit from the formation of the earth to about 570 million years ago during which life evolved in the oceans.

predation (prē dā′shən), the eating of one consumer by another.

predator (pred′ə tər), animal that hunts other animals.

preparator (pri par′ə tôr), person who works in a paleontology laboratory that cleans and prepares fossils for study.

prey (prā), animal eaten by predators.

producer (prə dü′sər), organism that converts light energy or chemical energy into sugars.

prokaryote (prō kar′ē ōt), organism made of a cell without membranes separating organelles from the cytoplasm.

protein (prō′tēn′), building-block molecule that forms the basic structure of living things.

protist (prō′tist), one of a kingdom of organisms that have varied characteristics; most are unicellular and nonphotosynthetic, others are unicellular or multicellular and photosynthetic.

protostar (prō′tə stär), beginning stage of a star brought about by gravity pulling together gas and dust into a ball.

pulsar (pul′sär), neutron star that sends out pulses of radiation, usually in the form of radio waves.

purebred (pyùr′bred′), organism that has two genes of the same kind, either both dominant or both recessive, for a trait.

purification (pyùr′ə fə kā′shən) **plant,** place where the public water supply is cleaned, treated, and tested to make sure it's pure and safe for drinking.

pylon (pī′lon), huge steel tower that carries high-voltage, bare-wire, transmission lines.

Q

quasar (kwā′sär), distant clusters of extremely bright stars billions of light years from the earth that have the largest known red shifts.

R

radioactive (rā′dē ō ak′tiv) **dating,** technique using radioactive elements to calculate how old rock is.

radioactive element, element whose atoms have nuclei that break apart naturally, changing them to atoms of a different element.

receptor (ri sep′tər), cell or group of cells sensitive to light stimuli.

recessive (re ses′iv) **gene,** a gene whose expression is prevented by a dominant gene.

red giant, star whose size has expanded greatly as it uses up its fuel.

red shift, change in a light wave from a retreating object to a color nearer the red end of the spectrum.

reflecting telescope (ri flek′ing tel′ə skōp), instrument that uses mirrors to gather light.

reflection (ri flek′shən), bouncing of light waves off a surface.

refracting telescope (ri frak′ting tel′ə skōp), telescope that uses lenses to gather light.

refraction (ri frak′shən), the bending of a light wave as it moves from one material to another.

reservoir (rez′ər vwär), an artificial lake that collects and stores water.

respiration (res′pə rā′shən), the process by which cells change sugar and oxygen into carbon dioxide and water, thereby releasing energy.

rod (rod), one of the microscopic sense organs in the retina of the eye that is sensitive to dim light; enables black and white vision in humans.

S

satellite (sat′l īt), object that revolves around another object.

second level consumer (sek′ənd lev′əl kən sü′mər), animal that eats first level consumers.

sediment (sed′ə mənt), soil, sand, and rocks carried by wind and water.

semen (sē′mən), liquid containing sperm.

sewage (sü′ij), mixed water and waste.

sewage treatment plant, place where waste water is cleaned before it is returned to the public water supply.

sexual (sek′shü əl) **reproduction,** reproduction by two parents.

sickle-cell (sik′əl sel), trait caused by a mutation that results in malformed red blood cells, which have a lessened ability to carry oxygen.

species (spē′shēz), group of organisms that naturally interbreed and produce offspring capable of reproducing.

spectrometer (spek trom′ə tər), an instrument that separates the different wavelengths in a beam of light.

sperm (spėrm), male sex cell.

spiral galaxy (spī′rəl gal′ək sē), galaxy shaped like a flying disc with a bulge in its center.

stable system, system that is in balance.

star life cycle, the complete process of a particular star's life from birth to death.

step-down transformer (tran sfôr′mər), transformer that decreases voltage.

step-up transformer (tran sfôr′mər), transformer that increases voltage.

structural (struk′chər əl) **adaptation,** adaptation that involves body shape or color.

subsystem (sub sis′təm), a smaller system that connects to a larger system.

supernova, brilliant explosion of a supergiant.

switch (swich), device that interrupts the flow of electric current in a circuit.

system (sis′təm), a set of parts that work together as a whole.

T

taxonomy (tak son′ə mē), the science of classifying organisms.

TCE, abbreviation for trichloroethylene, a chemical that causes cancer; found in water and certain manufactured products.

technology (tek nol′ə jē), the use of scientific knowledge to control physical objects and forces.

theory (thē′ər ē), one or more related hypotheses supported by data that best explains things or events.

thermal (thėr′məl) **pollution,** a heating of water that is harmful to living things.

THM, abbreviation for trihalomethanes, a chemical in chlorine that is added to purify water.

threatened species, species whose population is small enough that it might become endangered.

trait (trāt), characteristic.

transformer (tran sfôr′mər), a device that increases or decreases voltage of electric current.

tundra (tun′drə), the northernmost and coldest land biome.

turbine (tėr′bən), a machine with fanlike blades that can be turned by flowing gas or liquid.

U

ultraviolet (ul′trə vī′ə lit) **light,** light out of the range of human perception past the violet end of the spectrum.

understory (un′dər stôr′ē), middle layer in a forest where light is filtered by branches above.

V

variable (ver′ē ə bəl), anything in an experiment that can be changed.

vent, opening in the ocean floor.

vertebrate (vėr′tə brit), an animal with a backbone.

visible (viz′ə bəl) **light,** light that humans can see.

visible spectrum (viz′ə bəl spek′trəm), small range of wavelengths that humans can see.

volt (vōlt), unit to measure voltage.

voltage (vōl′tij), force needed to move an electron from one place to another, expressed in volts.

vulcanize (vùl′kə nīz), treat rubber with sulfur and heat to make it more elastic and durable.

W

warm-blooded, organisms whose body temperatures stay constant.

water table, layer of underground water that collects in an aquifer; the level below which the ground is saturated with water.

watt (wot), metric unit that measures power.

wavelength (wāv′lengkth′), distance from crest to crest or trough to trough on a wave.

wetland (wet′land′), area that is at or near the water table for at least part of the year.

white dwarf, star that is dimmer than other stars of the same temperature.

Index

Geothermal energy, D65, E91

Giant stars, A9

Global warming, E54

Glossopteris, C76

Glucose molecules, D8

Godowsky, Leo, D74-75

Goodyear, Charles, E63

Government. *See* United States Government

Gravity
　creation of universe and, A47, A48-49
　stars and, A10

Great Rift Valley, C80, C81

Greeks, astronomy and, A53

Groundwater, pumping, E18-20

Growth, B13

H

Habitats, F21
　rainforest, D33
　size decrease in, F14-15
　wildlife, F44-45

Hawking, Stephen, A49

Helium, A7, A48

Henry, Joseph, E35

Herbivores, C60

High-frequency waves, A40

High-tech, E7

Home, electric current in, E48-50

Hopi Indians, A55

Hormones, B60

Horner, Jack, C5-11, C30, C41-47, C58, C68-69

Hot water ocean vents, D60-65, D66-67
　chemosynthesis and, D68-71

How Things Work
　compound eye, D77
　DNA fingerprinting, B61
　radiocarbon dating, C93
　spectrometer, A77
　water heater, electric, E93
　wetland drainage, F77

Hubble, Edwin, A66

Hubble telescope, A68

Humans, C19
　eyes of, D12-13, D17
　population growth of, F21

Hybrids, B47, B48-49

Hydroelectric power, E38, E39, E53, E84-85

Hydrogen
　fusion of atoms of, A6-7
　in stars, A28

Hydrogen sulfide. *See* Chemosynthesis

Hydrothermal activity, in oceans, D60

Hypotheses, about dinosaurs, C8

I

Indians, corn and, B42-43

Information gathering about past, C66-93.
　See also Earth; Fossils

Infrared images, A42, A43, A44-45

Inheritance, B46-47, C24. *See also* Genes

Instincts, D22-23

Interactions
　in aquarium, F8-9
　in marshes, F34-43
　mutualism as, D37

Inventors and inventions, E86-87
　Goodyear, Charles, E63
　Matzeliger, Jan, E74

Invertebrates, C15

Iridium, C26, C27

Irregular galaxies, A16, A17

K

Keck telescope, A36, A37

Kilowatt-hours, E38, E51

Kingdoms, C30-32

L

Landfills, E80-81

Laws
　water pollution and, E29
　National Environmental Policy Act of
　　1969 (NEPA), F52-53

Lenses, A32-33

Lichens, B7

Life
  on Earth, B4-63
  materials of, B10-17
  molecules of, B14-15
  variations in, B36-63
Life cycle (of stars), A8-11
Life forms, B6-7. *See also* Crust, of Earth
  classifying, C28-29, C30-37
  fossils and, C4-75
  studying past, C4
Life processes, B12-13, D23
Light-year, A15
Light. *See also* Radiation; Spectrometers;
  Starlight; Sunlight
  bending of, A32-33
  bouncing of, A34-37
  chemosynthesis and, D68-71
  collecting, A32-39
  color and, D6-7
  filters, D58-59
  in oceans, D52-57
  perceivers of, D12-21
  pigments and, D8-9
Light bulb, E51
Light switch, as subsystem, E50, E51
Light waves, A25-29
Linnaeus, Carolus, C34, C35
Lithosphere, C79
Living things
  chemicals in, B10-11
  life processes of, B12-13
Local Group (of galaxies), A18, A19

M

Maiasaura fossils. *See* Duckbill dinosaurs
Malaria, B53
Mammals, types of, C82-85. *See also*
  Marsupials; Placentals
Mammals, Age of, C18
Mannes, Leo, D74-75
Mantell, Gideon and Mary Ann, C6
Mantle, C81

Manufacturing system
  factory and, E70-77
  for sneakers, E66-67
Marshes
  airport construction and, F51-59
  interactions in, F34-43
  salt, F26-31
Marsupials, C82-87
Mass, A48-49
Mass production, E71, E74-75
Matzeliger, Jan, E74
Mayan calendar, A55
Mayas, A59
MCLs, E29
Meiosis, B38
Melanin, B51, D9
Mesosaura, C76
Mesozoic Era, C12-13, C18
Metals, in water supplies, E29
Meteorite theory, of dinosaur extinction,
  C26-27
Mid-Atlantic Ridge, C78-79
Migrators, D45
Milky Way Galaxy, A16, A19, A42, A48,
  A66
Mirrors, light and, A34
Mitosis, B28-31, B32-33
Models, A60-63, A72
  of cell division, B32-33
  of dinosaurs, C62-63
  of DNA, B26-27
  of fossils, C48-49
  of genes, B56
  of molecules, B34
Molecules. *See also* Building-block
  molecules
  DNA, B22-23
  of life, B14-15
  polymer, E68-69
Moneran kingdom, C30, C31
Mutation, B50-55, D26

Mutualism, D37
    chemosynthetic bacteria and, D69
    in oceans, D57
Myths, about stars, A53-55

N

Naming. *See* Classification
NASA (National Aeronautics and Space
    Administration), A74
National Environmental Policy Act of 1969
    (NEPA), F52-53
Native Americans
    astronomy and, A55
    corn and, B42-43
    marshes and, F27
Natural resources, energy and, E90-91
Natural selection, C22-23, C24, D26
Nebula, A5, A10-11
Nests. *See* Duckbill dinosaurs
Newton, Isaac, A37
Niche, F6
Nitrogen cycle, F38-39
Nitrogen fixers, F38
Nocturnal animals, D16
Nuclear fission, E41, E86
Nuclear fusion, A6-11
Nuclear power, Chernobyl and, E60
Nuclear power plants, E41, E56-57
Nucleic acids, B14, B15
Nutrients, B12, B13. *See also* Building-
    block molecules
    in ecosystem, F8

O

Oceans
    hot-water vents in, D60-65, D66-67
    life in dark of, D60-65
    lights in, D52-57
    pressure and temperature in, D52
    temperatures in, D65
    zones in, D52, D53
Oersted, Hans, E35
Orders, C32

Organisms, B7
    characteristics of, B18, B20
    classification of, C28-29, C30-37
    differences among, B10-15
    DNA and, B21-27
    in ocean depths, D60-65
    of ocean zones, D52, D53
    in rainforest, D31-37
Origin of Species, On the, C22
Oxygen, A7, B11

P

Paleoecologists, C92
Paleontologists, C6, C7
    inferences of, C64
    skeleton recreations and, C62-63
Paleontology, labs for, C59
Paleozoic Era, C12-13, C15
Pangaea, C76, C77-78, C82, C87
Parents. *See* Reproduction
Pesticides, F37
Petrified tree, C52
Photography, color, D75
Photosynthesis, D9
    in aquarium, F9
    chemosynthesis and, D68-71
    ocean organisms and, D65
Phycobilins, D9
Phyla, C32
Physiological adaptations, D23
Picado, Claudio, D37
Pigments, D7-9, D10-11
    visual, D13
Placentals, C82-84
Plankton, poisonous, F42-43
Plants, B6-7. *See also* Arctic; Ecosystems;
    Life forms; Rainforest
    adaptations of, D23
    crowding of, F32-33
    kingdom of, C30, C31
    life functions of, B5
Plate boundaries, C80
Plate movements, C79, C81

Acknowledgments

Pupil Edition interior design
Ligature, Inc.
Rosa + Wesley Design Associates

Unless otherwise acknowledged, all photographs are the property of ScottForesman. Unless otherwise acknowledged, all computer graphics by Ligature, Inc. Page abbreviations are as follows: **(T)** top, **(C)** center, **(B)** bottom, **(L)** left, **(R)** right, **(INS)** inset.

Module A
Photographs
Front & Back Cover: Background: Anglo-Australian Telescope Board Children's Photos: Michael Goss for ScottForesman

Page A3(B) Milt & Joan Mann/Cameramann International, Ltd. **A5** California Institute of Technology **A6** Anglo-Australian Observatory, imaging by David Allen **A17** National Optical Astronomy Observatories **A17(BOTH INS)** U.S. Naval Observatory **A36** California Association for Research in Astronomy **A37** ©1990/Roger Ressmeyer/Starlight **A41(B)** David Young-Wolff/Photo Edit **A42-43** Mosaic NSf-COS-B **A43(T)** NASA **A43(C)** Lund Observatory **A43(B)** Dr. C.S.T. Haslam Max-Planck Institute for Radio Astronomy **A44(T)** Howard Sochurek **A45(T)** ©1990/Roger Ressmeyer/Starlight **A45(R)** Museo di Storia della Scienza, Florence **A49** David Gaywood/Gamma-Liaison **A53(T)** Courtesy of the Trustees of the British Museum **A54(TR)** Georg Gerster/COMSTOCK INC. **A54(B)** Georg Gerster/ COMSTOCK INC. **A55** Robert Frerck/ Odyssey Productions, Chicago **A58** Zentralbibliothek, Zurich **A59** The British Library **A60** Science Museum, London **A61(TR)** The Adler Planetarium of Astronomy Collection **A63(T)** California Institute of Technology **A66** National Radio Astronomy Observatory **A67(L)** SOVFOTO **A67(R)** Milt & Joan Mann/Cameramann International, Ltd. **A68(T)** NASA **A68-69** © 1989/Roger Ressmeyer/Starlight **A69(BOTH INS)** NASA **A70(ALL)** NASA **A71** Air & Space Museum, Photo by Robert Golden, Courtesy Harry N. Abrams, Inc. **A74,75** NASA

Illustrations
Page A8 Mark Paternostro **A10-11** Mark Paternostro **A14** Mark Paternostro **A18-19** Mark Paternostro **A42** Ed Schweitzer **A46-47** Mark Paternostro **A62-63** Mark Paternostro **A77** George Kelvin

Module B
Photographs
Front & Back Cover: Background: Will & Deni McIntyre/Photo Researchers Children's Photos: Michael Goss for ScottForesman

Page B2(TL) NASA **B2(TC)** Pat & Tom Leeson/Photo Researchers **B2(B)** Will & Deni McIntyre/Photo Researchers **B3(TL)** The Granger Collection, New York **B5, 6-7** NASA **B6(TL)** Rod Planck/Tom Stack & Associates **B6(TR)** David & Carol Hughes/Bruce Coleman, Inc. **B6(B)** Erwin & Peggy Bauer/Bruce Coleman, Inc. **B7** Willard Clay **B10(B)** Pat & Tom Leeson/Photo Researchers **B11** Bob & Clara Calhoun/Bruce Coleman, Inc. **B12-13** Dan Kline/Visuals Unlimited **B14(TL)**

POPULAR SCIENCE Magazine, © 1991 TIMES MIRROR Magazine, Inc. Distributed by Los Angeles Times Syndicate **B14(B)** Courtesy Ford Motor Company **B14-15** Wayne Floyd/ Unicorn Stock Photos **B24** Will & Deni McIntyre/ Photo Researchers **B30(T)** Biophoto Associates/Photo Researchers **B30(C)** Biophoto Associates/Photo Researchers **B30(B)** Biophoto Associates/Photo Researchers **B32(T INS)** Kjell B.Sandved/Visuals Unlimited **B32(B INS)** Kevin Schafer/Tom Stack & Associates **B37(L), 37(BR), 38(L&R), 39(INS)** Walter Chandoha **B40-41** Myron Wright/Alaska Photo/All Stock **B42** The Granger Collection, New York **B43(L)** Robert S. Peabody Museum of Archaeology, Andover **B43(C)** Robert S. Peabody Museum of Archaeology, Andover **B44(T)** Henry Doorly Zoo, Omaha **B44(B)** Dominique Braud/Tom Stack & Associates **B45** Henry Doorly Zoo, Omaha **B50** Jessica Ehlers/Bruce Coleman, Inc. **B51(B)** Laura Riley/Bruce Coleman, Inc. **B51(T)** Zig Leszczynski/ANIMALS ANIMALS **B52** P.A.Harrington/Peter Arnold, Inc. **B58** Larry Mulvehill/ Photo Researchers **B59** Paul Metzger/Photo Researchers **B60** Courtesy Dr. Betsy L.Dresser

Illustrations
Page B7 Walter Stuart **B22-23** Biomedia **B24-25** Biomedia **B28-29** Biomedia **B38-39** Biomedia **B61** George Kelvin

Module C
Photographs
Front & Back Cover: Background: Visuals Unlimited Children's Photos: Michael Goss for ScottForesman

Page C2(T) Terry Musebye/Discover Syndication/Walt Disney Publications **C2(TL)** Museum of the Rockies Photo **C2(BR)** Bruce Selyem/Museum of the Rockies Photo **C5(T)** Bruce Selyem/ Museum of the Rockies Photo **C5(B)** Terry Panasuk/Museum of the Rockies Photo **C6(TL)** The Natural History Museum, London **C6(TR)** The Natural History Museum, London **C6(B)** The Hulton Picture Company **C8** Field Museum of Natural History, Chicago **C10** Jerry Husebye/Discover Syndication/Walt Disney Publications **C17(INS)** Anglo-Australian Telescope Board **C21(L)** Crown copyright. Reproduced with the permission of the Controller of Her Majesty's Stationery Office and the Director, Royal Botanic Garden, Kew. **C23** From Merveilles de la Nature, from DARWIN AND THE BEAGLE **C24** Warren Garst/Tom Stack & Associates **C25(L)** Warren Garst/Tom Stack & Associates **C25(R)** Warren Garst/Tom Stack & Associates **C26** Courtesy The Lawrence Berkeley Laboratory **C31(ROW 1 L TO R)** David W.Dennis/Tom Stack & Associates, John Gerlach/Tom Stack & Associates, Rod Planck/Tom Stack & Associates **C31(ROW 2 L TO R)** John Gerlach/Visuals Unlimited, Scott, Foresman, Joe McDonald/Visuals Unlimited **C31(ROW 3 L TO R)** T.E.Adams/Visuals Unlimited, A.M.Siegelman/Visuals Unlimited **C31(ROW 4 L TO R)** Charles W.Stratton/Visuals Unlimited, David M.Phillips/Visuals Unlimited **C33(L)** Dr. Merlin D. Tuttle/Bat Conservation International **C33(R)** Dr. Merlin D. Tuttle/Bat Conservation International **C34(C)** E.R.Degginger **C35(T)** Linda H.Hopson/ Visuals Unlimited **C35** E.R.Degginger **C37** John Serrao/Visuals

Unlimited **C41** Bruce Selyem/Museum of the Rockies Photo **C42(TR)** Museum of the Rockies Photo **C42(B)** Bruce Selyem/ Museum of the Rockies Photo **C43(T)** Museum of the Rockies Photo **C43(B)** Museum of the Rockies Photo **C44(T)** Bruce Selyem/Museum of the Rockies Photo **C44-45** Steve Jackson/ Museum of the Rockies Photo **C46** Bruce Selyem/Museum of the Rockies Photo **C47** Jerry Husebye/Discover Syndication/Walt Disney Publications **C51(T)** James L.Amos/Photo Researchers **C51(B)** John Gerlach/Visuals Unlimited **C52(T)** Visuals Unlimited **C52(C)** Cabisco/Visuals Unlimited **C52(B)** A.J.Cunningham/Visuals Unlimited **C53** E.R.Degginger **C55** Photo by Joel Dexter, Illinois State Geological Survey **C58** Steve Jackson/Museum of the Rockies Photo **C59(T)** Phil Degginger **C59(BR)** Phil Degginger **C60(ALL T)** Bruce Selyem/Museum of the Rockies Photo **C61(T)** A.J.Copley/ Visuals Unlimited **C61(B)** John D. Cunningham/Visuals Unlimited **C67** Bruce Selyem/Museum of the Rockies Photo **C71** Donna Braginetz, illustrator, Natural History Magazine **C76(T)** Breck P.Kent/Earth Scenes **C76(B)** Albert J.Copley/ Visuals Unlimited **C78-79** THE FLOOR OF THE OCEANS, Bruce C. Heezen and Marie Tharp ©1980 by Marie Tharp, reproduced by permission of Marie Tharp **C80** Tom Kitchin/Tom Stack & Associates **C81** E.R.Degginger **C82(L)** Dave Watts/ Tom Stack & Associates **C82(R)** J.Cancalosi/Tom Stack & Associates **C83(T)** EPI/Nancy Adams/Tom Stack & Associates **C83(B)** John Cancalosi/Tom Stack & Associates **C84-85** Painting by Jay H.Matternes ©1982. **C90(T)** Paul A. Gardner **C90-91** Bruce Selyem/Museum of the Rockies Photo **C90(T)** Paul A.Gardner **C91(T)** Courtesy of Robert Kahle **C91(B)** Paul A.Gardner **C92** Courtesy of Julio Betancourt

Illustrations
Page C3 Gary Torrisi **C11** Walter Stuart **C14-15** Laurie O'Keefe **C16-17** Laurie O'Keefe **C18-19** Laurie O'Keefe **C27** JAK Graphics **C32** Nancy Lee Walter **C41** Ebet Dudley **C50** Charles Thomas **C62-63** Gary Torrisi **C72-73** Laurie O'Keefe **C93** Laurie O'Keefe

Module D
Photographs
Front & Back Cover: Background: Kjell Sandved/Visuals Unlimited Children's Photos: Michael Goss for ScottForesman

Page D2(BR) John D. Cunningham/Visuals Unlimited **D3(BC)** WHOI/Visuals Unlimited **D3(C)** WHOI, D. Foster/ Visuals Unlimited **D5(T&B)** Thomas Eisner **D5(INS)** E.R.Degginger **D8** R. Howard Berg/Visuals Unlimited **D12(R)** From THE INCREDIBLE MACHINE/Lennart Nilsson/Bonnier/ Fakta **D13(L)** E.R.Degginger **D13(R)** David Scharf/Peter Arnold, Inc. **D14(L)** AP/Wide World **D16(T)** E.R. Degginger/ Bruce Coleman, Inc. **D16(C)** E.R.Degginger **D16(B)** Joe McDonald/Tom Stack & Associates **D17(TL)** Stuart Craig Jr./Bruce Coleman, Inc. **D17(TR)** Stuart L. Craig Jr./Bruce Coleman, Inc. **D17(CL)** Sandra Sinclair **D17(CR)** Sandra Sinclair **D17(BL)** Wendell Metzen/Bruce Coleman, Inc. **D17(BR)** Wendell Metzen/Bruce Coleman, Inc. **D18(T)** Stuart Craig, Jr./Bruce Coleman, Inc. **D18(C)** Wendy Shatth/Tom Stack & Associates **D18(B)** E.R.Degginger **D19** Allan Roberts **D22(T)** Tom Stack & Associates **D22(B)** John Cancalosi/Tom Stack & Associates **D23** Walt Anderson/Visuals Unlimited **D24(T)** Dave B.Fleetham/Visuals Unlimited **D24(C)** Tom Leeson/Photo Researchers **D24(B)** Stephen Dalton/ ALLSTOCK,INC. **D25(T)** John D. Cunningham/ Visuals Unlimited **D25(C)** E.R.Degginger **D25(B)** Visuals Unlimited **D27(T)** W.Perry Conway/Tom Stack & Associates

D27(C) Thomas Kitchin/Tom Stack & Associates **D27(B)** Field Museum of Natural History, Chicago **D31** Tom Stack & Associates **D32** E.R.Degginger **D33** Wolfgang Kaehler **D33(T INS)** E.R.Degginger **D33(B INS)** Bruno J.Zehnder/Peter Arnold, Inc. **D34(T)** Kjell Sandved/Visuals Unlimited **D34(B)** Patti Murray/Earth Scenes **D35(T)** Alex Kerstitch/Sea of Cortez Enterprises **D35(B)** Kevin Schafer/ Martha Hill/Tom Stack & Associates **D36** John D. Cunningham/ Visuals Unlimited **D36(TL-INS)** Raymond Mendez/ANIMALS ANIMALS **D36(TR-INS)** Raymond A Mendez/ ANIMALS ANIMALS **D36(B-INS)** Andrew Odum/Peter Arnold, Inc. **D40(TL)** N. Pecnik/Visuals Unlimited **D40(TR)** Stephen J Lang/Visuals Unlimited **D41(R)** Stephen J. Krasemann/ ALLSTOCK,INC. **D41(L)** Wolfgang Kaehler **D42-43** Wolfgang Kaehler **D42(INS)** Wolfgang Kaehler **D43(INS)** Rod Allin/Tom Stack & Associates **D44(T)** Wolfgang Kaehler **D44(C)** Visuals Unlimited **D44(B)** Johnny Johnson/ Alaska Photo/All Stock **D55** Larry Lipski/Tom Stack & Associates **D56(T)** Howard Hall **D56(B)** Robert Wu/Peter Arnold, Inc. **D57** Planet Earth Pictures **D60** Scripps Oceanographic Institute, Univ. of Calif. San Diego **D61** Robert Hessler/Scripps Oceanographic Institute, Univ. of Calif. San Diego **D64(T)** WHOI/D. Foster/Visuals Unlimited **D64(B)** Larry D. Tackett/Tom Stack & Associates **D68** WHOI/Visuals Unlimited **D69** J. Frederick/Woods Hole Oceanographic Institute **D74** Courtesy of Eastman Kodak Company **D75(T)** Courtesy The Museum of the Confederacy, Richmond, Va.

Illustrations
Page D2 Laurie O'Keefe **D14-15** Laurie O'Keefe **D53** Todd Telander **D54** Todd Telander **D62-63** Jacque Auger **D70** Nancy Lee Walter **D77** Laurie O'Keefe

Module E
Photographs
Front Cover Children's Photos: Michael Goss for ScottForesman

Page E2 Richard Hutchings/InfoEdit **E3** Illustration from SNEAKERS, THE SHOES WE CHOOSE by Robert Young, ©1991, by Dillon Press Inc. All rights reserved **E18(L)** Milt & Joan Mann/Cameramann International, Ltd. **E20(ALL)** Courtesy California Department of Water Resources **E25(L)** G.Azar/The Image Works **E25(R)** Paul Shambroom/Photo Researchers **E28** Richard Hutchings/InfoEdit **E35** The Granger Collection, New York **E52** Courtesy Northeast Power Coordinating Council. **E56** Milt & Joan Mann/Cameramann International, Ltd. **E57** Courtesy Department of Energy **E64(TL)** Illustration from SNEAKERS, THE SHOES WE CHOOSE by Robert Young. ©1991 by Dillon Press, Inc. All rights reserved. **E64(BR)** Courtesy Sears, Roebuck & Co. **E65(TL)** Courtesy Converse, Inc. **E65(TR)** Courtesy Reebok **E65(B)** Courtesy New Balance **E72-77** Courtesy Converse, Inc.; Photos by Cramer Gallimore for ScottForesman **E74 (BL)** Courtesy U.S. Postal Service **E80-81** Courtesy Converse, Inc.; Photos by Cramer Gallimore for ScottForesman **E84** Copyrighted, Chicago Tribune Company, all rights reserved, **E85** Photo Researchers **E87(T)** Biomechanics Lab, Southern Illinois University **E87(BL)** Popperfoto **E90** Milt & Joan Mann/Cameramann International, Ltd. **E92** Ames Research Center/NASA

Illustrations
Page E2-E3 Gary Torrisi **E3(T)** Gary Torrisi **E8** Gary Torrisi **E10-11** Jacque Auger **E12-13** Jacque Auger **E16** Jacque Auger **E18-19** Jacque Auger **E26-27** Paul Blakey **E37** Steve Fuller

E38-39 Gary Torrisi **E40-41** Gary Torrisi **E44-45** Jacque Auger **E46-47** Jacque Auger **E50** Steve Fuller **E54-55** Paul Blakey **E63** Steve Fuller **E70-71** Simon Galkin **E78-79** Simon Galkin **E85** Gary Torrisi **E86** Jacque Auger **E91(T,M,B)** JAK Graphics **E93** George Kelvin

Module F
Photographs
Front & Back Cover: Background: Gary R.Zahm/DRK Photo Children's Photos: Michael Goss for ScottForesman

Page F3(BR) S.Lang/Visuals Unlimited **F25** John D. Cunningham/Visuals Unlimited **F25(INS)** John Gerlach/ Visuals Unlimited **F26-27** National Audubon Society Collection **F28-29** Michael Rigsby/Scott, Foresman **F30(T)** Wayne Lankinen/DRK Photo **F30(C)** S.Nielsen/DRK Photo **F30(B)** Tom & Pat Leeson/Photo Researchers **F31** Doug Sokell/Visuals Unlimited **F40(T)** S.Lang/Visuals Unlimited **F40(B)** Wendell Metzen **F41** Leonard Lee Rue III/DRK Photo **F44-45** Larry R.Ditto **F46-47** Zig Leszczynski/Earth Scenes **F51** Marshland, Tom Bean/DRK Photo **F51** Airport model-Dan Corniah/ESTO

F52-53 Michael Rigsby/Scott, Foresman **F58** Stephen Frisch/Stock Boston **F59** Courtesy Murphy/Jahn Architects **F59(INS)** Laima Druskis/Stock Boston **F60(T)** Jim Brandenburg/ Bruce Coleman, Inc. **F60(B)** Jack Wilburn/ANIMALS ANIMALS **F61(T)** John Bova/Photo Researchers **F61(B)** Doug Perrine/DRK Photo **F62** John Sohlden/Visuals Unlimited **F62(INS)** Arthur Morris/Visuals Unlimited **F63** Peter Ziminski/Visuals Unlimited **F66-67** Shattil and Rozinski/Tom Stack & Associates **F68(L)** Alice Q.Hargrave/The Nature Conservancy, Chicago **F68-69** Kirk Woolford/The Nature Conservancy, Chicago **F70(T)** Lisa Law/The Image Works **F74(L)** Courtesy of Galien Bell **F74(R)** Michael Rigsby/Scott, Foresman **F75(T)** C.C.Lockwood/Cactus Clyde Productions **F75(B)** Courtesy of John Arana **F76** Michael Rigsby/Scott, Foresman

Illustrations
Page F35-36 Precision Graphics **F38-39** Ebet Dudley **F77** Laurie O'Keefe